Religion, Law and Power

Religion, Law and Power

Tales of Time in Eastern India, 1860–2000

Ishita Banerjee-Dube

ANTHEM PRESS
LONDON · NEW YORK · DELHI

Anthem Press
An imprint of Wimbledon Publishing Company
www.anthempress.com

This edition first published in UK and USA 2009
by ANTHEM PRESS
75-76 Blackfriars Road, London SE1 8HA, UK
or PO Box 9779, London SW19 7ZG, UK
and
244 Madison Ave. #116, New York, NY 10016, USA

British Library Cataloguing in Publication Data
A catalogue record for this book is available from the British Library.

Library of Congress Cataloging in Publication Data
A catalog record for this book has been requested.

ISBN-13: 978 1 84331 783 8 (Pbk)
ISBN-10: 1 84331 783 4 (Pbk)

1 3 5 7 9 10 8 6 4 2

Printed and bound in Great Britain by Marston Book Services Limited, Oxford

CONTENTS

	Page
Preface	vii
Maps	xiii
1. Introduction: Tales of Time	1
2. Formations of Faith	25
3. Poets and Texts	69
4. Ascetics, Histories and the Law	117
5. Contemporary Contours	159
6. Epilogue	193
Bibliography	197
Appendix	211
Glossary	213
Index	217

PREFACE

Well over a decade ago, I began a somewhat inchoate project on the religion of a subaltern people in eastern India. Following a long, meandering course the project has resulted in a book on discrete expressions of time and temporality – and their intricate interplay with articulations of pasts and histories – among members of a subordinate religious order. The explorations of Mahima Dharma have further revealed wider entanglements of religion, law and power, especially as they are played out in everyday arenas.

The study draws on the concerns and methods of history and anthropology and on perspectives provided by critical trends within the disciplines in order to present a textured account of the distinct trajectories and lives of Mahima Dharma. The diverse yet jumbled pasts of the subaltern religious formation, rich in composite configurations of temporality and time, faith and reason, religion and law, state and community and the written and the oral, crucially question the modular division of social worlds premised on analytical binaries. The story of Mahima Dharma also allows insights into discrete perceptions of history.

I began the research on Mahima Dharma supported by a doctoral fellowship from the Indian Council of Social Science Research at the Centre for Studies in Social Sciences, Calcutta. The vibrant atmosphere of 10 Lake Terrace – the stimulating faculty, the helpful personnel and the camaraderie of fellow research scholars there – made the work both challenging and rewarding. I thank everyone associated with the Centre in the 1990s and in particular, Amiya Bagchi, Pradeep Bose, Partha Chatterjee, Keya Dasgupta, Barun De, Anjan Ghosh, Sushanta Ghosh, Tapati Guha Thakurta, Hitesh Ranjan Sanyal and Manahswita Sanyal, the entire staff of the library and my friend Bansari Guha.

To Gautam Bhadra, my teacher and supervisor, I owe an enormous intellectual debt and much gratitude. He has nurtured the project with exceptional care, concern and enthusiasm from the beginning through to the end. I cannot thank him and Narayani Banerjee enough for the long hours of passionate discussion, the innumerable instances of advice and help, and the tea and eats invariably provided at their home.

Kalpana Das devoted months teaching me to read and write Oriya and then spent years helping me to translate the difficult works of Bhima Bhoi. This study would have collapsed without her unconditional help. It is difficult to adequately acknowledge the warmth and hospitality I received during my several years of field-work in Orissa. Teachers of the Philosophy and History Departments of Utkal University, Bhubaneswar, variously helped out in the initial stages. Pritilata Bardhan and Chanda Singh provided hospitality on several occasions. Shatrughna Nath gave freely of his time to discuss and explain the doctrines of his faith and put me in touch with several other members of Mahima Dharma. Uddhab Nayak accompanied me to Joranda and other *ashramas*. The Patel and the Misra families were vital in making my trips all over Orissa happen. I treasure the memory of the affection and kindness I received from Bapa and Mama (Sri and Srimati Misra) and Renu Didi (Renuka Misra) of Sonepur.

My host and friend Sanjukta Jena and other teachers of the Mahima Mahavidyalaya, Joranda, made the induction into field-work pleasurable and productive. Ascetics and lay disciples of Mahima Dharma generously allowed me access into their faith and its worlds. Their anecdotes and explications as well as the invitation to participate in several ceremonies have proved priceless toward my learning not only about Mahima Dharma but about the disciplines themselves.

A grant from the German Academic Exchange Service enabled me to spend three months in Germany working in the archive of the Orissa Research Project and the Eschmann Collection. The convivial surroundings of the South Asia Institute, Heidelberg and the special kindness of several persons made my stay fruitful and memorable. I particularly wish to thank Hermannn Kulke, Charlott Eschmann, Martin Brandtner, Birgit Mayer, Dietmar Rothermund, Jürgen Lutt, Heinrich von Stietencron, the late Richard Burghart and the late Günther-Dietz Sontheimer. A year in England added fresh dimensions to the work. My thanks go to Javed Majeed, Kislay Prasad, Nikhil Tandon, Sandeep Kapoor and Mamata Murthy, Allan Findlay, Henry Hurst, Gordon Johnson and Rosalind O'Hanlon.

The staff and members of several libraries, archives and repositories have immensely aided my work. I am grateful to Safalya Nandi of the Oriya Section of the National Library, Calcutta; Lionel Carter of the Centre of South Asian Studies, Cambridge; the Superintendent of West Bengal State Archives, Calcutta; the Superintendent, Archivist and staff of the Reading

Room of Orissa State Archives, Bhubaneswar; and the Archivist of the Baptist Missionary Society archive, Regent's Park College, Oxford. I also wish to thank the staff of the Reading Room of the National Library, Calcutta; of the library of the Asiatic Society of Bengal, Calcutta; of the State Museum Library, Bhubaneswar; of the Office of the Religious Endowments Commissioner, Bhubaneswar; of the Record Room of the Board of Revenue, Cuttack; of the National Archives of India, New Delhi; of the Nehru Memorial Museum and Library, New Delhi; and of the libraries of Utkal University, Sambalpur University and Berhampur University, all in Orissa.

The lively intellectual environment of El Colegio de México, Mexico City has made for a perfect setting for the completion of the project. Colleagues, friends, students and staff of the Centre for Asian and African Studies have contributed in numerous ways. David Lorenzen has provided warmth, friendship and sustained intellectual feedback. Celma Agüero, Flora Botton, Benjamín Preciado, Mercedes Barquet, Rubén Chuaqui, Agnes Pan, Anne Staples, Andrés Lira, German Franco, Gilberto Conde, Amaury Garcia, Gabriela Lara, Pilar Camacho and Magdalena Bobadilla have been supportive friends. Mario Rufer and María Fernanda Vázquez have helped enormously in the final stages of the book. Angelica Vargas, Alicia Hatzue, Karin Teran and members of the Computer Centre have offered unfailing support.

Paolo Cabrelli at Anthem Press has been a patient, considerate and efficient editor. Collaboration of the Anthem team has been vital for the speedy publication of the book.

Over the years, interactions with a host of individuals have helped to shape my thinking and writing in important ways. I would specially like to thank Richard Eaton, Ann Gold, Dipesh Chakrabarty, Ashis Nandy, Shahid Amin, Ajay Skaria, Crispin Bates, Bishnu Mohapatra, Romila Thapar, Benoy Bhushan Chowdhury, Sekhar Bandyopadhay, Gyanendra Pandey, Gyan Prakash, Milind Wakankar, Anupama Rao, Arvind Rajagopal, Wendy Doniger, Laurence Moore, Daniel Gold, Grant Farred, Walter Mignolo, Giovanni Levi, Craig Calhoun, Indivar Kamtekar, Kalpana Sahni and Romi Khosla.

My friends Sarvani Gooptu, Moushumi Mukherjee, Anuradha Gupta, Rupa Datta, Sayanti Mukherjee, Susmita Mukherjee and Sushweta Ghosh have been around whenever I needed them. Relatives on both sides of the family, the Gangulys, Chatterjees, Bagadtheys and Mukherjees have been invaluable sources of support.

Religion, Law and Power has benefited much from the advice and encouragement of Leela and S. C. Dube and the editorial skills of Mukul Dube. Paramita Banerjee has helped to tie up several loose ends. Gitasree Banerjee has been a constant source of comfort and strength. Saurabh Dube has shared the pleasures and pangs of the project over the years and his excitement and passion regarding the study urged me on when the going got tough.

Long before the beginning of this project, S. P. Banerjee set an example for me through his zest for life and pleasure in learning. His remarkable capacity to completely understand his daughter and his unabashed pride in her achievements nourished the study in inexorable, if inexpressible, ways. The sad-happy thought that he is impatiently waiting to announce the publication of this work to his fellows and friends in an after-world compelled me to complete it. The book is dedicated to him.

Kolkata
August 2006

S. P. Banerjee (1929-2003)
Father and Philosopher

MAPS

Tributary States of Orissa in the late 19th century

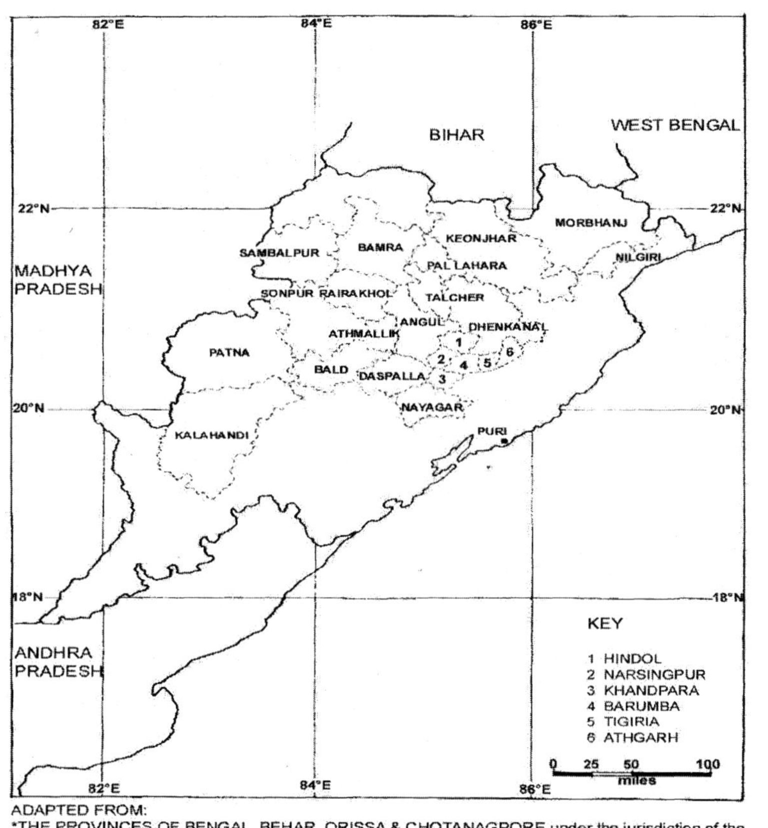

ADAPTED FROM:

*THE PROVINCES OF BENGAL, BEHAR, ORISSA & CHOTANAGPORE under the jurisdiction of the Lieutenant Governor of Bengal, 1884 (Survey of India Office, Cal., 1686)

*THE CENTRAL PROVINCES showing the bounsaries of districts, Tahsils, Feudatory Chief-Ships, Zamindaries & Govt. Forests, 1885 (Survey Gen. of India Off., Calcutta)

Map of India in the 19th century
(Orissa highlighted)

(Source: www.wmcarey.edu/carey/maps/1857indiampa.jpg)

CHAPTER 1.

Introduction: Tales of Time

Time and temporality lie at the heart of configurations of history. They provide history writing with vital organizing principles. All too often, these concepts and entities are held in place by the historian in chiefly implicit ways. At other moments, time and temporality occasion the most severe disagreements among the practitioners of the discipline. This is because 'history' as we know and understand it is defined by a marking out of the past from the present, premised upon an implicit belief in a linear progression of time. The stark separation of the past from the present, a foundational element of the 'rupture' believed to have been occasioned by modernity, is considered to be based on rational modes of taking stock of time, modes that make history a scientific discipline clearly distinct from myth.[1] This hidden hierarchy of time in history — accompanied by evolutionary principles that have variously shored up a great deal of modern anthropology — divided the world in terms of temporal sequence between Western societies grounded in history and reason and non-Western cultures held in place by myth and ritual.[2]

Such presumptions have long and chequered genealogies that go back to the Enlightenment and earlier. In addition, they are intimately linked to the gradual secularization of Judeo–Christian time which entailed a changeover from time conceived as the medium of a sacred history specific to a chosen people to a generalization and universalization of time by denuding it of its specificity.[3] What lay at the heart of the transformation of particular time to general time was a corrosion of the eschatological content of time, leading to a break from 'a conception of time/space in terms of a history of salvation' to 'a secularization of Time as natural history.'[4] It bears pointing out here that European Enlightenment itself was marked by formative differences that make it difficult to speak of a single Enlightenment. It is also true that the 'secularization' of Judeo–Christian time formed an 'influential' idea but a 'circumscribed' process.[5] This is because Enlightenment philosophers could not by themselves bring about the secularization of Judeo–Christian time in broader social and political contexts, tasks that had to be undertaken by the state.[6] At the same time, neither philosophers nor governments had complete control over the manner in which their ideas and reforms were 'understood and articulated by citizens and subjects'.[7] Unsurprisingly, messianic time has shown deep provenance and wide prevalence in western worlds, continuing up to the present.[8] Such qualifications notwithstanding, it must be registered that by the second half of the nineteenth century secularized time acquired a natural aura, at the very least in the protestant West. This naturalized time in turn provided the basis for the mapping of peoples and cultures hierarchically in the developmental schemes that underlay the grand designs of human history.[9] Universal time and universal history evolved in conjunction, simultaneously marking out 'others' — societies and cultures where time and temporality were construed differently.

Changes in notions of time were accompanied by shifts in 'technologies in measurement', signalled by the changeover from stationary clocks that showed the hour alone in late medieval Europe through to watches that displayed minutes and seconds and then onto bureaucratic, industrial structures of time, a process that took almost five hundred years.[10] These long drawn out and fiercely contested alterations in conceptualizations of time and time-reckoning formed part of wider articulations of capitalism and colonialism. All of this established Europe as the site and the centre of the modern. Here, the break with the past turning on the modern West brought in its toe other dichotomies, such as those between myth and history, ritual and rationality, religion and politics, community and state and emotion and reason.[11] Together, the enduring legacies of developmental schemas of a natural, universal history and of dominant representations of an exclusive, western modernity have made the past of Europe into the standard through which to assess other societies. The world stands divided into modern, dynamic societies and static, enchanted communities, placed upon an axis of space and time, gauged on the basis of the distances cultures had advanced on the path of modernity, a modernity that is seen as nothing but the West. Needless to say, the milestones on this path have been determined by the place and the presence of history.

The alleged indifference to historical consciousness in India was often mentioned by early travellers and forcefully reiterated by British administrators and scholars. It served to reinforce the definition of India as 'traditional' and 'static' by early colonialists. Volumes were written by Indologists and Orientalist scholars on the notion of 'cyclical' time depicted in Sanskrit texts of classical Hinduism, where four ages Satya, Treta, Dwapar and Kali, defined by definite norms and specific values, were meant to succeed each other in endless cycles. Tied to the notion of the cycle but of even greater significance was that of 'duration'.[12] Early Europeans were intrigued and troubled by the very long time span of Hindu ages contrasted with the short extent of Biblical times.[13] The supposed inconsequentiality of duration in Hindu time was strengthened by the scheme of the cycle where the end of the era was to be marked by a deluge and the appearance of an incarnation, which was to herald a 'return' to the earlier age. This idea embedded in the *Mahabharata* and the Puranas and current in the Vaishnavite tradition of Hinduism formed the basis for Mircea Eliade's well-known thesis on the 'myth of eternal return'.[14] The rotation of time in cycles posited on eternal return was, in Eliade's opinion, a direct opposite of the Judeo–Christian concept of linearity which had made possible the emergence of modern time.

In recent years, important works in history and anthropology have thoroughly questioned the presumed binary of linear-cyclical time. Studies of societies from different parts of the globe have demonstrated with clarity the co-existence and combination of the two conceptions.[15] With regard to India, it has been argued that the notion of the four Yugas is sequential since they follow each other in a particular order.[16] It needs to be stressed here that sequence is significant since there is a progressive degeneration in morality, a vital element of time, in each succeeding epoch. This confers on each era distinctive qualities making a change of Yuga as much a new beginning as a return to the old.

In a different vein, scholars have also interrogated the Indological assumption of the prevalence of a single notion of time in pre-colonial India. Apart from the fact that there were Indo-Islamic configurations of time, texts of pre-Islamic India bore testimony to the presence of different modes of time reckoning.[17] If cyclical time featured in the *Mahabharata* and certain other Sanskrit texts, chronicles of rulers and genealogies of dynasties displayed perfect familiarity with linear time. Indeed, it has been argued that the Puranic tradition itself was not bereft of historical content. The tradition was actually that of *itihasa-purana* in which *iti-ha-asa* literally translated as 'so it has been'. Hence the compound word signified a conjunction of perceived past and historicity and texts represented a move from 'embedded history' to the 'prising of historical consciousness' in ancient India, which was a corollary to the transformation of the political order from lineage-societies to state-systems.[18] This has been further extended in analyses demonstrating the 'completely unproblematic' transition from the mythic to the contemporary in the rendering of 'histories' of ruling dynasties in *puranetihasa* (*purana-itihasa*).[19]

While there is consensus on the currency of distinct temporalities in India, there is disagreement over whether consciousness of the past in pre-colonial India can be termed 'historical'. The issue assumed urgency in the early 1990s in the context of the political success of parties of the Hindu right and their strident demands for a history based on a specific, singular construction of the past. The participation of right-wing and 'secular' historians in a vigorous debate that ensued on the veracity of the claims made on the past — and on the nature of the 'facts' adduced — led some prominent thinkers to foreground basic assumptions about modernity and history. Historical consciousness in the 'modern' sense of the term, argued Ashis Nandy, was absent in India since history itself originated with modernity which in turn was a result either of Enlightenment or colonialism and nationalism.[20] Hence, the ways in which the past and its relationship with the present were perceived in India prior to British rule did not in any way conform to the standards of western history.

This stance was extended further to valorize the 'ahistoricity' of India.[21] The idea of progressive degeneration in successive Yugas and the characterization of evolution 'as a move from authenticity to inauthenticity' in certain important trends of Hindu thought were taken to be crucial indicators of the 'rejection' of history in early India. Arguing that this was one of the most attractive features of pre-colonial India, Vinay Lal concluded that 'the past of India' cannot be 'read from historical records' since a tradition of historical enquiry and writings did not exist for 'compelling reasons'.[22] The need to establish the early traditions of ordering the past as 'historical', he stated, stemmed from a naïve belief in and uncritical acceptance of modernist traditions. Though persuasive and thought-provoking, these arguments in privileging the 'ahistoricity' of India seem to abide by the same rigid notion of history as 'rational' and 'scientific' they accuse others of subscribing to. Such a point of view identifies history as an essentially modern discipline intimately tied to the nation and construes the earlier imaginative and 'irrational' modes of ordering the past as not-modern and hence ahistorical, ruling out the possibility of a wider and more comprehensive definition of history.

Changing Times

What I have said so far point to the critical reflection on the uses of time in history and anthropology. A wide range of scholars, with different backgrounds and orientations have probed the process that led to the separation of the past and the present and problematized the switch from religious time to clock time. This has involved contemplation on the 'pertinence' of the opposition between the past and the present in different societies and the ramifications of this demarcation on the future,[23] provocative suggestions about the disciplinary aspects of modern clock-time in the West[24] as well as a searing critique of 'distancing' posited on 'temporalization' and the denial of co-evalness between anthropological discourse and its referents.[25] These extremely valuable contributions however, have not negated the premise that there has been a definite changeover — albeit awkward and somewhat incomplete — from sacred time to modern 'secular' time.

The discussions with regard to India also seem to follow the same pattern, postulating a presence of distinct temporalities in pre-colonial India yet holding on to the move from religious to secular time during the period of colonial rule.[26] As noted above, this transformation has been associated with the emergence of modernist history in India. The break with religious time is also seen to have effected a rupture with the *itihasa-purana* tradition. From the late-nineteenth and increasingly over the twentieth century history in India has come to be determined by 'what happened' and not 'what is imagined', displaying a particular preference for events and facts. This has resulted either in a lack of interest or understanding of modes of ordering the past that blend sacred and secular time or a celebration of the non-modern who understands his/her past 'mythically' as a resistant subject who has successfully evaded the tropes of modernity.[27] Time in and for History, is widely believed to have changed irrevocably from sacred and salvational to linear and progressive. The remnants of distinct ways of perceiving the past are seen as non-historical and not-modern.

As stated before, these dichotomies — the founding 'myths' of modernity — have been seriously questioned in recent years.[28] And yet, they continue to exert influence both as categories of thought and as ways of understanding societies. This is because 'these oppositions emerged within formidable projects of power and knowledge, turning on modernity, Enlightenment, empire and nation.'[29] These conscious projects did not simply look at and record but 'recorded and remade' the world.[30] Although these projects were neither singular nor uniform and often combined contradictory trends of thought that lay at the heart of modernity, through their ambivalences and inconsistencies they came to acquire salience as they were 'assiduously articulated'.[31] The significance of such antinomies is only too palpable in the way the world continues to be perceived in terms of 'enchanted spaces and modern places.'[32] As such, it is not enough to have a 'new and inoffensively correct consensus' on the interpenetration of the oppositions.[33] What is required is the assertion of the validity and legitimacy of thought and understanding that fuse and scramble dichotomies and through it question the authority of thought that relies on these oppositions. Such moves, affirms Fernando Coronil, turn our attention to an understanding of the 'relational nature of representations of human collectivities' and reveal 'their genesis in asymmetrical relations of power, including the power to obscure their genesis in inequality, to sever their historical connections, and thus to present as the internal and separate attributes of bounded entities what are in fact historical outcomes of connected peoples.'[34]

To reiterate, *Religion, Law and Power* does not simply invert binaries, it questions the implicit assumption of an earlier *Ur* moment in which the dualisms bore an original, unadulterated character. While it acknowledges the lasting presence of such analytical oppositions, my account interrogates their modular division of social worlds by attending to the murkiness and jumbles that characterize such worlds. Further, my exploration of the intermeshed workings and novel combinations of several dualities in the career of Mahima Dharma brings into relief varied articulations of history, innovative reformulations of Hinduism through the construction of a modern 'timeless religion', and discrete engagements with stipulations of the state and the law by a contingent community. This in turn, serves to unpack the wider entanglements of history, religion, law and power. All along, the analysis is informed by and grounded in important debates and reflections that have caused significant shifts in understandings of history.

History, Event, Narration

History is a true novel, writes a French historian and historians tell of true events in which man is the actor.[35] This apparently simple response to what history is raises some critical issues challenging history. What constitutes an 'event' and how true is the representation of the 'true event' in historical narratives? Do the perception and understanding of events remain constant over time? How does history deal with its inherent ambivalence relating to the interface of action and narration, of what happened and what is said to have happened? Indeed, it is this unresolved ambiguity that causes wide divergence in historical narratives and interpretation and renders the past 'unpredictable'.

For some, the 'unpredictability of the past' is salutary rather than problematic since it adds to the vivacity of thought.[36] History, in the words of a celebrated American historian, 'is never, in any rich sense, the immediate crudity of what "happens", but the finer complexity of what we read into it and think in connection with it.'[37] Such historians readily accept that the understanding of standard historical occurrences inevitably varies from generation to generation because, of necessity, the occurrences are viewed through the prism of a changing present. If this makes historians operate in 'cycles of historical interpretations', in the end they come up with increasingly sophisticated understandings of the past.[38] In the 1940s, the French historian Marc Bloch had stressed that although nothing in the future can change the past, knowledge of the past 'is something progressive which is constantly changing and perfecting itself.'[39]

This healthy spirit notwithstanding, practitioners of the discipline have not made their peace with one area of historical unpredictability: that of changing notions of what events and which people should constitute the focus of the historian's study. Over the past few decades, dissatisfaction with the content of history and efforts to democratize the discipline have resulted in some of the most exciting departures in the writing of history. Starting with E. P. Thompson's social history of the English working class and efforts to write 'histories from below' and the exciting works of Natalie Zemon Davis and Eugene D. Genovese through to histories of everyday life (*Alltagsgeschichte*), micro-history and concerns of the subaltern studies collective to reclaim the subaltern as the subject of history, history writing has taken significant turns that have transformed notions of history. Realms of experience and emotion have been given the pride of place in historical accounts with a primary focus on the everyday lives of ordinary men and women.[40] Alongside, there has been a coming together of the disciplines of history and anthropology, a sharing of and learning from each others methods and perceptions in an attempt to overcome the limits of both.[41] Together, all these moves have shaken settled verities and opened new vistas for approaching and understanding the past and the writing of history. They have also produced a growing consensus among historians that history 'as a form of knowledge about the past is itself worthy of study.'[42]

This book does not provide an analysis of the philosophical and theoretical traditions that have 'studied' history, nor does it advance a 'social history of historiography', the lack of which has been lamented by renowned historians.[43] Rather, it draws upon insights offered by distinct trends of historiography and the discussions within the discipline to reflect on some urgent questions that underlie the production of historical narratives. *Religion, Law and Power* constructs an anthropological history of a subaltern religious formation — Mahima Dharma of Orissa, eastern India — in a way that allows the different pasts of the group to come through and engage with each other producing a creative tension.[44] The multiple stories of single community, related yet separate, bring into relief different pathways of historical consciousness and varied conditions under which the past is perceived, represented, invoked and deployed. Apart from revealing diverse historical sensibilities and changing notions of history they underscore its salience as the mediator in the construction of identity by a contingent community at critical moments of its existence.

At the same time, the pasts of Mahima Dharma — informed by different registers of temporality and intricate conceptions of faith and reason, divinity and veracity, legality and history, writing and orality — throw a single, coherent historical account into disarray by their very fuzziness. My account unties the tangled stories of a radical yet marginal group only to underscore the wider entanglements of history, religion, law and power in the formation and preservation of a religious community over almost a century and a half.

Formation

Mahima Dharma was founded by Mahima Swami, an abstemious, itinerant ascetic in the 1860s when Orissa was rocked by a devastating famine. The Dharma advocated devotion to an all-pervasive, formless Absolute — equally accessible to all — as the only way of salvation. This seemingly simple message rendered redundant worship of idols, including that of Jagannath, the central deity of Hinduism in Orissa and the state deity for centuries, and questioned complex hierarchies of caste and kingship, and the role of the Brahman as mediators between gods and men. The radical message, which pooled thoughts and ideas from different trends of religious thought — 'high' and 'low', classical and popular — was accompanied by a contravention of the rules of caste and norms of commensality.[45] Directly challenging the injunction on sharing of cooked food by members of different castes, Mahima Swami asked for cooked rice as alms and ate it together with his disciples from the same pot.[46] Moreover, he accepted cooked rice from all including the untouchables but refused to accept it from the Brahmans, ritually the purest. In accepting cooked food from the lowest castes the Swami absorbed their pollution and made them pure. On the other hand, he showed his disregard for and his superiority to the Brahmans by refusing to accept cooked food, the carrier of pollution, from them.

These ingenious inversions and combinations were also reflected in his engagement with the opposition between *kshetra* and *vana*, settled space and the uninhabited, dangerous zone. Mahima Swami preached his faith in the far-flung territories of the tributary states, inhabited predominantly by low-caste, untouchable and indigenous peoples, settled spaces that were simultaneously liminal.[47] His mobility and extreme detachment were further statements against authority and establishment. Although the Swami followed distinct practices of asceticism in his own life, he initiated both renouncers and householders in his faith, opening for them the way to salvation through pure devotion.[48] All this made Mahima Dharma attractive to subordinate groups of men and women, whose lives the faith invested with new significance.

The force of the message of Mahima Swami and its creative reworking found expression in a dramatic event. On 1 March 1881 a small group of anonymous men and women from western Orissa, householder devotees of Mahima Dharma, entered the main temple of Jagannath in the pilgrimage centre of Puri with the express intention of dragging out and burning the images of Jagannath, his brother Balaram and sister Subhadra. The person who led the group had been commanded in a dream by Mahima Swami (who had died in 1875), to embark on this daring mission. These ordinary men and women failed in their task. But the 'audacity' of their mission caused consternation among Oriya elites and brought the faith to the notice of the colonial government. The dramatic 'event' of the 'attack' on the temple, marked the entry of the new faith into colonial records as 'A sect of Hindu dissenters'.

Thorough enquiries were carried out and detailed reports drawn up on the sect, its founder, its beliefs and practices. An itinerant ascetic who had been variously referred to as a Gosain (renouncer, a term commonly used for Vaishnava ascetics) who covered his body with ashes, lived on fruit, milk and water coalesced in the figure of Mukunda Das who had come to be called Mahima Swami by his followers. The touch of the magical that constituted a major element of his charisma for his disciples was carefully removed in these reports, and the belief in his divinity explained as the result of gullibility on the part of poor and illiterate people. It is striking that various records mentioned that *malikas* — texts which spoke of the evil era of Kali and predicted its destruction through the appearance of an incarnation — were in wide circulation in Orissa and that the adherents of Mahima Dharma were 'in possession of a book of predictions'. However, the significance of Kali Yuga for perceptions of a difficult present and the identification of Mahima Swami as the human form of the Absolute he spoke about were dismissed as instances of irrational thought on the part of simple, unlettered folk. Mahima Swami was firmly established as a historical figure with clear antecedents and his deification ascribed to the credulity of innocent people. Innovative combinations of real and mythical time in understandings of the present were not considered worthy of enquiry.

Of greater significance is the fact that the 'event' which occasioned the entry of Mahima Dharma into official records, has almost disappeared from the 'collective memory' of present day followers.[49] In the course of its existence, the faith has redrawn its boundaries with Hinduism and changed its stance of direct opposition to the central cult.[50] The 'attack' is seen as an embarrassment or sought to be rationalized as irresponsible behaviour of householder devotees with no involvement of the leaders. The common men and women from western Orissa, who had momentarily seized history for themselves on the force of conviction in a divine mission, have been relegated to the anonymity they were subjected to prior to the incident.

It is true that the memory of the incident survives, particularly among the marginalized section of the followers, and innovative appropriations of teachings of the faith that had occasioned the march to the temple of Jagannath continue. However, reasoned explications of Mahima Dharma and official histories of the faith written by scholar ascetics of the twentieth century have, by making no mention either of the Dharma's intimate relationship with the cult of Jagannath or of the incident of 1 March 1881, induced a selective amnesia that has turned it into a non-event. This, apart from throwing insight into how history and memory get configured, demonstrates with spectacular clarity the ambiguity and overlap of event and narration — of what happened and what is said to have happened — that history embodies.[51] It also highlights the crucial role played by power in the construction and legitimization of historical narratives.

Elaboration

The spirit and force of Mahima Swami's teachings were continued, disseminated and given new significance in the compositions of Bhima Bhoi, a blind poet of tribal origins who grew up with no formal education. Bhima Bhoi's lyrics, inspired utterances noted down by scribes, not only gave Mahima Dharma its first written texts they also formed the core of the theosophy–philosophy of the faith. Bhima Bhoi, believed to have been born blind to very poor parents, tutored himself through aural comprehension of readings of popular religious texts in the village. His innovative mind blended ideas and motifs of different trends of thought current in Orissa to churn out compositions that combined high philosophy with everyday metaphors to speak of an Absolute who was at once all-powerful and indescribable and accessible to all through devotion. The lyrics also stressed the urgency of taking shelter in the Absolute to avoid being engulfed by the vices of Kali. The incarnation had already appeared in the form of Mahima Swami, the Guru of the world and the personal preceptor of Bhima Bhoi. Lord Jagannath had recognized the Guru and had left Puri to become his first disciple. But other followers had failed to follow suit. The human form of the Absolute had left the world but Kali Yuga had not come to an end. If the true devotees were to realize their mistake and take refuge in the Absolute he will show the way again. Bhima Bhoi played a key role in the spread of Mahima Dharma from the 1870s to his death in 1895.

A creative genius not restrained by the dictates of one faith, Bhima Bhoi broke the norms of celibacy, cut off his links with ascetics who decided to construct a memorial for the Guru in central Orissa, set up his own *ashrama* in western Orissa and aroused the ire of the ascetics by allowing women into the monastic order.[52] Bhima Bhoi's life became a rich source of legends that led to his deification among his followers in western Orissa and his works formed a perpetual source of inspiration for the devotees of Mahima Dharma.[53]

The vitality of diverse messages conveyed through the lyrical compositions replete with meanings would be proved again and again in the life of Mahima Dharma. The incident of 1881 is one example of the apprehension of the teachings of Mahima Swami and Bhima Bhoi by householder devotees. The appearance of *malikas* in Bhima Bhoi's name in the 1920s and 30s when the faith was threatened with dissension, provides another brilliant example of the surfeit of meanings generated by collective recitals of Bhima Bhoi's compositions and their understandings by the 'interpretive community'. Drawing strength from Bhima Bhoi's message that the Guru would lot leave his true followers, these new *malikas* would predict the reappearance of the Guru in the form of Mahima Swami, Kalki and Gandhi to lead the war against the British and the forces of evil. Organic combinations of the sacred and the secular, the spoken and the written, faith and reason, myth and history, these texts illustrate the immense import of distinct registers of time that occasion discrete articulations of the religious and the political in the everyday lives of common people and provide them with hope by pointing to a way out of the predicament.

Institutionalization

Mahima Dharma underwent significant transformation in the twentieth century. Variously known as Alekh and Kumbhipatia Dharma in the nineteenth century, it evolved as Mahima Dharma, a sect within Hinduism in the twentieth.[54] The Dharma faced a serious crisis after the death of its founder in 1875/76. His followers had not expected him to die. The Swami in turn, had made no arrangements for the continuation of the faith. There was no nominated successor, no permanent structure and no nucleus. While Bhima Bhoi's compositions played a crucial role in the spread of the faith, his unorthodox lifestyle caused indignation among the ascetics. Bhima Bhoi set up his own *ashrama* in Khaliapali in western Orissa. The ascetics decided to construct a memorial for the Guru at Joranda in Dhenkanal.

The replacement of a mobile preceptor by a static memorial symbolized the beginnings of the institutionalization of Mahima Dharma. Over the twentieth century, the memorial got transformed into the locus of the Guru's authority and the headquarters of the faith with set ceremonies, liturgies, rituals and services. Two orders of ascetics clashed over rights of precedence in the offering of ritual services at the memorial. Unable to resolve disagreements through deliberations, the ascetics turned to the legal machinery of the colonial state. The language and requirements of the legal apparatus dictated and invited unique understandings and configurations of the Dharma. The emphasis of the law in framing the faith through fixed and formal, unambiguous and authoritative written evidence went hand in hand with the ascetics' urge to form a bounded community out of a disparate group of followers. Together, they occasioned significant shifts within the faith. The drive for uniformity and the demand of the legal apparatus for written evidence induced scholarly ascetics to produce authoritative explications and authentic histories of Mahima Dharma. These written texts brought order and homogeneity to divergent tenets open to myriad perceptions by forging tendentious relationships with the Vedantic tradition of Hinduism, by marginalizing its complicated relationship with the cult of Jagannath and finally by reformulating Mahima Dharma as a sect that represented the very essence of eternal (*sanatan*), pristine Hinduism. This was accompanied by a search for adherents and sympathizers among the urban literati which reinforced the shift in accent, already under way, from the periphery to the centre, from the oral to the written.

Lawyers and judges, of independent India in particular, vigorously dispensed with their role as the arbiters in charge of the proper functioning of religion by formulating their own definitions of and prescriptions for Mahima Dharma. The twin processes fed into each other. Mahima

Dharma, which started its career by positing a distance and difference from high Hinduism rearticulated itself as an established sect within the universe of Hinduism.

If this long and convoluted relationship of Mahima Dharma with the legal machinery of the state tends to reiterate Marc Galanter's argument that the judiciary of independent India has acted as a sponsor for reform within Hinduism, it also opens up other issues relating to the interaction of the state and the community and the way they impinge on each other. The ascetics' decision to move to the law courts and the salience of legal idioms in the subsequent reshaping of the community lucidly portray the acute presence of the state in the life of the community. At the same time, the renouncers had their own uses and understandings of state power and the decrees of courts. Indeed, through their texts and histories they sought to construct a community and posit it as already existing.

What is of singular importance is the nature of the *Itihasas* (histories) of Mahima Dharma produced by the ascetics. Composite blends of modern history and *itihasa-purana*, these texts situated Mahima Dharma within a linear chronology and located the founder in history while positing their claims to truth on the divinity of Mahima Swami. The founding concerns of chronology and temporality of modern history were paid attention to and overturned by a particular a notation of time which marked the precise year of the 'appearance' of the founder in Orissa as the beginning of the new era of Mahima (*Mahimabda, Mahima abda*) and invocations of the timelessness of the founder. These texts thus acceded to and exceeded the norms of history writing. The excess engendered by the intermingling of history and *itihasa* opened up the written texts to diverse interpretations and allowed the ascetics to use their own texts to question the definitions of judges and connive at their rulings.

Groups of lay followers, on the other hand, have used the texts of Bhima Bhoi to counter the elucidation contained in the texts of twentieth century. Equally, they have drawn upon both the compositions of Bhima Bhoi and the reasoned explications of Mahima Dharma to formulate their own understandings. Such differential perceptions have undercut moves at uniformity and standardization and given rise to further contingent communities. My account outlines how, under the aegis of legal and ritual power and through specific claims of being a modern yet timeless religion, Mahima Dharma has evolved as an ordered sect but one with many contentions, pasts and orientations.

Contention

Religion, Law and Power combines the methods of history and anthropology to provide a situated and textured analysis of the different trajectories of Mahima Dharma. It locates the members of a critically marginal community within the interstices of power over a century and a half in order to examine the imbrication of domination and subordination, *Herrschaft* (state power) and community and resistance and incorporation.[55] Here records of the archive engage in a dialogue with material yielded by extensive fieldwork — formal and informal interviews, conversations with ascetics and householders and participation in ceremonies and festivals of the faith — in an attempt to recreate the world of the followers of Mahima Dharma. I do not use interviews and 'oral history' 'as a seasoning to enliven documentary evidence'. Rather, my effort is to arrive at 'enmeshed, intertwined and imbricated web of narratives from every available source'.[56] The ethno-historical account of a subaltern religious formation I offer is informed by an attention to detail and a tendency to desist from structuring. My purpose is to stay with the problems and tensions that a singular, coherent historical narrative embodies and hides.

The distinct yet overlapping pasts of Mahima Dharma bring to the fore a clutch of empirical and theoretical issues. To begin with, a focus on how a scattered religious formation came to be crystallized into an institutionalized sect reveals the inherently historical nature of religion, its key attributes as process and its linkages with power. This gives the lie to yet another enduring dichotomy — that between religion and politics — one that owes its origin to the same legacy as that of the secularization of Time and History. The innate separation of religion from power/politics, premised on the universal definition of these categories, masks the genealogies of their own construction and confers on religion an unchanging essence.[57] My study views religion and power as spheres that mutually structure and transform each other in specific colonial and postcolonial contexts. It probes pervasive projections of religion as an insular domain of the sacred and of power as pure force unto itself. Here, explorations of the formulation, rearticulation and consolidation of a subaltern religious order are not marked off from but unravel the mechanisms and measures of the modern state and dominant Hinduism.

Second, a close examination of the tenets, practices and philosophy of Mahima Dharma in the context of particular understandings of time and temporality in which they acquire importance, serves to underscore unique combinations of 'great' and 'little' traditions, secular and religious time and faith and reason in the everyday lives of ordinary men and women. The doctrines of the founder and its poet-philosopher and their individual practices throw into disarray neat classifications of the classical and the popular and influential formulations of the opposition between the man-in-the-world and the individual-outside-the-world, the householder and the renouncer, apart from providing valuable insights into notions of asceticism as well as that of the preceptor and the disciple. More significantly, the reshaping of Mahima Dharma in concordance with the requirements of the law foreground the subaltern and ascetic negotiations of modernity in institutional and quotidian arenas through the delineation of new temporalities and creation of 'timeless' traditions. This challenges the distinction between the modern and the non-modern by showing the very modern venture of creating tradition and community. It also offers a rare glimpse of the perception and deployment of legal idioms in the construction and demarcation of a bounded community by subaltern subjects.

Third, the manifold understandings of the teachings and practices of the faith by its lay followers and renouncers — that course through the life of Mahima Dharma — emphasize the need to attend to the experiential, subjective domain of subordinate peoples and quotidian cultures. In different ways and in diverse contexts, this has been stressed in the works of Michel de Certeau as well as by the proponents of history-from-below in England, Alltagsgeschichte in Germany, microhistoria in Italy and subaltern studies in South Asia. My work extends these concerns with its own accents. It uses the discrete perceptions of Mahima Dharma by its adherents as a point of entry into practices of 'reading' and understanding of texts by its interpretive community highlighting thereby the creative potential of such exercises. Moreover, by probing the divergent, purposeful expressions of religious idioms in the lives of ordinary members of Mahima Dharma, this study illustrates the conjunction of authority and approbation in daily lives and of religion as a worked-over entity and a political, changing domain.

Fourth, this serves to unpack the implications of constellations of power and religion that have been indicated but not sufficiently worked out in scholarship on South Asia, particularly subaltern studies. Indeed, a close examination of the process through which a marginal 'religious tradition' comes into being and gets established acutely highlights the mutual imbrications and constant interaction of religion and power as they shape each other in the realm of the everyday. *Religion, Law and Power* looks at religion as a key dimension of cultures of subalterns without romanticizing either the subalterns or their religions. It tracks the divergent and discordant ways in which the message of the faith has been perceived and grasped by subordinate subjects, diverse perceptions that have occasioned dissension among different groups of renouncers and contentions between ascetics and householder disciples. Moreover, the hierarchy of the monastic and lay orders — something that is assumed in the 'natural' right of ascetics to interpret the teachings of the faith and regulate the fortunes of the community — adequately exhibit the necessity of using the subaltern as a relational category. An attention to subaltern as perspective, in fact, lays bare its multiple registers and immense possibilities.

Fifth and finally, this work tracks the ragged routes of Mahima Dharma in order to portray the polyvalence of history that inheres in the ambiguity and overlap between event and narrative at the core of configurations of past and present. The truth-claim of historical narratives invites the play of power, legitimizing some as historical and dismissing others as mere myth. And it is precisely different perceptions of truth and belief in distinct temporalities that enable the followers of Mahima Dharma to chart diverse pathways of historical consciousness. Their formal histories and 'rational' explications of the Dharma are based on evidence and strongly advocate the necessity of written texts for the 'progress' of the religious order. Yet, as stated before, these accounts claim to be true on grounds that they are about the divine founder. Apocryphal texts use specific markers of linear history and popular notions of cyclical time, jumbled up 'political' idioms of the nationalist struggle against British rule with 'religious' motifs of epic battles to undo and traverse the worlds of myth and history, faith and reason and orality and writing. These mix-ups produce competing conceptions of Mahima Dharma that result in divergent practices, simultaneously generating tensions and contradictions and marking off its members as a bounded community. It is this cluttered world of fusions and inconsistencies, friction and solidarity that my account seeks to bring to life.

Chapters

Religion, Law and Power constructs an account of Mahima Dharma which focuses on particular themes and moments in the life of the faith without foregoing an attention to chronology. It traces the ragged paths in the emergence, establishement and evolution of a new religion and unpacks the several enmeshments of religion, reason, politics, law and history that underlie these steps. Following the introduction, which sets out the main arguments and concerns, the second chapter locates the faith and its founder in the wider context of socio-economic, religious conditions of Orissa in the nineteenth century. The chapter juxtaposes information on the preceptor provided by a few fragmentary references in Oriya newspapers with the coherent reports produced by colonial administrators, Protestant missionaries and the formal *Itihasa* of the faith in order to bring into relief both the plurality of perceptions of history and the creative tensions of faith and reason. Through a detailed analysis of the troubled conditions of Orissa, the significance of the metaphor of Kali Yuga and the immense import of the teachings of Mahima Swami, it tries to explain why Mahima Swami gained immediate success and became deified in his lifetime as the incarnation of the Absolute he spoke about. It also analyses why the new Dharma appealed primarily to subordinate groups of men and women. Finally, the chapter offers a critical account of the 'attack' on the temple of Jagannath in 1881. Once more, contrasting the disparaging tone of reports of administrators and Oriya periodicals with divergent understandings of the incident among followers of the faith, the chapter raises important issues of history, memory and power and the ambiguity of action and narration that underlies history writing.

The third chapter focuses on Bhima Bhoi, the main poet-philosopher of Mahima Dharma. It offers a detailed analysis of the life and some key works of a non-conformist poet and underscores how both were amenable to distinct apprehensions. The combination of the life of a householder with that of a religious preacher made Bhima Bhoi's life a rich source of legends. Ingenious and inextricable blending of high philosophy and everyday metaphors, the oral and the written in the inspired lyrical compostions of a blind poet lent his works to varied perceptions. Staying with the wide-ranging implications of this interface, the chapter discusses distinct practices of 'reading' and interpretation occasioned by oral recitation and singing of the devotional lyrics at collective gatherings of unlettered devotees.[58] It analyses the singular significance of the recurrent reference to Kali Yuga and the prediction of its imminent destruction in the works of Bhima Bhoi, in apprehensions of Bhima Bhoi's works and in perceptions of a difficult present by lay followers. The chapter extends the analysis by a critical focus on the way both Bhima Bhoi and his works have been perceived and apprehended by members of the community in the twentieth century.

The fourth chapter — Ascetics, Histories and the Law — chalks the course of Mahima Dharma from the death of Mahima Swami to the end of the twentieth century. It focuses on the efforts of leading ascetics of the faith to configure and conserve a community. Noting the crisis engendered by the death of the charismatic founder, the chapter discusses how the need to find a rallying point to hold the disparate group of followers together prompted the ascetics to construct a memorial for the Guru. Further, it examines the wide-ranging ramifications of the substitution of a mobile preceptor by a static memorial, followed by the introduction of ritual services at the memorial and the discord between two groups of renouncers over the right to offer services. This discord eventually results in a complete breach with the intervention of the legal machinery of the state. Processes of institutionalization are given a fillip by dictates of the law as ascetics end up writing detailed explications and formal histories of the Dharma to be used as written evidence in court. This division also encourages the two groups to look for sympathizers among the Oriya literati which results in a further shift in emphasis from the periphery to the centre and from heterogeneity to homogeneity.

At the same time, the histories (*Itihasas*) written by the renouncers simultaneously draw upon traditions of modern history and *itihasa-purana* by situating Mahima Swami in chronology but positing the veracity of the history on the divinity of the founder. The fundamental importance of the divine founder in the history of the faith is emphasized in the use of a new era for marking time: the age of Mahima Dharma which is said to begin in 1826, when Mahima Swami appeared in Puri. The *Itihasa* and several other texts of the ascetics inscribe the *Mahimabda* (Mahima *abda*, era) as the authoritative mode of measuring time for the followers of the faith who live their lives within the sacred spatial and temporal realms of the faith. The special blend of history and *Itihasa* posited on secular-chronological time make the formal histories amenable to various perceptions, which destabilize their own projects of standardization.

Moreover, the lawyers and judges of independent India advance their own interpretations in characterizing Mahima Dharma as a sect within Hinduism. The ascetics carefully redraw the Dharma's boundary with Hinduism but with their own emphases which allow them to evade the rulings of law courts. Finally, lay followers use both the written histories and the works of Bhima Bhoi in their understandings of the faith. The long and convoluted relationship with law throws valuable insight into the interaction of *Herrschaft* and community, each in a process of change and accommodation, impinging upon and shaping the other. Moreover, the different trajectories make for the evolution of Mahima Dharma as a sect, but not a singular one.

The fifth chapter brings the everyday lives of householder devotees into perspective. It explores the reasons that have drawn people into Mahima Dharma and explores the tensions and negotiations of caste, sect and gender that are played out in the quotidian arena. This serves to highlight the many meanings of belonging to a distinct faith. The chapter probes Dumont's overarching theory on caste and sect and the dominant understandings of conversion as a fundamental break with an earlier faith. Further, it examines the lives of different groups of renouncers and varied ceremonies and festivals of the faith that reinforce the borders of a bounded community. This is complemented by accounts of the annual pilgrimage to Mahima Swami's memorial and to Bhima Bhoi's *ashrama*. The distinct participants of the two pilgrimages and the differences in the rituals illustrate the different tracks that Mahima Dharma continues to follow, in spite of sedentarization and institutionalization.

Finally, a brief epilogue comments on recent developments within the faith. It underscores further the variations in the perception of tenets and the elaboration in practices, particularly in novel configurations of temporalities and expressions of direct communication with the founder. Mahima Dharma retains its independence and uniqueness, offering to its many members multiple and overlapping modes of coping with life.

Notes

1. This has been affirmed by a wide range of scholars with different emphases. David Lowenthal, for instance, argues that the clear separation of the past from the present is what made for the emergence of history. D. Lowenthal, *The Past is a Foreign Country* (Cambridge, Cambridge University Press, 1985). A critical discussion of all these distinct approaches can be found in Ajay Skaria, *Hybrid Histories: Forests, Frontiers and Wildness in Western India* (Delhi, Oxford University Press, 1999), pp. 6–10.
2. This division, in fact, has been critically considered in the disciplines of anthropology and history. See, for instance, Bernard S. Cohn, 'History and anthropology: The state of play', *Comparative Studies in Society and History,* 22:2, 1980, pp. 198–221; Hans Medick, 'Missionaries in a row boat? Ethnological ways of knowing as a challenge to social history' in Alf Lüdtke (ed.), *The History of Everyday Life: Reconstructing Historical Experiences and Ways of Life,* tr. William Templer (Princeton, Princeton University Press, 1995) pp. 41–71; Johannes Fabian, *Time and the Other: How Anthropology Makes its Object* (New York, Columbia University Press, 1983). For a detailed and incisive analysis of these positions and the wider issues at stake here see, Saurabh Dube, 'Anthropology, history, historical anthropology' in S. Dube, (ed.), *Historical Anthropology* (Delhi, Oxford University Press, forthcoming).
3. J. Fabian, *Time and the Other*, p. 2.
4. *Ibid.*, p. 26.
5. S. Dube, 'Anthropology, history, historical anthropology'.
6. Nancy Munn has discussed how efforts to establish the historical-temporal break between the past and the present after the French Revolution entailed wide-ranging measures of governance including the French Republican calendric reform, which grounded time in a new vision of socio-economic foundation of political power. Nancy D. Munn, 'The cultural anthropology of time: A critical essay', *Annual Review of Anthropology*, 21, 1992, pp. 93–123.
7. S. Dube, 'Anthropology, history, historical anthropology'.

8. See, for instance, R. Laurence Moore, *Touchdown Jesus: The Mixing of Sacred and Secular in American History* (Louiseville, Kentucky, Westminster John Know Press, 2003).
9. S. Dube, 'Anthropology, history, historical anthropology'.
10. The literature is vast. See, for instance, David Landes, *Revolution in Time: Clocks and the Making of the Modern World* (Cambridge, Mass., Harvard University Press, 1983). For an analysis of some of the key issues from a perspective of modern Indian history see, Sumit Sarkar, 'Colonial times: Clocks and Kaliyuga' in Sumit Sarkar, *Beyond Nationalist Frames: Relocating Postmodernism, Hindutva, History*, (Delhi, Permanent Black, 2002), pp. 10–37, 10–11, in particular.
11. John Comaroff and Jean Comaroff, *Ethnography and the Historical Imagination* (Boulder, Westview, 1992); Saurabh Dube, *Untouchable Pasts: Religion, Identity, and Power among a Central Indian Community, 1780–1950* (Albany, State University of New York Press, 1998).
12. For a useful discussion of different approaches to time and duration in anthropological scholarship see Arjun Appadurai, 'The past as a scarce resource', *Man* (N.S.), 16:2, 1981, pp. 201–19.
13. I thank David Lorenzen for this point. To substantiate it further, Hindu Yugas last aeons of years as compared to 6000 years of Biblical time. Kali Yuga, the last one is meant to go on for 432, 000 years. It is not yet over. We will see the salience of the ever-present Kali in understandings of the past and the present in the following chapters.
14. Mircea Eliade, *The Myth of Eternal Return*, tr. Willard R. Trask, (Tennessee, Pantheon, 1954).
15. Nancy M. Farris, 'Remembering the future, anticipating the past: History, time and cosmology among the Mayas of Yucatan', *Comparative Studies in Society and History*, 29: 3, 1987, pp. 566–93.
16. Sarkar, 'Colonial times', p. 12.
17. For an insightful analysis of the heterogeneity of time reckoning among medieval chroniclers of the Indo–Persianate tradition see Sudipta Sen, 'Imperial orders of the past: The semantics of history and time in the medieval Indo–Persianate culture of north India' in Daud Ali (ed.), *Invoking the Past: The Uses of History in South Asia* (Delhi, Oxford University Press, 1999), pp. 231–57.
18. Romila Thapar, 'Society and historical consciousness: The *itihasa-purana* tradition' in Sabyasachi Bhattacharya and Romila Thapar (eds), *Situating Indian History for Sarvepalli Gopal* (Delhi, Oxford University Press, 1986), pp. 353–83. For an insightful account of the uses of time and history in ancient India see, Romila Thapar, *Time as a Metaphor of History: Early India* (Delhi, Oxford University Press, 1996).
19. Partha Chatterjee, 'Itihaser Uttardahikar', *Baromas*, 12: 2, 1991, pp. 1–24; P. Chatterjee, 'Claims on the Past' in David Arnold and David Hardiman (eds), *Subaltern Studies VIII: Essays in Honour of Ranajit Guha* (Delhi, Oxford University Press, 1994), pp. 1–49.
20. Ashis Nandy, 'History's forgotten doubles', *History and Theory*, 34, 1995, pp. 44–66.
21. Vinay Lal, *The History of History* (New Delhi, Oxford University Press, 2003).
22. *Ibid.*, p. 65.
23. Jacques Le Goff, *History and Memory*, tr. Steven Rendall and Elizabeth Claman (New York, Columbia University Press, 1992).
24. E. P. Thompson, 'Time, work-discipline and industrial capitalism', *Past and Present*, 38, 1967, pp. 56–97; reprinted in E. P. Thompson, *Customs in Common* (New York, The New Press, 1993), pp. 354–403; Michel Foucault, *Discipline and Punish: The Birth*

of Prison, (New York, Vintage, 1977).

25. Fabian, *Time and the Other.*
26. According to Sumit Sarkar, the Kali Yuga texts of Bengal demonstrate that the 'changeover' from cyclical Hindu time to linear western time was neither 'total' nor 'painless'. Sarkar does not, however, question either the binary or the changeover. In a later essay, he interrogates the binary but not the changeover. Sumit Sarkar, 'Renaissance and Kaliyuga: Time, myth and history in colonial Bengal' in Sumit Sarkar, *Writing Social History* (Delhi, Oxford University Press, 1998), pp. 186–215; Sumit Sarkar, 'Colonial times', pp. 10–37.
27. Lal, *The History of History.*
28. For a recent, thorough and thoughtful critique of modernity see, Dipesh Chakrabarty, *Provincializing Europe: Postcolonial Thought and Historical Difference* (Princeton, Princeton University Press, 2000); and D. Chakrabarty, 'Postcoloniality and the artifice of history: Who speaks for "Indian" pasts?' in Ranajit Guha (ed.), *A Subaltern Studies Reader 1986–1995* (Minneapolis, University of Minnesota Press, 1997), pp. 263–94, for a reflection also on the arrogance and power that underlies the western notion of History.
29. Dube, 'Anthropology, history, historical anthropology'.
30. Talal Asad, *Genealogies of Religion: Discipline and Reasons of Power in Christianity and Islam* (Baltimore, The Johns Hopkins University Press, 1993), p. 269. One of the most important and influential formulations and critiques of the western project of power-knowledge in relation to colonialism was advanced by Edward Said's *Orientalism*, (London, Routledge and Kegan Paul, 1978).
31. Dube, 'Anthropology, history, historical anthropology'.
32. For a critical discussion see, Saurabh Dube, *Stitches on Time: Colonial Textures and Postcolonial Tangles*, (Durham, Duke University Press, 2004), chapter 7.
33. This has been stressed with regard to the duality of orality and writing by Ajay Skaria. A. Skaria, 'Writing, orality and power in the Dangs, western India, 1880s–1920s' in Shahid Amin and Dipesh Chakrabarty (eds), *Subaltern Studies IX: Writings on South Asian History and Society* (Delhi, Oxford University Press, 1997), pp. 13–58.
34. Fernando Coronil, *The Magical State: Nature, Money, and Modernity in Venezuela*, (Chicago, The University of Chicago Press, 1997), p. 14. Coronil elaborates the idea of Occidentalism by way of both extending and critiquing Said's Orientalism. Occidentalism, in his words, is 'the expression of a constitutive relationship between western representations of cultural difference and worldwide Western dominance.' *Ibid.*
35. Paul Veyne, *Writing History*, tr. Mina Moore-Rinvolucri (Middletown, Wesleyan University Press, 1984), 1st French edition, 1971, prologue.
36. Lawrence W. Levine, *The Unpredictable Past: Explorations in American Cultural History* (New York, Oxford University Press, 1993), p. 4.
37. Henry James, 1946, cited in Levine, *The Unpredictable Past*, p. 4.
38. Levine, *The Unpredictable Past*, p. 4.
39. Marc Bloch, *The Historians Craft*, tr. Peter Putnam, (New York, Vintage, 2nd edition 1953), p. 58.
40. It is difficult to provide a comprehensive list of the vast literature that these different trends have produced. Here are some representative examples, E. P. Thompson, *The Making of the English Working Class* (New York, Vintage, 1963); Natalie Zemon Davis, *Society and Culture in Early Modern France: Eight Essays by Natalie Zemon Davis* (Stanford, Stanford University Press, 1977); Eugene D. Genovese, *Roll Jordan Roll: The World that Slaves Made* (New York, Pantheon, 1977). A substantive statement of

the project and programme of *Alltagsgeschichte* is contained in Alf Lüdtke, 'Introduction: What is the history of everyday life and who are its practitioners?' in A. Lüdtke (ed.), *The History of Everyday Life*, pp. 3–40. Another significant work of this school is David Warren Sabean, *Power in the Blood: Popular Culture and Village Discourse in Early Modern Germany* (Cambridge, Cambridge University Press, 1984). Important writings of micro-history include, Carlo Ginzburg, *The Cheese and the Worms: The Cosmos of a Sixteenth Century Miller*, tr. John and Anne Tedeschi (Baltimore, Johns Hopkins University Press, 2nd edition, 1980); Edward Muir and Guido Ruggiero (eds), *Microhistory and the Lost Peoples of Europe*, tr. Eren Branch (Baltimore, Johns Hopkins University Press, 1991). There have been 12 volumes of *Subaltern Studies* published between 1982 and 2005. Some other key works by individual members of the collective are: Ranajit Guha, *Elementary Aspects of Peasant Insurgency in Colonial India*, (Delhi, Oxford University Press, 1983), Dipesh Chakrabarty, *Rethinking Working Class History: Bengal 1890–1940* (Delhi, Oxford University Press, 1989); David Arnold, *Colonizing the Body: State Medicine and Epidemic Disease in Nineteenth Century India* (Delhi: Oxford University Press, 1993); Partha Chatterjee, *The Nation and Its Fragments: Colonial and Postcolonial Histories* (Princeton, Princeton University Press, 1993); Shahid Amin, *Event, Metaphor, Memory: Chauri Chaura 1922–1992* (Berkeley and Los Angeles, University of California Press, 1995); David Hardiman, *The Coming of the Devi: Adivasi Assertion in Western India* (Delhi, Oxford University Press, 1997); Gyanendra Pandey, *Remembering the Partition: Violence, Nationalism and History in India* (Cambridge: Cambridge University Press, 2001); and, in Bengali, Gautam Bhadra, *Jal Rajar Katha: Bardhamaner Pratapchand* (Calcutta, Ananda Publishers, 2002).

41. Several works have discussed both the problems and possibilities of the dialogue between history and anthropology and applied the methods in their analyses. Moreover, *Alltagsgeschichte, micro-historia* and subaltern studies have all engaged with historical anthropology with distinct emphases. I offer a few examples. For early statements on and fruitful engagements with historical anthropology see, Bernard Cohn, 'History and Anthropology', Renato Rosaldo, *Ilongot Headhunting 1883–1974: A Study in Society and History* (Stanford, Stanford University Press, 1980); Gananath Obeyesekere, *The Cult of the Goddess Pattini* (Chicago, University of Chicago Press, 1984); Nicholas Dirks, *The Hollow Crown: Ethnohistory of an Indian Kingdom* (Cambridge, Cambridge University Press,1987); John and Jean Comaroff, *Ethnography and the Historical Imagination*; Emiko Ohnuki-Tierney, 'Introduction: The historicization of Anthropology' in E. Ohnuki-Tierney (ed.), *Culture Through Time: Anthropological Approaches* (Stanford, Stanford University Press, 1990), pp. 1–25. For recent imaginative engagements and extension of the methods of historical anthropology in works in South Asia see, Saurabh Dube, *Untouchable Pasts*; Ajay Skaria, *Hybrid Histories*. Two critical and comprehensive accounts of the distinct trends and debates of historical anthropology can be found in Brian K. Axel (ed.), *From the Margins: Historical Anthropology and its Futures* (Durham, Duke University Press, 2002); and Saurabh Dube (ed.), *Historical Anthropology*.
42. Daud Ali, 'Introduction' in Daud Ali (ed.), *Invoking the Past*, p. 1.
43. Sumit Sarkar, *Writing Social History*, p. 1.
44. I have gained from Robert Borofsky's critical reflections on anthropological constructions of knowledge premised on an insightful account of the different ways of knowing and reviving the past among a Polynesian community. R Borofsky, *Making History: Pukapukan and Anthropological Constructions of Knowledge* (Cambridge, Cambridge University Press, 1987).

45. Robert Redfield's well-known formulation of the 'great tradition of the reflective few' and the 'little tradition of the largely unreflective many' in Hinduism has had an important bearing on the demarcation of the high and low, classical and popular traditions of Hinduism. Robert Redfield, *Peasant, Society, and Culture* (Chicago, University of Chicago Press, 1956). This division was worked out in a different way in the concept of Sanskritization developed by M. N. Srinivas in the early 1950s and elaborated in 1962. M. N. Srinivas, *Society and Culture among the Coorgs of South India,* (Oxford, Clarendon Press, 1952). A persuasive critique of the dichotomies of both 'great' and 'little' and Sanskritic and non Sanskritic traditions in Hinduism was offered by Lawrence Babb in his study of popular Hinduism in central India. Lawrence A. Babb, *The Divine Hierarchy: Popular Hinduism in Central India* (New York, Columbia University Press, 1975), pp. 23–6 in particular. Several works have pointed to the intermingling of high and low traditions within trends of *bhakti*. See, for instance, the essays contained in, David N. Lorenzen (ed.), *Bhakti Religion in North India: Community Identity and Political Action* (Albany, State University of New York Press, 1995). The point, however, is that the problem lies in thinking of the two trends as completely separate entities that then interact with each other. In a different context, Carlo Ginzburg provides a fascinating account of the ways in which ideas travelled back and forth between 'high' and the 'low' cultures and how each shaped the other. C Ginzburg, *The Cheese and the Worms*.
46. Complex norms and asymmetrical patterns of food exchange maintain the norms of purity and express the rank in caste hierarchies. Cooked rice, in particular, 'readily absorbs pollution from those who prepare and serve it, and accepting cooked rice from a person belonging to another caste would, in effect, be symbolically accepting a relatively high degree of pollution from the giver'. L. A. Babb, *Divine Hierarchies*, p. 55. Mahima Swami, in accepting cooked rice from the lowest castes but not from Brahmans and kings was playing havoc with this strict code and demonstrating his confidence in accepting the highest degree of pollution.
47. I discuss this at greater length in the following chapter.
48. What we find here is another reversal of hierarchy between the monastic and lay orders. Mahima Swami, in preaching that salvation was open to all through devotion, was erasing the boundary between and the renouncer and the householder. Even a radical, 'dissenting' sect such as Theravada Buddhism lays down several precepts only for the monks to attain salvation. 'Merit accumulation' is what the householders are entitled to do. See, Ilana Sibbler, 'Dissent through holiness: The case of the radical renouncer in Thervada Buddhist countries' in S. N. Eisenstadt, R. Kahane and David Shulman (eds), *Orthodoxy, Heterodoxy and Dissent in India* (Berlin and New York, Mouton Publishers, 1984), pp. 85–104.
49. A critical discussion of the nature of 'collective memory' can be found in Ann Grodzins Gold and Bhoju Ram Gujar, *In the Time of Trees and Sorrows: Nature, Power and Memory in Rajasthan* (Durham, Duke University Press, 2002).
50. I draw upon the critical discussion of differential perception of 'events' among different groups in Gyanendra Pandey, '"Encounters and calamities": The history of a north Indian Qasba in the nineteenth century' in Ranajit Guha (ed.), *Subaltern Studies III: Writings on South Asian History and Society*, (Delhi, Oxford University Press, 1984), pp. 231–70.
51. For a sensitive discussion of this ambiguity and the role of power in History see, Michel Rolph-Trouillot, *Silencing the Past: Power and the Production of History* (Boston, Beacon Press, 1995).
52. These steps are significant. On the one hand, Bhima Bhoi challenged the notion of

superiority of the renouncer and his greater claim as a religious preacher by becoming a householder. On the other hand, he erased gender inequality by allowing women to renounce the world.

53. For an early nuanced account of the making of a prophet among the *adivasi* see K. S. Singh, *The Dust Storm and The Hanging Mist: A Study of Birsa Munda and His Movement 1874–1904*, Calcutta, Firma K L M, 1966.
54. I do not want to enter the extensive debate within religious studies on the nature and meanings of sect, of whether and how far Hindu sects can be called sects. The two principal theories that have inspired and framed a lot of this discussion are Max Weber's analysis of othorodoxy and heterodoxy and Louis Dumont's discussion of renunciation in Indian religions and of sects degenerating into castes. I will briefly engage with this theory of Dumont in the last chapter. See Max Weber, *The Sociology of Religion*, tr. by Ephraim Fischoff (Boston, Beacon Press, 1969); Louis Dumont, 'World renunciation in Indian religion', in *Religion/Politics and History in India: Collected Papers in Indian Sociology* (Paris and The Hague, Mouton, 1970). For a critical reflection on problems produced by analyzing sects with reference to these theories see, R. Blake Michael, *The Origins of Virasaiva Sects: A Typological Analysis of Rituals and Associational Patterns in the Sunyasampadane* (Delhi, Motilal Banarsidass, 1992), chapter 1. For a different and critical take on Dumont's theory of caste and sect see, David N. Lorenzen, 'Traditions of non-caste Hinduism: The Kabirpanth', *Contributions to Indian Sociology*, 23:1, 1987, pp. 263–83. For a recent analysis of a sectarian tradition which discusses the problems of taking tradition as static see, Vasudeva Rao, *Living Traditions in Contemporary Contexts: The Madhava Matha of Udipi* (Hyderabad, Orient Longman, 2002).
55. I take the German term *Herrschaft* from David Waren Sabean. *Herrschaft* 'expresses relationships of power' but in a way not covered by any of the competing terms in English. *Herrschaft* is 'over-laid by historical specificity on the one hand and by ideological dispute on the other'. Sabean, *Power in the Blood*, p. 21. It is in this sense that I want to use authority and state power.
56. Here I closely follow the arguments advanced in Shahid Amin, 'They also followed Gandhi' in Saurabh Dube (ed.), *Postcolonial Passages: Contemporary History-writing on India*, (New Delhi, Oxford University Press, 2004), pp. 132–58; and Shahid Amin, *Event, Metaphor, Memory*.
57. I draw upon Talal Asad's important insights concerning the configuration of religion as a universal, a priori category in the modern West. Talal Asad, 'The construction of religion as an anthropological category' in Asad, *Genealogies of Religion*, pp. 27–54.
58. The dichotomy of the oral and the written has been seriously discussed and questioned over the past several years, particularly by important studies on Africa. These have involved attempts to establish oral traditions as history and thorough critiques of the stereotypes that hold the binary in place. My work uses and extends these with its own emphases. See, for instance, Jan Vansina, *Oral Tradition as History* (London, James Currey, 2nd edition, 1985); Ruth Finnegan *Literacy and Orality: Studies in the Technology of Communication* (Oxford, Blackwell, 1988).

CHAPTER 2.

Formations of Faith

How do new religious traditions emerge and legitimize themselves? What is the role of relationships of power in these processes? This chapter addresses such questions by tracing the emergence and establishment of Mahima Dharma. I begin by tracing the construal of the figure of the founder of the faith by colonial administrators, Protestant missionaries, Oriya intellectuals and followers of Mahima Dharma, further exploring creative tensions between 'reason' and 'faith' in portrayals of Mahima Swami as a historical figure and a divine ascetic. Next, I discuss the precepts and practices of Mahima Swami and their implications for the members of the new faith, who were mainly low-caste and tribal peoples, in the wider context of the socio-economic, religious and political conditions of Orissa in the mid-nineteenth century. As a last step, I offer a critical analysis of a dramatic event: an 'attack' on the temple of Jagannath in Puri by a small group of men and women from western Orissa, which has wide implications.

This short-lived drama brought Mahima Dharma to the notice of British administrators and caused consternation among middle-class Oriyas. A handful of lay adherents of the Dharma desecrated the sanctity of the temple and tried to destroy the image of Jagannath, a deity whose status as the Lord of the Universe rested on the inextricable links between religion and politics, ritual and power. In doing so, they gave a new meaning to Mahima Swami's questioning of hierarchy and authority, especially underscoring the potential of innovative appropriations of the teachings of the founder. Yet, this dramatic event has left seemingly little or no trace on the subsequent development of the faith and appears to have disappeared from the collective memory of its followers. Focusing on this apparent paradox as part of the interface between the past and the present and religion and power, the chapter explores the ambiguity and overlap between action and narration, between 'what happened' and 'what is said to have happened' in history.[1]

The Making of Mahima Swami

The first known report about Mahima Swami came only a few years after he had launched on his career as a holy man and appeared in the Oriya newspaper *Utkala Deepika* on 1 June 1867.[2] It claimed that a new faith was spreading in the princely states bordering Cuttack. This faith had been founded by a *phalahari sanyasi* (an ascetic who survived on fruits) who lived on Kapilas hill in Dhenkanal. The ascetic had initially subsisted on fruits alone, later had drunk milk, but in the end he lived only on water. He worshipped Siva. One day, on the directions of *śunya* (the great void) he cut his matted locks and gave up his vocation as a mere renouncer. He began wearing the bark of a tree and spread a *dharma* that disregarded caste distinctions, forbade idol worship and rituals — for example, *śraddha* (death rites and ceremonies) — and advocated a belief in one *iśwara* (god). The *sanyasi* was described as *ati nirlobh* (completely free of greed) and praised for his efforts to feed people at a time of scarcity. He constructed large temporary houses where he fed forty to fifty thousand people. He then burnt these houses and moved on at will. The ascetic was said to command great respect. These bare details as they are set out in the first report of the newspaper underwent embellishments and mutations over the next fifty years during the construction and legitimization of the figure of Mahima Swami, the founder of Mahima Dharma.

Utkala Deepika also provided a second report six years later in 1873. By now the *phalahari sanyasi* had become 'Mahima Babaji' and his preaching and practices had started causing concern.[3] It was precisely the precepts of the Babaji and their success in attracting people that got the Baptist missionaries interested in him, and they went through a 'good deal of enquiry and difficulty' to meet him. The missionaries were impressed by what they saw: 'We found him to be a man of perhaps sixty years of age, tall and thin, with an intelligent and benevolent countenance.'[4] Rev. Miller looked upon the 'new religious teacher' favourably as a person who was paving the way for the spread of Christianity. He called him 'Dhulee Babajee' and felt that the name had originated from this teacher's habit of sleeping on bare ground. He further stressed that this ascetic 'never sleeps two nights in one place, and is constantly on the move among his followers'. The Babajee was commended as 'a very abstemious man'. He has 'but one meal a day, drinks only water or milk, never indulges in narcotics. He denounces idolatry, caste, the Brahmans, the use of narcotics and spirituous liquors. He inculcates the worship of the Creator and Preserver of the world, and the practice of devotion to God, truth, charity and chastity'.[5]

Colonial administrators, asked to enquire into the beliefs and practices of the people who attacked the temple of Jagannath in 1881, were the first to embark on a project of constructing a life history of the founder of Mahima Dharma. Their writings drew upon local traditions that had gathered around the renouncer but they consciously tried to forsake 'myths' in an attempt to provide an accurate account. In legend-history and myths a *dhulia/dhulee babaji*, a *phalahari sanyasi*, and a *kshiranira payee* (one who drinks milk and water) seemed to coalesce in the figure of Mahima Swami. Administrators' reports referred to these three different epithets of the founder, but claimed that they referred to separate stages of his life, thereby negating the possibility of a conflation of identities. Their accounts allow us to identify three phases, steps as it were, in the life of the religious leader.

In the first phase, the founder whom the administrators identified as 'one Mukund Das', was an 'Achari Boishnab' (practising Vaishnav, worshipper of Vishnu) who believed in and worshipped Hindu deities.[6] At the same time, he followed the practice of Śaiva ascetics in daubing his body with ashes, which earned him the cognomen of *dhulia babaji*. The second phase was spent on Kapilaś hill, 'a celebrated holy place' in Dhenkanal.[7] His sojourn at Kapilaś was a long one. In the first twelve years of his stay there he lived on fruits and for the next twelve years on milk and water. He came to be known respectively as *phalahari babaji* and *kshiranira payee*. During this period Mukund Das was a devout worshipper of Chandrasekhar–Śiva. He lived near Śiva's temple and 'took much pains in improving the place by cutting the jungle, making gardens, looking after the Bhog or sacred food of the idol, and taking care of the pilgrims who visit the hills periodically'.[8] Mukund Das earned the respect of the mother of the Raja of Dhenkanal. The Raja supplied him with milk. 'Popular belief' granted him special status as the intermediary between men and god. People of the surrounding villages became convinced that he was in secret communion with the idol and 'could intercede with it on behalf of its votaries'. The basis of this belief lay in the Babaji's practice of visiting the temple at dead of night, when others were asleep, and in his success in healing the sick pilgrims who visited Kapilaś.[9]

Clearly the long stay at Kapilaś constituted a critical stage in the career of the founder. It was at this site that he earned fame, respect and veneration and found his name and identity transformed. He rose from the position of an ordinary ascetic to that of the favoured devotee of Mahadev (Śiva). He became a human being with superhuman powers. He was ready for his vocation as the preacher of a new religion. The first noticeable change was in his garb. Throughout his sojourn at Kapilaś, as a worshipper of Śiva he had continued to wear the *kaupin* (waist-cloth) and *kanthi* (wooden beads worn around the neck): 'the two distinctive features in the raiment of a Vaishnava'.[10] It was only after he had finished his experiments with Hindu asceticism and decided to preach his own faith that he 'eschewed' the *kaupin* and *kanthi* and wore *kumbhipat* (the bark of the *kumbhi* tree). This symbolic act snapped his links with Hinduism and set him off on his own as the founder of a new *dharma.*

The third and final stage saw the ascetic preaching a new faith, Mahima Dharma. It also marked the culmination of his gradual elevation in status: the Babaji became Mahima Swami, an incarnation of the all-powerful Absolute whose glory he preached. Extensive and constant mobility were distinctive features of this phase. The ascetic ended his long period of meditation; with a new zeal he now set out to spread the message of *satya dharma* (true faith). From Kapilaś he went to Puri and then to Darutheng in Khurda, where he set up a *tungi*, a small hut that served as a place of worship, and began preaching the new doctrine.[11] He declared that Mahadev and other divine beings worshipped by the Hindus were nothing but destructible idols of stone and wood whose worship was useless. 'The Creator of the universe was *alekh* (indescribable) or *mahima* (glorious), a spiritual Being without form, omnipresent and omniscient.'[12] This was the only proper object of worship. The ascetic claimed to possess the power to communicate with this Absolute and to have his prayers answered.

The preacher's message was received favourably. The village of Darutheng provided him with his first two disciples, Govinda Das and Narsing Das. The site also witnessed the beginnings of his deification and transformation into Mahima Gosain. His first disciples initiated several others into the faith, who in turn dispersed 'on all sides' to spread the Dharma. The Swami himself took an active part in proselytizing. He traveled extensively in the Garhjats (tributary states under Oriya rulers) to spread his message. He led a very simple life: slept on bare ground, ate only one meal a day which consisted of cooked food obtained as *bhiksha* (alms), and acquired no personal property. The rigid renouncer even burnt the *tungis* before leaving a particular place. After destroying the *tungi* at Darutheng he built another one at Andharua. He subsequently built *tungis* at Damna in Patia and at Khuntuni in Athgarh. At Khuntuni 'he gave a great feast and attracted the general faith and worship of common people and the reputation of his excellencies spread far and wide.'[13]

At his next stop, Malbaharpur in Banki, the Swami with the help of his followers constructed a large house where he lit a *dhuni*, a sacred fire.[14] The *dhuni* was not to be extinguished. Narsing Das was left in charge of it while the Swami moved on to Dhenkanal, Angul, Talcher and Khurda and then returned to Malbaharpur. He 'stopped and ate at a distance of 300 hats from the house and gave some great feasts on the banks of the marsh called Ainspa. Numerous persons wore "Kumbhipat" in the Dhuni house under the Mahima's orders and they went to several parts of Orissa and to Sambalpur and Ganjam districts to propagate the creed'.[15] Large numbers of married men and women became devotees of Mahima Swami. They continued to lead the life of householders and were designated as *aśritas*, beings under the protection of Mahima. In 1869 the *dhuni* at Malbaharpur was destroyed. Mahima Swami visited various places in Banki and other feudatory states before coming to live at Joranda in Dhenkanal, where he died in 1875 [or 1876].[16]

The administrators' accounts of the activities of the Swami reveal a clear pattern. His constant mobility was complemented by short intervals when he stayed at a particular place, built a *tungi* and gathered large numbers of followers. The *tungi* became the site where devotees would congregate to hear the oral instructions of the new preacher.[17] The initiates, particularly the *aśritas*, stayed behind while his *sanyasi* disciples moved on. The ascetics propagated the message of the new faith while the lay disciples formed its permanent bases of support. The *aśritas* wove the threads of the memory of the Swami into the fabric of legend-history and continued to conduct their lives according to his precepts. Slowly but steadily, Mahima Swami's fame grew.

One marker of his increase in popularity was the growth in size and dimension of the successive *tungis* that were constructed and the money spent on them. While the first *tungi* at Darutheng was built at a cost of only 150 rupees, that at Malbaharpur, which was built in about 1869, involved an outlay of 2000 rupees. The size of *tungis* grew from 21 *hats* to 84. A second indicator of Mahima Swami's success was his practice of giving large feasts. Within a few years he had gathered enough followers to muster the resources to feed large numbers of people. These feasts acquired particular importance against a backdrop of scarcity and starvation: Orissa went through the worst famine of the century in 1866, a subject that will be discussed in greater detail in the following section. The feasts provided an occasion for the adherents of Mahima Dharma to come together, a chance for them to get *darśan* (sight) of the founder, whom they had come to regard as a divine being. They also acted as catchments for fresh converts and brought to the fore the immense power of the new religious leader.

At the same time, Mahima Swami persisted on the path of total detachment and shunned property. He never set himself up as the proprietor of a *tungi* with resident monastic and lay orders. He did not stay in a particular region or acquire landed property. *Tungis* were constructed with donations from *bhaktas* and were pulled down at the will of the founder. Indeed, Mahima Swami's constant mobility, his practice of sleeping on bare ground as well as of eating one cooked meal a day got as alms were direct disavowals of acquisitive tendencies. Such simple and appealing style of life was combined with an attractive message of devotion toward an all-powerful but accessible Absolute and a practical disregard of caste and other hierarchical social distinctions. All this made the Swami appear as a true benefactor to many. His practice of feeding people during times of scarcity, and a capacity to heal sick bodies fuelled the belief that he was in constant communion with the Absolute and contributed to Mahima Swami's deification.

Colonial officials did not stop at providing the 'facts' — the details of the life and activities of Mahima Swami, a human preceptor. They also sought to explain his deification as the result of the ignorance of common people. The illiterate and gullible people of Orissa, the administrators suggested, had interpreted the ascetic's claim that he preached what the Absolute had ordered, to mean that he was himself an incarnation of the Absolute. The Manager of Dhenkanal, in particular, the only official who had met the Guru, categorically denied that the Swami ever claimed to be the Lord. 'I never heard from him that he professed to be the Creator of the world as his disciples and followers believed him to be. From what I heard from him, I concluded that the Creator of the world was a spiritual Being, omnipresent and omniscient, without form, whom he called Mahima and also Prabhu, and that he alone could communicate with Alekh Prabhu and get down what he wished.'[18] All this, of course, bore testimony to the administrators' desire to establish Mahima Swami as merely a historical character.

The *Utkala Deepika* and the Baptist missionaries did not share the administrators' concern about establishing the historicity of Mahima Swami. The *Deepika* was content to refer to him as a *phalahari sanyasi*, and as Mahima Babaji, and paid greater attention to his teachings and practices.[19] Its first account praised the *sanyasi* for being *ati nirlobh*, free of greed, though there was just the hint of anxiety at his disregard of Hindu rites and rituals, which became a major concern by the time it published a second report in 1873. The Baptist missionaries, in their turn, were interested in the antecedents of the Swami in order to gauge the genesis of his ideas, and the extent to which his denunciation of caste and idolatry could help clear the path for the spread of Christianity. 'He [Mahima Swami] was very reserved as to his former history, when and where he got hold of his present views. It seems that he lived near Choga some years ago, and there had several interviews with the native preacher. This may account for some of his ideas.'[20] The messengers of Christ had found what they were looking for: it was the teachings of *their* Lord that had inspired the new religious leader to take up his vocation. Would this not lead the followers of the new faith to the truth of Christ?

The Swami and his followers have charted their own course irrespective of the concerns of colonial officers, Oriya intellectuals and Christian missionaries. The belief in the divinity of the founder has come to stay among the believers of Mahima Dharma; his identification with a particular human being remains a bone of contention. Scholars to this day squabble about whether he was indeed 'Mukund Das', mentioned by the Tehsildar (revenue collector) of Banki as the founder of Mahima Dharma.[21] N. N. Vasu, who discovered *Kali Bhagabata*, *Alekh Leela* and *Yaśomati Malika* — important religious books of Mahima Dharma — in the state of Mayurbhanj in the first decade of the twentieth century, added an interesting twist to the tale. He claimed that the founder of this 'crypto-Buddhist' sect was none other than Bhagavat Buddha himself, who had taken human form at the instance of Alekha Brahma or the Great Void.[22] The function of this human incarnation, however, was limited only to initiating Lord Jagannath, who had left Puri to join him in the village Golasingha of the feudatory state of Baud. Buddha initiated Jagannath into the doctrines of the true faith, delegated all his powers to him, and asked him to go to Kapilaś in Dhenkanal and 'remain stock-still in a trance'. In Kapilaś, Jagannath came to be known as Govinda. And here, 'for the good of humanity he remained absorbed in a trance for a period of full twelve years. His staple food, then, was simply a small quantity of milk and fresh water'.[23] We have here a double confusion, a conflation of identities between the Buddha and the founder of Mahima Dharma, and between the latter and his first disciple Govinda, who is widely believed to be Jagannath. I will discuss the problem and possibilities of this intricate relationship with the cult of Jagannath in the final section of this chapter and the chapters that follow. For the present, I want to underscore the persistence of fluidity in the figure of Mahima Swami, in spite of the presence of certain recurrent motifs, and despite the attempts of British officials to pin down his identity.

Satya Mahima Dharmara Itihasa of Biswanath Baba, the formal history of the faith written in the 1930s, began on the premise that Mahima Swami was *prabuddha narayan* (enlightened Supreme Being) and *iśwar purush* (male godhead) whose human form was *ajoni sambhuta* (not born of a womb).[24] Biswanath Baba also took care to establish Mukunda Das as a close companion of Mahima Swami, a claim upheld by his present followers. According to the *Itihasa*, Mahima Swami appeared in Orissa in 1826 and toured the regions of Puri, Khurda, Udaygiri and Khandagiri before moving on to Kapilaś. A prolonged period of meditation here cleansed the human form of the Absolute of his impurities and prepared him for the task of preaching *satya dharma*. *Sebakalara Katha*, a manual on the less known religious sects and places of pilgrimage in Orissa published in 1941, identified Mahima Swami with Balakrishna Das, a monk who performed *sadhana* in Udaygiri and Khandagiri before arriving at Kapilaś. There he met the old king and queen, got a *tungi* built, and spent 12 years drinking only milk before starting to give 'valuable advice' like Budhhadev.[25] While closely following Biswanath Baba's account, this short text revealed a possible influence of N. N. Vasu's argument in the author's interpretation of *prabuddha* (knowing/knowledgeable) as the Buddha of Buddhism. Mahima Swami's identity continued to defy any historical consensus.

Biswanath Baba, his particular concerns for writing an 'official' history of Mahima Dharma notwithstanding, was drawing upon legends and traditions that had gathered around Mahima Swami. As stated before, Mahima Swami had become deified during his lifetime. Indeed, the change of name from *dhulia babaji* and *phalahari gosain* to Mahima or Alekh Swami was a consequence of this elevation in status. Colonial administrators, who carefully crafted the figure of the founder hardly ever referred to him as Mahima Swami in their reports written in 1881. However, the feature on the ascetic published in *Utkala Deepika* in 1873 was titled 'Mahima Babaji'. This was a first indication that the adherents of the renouncer had started calling him by that name, believing him to be the incarnation of the indescribable Absolute, whose *mahima* he spoke about.

Biswanath Baba's *Itihasa* felt no need to justify the divinity of the founder. It was an established fact, particularly so because the arrival of this divine incarnation had been prophesied in important religious texts.[26] The opening statement clarified how in response to prayers of self-realized saints to purge the world of sin, the omnipotent, indescribable Absolute came down to earth as Mahamahima Swami. After travelling all over India in a secret form, he appeared in Orissa in 1826. It is said, asserts the *Itihasa* that Mahima Prabhu lay in the dust of the *bada danda*, the grand road in front of the Jagannath temple of Puri, thus acquiring the name of *dhulia gosain*. It is significant that the Swami made his appearance in the human form in Puri, the abode of Lord Jagannath, in close proximity to his temple. The *satya dharma* he eventually preached discarded the worship of the wooden image of the Lord of the Universe. Mahima Swami's sojourn at Kapilaś began after he had toured Udaygiri, Khandagiri, Dhauligiri, Bhubaneswar and neighbouring places for twelve years drinking only water. At Kapilaś, he cast off his saffron cloth and matted locks, and took to wearing the bark of *kumbhi* tree as preparatory to his vocation as a preacher. There was, of course, no need for any experiments with different versions and popular forms of Hinduism. The human form of the Absolute had come down to earth with a definite mission, to re-establish true faith. Resting on a round stone at the summit of Kapilaś hill, *prabuddha narayan* decided to take *samadhi* (living-death) in his glorious form for 21 days.

It was Sadanand, a Śavar, who had the first vision of the Swami in his state of *samadhi* at Kapilaś. Sadanand was also the person who supplied the *sanyasi* with fruits as he emerged from his *samadhi*, ready to save society and humanity by preaching *satya dharma*. Sadanand thus was the crucial link in the transformation of the Absolute into the founder of Mahima Dharma. After the Raja of Dhenkanal got to know of the ascetic through Sadanand, the Śavar took the Guru the milk supplied by the Raja.[27] All this involved a play with the figures and symbols associated with Jagannath. Jagannath, according to local traditions, was a *śavar-devata* (god of the Śavars, hunter-gatherers) whose worship was later taken over by kings who made him the *rashtra-devata* (state deity).[28] The career of Jagannath displayed the wresting of authority from *adivasis* (literally, original inhabitants) by rulers and upper-castes, accompanied by a shift in the locus of the cult from the *vana* (forest) to the *kshetra* (field). The story of Mahima Swami as narrated by Biswanath Baba effected an inversion: the Śavar was given priority over the Raja as the only person who had direct access to the Swami. We do not know whether Biswanath Baba was consciously trying to portray Mahima Swami as superior to Jagannath or merely rehearsing a belief that had developed over the nineteenth century. What is clear, however, is that the staging of Mahima Swami's encounter with the Śavar and the Raja underscored the interrogation of high Hinduism inherent in Mahima Dharma.

This was poetic justice. The Swami had ingeniously combined the dichotomies of *vana* (forest/ desert, uninhabited dangerous space lurking at the edges of settled areas) and *kshetra* (field, habited space) and *nagar/pura* (city/town) and *grama* (village) prevalent in different traditions of literature since the time of the Vedas and simultaneously given precedence to the *vana* and the *grama*.[29] He had chosen to preach in the remote villages of the Garhjats predominantly inhabited by *adivasis* and lower caste people. These villages, located at a distance from Puri and Cuttack, areas under direct

British administration and urban centres of religio-political power, were symbolic of inhabited space with forest-like, liminal attributes. In according primacy to tribal peoples, the Swami had sought to reverse a process set in motion by the steady elevation in status of Jagannath, the Lord of the Universe, from a tribal god to the state-deity of Orissa, a preserve of Brahmans and kings. Biswanath Baba's *Itihasa* gave it recognition and legitimacy. The making of Mahima Swami had reached its culmination.

Precepts and Practices

What did Mahima Swami preach and what was its significance in the nineteenth-century conditions, particularly in the tributary *mahals*, of Orissa? Let us turn to the features that can be culled from the fragmentary reports cited so far. According to the *Utkala Deepika*, the *phalahari sanyasi* preached 'a *dharma* that disregarded caste distinction, forbade idol worship and rituals and advocated a belief in one god.' We know from the accounts of missionaries and colonial officers that this god was the all-powerful, indescribable Creator and Preserver of the world. The accounts also stress the ascetic's extreme detachment and lack of greed, his inculcation of truth, charity and chastity, his constant mobility, his refusal to acquire property or accept anything but cooked food as alms and hint at his rejection of the Brahman.

The teachings of Mahima Swami, then, were characterized — at the level of dictates, implicit meanings and actual practices — by a challenge to the patterns of hierarchy and authority embedded in structures of dominant Hinduism, which involved a tie-up between the dharmic hierarchy of purity and pollution and the ritually fashioned kingship of Orissa. In speaking of an omniscient, omnipresent, all-pervading, formless, indescribable Absolute, the creator of the universe, as the only object of devotion, Mahima Swami rejected the deities of the Hindu pantheon, stressed the redundancy of temples and rituals and did away with the Brahman's role as the mediator between god and human beings. This implied a questioning of the close connections between divine, ritual and social hierarchies. The denunciation of idols as lifeless images of stone and wood was a corollary to this questioning of authority. Moreover, the preceptor's incessant movement and persistent refusal to acquire property were definite statements against establishment and authority. Mobility/movement (*jangama*) as a mode of interrogating something inert and established (*sthabara*) had a long tradition: it had been in vogue among Virasaiva ascetics of the South.[30]

The Swami's novel practice of accepting cooked food from every household and of eating it together with his devotees concretized the challenge to the norms of caste and the rules of commensality. As mentioned in the introduction, cooked rice symbolically transferred pollution from the donor to the receiver. Mahima Swami's practice of accepting cooked rice from untouchable and lower caste people thus, was of immense significance. The 'pure' ascetic absorbed the pollution of the impure people lowest in the caste hierarchy and made them pure. At the same time, the founder denied the Raja, the Brahman, the *bhandari* (barber) and the *dhoba* (washerman) the right of giving *bhiksha* to him and his followers. The Brahman and the Raja constituted the key figures who articulated the exercise of domination through the inextricable bounding of the arenas of ritual and politics, while the *bhandari* and the *dhoba* (the traditional service castes) were instruments in the effective functioning of the ritual-social hierarchy.[31] The Swami displayed his superiority to and contempt for the ritually pure Brahman in refusing to accept cooked food from him while he deprived the Raja and members of service castes of the opportunity of becoming pure by serving cooked rice to the *sanyasi*. It was this challenge to the power exercised through and encoded within religion that made Mahima Swami appear as a genuine benefactor to those groups in Orissa whose subordination had been secured through the close intermeshing of religion and politics.[32]

Contemporary reports bear testimony to the impact of the Swami's preaching. In its first report on the religious leader the *Utkala Deepika* commented, perhaps with a hint of irony: 'The said ascetic is commanding such total devotion from the inhabitants of the places to which he is going that no one is daring to disregard his wishes; they are giving him whatever he is asking for'.[33]

After six years the *sanyasi*, now called Mahima Babaji, had become a threat, a danger. The second report of the *Deepika*, which appeared on 6 September 1873, stated that the *sanyasi* disciples of the Babaji were all out to destroy *jati dharma* (the norms of caste). Their activities had compelled the ruler of Madhupur to drive them out of his territory. Some of them had come to Jajpur and managed to gather a large number of followers. All these men were moving from door to door asking for food and eating together from one bowl to the complete disregard of the rules of commensality. The extent of the outrage they had perpetrated was all too evident: they did not even hesitate to accept food from Christian households. At the same time, they desisted from entering the house of a Brahman, a *bhandari*, a *dhoba*, a *mali* or a *dari*. The Brahmans of Jajpur, incensed by such scandalous behavior, had ruled that all followers of the Babaji would be rendered outcastes and socially ostracized till they performed *prayaścitta* (penance).

The *Deepika* also expressed anxiety over the sect's professed condemnation of the raja. It gave vent to upper-caste loyalist sentiments by stating that as long as the rejection remained confined to the rulers of the Garhjats there was no cause for worry. It would, however, be a matter of grave concern if the sect extended its challenge to British rule.[34] The concerns of the *Deepika* notwithstanding, the content of the report was indicative of the fact that the new faith had become a force to reckon with. It had forced the Brahmans and the rajas to range themselves against Mahima Dharma.

The missionaries hailed Mahima Swami as the leader of a 'very extensive religious movement in the Garjats'.[35] 'His disciples already number many thousands, and are composed of nearly every caste.'[36] Rev. William Miller, for instance, was duly impressed by a man whose teachings had induced 'whole villages to give up idolatry as far as the worship of village idols is concerned.'[37] The followers of the new faith were 'prepared to a great extent' to hear the message of the missionaries and were free 'from those foolish prejudices which often close the ear and the heart of others to the truth'.[38] The missionary was optimistic that 'this movement' was 'destined to have an important bearing on the spread of Christianity in the Garjats'.[39] The missionary's specific concern may have prompted him to misread the implications of the Guru's teachings. At the same time, his statements underscored the extent of the Swami's success. The report corroborated the fact that the Brahmans were reacting strongly against the new faith. The Guru was said to refer 'very feelingly' to the hostility of the Brahmans and the priests towards the movement.

The Hindu officials of the colonial government displayed somewhat divergent sentiments in their assessment of the Swami's impact. The Tehsildar of Angul, exposing an administrator's characteristic concern with law and order and an uncritical acceptance of classificatory categories being introduced by colonial ethnography, congratulated Mahima Swami for bringing about a marked improvement in the character of the low-caste people who filled the ranks of his followers.[40] 'The principles of Mahima appear to have worked a very good example amongst the Pans of Angul who, on accepting them, seem to hate burglary, a practice not uncommon among their Hindu brethren.'[41] The Manager of Dhenkanal, on the other hand, dismissed the Swami's appeal as being limited to 'ignorant and illiterate people of the lower classes of the Hindu community'. These people, the Manager argued, had been 'induced to adopt the new religion by hopes of enjoyment if they followed and threats of perdition if they did not follow the precepts'.[42] The Tehsildar of Banki echoed this view. Speaking of the *aśritas* he commented: 'In fact they never learnt or understood what it [the new religion] really was but adopted it and had blind faith in it, in ignorance being misled by the show of extraordinary qualities which they took to be superhuman and divine in the Mahima Gosain.'[43] Grudgingly and critically or in open admiration, contemporary observers acknowledged the devotion the Gosain commanded from his *bhaktas*.

Kali and Colonialism

Why did opposition to caste and idolatry appeal to sections of the Oriya people? Rather than try and offer definite answers in a cause-effect mode, I will outline some distinctive features of early and mid-nineteenth century Orissa, in order to provide the background against which Mahima Dharma emerged and spread. Here, it is crucial to keep in mind that the changes and turmoil of the times were often understood through the concept-metaphor of Kali Yuga, the last and the most evil of the four eras according to classical Hinduism.[44] The long-lasting Kali Yuga is meant to be brought to an end by the appearance of an *avatar*, a human incarnation of the divine, who will purge the world of sins through a devastating war, annihilate Kali and re-establish *satya-dharma* (true faith) heralding Satya Yuga (the pristine era of truth). This belief, current in the Vaishnavite tradition and mentioned in the Puranas, gained wide currency in Orissa from the late sixteenth century through the appearance and circulation of *malikas*[45], apocryphal texts that were ascribed to the Panchasakhas (Five Friends), the five eminent medieval mystics.[46] *Malikas* and texts of a similar vein, written in verse in the form of a dialogue, easy to recite in large gatherings of people without formal education, not only concretized the intermingling of 'great' and 'little' traditions and the oral and the written, they kept alive and rendered acutely palpable the notion of Kali. This made the imminent destruction of the evil age by the arrival of an incarnation immensely probable.

Conditions of nineteenth century Orissa added fresh vigour to the idea of Kali. The century opened with the advent of British rule. It is true that the stepping in of a new government did not bring about a complete rupture with the past. There were perceptible continuities with the administrative structure of Mughal and Maratha regimes which had in turn retained many features of the agrarian and fiscal systems elaborated by Hindu rajas of the region.[47] At the same time, there were significant shifts in emphases in revenue administration. Constant experimentation with various modes of revenue assessment and increased rigour in revenue collection engendered uncertainties and complications and created hardships for tenants and proprietors of land.[48] While resistance from Oriya princes and peasant uprisings accompanied the elaboration of the East India Company's rule in Orissa, the introduction of English education and the ventures into social reform occasioned intense reflections on the part of the elites in the province of Bengal, who were not new to traditions of Hindu and Islamic rational argument and among whom causality and verification of intuitively perceived 'truths' were not unknown.[49]

Moreover, colonial take-over of Orissa in 1803 was followed by the entry of Protestant missionaries.[50] Earnest in their efforts to spread the gospel of truth, these messengers of Christ were baffled by the overwhelming presence of Jagannath, the Lord of the Universe and the central deity of Hinduism in Orissa. Trenchant criticism of the caste system and an all-out attack on Jagannath, whose worship, the missionaries felt, the British government was patronizing, were inherent features of the missionaries' propagation of Christianity.[51] Although Orientalist scholars, British administrators and missionaries differed widely in their approaches to caste and Hinduism, they all concurred in differentiating 'traditional' India from the modern West, defining religion and the 'religious' institution of caste to be the grounding principles of Indian society.[52]

All this produced intriguing consequences. On the one hand, there was a renewed questioning of 'tradition' on the part of a section of the English-educated Hindu intelligentsia and on the other there was a greater zeal to hold on to the 'traditional' norms of society.[53] In Orissa, which according to the census report of Bengal for 1881, was 'the most essentially Hindu portion of Bengal', where '9 out of 10 persons is a Hindu',[54] upper-castes by and large began to reinforce tradition. This perhaps accounted for the blanket condemnation of the Oriyas by W. W. Hunter: they were described as 'a priest ridden race kept in subjection by the Brahmins and subject to all paralysing influences of religious superstition and caste prejudices. Nowhere else do the ancient caste rules exercise such an influence.'[55] There are evident problems with such representations; but they do point to the increasing rigidity of the norms of caste in Orissa in the nineteenth century.

The changes in practices at the Jagannath temple in Puri, the abode of the great Lord of Orissa, provide us with a prism through which to view these processes. In 1882 Hunter, in his *A Statistical Account of Bengal*, noted that 'the temple of Jagannath in which every creed obtained an asylum and in which every class and sect can find its god now closes its gates to the low caste population'.[56] The same work also provided a list of the castes that were denied entry into the inner sanctum of the temple.[57] L.S.S. O'Malley's *Gazetteer* incorporated the list.[58] Observance of caste discrimination undoubtedly went against the basic principle of universality that was widely believed to underlie the cult of Jagannath. It seriously compromised Jagannath's position as the Lord of all, high and low. This universality, stressed alike by administrators, scholars and historians, is manifest in the movement of the deity from distinctly tribal beginnings to the position of *bara thakur*, the Great Lord of Orissa.[59] In its rise to eminence the auspicious trinity of Jagannath, Balabhadra and Subhadra assimilated and incorporated all the major religious trends that had gained a foothold in Orissa. Jagannath is at once *śavar-devata* and Buddha-Jagannath, the ninth incarnation of Vishnu; a symbol of openness and syncretism.

Indeed, the importance of Jagannath in Orissa cannot be over-emphasized. It forms the pivot around which constructions of Oriya cultural identity revolve. The interpenetration of ritual and politics contributed to the strength of the cult of Jagannath. Jagannath became the *rashtra-devata* (state deity) under the Ganga dynasty in the twelfth century and retained this elevated status under the Suryavamsa rulers who succeeded the Gangas. These kings claimed to rule Orissa as the *rauttas* (viceroys)[60] or *sevakas* (servants)[61] of Jagannath. It is not only that the will of Jagannath underlay their collection of taxes, it is also that the Suryavamsi rulers declared that opposition to them and their policies amounted to *droha*, revolt, against the Lord.[62] Political rivals to the throne and dissatisfied subjects were not the only targets of this declaration: the priests of Puri, whose position had been strengthened through the acceptance of the over-lordship of Jagannath by the Oriya rulers, were sought to be contained as well. As central authority weakened and political control came to be concentrated in the Khurda region, the rulers clung to Jagannath with greater zeal. It helped them maintain their symbolic superiority over the kings of the Garhjats.[63]

The strategy worked. In the sixteenth century the Khurda rajas were recognized by the Mughals as successors to the last Hindu dynasty in southern Orissa. The Garhjat rulers continued — albeit nominally — to recognize the elevated position of the Khurda rajas. These perceptions and practices persisted under the Marathas, although now these kings were reduced to little more than rulers of Puri. Under Company rule, which commenced at the end of 1803, the territories of Mukunda Deva II, the ruler of Khurda/Puri, were seized following a revolt against the British. At the same time, an Act of 1809 gave the superintendence of the Jagannath temple to the Khurda prince. These rajas, once again, were accorded a pre-eminent position in the hierarchy of the feudatory rajas of Orissa. The British rulers themselves, it has been argued, committed themselves to the management of the temple in the initial phase of their occupation, because they 'wanted the idol of Jagannath's seal of approval on their rule of

Orissa'.[64]

The wide-ranging changes occasioned by British rule together with the reinforced exclusivity of Jagannath and growing rigidity of caste norms generated a situation of extreme stress and uncertainty. This was reflected in the unrest of peasant and tribal peoples as well as in the proliferation of new religious sects. The strong undercurrent of non-conformist religion and practices of yogic and tantric *sadhana* centred on the training of the body prevalent in the region since the time of the Nath yogis came out in the open with new vigour in these turbulent times. Circulation of *malikas* and other apocryphal texts that spoke of the end of the world and the evil era of Kali went hand in hand with the emergence of new religious leaders who were taken to be incarnations come down to earth to deliver divine dispensation. We will return to this point a little later.

The sense of imminent disaster was made tragically real by the great famine of 1866, the worst that Orissa suffered in the century.[65] The famine, a consequence of man-made problems and natural calamities, apart from wiping out one third of the population of the province, made the predicted destruction of the world acquire new significance.[66] Miseries born of scarcity were exacerbated by the upper-castes' concern with the norms of caste. The active role of missionaries in relief operations during the famine and the serving of cooked rice from the *chatras* (relief houses) by the government raised a furore. All *chatrakhiyas* (people who had eaten in *chatras*) were ostracized.[67] Undoubtedly, it was a period of strain, a time of contrary pulls — an epoch when Kali held sway.

The situation was somewhat different in the tributary states, which were internally autonomous under the Mughals and the Marathas and under Company and imperial rule.[68] These states were not plagued by the problems of temporary revenue settlements and rigorous collection of revenue, like the districts under direct colonial administration. The land revenue system common to almost all these states was 'very simple'.[69] Ownership of land vested in the State, the actual cultivator enjoying occupancy rights as long as he paid the rent. Sub-infeudation was virtually unknown and the sale or transfer of land was illegal. However, there were a number of large estates and *gaontias* (village headmen) enjoyed special privileges as rent collectors. Annual administrative reports of the Tributary Mahals written in the 1860s generally stated that conditions were peaceful and satisfactory.[70] These states were not as badly hit by the famine as were the districts under direct British administration.

The annual administrative reports, however, did not provide a true picture of the situation. There was no reflection of the general discontent prevailing among the subjects, particularly the aboriginal population, which came into the open in a series of revolts in the feudatory states throughout the nineteenth century.[71] The subjects of the Garhjats shouldered the burden of certain feudal practices. They had to render *bethi* (paid forced labour) and *begar* (unpaid forced labour) by digging canals, building roads, carrying luggage and thatching roofs. They provided domestic service to chiefs and supplied them and their officials on tour with provisions (*rasad*).[72] Rural indebtedness was common and instances of *goti* (debt bondage) were not unknown. As late as in 1919, Mansfield, the Additional Political Agent in the Orissa Feudatory States, wrote in a letter to his parents: 'the inhabitants [of the feudatory states] have to perform duties, and the lower castes to do cooly work at the bidding of the chief, just as in medieval England. Many of the tenures are based on services and the Raja can do very much as he likes ...'[73]

Various measures adopted by the colonial government compounded the problems of these states' subjects. Though the British did not actively interfere in the internal affairs of the tributary states, their rule began a process of integration of the Garhjats with the mainland of Orissa. The Superintendent of the Tributary Mahals and the Political Agent who closely watched the activities of these states also encouraged the rulers to improve transport and communication and to undertake survey and settlement operations.[74] The colonial masters and Oriya intellectuals became concerned about the 'backward' condition of the Garhjat population.[75] Schools were set up to impart formal education to the uneducated masses and vigorous campaigns were undertaken by enthusiastic English officials against 'barbaric' Hindu and tribal practices.[76] These efforts disrupted the rhythm of life of the Garhjat subjects, composed, in the main, of *adivasis* and low-castes.

Close supervision by the British government reduced boundary disputes and wars of succession among the feudatory chiefs. Internal peace and stable law and order freed the chiefs of their dependence on subordinate networks. The projection of an elevated self-image to the outside world became their chief concern: they tuned their practices to an emerging dominant construct of royalty and regal power.[77] The Khurda rajas became their model. Jagannath was sought to be appropriated as a mode of augmenting royal power and dignity.[78] Until the sixteenth century Suryavamsi rulers had monopolized the worship of the great Lord. They had not allowed Jagannath temples to be built outside Puri and Cuttack. The collapse of their central power in the sixteenth century saw the spread of the cult to other areas. In the Garhjats, however, the deity did not become a significant presence. The subjects persisted in their worship of ancestral gods and *grama devatas* (village deities) while the chiefs[79] displayed their respect for the central god through occasional trips to Puri, where they received special treatment from the Khurda raja.

The nineteenth century witnessed a worsening of relations between the Raja of Khurda/Puri and the feudatory chiefs. The Raja of Puri, now devoid of his kingdom, hung on with great fervour to whatever semblance of symbolic authority that he still possessed. Ill-treatment of the chiefs of the Garhjats was an exercise in power. They were denied the special favours they had traditionally received.[80] The Garhjat rulers, for their part, were no longer prepared to accept their position of notional subordination. Jagannath was as much their Lord as that of the Raja of Puri. Hermann Kulke has pointed to the fact that the mid-nineteenth century saw an upsurge of grand constructions in the feudatory states: royal palaces and temples of Jagannath displayed regal attributes and authority. In nine of the twelve Garhjat states of central Orissa, 'Jagannath temples were built in the immediate vicinity of the palace'.[81] Jagannath, once again, was made to provide divine-ritual sanction for exploitation. The rajas increased the tax burden and demanded *bethi* from subjects for the construction of temples. What is more important, they started making lavish land grants to these temples and to priests and other Brahmans. Consequently, there was an increased encroachment by upper-caste Hindus on lands held by tribal peoples.

The report of the land revenue settlement of Sambalpur made a mention of the excessive alienation of land to priests, temples and adherents of rulers that had begun from 1829.[82] The District *Gazetteer* of Sambalpur came up with a clear and categorical statement: 'There seems little doubt that the power of the aboriginal owners of the soil is gradually being broken.'[83] The same was true of other states, particularly Dhenkanal. Here the 'large percentage of Brahman population compared with the other Garhjat states' was accounted for 'by the fact that the previous chiefs, and more particularly Maharaja Bhagirathi Mahendra Bahadur, an enlightened ruler and a lover of Sanskrit literature, made extensive grants of *lakhiraj* [rent-free] lands to learned Brahmans and induced them to settle down in the State with a view to raise the standard of public morality'.[84] Rulers and Brahmans were again using Lord Jagannath to consolidate and strengthen subservience and oppression. It was beyond doubt a time when the evil Kali reigned supreme.

Meanings and Actions

The teachings of Mahima Swami acquire their specific meaning against this background. We have seen that the precepts and practices of Mahima Dharma contested the power of rajas, Brahmans and deities. Alongside, they helped its adherents acquire a sense of self-worth. As such, despite the suppositions of colonial officials, it was not ignorance and gullibility which made large sections of the Garhjat population look upon Mahima Swami as an incarnation of the Absolute. Rather, it was the significance of the ever present Kali Yuga — which the taxing times had made particularly potent — and a belief in its ultimate dissolution through the appearance of a redeemer that resulted in Mahima Swami's deification.

Earlier, I have referred to the genre of *malikas* that have been current in Oriya literary and oral traditions since the sixteenth century. Cast in the mode of classical Puranas, *malikas* deal with the theme of Kali, the era of evil, and predict its dissolution through the appearance of a redeemer and the establishment of true faith. While the ascription of their authorship to the Panchasakhas lends credibility to the prophesies of the *malikas*, the attribution of woes to the evil era of Kali, the assurance of an eventual dissolution of sufferings and the ultimate triumph of good over evil, account for their continued presence and popularity. Belief in the divination of the *malikas* underscored the inevitability of the appearance of an *avatar*.[85] And identification of Mahima Swami as that incarnation was an easy step from there.

Official reports, drawn up in the 1880s on 'The sect of Hindu dissenters', mention the followers of the sect to be in possession of a book of predictions. This book treated 'the incarnation of Alakh in the shape of Mahima Swami to save the world from the burden of sin and pave the way towards salvation.'[86] N. N. Vasu, a scholar-cum-administrator, chanced upon *Yaśomati Malika* in Mayurbhanj in early twentieth century, which he claimed to be a major scripture of Mahima Dharma. This *malika*, according to Vasu, clearly established the preceptor of the new faith to be Buddha, a claim that underscored the divinity of Mahima Swami.

We have further corroboration of the fact that *malikas* were in wide circulation in Orissa around this time. In an amusing anecdote published serially in the journal *Sajantoshini Patrika*, a Bengali Deputy Magistrate of Puri recorded his encounter with a 'fake' *avatar*. In 1870–71, this ascetic — Bishkishan — had established himself as the leader of a Vaishnavite sect by proclaiming himself to be Mahavishnu (great Vishnu) who, their *malika* said, was to reappear.[87] The Deputy Magistrate affirmed that Bishkishan was not the only one of his kind. There were others who were giving themselves out to be Chaitanya, Krishna or Baladev, using 'false' manuscripts (*jal punthi*) that declared that Chaitanya would come again.[88]

The *Census of India, 1911*, in its detailed account of the 'Kumbhipatia sect', referred to one group in Puri, also called Alekh, which is 'said to be distinct from other sections'.[89] But their doctrines, according to the *Census*, were 'much the same'. The founder of this group was one Artatran Das, 'who flourished about 60 years ago'.[90] He preached the doctrines of Alekh, the formless one, denounced idolatry, composed religious poems and 'gave utterance to mysterious sayings' (*malikas*). The report went on: 'when disease, drought etc. come, the people refer to these sayings as prophetic.'[91] Yet another religious leader was preaching devotion to the formless Absolute and making use of prophetic sayings in which people believed. In the Khurda-Puri region, Banamali Das founded the *abadhuta* sect in the early 1860s which advocated belief in one god and opposed distinctions of caste.[92] The 1860s in Orissa were, indeed, times of scarcity and famine. The prevalence of new sects that discarded idolatry and the circulation of *malikas* in the district of Puri, where the temple of Jagannath is located, is a further indication that belief in the great Lord was failing to provide answers and making people search for alternatives.

A proliferation of sects and *malikas* was not particular to the second half of the nineteenth century. In the late 1830s Sundar Das, a resident of Kujibur in Athgarh, a tributary state close to Dhenkanal, had gathered a large number of followers by preaching monotheism and ridiculing the practices of dominant Hinduism. He authored a manuscript, *Kujibar Patra,* to propagate his ideas. His initiative, however, petered out as his followers *en masse* adopted Christianity, signalling the success of proselytizing efforts of the Baptist missionaries.[93] At the same time, this and other faiths that advocated analogous messages bear testimony to the general restlessness that characterized Orissa in the nineteenth century.

How then was Mahima Dharma distinct and different? The tenets and practices of the Dharma, one can argue, were drawn from existing beliefs and symbols. To begin with, traditions of *bhakti* (devotion) to a formless god had been current in Orissa since the eleventh and twelfth centuries. The Naths and other cults devoted to (Alekh) Niranjan flourished in Orissa long before the emergence of the medieval *Sants*.[94] After going through various phases they found their culmination in the Panchasakhas, the five medieval mystics, who worshipped Krishna-Jagannath in his absolute form as *nirakar* (formless). Ideas of an indescribable Absolute were also evoked by Sarala Das's *Mahabharata* and Jagannath Das's *Bhagabata* — vernacular renderings of the epic and the life of Krishna — extremely important texts which at once signalled the autonomy of the vernacular and substituted the originals in Sanskrit in the region from the fourteenth and fifteenth centuries. These texts remained ever attractive through constant narrations and provided modes for the understanding and deployment of ideas of classical Hinduism at 'popular' levels. Moreover, belief in the appearance of an incarnation to purge the world of sin, integral to the tradition of Vaishnavism, had been given wide currency by the *malikas* for a long time prior to the advent of Mahima Swami.

And yet, existing ideas and traditions were blended and perceived in novel ways that imbued them with new meanings that were tuned to the conditions of the times. The rules that Mahima Swami laid down for the conduct of daily lives conferred on his disciples a new identity. The followers were divided into two well-defined orders: the *sanyasis* (renouncers) and the *aśritas* or *gruhi bhaktas* (lay disciples). The *sanyasis* were grouped into *kumbhipatias* (wearers of the bark of the *kumbhi* tree) and *kanapatias* (wearers of waist-cloth). The central feature of the life of all Mahima Dharmis was total devotion to the formless Alekh Prabhu. 'The disciples of Mohima Swami inculcate self-denial and surrender to god as the sources of salvation; they do not aspire after worldly greatness or pleasure; extreme humility is one of their characteristics. They have no prescribed mode of worship except praise of god and pray for his mercy.'[95] 'They turn their faces towards the sun at its rise and set and prostrate themselves seven and five times to Alekh. They believe in the existence of Hindu deities but do not obey them, asserting that it is not necessary to obey the servant, but only the master.'[96] In fact, lack of regard for the Hindu deities was pronounced: it was not only the idols that were discarded, the symbols of these gods and goddesses also suffered the same fate. The judicial resolution of the Government of Bengal of 21 October 1881 commented: 'There is indeed reason to think that unlike the followers of Ramanand, Kabir and Chaitanya, they [the Kumbhipatias] have an antipathy to them [Hindu gods and goddesses] as they dislike to touch the tulsi plant, because it is held sacred by the Hindus, and will not eat the flesh of a goat, because it is offered in sacrifice to the Hindu goddess Kali.'[97]

The Mahima Dharmis (followers of Mahima Dharma) did not deny the existence of gods and goddesses but deprived them completely of all efficacy and significance. The act of discarding the icons and symbols underscored the contempt with which the followers of Alekh treated the Hindu divinities. Similarly, they read the *Bhagabata* but interpreted it differently from the Hindus. It is probable that this *Bhagabata* was the *Kali Bhagabata*, a particular rendering of the life of Krishna suited to Kali Yuga, a text akin to *malikas* that has undergone different incarnations. The important religious texts of the followers also included a *malika*, and other works which contained 'songs and dialogues interpreting the truth of Alakh'.[98] A differential reading of conventional texts went hand in hand with the creation of Mahima Dharmi scriptures, forcefully demonstrating the 'innovative' impetus of practices of reading and understanding in transforming meanings.

The Kumbhipatia and Kanapatia *sanyasis* led celibate lives. They were stated to have been 'of very dirty habits'.[99] Was this an inverse confirmation of their disregard for the norms of caste? Austerity and detachment formed the essence of the lives of these renouncers. They moved constantly from place to place, spending just one night in a village, and taking food but once which they accepted from any house without heed to caste distinctions. They did not 'take their meals within houses or in plates but in the open air and from earthen pots'.[100]

The *aśritas* of the faith did not renounce the social order and their families but were expected to shun extravagance and ostentation. They wore *geru basan*, or cloth dyed with red earth, and looked upon the ascetics as their spiritual guides. A living out of the Guru's teachings and a rejection of authority formed the core of their mode of existence. They 'did not perform any Hindu ceremony or festival', nor did they call upon the Brahman priests to officiate in their life cycle rituals. Their marriage ceremony was remarkably simple. It was performed by 'the side of a road or public thoroughfare'. The bride put a garland of flowers around the neck of the bridegroom 'in token of offering herself to him', and the friends and relatives of both loudly '[called upon] Alekhswami to protect the new pair in their career through life'.[101] Polygamy was prohibited. For any misconduct an offender was made to do penance by drinking a solution of cow-dung.

The prescribed code of conduct set the Mahima Dharmis apart. Total devotion to the omnipotent, formless Absolute that made belief in the gods and goddesses of the Hindu pantheon redundant, also made the Brahmans — the mediators between gods and human beings — useless. This coupled with a discarding of elaborate rituals of worship, and performance of separate life cycle rituals, arguably gave the followers of Alekh a distinct identity. For the ascetics detachment and renunciation were the order of the day; the lay disciples could function with the principles of the transient universe of the renouncers even as they lived within the organic world of the householder. It is not a matter of surprise, then, that members of low-caste and tribal groups formed the majority of the Swami's following. The message and practices of the Dharma enabled them to counter their low ritual and social status. They had become members of a group that had the all-powerful maker of the universe as its protector and saviour. Did all these not confer on them a new sense of self-assurance?

Mahima Swami, in combining high philosophy with a simple, austere way of life, in preaching an easy message of devotion and in exemplifying in his life the challenge to property and authority, showed to many a way out of the torments of life. The Guru became the Lord to his followers, a living incarnation of the Brahma he spoke about. They treated him in a way that befitted the gods. 'On his arrival at every tungi his feet were washed by his followers and ashritas with Saptamruta, being a mixture of milk, curd, sugar, honey, sandalwood powder and camphor, differing from the Panchamruta of the Hindus by the addition of camphor and sandal, which they used to drink as something holy for their salvation.'[102] The slight variation in the preparation of the mixture revealed Mahima Dharma's deployment of existing traditions. The notion of the beneficial effect of *panchamruta* was accepted, but the mixture was made Mahima Dharma's own by the addition of two new ingredients.

The practice of the ascetics of Mahima Dharma of surviving on *bhiksha* was in line with that of several other categories of wandering ascetics. At the same time, the renouncers of the faith distinguished themselves by asking for cooked food. Apart from challenging and inverting the norms of caste and commensality, the exercise enabled them to maintain their principle of simplicity and non-attachment: acceptance of uncooked rice or cash carried with it the danger of creating the tendency to accumulate. As stated before, the injunction against accepting food from Brahman households contained a play with the notion of *dana* as a carrier of pollution. The Brahman, specially the purohit/priest, was impure because he accepted gifts from his patrons. The founder demonstrated his superiority by refusing to take *dana* from the Brahmans.[103]

An administrator's account contains an interesting anecdote. Mahima Swami had developed the practice of feeding a large number of people at the places where he lived. As the faith gained a significant number of followers, fairs started being held on a regular basis near the *tungis* of the Guru. At the time of these fairs a *dhuni* was lit, to which the devotees made offerings of *ghee* (clarified butter). One such fair was held at Jaka in Dhenkanal on *kartick purnima* (full moon in October–November), shortly before the founder's death. A large body of followers assembled with rich presents for the Swami. The Swami did not accept them; instead he offered them to the Raja of Dhenkanal. When the Raja declined, the gifts were openly burnt in the *dhuni*.[104] The Guru's act upheld the principle of personal detachment and interrogated the authority of the king. There was a reversal of roles between the patron and the receiver of the donation: the king, who had been the patron traditionally, was relegated to the position of recipient by the ascetic.[105]

The practice of feeding a large number of people was, in itself, quite significant. We have seen that it was a time of scarcity. The great famine had produced hordes of starving men and women who needed to be fed. In taking over the responsibility the Swami came to rival the State and the king, whose duty it was to look after the well-being of the subjects. Interestingly, the Raja of Dhenkanal was perhaps the only one among the rulers of feudatory states who took 'special care' of the famine-stricken people by opening an *annachatra* (relief house where food was served) and by donating rupees 5000 to the famine relief fund. For these and other commendable measures, he was raised to the status of a Maharaja from that of a Raja by the British Governor General.[106] Earlier, we have noted Bhagirathi Mahindra Bahadur's love for Sanskrit literature and his efforts at 'raising the standard of public morality' through the grant of rent-free lands to Brahmans to induce them to settle in Dhenkanal. Here we get proof of his loyalty to the colonial state. At the same time, he held Mahima Swami in great respect. Why did the founder of Mahima Dharma decide to hold feasts mainly in Dhenkanal? Why did he offer the gifts meant for him to Bhagirathi Mahindra Bahadur? Was the Swami trying to scorn the Raja's fascination with authority and his eagerness to get rewards? Was he also making a statement about the elevated nature of the relief he provided in comparison to the relief measures of the Oriya ruler? The ascetic did not only provide food. He healed bodies and minds by preaching the message of a higher faith.[107]

The Swami had indeed attained a remarkable degree of success. It lay not only in the fact that his message had spread over a large part of Orissa and in neighbouring states, that numerous people had started conducting their lives in accordance with his precepts and had conferred divinity on him. His real impact was the social space he created within the structure of dominant Oriya society, a space in which ordinary men and women gained new confidence, a new meaning for the self which prompted them to lead their lives in a prescribed manner in the hope of securing a better future.

The sources do not allow us to ascertain the exact number of followers of Mahima Swami. What is clear from the contemporary reports of newspapers, missionaries and administrators is that the Guru made for a significant presence. These sources estimated his following at about twenty to thirty thousand people. On the other hand, census figures, drawn up within a few years of the death of the Swami, showed the number of

Mahima Dharmis to be extremely small. The *Census of the Central Provinces, 1881* which alone included separate statistics on the Kumbhipatias[108] returned 931 from the Sambalpur district of the province.[109] The group did not find mention in the census of Bengal till 1911.[110]

The apparent contradiction between census figures and the estimates of contemporary observers may be due to the fact that the census enumerators returned most of the householder devotees, who formed the majority of the following, as Hindus. It may also be that the sect suffered a setback after the death of Mahima Swami in 1875/76. Indeed, the reports of officials point to the fact that the death of the founder produced a crisis within Mahima Dharma: the belief in the divinity of the Guru was so strong that his death shocked his followers. Many lay disciples reverted to Hinduism,[111] while those who persisted in Mahima Dharma were left without a recognized leader.[112] Sambalpur emerged as the new centre of the faith, where the songs and verses of Bhima Bhoi sang the praises of the Guru and proclaimed the superiority of his *dharma.* Many followers again, did not 'recognise the demise of "Mahima Swami" and said that he had disappeared and may at any time come to them as their saviour'.[113] The truth of this almost disparaging statement of a 'rational' colonial official was to be proved again and again by the members of Mahima Dharma in their effort to grapple with crises in their lives engendered by a crisis in their faith. Let us now turn to the first and the most dramatic of such expressions, and 'attack' on the temple of Jagannath in Puri. This event also provides a rare glimpse into one of the various ways in which the teachings of Mahima Swami and Bhima Bhoi were understood, interpreted and appropriated by their followers.

Deities and Desecration

> For two weeks now there has been a rumour that a group of men and women had entered the temple of Jagannath in Puri by force with a pot of rice. That time the *bhog* of Jagannath was being served. The men and women refused to listen to the doorkeepers and tried to move towards the idol of Jagannath. A tussle broke out between the doorkeepers and the attackers in which one member of the group died on the spot. The others threw cooked rice all over the place, desecrated the *bhog* of Jagannath, threatened to burn Jagannath and left the place. A serious offence was committed within a few moments; but up until now there has been no news of the arrest and trial of offenders. If there

> is any semblance of truth in the rumour, Jagannath is in great danger. It is surprising that no serious step has so far been taken for the protection of Jagannath.[114]

These statements of the *Utkala Deepika* echoed the sentiments of all the devotees of Jagannath. The rumour was indeed unnerving. A small group of uneducated, uncivilized, lowly men and women had dared to threaten the sanctity of the mighty *bara thakur* (great Lord) of Orissa. How were the 'Jagannathis' to react to this act of extreme audacity? The issue of the daily of 26 March 1881 carried a detailed account of the scandalous incident. I provide here a summary of the report.

On Tuesday, 1 March 1881, around two in the afternoon, a group of sixteen naked men and women tried to enter the temple of Jagannath in Puri with a pot of cooked rice. When the doorkeeper and guardians of the temple tried to prevent them from entering the temple by closing the Lion Gate (the eastern gate, the main entrance to the temple), the group left the pot of rice near the Garura pillar, pushed the gate open, broke the door of the *bhoga mandap* (a room where offerings to Jagannath are kept) and headed for the Jai-bijai door (the door which leads to the inner sanctum). The doorkeeper closed the Jai-bijai door and the southern door of the temple. The group failed in its attempt to reach the throne of Jagannath. They were somehow driven out by the guardians of the temple and the pilgrims. The men and women were naked and appeared to be drunk. They had never been inside the temple. When they were pushed back to the *bhoga mandap*, their leader Dasaram, who had made great efforts to break the temple door, fell on the stone pavement near the temple of Agniswar Mahadev and lost consciousness. His friends carried him to the Garura pillar and fed him rice. The man died within an hour. The police came and sent his body to a doctor. The doctor stated that the death had not been caused by beating.

The colonial government, ever anxious to preserve law and order, ordered enquiries into the incident. Detailed reports on the group, their beliefs and practices, and the act they performed were drawn up by several officials. The Magistrate of Puri incorporated the information provided by various reports in his accounts of the incident sent to the Governor General of Bengal.[115] I paraphrase the account of an eyewitness, a doorkeeper of the temple who stood on duty at the Lion Gate at the time of the incident, which found a place in the magistrate's report. About twenty naked men and women came up to the temple shouting 'Alekh! Alekh!' They were carrying a pot of cooked rice and it was evident from the state of their hands that they had recently eaten. They were about to enter the temple when the doorkeeper shut the gate, which, however, they pushed open. The group went in and was followed by about two hundred pilgrims. A member of the group still held the pot of rice. He left this outside only after the doorkeeper objected to it strongly. They then broke down the door of the *bhoga-mandap* which, at that stage, was empty. The men and women proceeded to the great hall in front of the shrine. The crowd of spectators had doubled by then. On finding the Jai-bijai door shut the group went out into the enclosure and rushed about like mad men and women to find some other entrance. In the hustling that followed, one of them fell on the stone pavement. Two or three others lifted him up and helped him out of the temple.

The Assistant Superintendent of Police of Puri was 'speedily at the spot' and arrested seven men and one woman. The others ran off but were pursued and arrested. The man who had fallen died. The arrested were 'lunatically inclined' and spoke of a 'band of fanatics' who were coming down the Cuttack road to burn Jagannath. A police patrol was dispatched and arrested six men and eleven women who had eleven small children with them. This group was a part of the larger 'band'. They, once again, reiterated the need to burn Jagannath.[116] All the arrested men and women were placed under trial before Kamal Nath Ghosh, the Deputy Magistrate of Puri. He sentenced the members of the first group to three months' rigorous imprisonment. Of the members of the second group, four men were sentenced to seven days' rigorous imprisonment and the rest acquitted.[117]

As might be expected, the attack on the temple caused consternation in the upper-class circles of Oriya society. The accounts they drew of the incident reflected their bias and prejudices very clearly. The tone all through was one of condemnation. If law-keepers of the colonial state underscored the irrationality of the followers of Mahima Dharma by defining them as a lunatically inclined band of fanatics, *Utkala Deepika* stressed the unreasonableness of the incident by harping on the lowly origin and filthy habits of the 'attackers'.[118] They were denigrated as 'extreme mlechhas' (outcastes) who neither bathed nor cleaned themselves after defecation. It was not yet clear how and why they had taken to their faith and what caste and religion they belonged to prior to the acceptance of it. One could, however, easily guess that they belonged to some 'wild' and 'uncivilized' tribe like the Santhals and had come under the spell of some cunning man who was fooling them by posing as their Guru.[119]

The same bias, though to a lesser degree, attended the trial of the group. The Deputy Magistrate took the trouble to visit the temple and assess the damage done, called upon witnesses to furnish details of the attack and of the circumstances leading to the death of Dasaram, the leader, and examined the post mortem report of the police surgeon before passing his judgement. At the same time, he revealed a tendency to believe the witnesses far too easily. There were marks of injury on the bodies of the dead man and other members of the first group. The police superintendent stated them to have been caused by the *ratans* (sticks) used by the 'guardians' of the temple.[120] None of the witnesses admitted to the use of the instrument by the doorkeepers at any stage in the scuffle. The civil surgeon who examined Dasaram declared 'shock', caused by a fall on a full stomach, to be responsible for his death.[121] The marks of injury were not taken seriously; the exact conditions in which the fall had occurred were not probed into. The death was taken to be 'accidental', the 'guardians' of the temple and the pilgrims who had taken active roles in the 'scuffle' escaped without a taint of guilt.

The judgement on the group of attackers overtly expressed the sentiments of the Deputy Magistrate: 'The evidence of the witnesses proves that the Defendants broke down the door and entered the great hall in the temple. Under the circumstances the Defendants are guilty of rioting punishable under section 147 of the Indian Penal Code. They are also guilty of committing trespass into a place of worship punishable under Section 297 of the same code, because although they might have had no intention to wound the religious feeling of any person, but they could not fail to know that by taking out and burning the image of Jagannath, the feeling of his worshippers are likely to be wounded. Besides low-caste people and barbarous people who have no distinction of caste such as the Defendants are not allowed to enter the temple of Jagannath.'[122] The last statement sealed the fate of the 'barbarous people'; their entering the sacred space of the temple was in itself a violation, and punishment was their due from the beginning of the act.

The act in question was indeed remarkably significant. Its most striking feature was the stunning contrast between the opponents. The contemptuous tone of the reports, the comment of all the observers that the attackers were very scantily dressed and that they were 'uncivilized', underscored their lowliness. They were also very poor. In his judgement on the second 'band of fanatics' the Deputy Magistrate declared that he was acquitting most of the members of the group because they were 'beggars' like hundreds of others who throng the streets of Puri.[123] There could not have been a more emphatic statement on the anonymity of the Mahima Dharmis. A group of obscure, marginal men and women from Sambalpur threw a direct challenge to the central deity of dominant Hinduism in eastern India, the *rashtra devata* of Orissa for centuries. In doing so they came dangerously close to destroying the pivot of Oriya life and cultural identity.

What gave these poor, 'lowly' men and women the courage to commit such an act? Biswamoy Pati has argued that the idea that the Mahima Dharmis had come to Puri to burn the image of Jagannath is a misconception of colonial administrators and upper-caste officials. The attack on the temple, according to him, was symbolic of the attempt of tribals and low-castes to go into the 'presence' of the great Lord who had been 'stolen' by Brahmans and upper-castes.[124] While it is important to remember the problems related to the reading of colonial archives,[125] it is equally important to point out, as has been done by members of subaltern studies and David Warren Sabean, among others, that the problem of testimonies of subordinate subjects reaching the historian only through official documents can in fact be a strength rather than a weakness.[126] Pati also ignores the 'evidence' of the statements of the 'attackers' contained in almost every report. The men and women persistently affirmed that their sole purpose behind the trip to Puri and the temple was the burning of the idol of Jagannath. Pati takes no trouble to explain why in going into the 'presence' of their great Lord — Jagannath — these people invoked Alekh, the Absolute. It is perhaps, worthwhile to look at the relationship of Mahima Dharma with Jagannath to find an answer to the question.

Legends hold that Mahima Swami appeared in Puri. Wearing the garb of a follower of Vishnu, whose manifestation Jagannath is, he lay on the *bada danda*, in close proximity to the temple of Jagannath. Significantly, the ascetic had not yet begun preaching. He went through a long period of mediation before becoming the preceptor of the true faith. By this time, there was a reversal of roles: Jagannath had recognized the ascetic as the incarnation of the all-powerful Absolute, and had left Puri to become the Swami's first disciple Govinda. This belief, mentioned in various texts and reports with slight variations, had been given legitimacy and currency by the works of Bhima Bhoi, the poet philosopher of the faith.[127] Amidst the crisis of the faith following the death of Mahima Swami, Bhima Bhoi emerged as the main leader, and the Sonepur-Sambalpur region as the stronghold of the faith. The men and women had marched to Puri from Sambalpur. If we are to believe the reports, they were unlettered. Bhima Bhoi's works, as we will see in the chapter that follows, spread through recitation and singing, rendering them amenable to distinct perceptions and understandings.

Let us take a fresh look at the death of Mahima Swami in the context of this belief. Alekh Swami had come down to earth to establish *satya dharma*.

Jagannath had left Puri to become his disciple. But the situation had not changed. Idol worship continued, as did the domination of Brahmans and rajas. The new vision of life, the assurance and confidence that the Guru had given, was losing ground. To make matters worse, the divine preceptor had left the world. There was no one to guide the true devotees. Bhima Bhoi, who had emerged as the leader had taken to the life of a householder. Many of his disciples were unnerved by the fact that two of his consorts had become pregnant.[128] The followers of Alekh were faltering. The image of Jagannath, ensconced in the temple of Puri, the centre of royal and priestly domination, had, in the eyes of these Mahima Dharmis, become the main obstacle to the spread of the true faith preached by Mahima Swami. A resolution of their sufferings lay in the storming of the bastion of idolatry. Alekh Prabhu, who had disappeared from earth of his own volition, again showed the way: he appeared in a dream to the humble and unknown Dasaram of the village Chunderpur in Sambalpur and commanded him to lead an attack on Jagannath.[129] Members of his village, charged by a divine mission, began a long march to Puri that culminated in the incident of 1 March 1881.[130]

Through this audacious act, the poor 'uncivilized', 'barbarous' men and women were at once trying to expose the inefficacy of the wooden image of Jagannath and his abode, Puri; and lashing out against the exclusiveness, domination and power with which Jagannath had come to be associated. Their failed attempt marked a debunking of the myth about the universality of the *bara thakur*, the great Lord of Orissa. This explains the consternation in upper-caste Oriya circles.

The challenge to authority was worked out in concrete ways. Devotees of Jagannath are not meant to enter the temple after a meal; cooked food is not allowed inside the temple; the *mahaprasad* of Jagannath consists, among other things, of boiled rice. The followers of Alekh went into the temple just after they had eaten. They had not even bothered to wash their hands — this amounted to a contravention of temple rules and to a repudiation of Jagannath. It had the desired effect. It created fear and uncertainty among the *bhaktas* of the Great Lord. Rumour spread that the attackers had actually desecrated the unpollutable *mahaprasad* by scattering cooked rice over the temple courtyard.[131] The cries of 'Alekh, Alekh' as the group entered the temple underscored *his* pervasive presence and all-conquering supremacy. It was Alekh who was all-important. It was to carry out the orders of Alekh that the group had come to Puri. When the execution of the order was obstructed and a gate closed, the group behaved like 'mad men and women'. Belief in the necessity of the task they had undertaken did not desert the members of the group for a moment: the clarity and confidence with which they explained their motive of coming to Puri carried the force of divine conviction. They even regarded the death of Dasaram to be the result of the Guru's wish. 'Their [the defendants'] religious frenzy is so deep rooted that some say that the Guru has taken him [Dasaram] away.'[132]

The small group of marginal people from Sambalpur had, in throwing a dramatic challenge to Jagannath, given concrete shape to the questioning of the authority of the Raja and the Brahman-*purohit* and to the rejection of caste and of the Hindu pantheon. It is not surprising then that the incident had a powerful reverberation all over Bengal. Kshitimohan Sen, one of the very early scholars to work on 'medieval mysticism' and its impact on later sects described the followers of 'the Mahimapanth and the Kumbhipatia sect' thus: 'Their dislike of the idol is so great that they are known to have once made an attempt to demolish the famous temple of Jagannath in Orissa.'[133]

Yet, with the lapse of a hundred years, the event has taken on a different character within the faith — it has become an embarrassment to the present followers and sympathizers of Mahima Dharma. The conviction that had given a small group of marginal men and women the courage to claim history for themselves has now made them 'impetuous and irresponsible' people who acted on their own without the sanction of their leader, Bhima Bhoi.[134] Eschmann, who worked on Mahima Dharma in the 1970s, held that the incident was 'neither typical nor important'.[135] The men and women from Sambalpur have been marginalized once again; the narration of their action has been taken out of their hands.

What role does power play in all this? As we will see in the following chapters, over the course of the twentieth century Mahima Dharma has rearticulated its position and redefined its boundaries with Hinduism. Actively seeking support from middle-class Oriya society for its propagation, the leaders of the dominant segment of the faith have aligned it closely to the Advaita Vedantic tradition of Hinduism, carefully circumventing any direct engagement with the cult of Jagannath. Scholars and intellectuals, in an attempt to canonize Bhima Bhoi as the 'greatest adivasi poet and philosopher of Orissa', have also sought to negate any link between the teachings of Bhima Bhoi and the 'attack' on the temple. Leaders of Mahima Dharma and intellectuals of Orissa have acted separately and in conjunction to relegate the group from Sambalpur to the position of anonymity to which they belonged prior to act of 1 March 1881. The master narrative of Mahima Dharma has induced a selective amnesia with regard to this event that fits awkwardly and inconveniently with its neatly woven pattern. The attack, excised from a series in terms of its 'denouement and consequence' has been discarded as a single untoward incident.

How masterful then is the master narrative? According to Johannes Beltz, the wide identification of Govinda Baba — the first disciple of Mahima Swami — as Jagannath in later texts, stories and 'myths' of Mahima Dharma explains why the present day followers give little importance to the incident of 1881. The attack on Puri was only 'a protest against the hegemony of Puri's Brahmanic culture and social discrimination', launched by 'a rather militant branch of the Mahima movement', not an attack on Jagannath.[136] The institutionalized discourse of history thus, has no 'conceptual need' for the narrative of 1881. The present followers believe that Mahima Goswami is mightier than Jagannath and other centres, holier and more important have replaced Puri.

Wasn't it precisely this belief that led the militant group of followers to attempt to do away with the image of Jagannath? After all, the myths and stories about Jagannath leaving Puri to become Mahima Swami's disciple are not later day innovations. They have been propagated through the texts of Bhima Bhoi almost since the inception of the faith. Moreover, the importance of Jagannath and Puri has not decreased over time. Rather, as stated above, Mahima Dharma has worked out a different relationship with the cult. Besides, it would be a mistake to assume that the event has left no trace on the 'collective memory' of the people of the region. I quote here a popular rhyme from western Orissa: 'There runs the Kumbhipatua rebel/Gulping down everything/With food in his hand/And more food on his shoulder/There runs the Kumbhipatua rebel.'[137]

Within Mahima Dharma itself, the event continues to remain significant among its marginalized sections. In early 1993, a Kaupindhari ascetic who preaches to the former untouchable members of the sect in the Barpali region of western Orissa asserted that the attack of 1881 had divine sanction. At the end of 1880, a vulture had sat on the top of Nilmadhab (Jagannath as worshipped by the Savars, whose temple is located within the Jagannath temple complex in Puri) and cast its shadow on the Jagannath temple. The great *nullah* next to the temple had been filled with worms. Were the twin signs not ominous? Did they not signify that Jagannath's days were numbered?[138]

Notes

1. I draw upon the sensitive discussion of this ambiguity contained in Michel-Rolph Trouillot, *Silencing the Past.*
2. *Utkala Deepika*, 1 June 1867, Part 2, No. 22. Also contained in S. Patnaik,

Sambadpatraru Odisara Katha, vol. 1 (Cuttack, Grantha Mandir, 1972). A translated version of the report is found in S. Patnaik, 'Orissa in 1867', *Orissa Historical Research Journal*, 10:3, 1961, pp. 61–73. See also S. Nath, 'Mahima Dharma', in M. N. Dash (ed.), *Sidelights on History and Culture of Orissa* (Cuttack, Grantha Mandir, 1977), pp. 450–51.

3. *Utkala Deepika*, 6 September 1873, Part 8, No. 36.
4. 'Indian Report of the Orissa Baptist Mission for 1873–74', Baptist Missionary Society (BMS) Archives, Angus Library, Regent's Park College, Oxford.
5. *Ibid.*
6. The colonial government first took notice of the sect after the attack on the Puri temple. Several reports were drawn up by government officials after the incident. They include the reports of the Tehsildar (revenue collector) of Banki, the Tehsildar of Angul, the Manager of Dhenkanal and the Deputy Commissioner of Sambalpur. The Commissioner of the Orissa Division, in his report to the Government of Bengal, summarized the information supplied by these officials. This report was entitled 'On the origin and growth of the sect of Hindu dissenters who profess to be the followers of Alekh' ('The sect of Hindu dissenters') and incorporated in the *Proceedings of the Asiatic Society of Bengal 1882*. The reports were also incorporated in the *Jagannath Temple Correspondence*, Part VI, 1880–84. The report of the Tehsildar of Angul clearly marked the distinct phases in the life of the ascetic. The report of the Tehsildar of Banki provided the identification of Mahima Swami with 'Mukund Das'. This identification found its way into later official publications like censuses and gazetteers. B. B. Misra drew upon these sources to argue that Mahima Swami was none other than Mukunda Das, despite the objections raised by Mahima Dharmis. B. B. Misra, 'Rise and Growth of the Mahima Cult in the Nineteenth Century' (M. Phil. Dissertation, Sambalpur University, 1984), p. 17.
7. 'Tehsildar of Angul to the Commissioner of Orissa', Cuttack, 12 August 1881, Board of Revenue Document No. 443, Orissa State Archives (OSA), Bhubaneswar; Jagannath Temple Correspondence, Part 6, 1880–84, No. 513, Record Room (RR), Board of Revenue, Cuttack, pp. 1328–33.
8. 'Report of the Commissioner of the Orissa Division', Board of Revenue Document No. 445/1, OSA, Bhubaneswar; 'The sect of Hindu dissenters', *Proceedings of the Asiatic Society of Bengal 1882*, pp. 2–6.
9. *Ibid.*
10. *Ibid.*
11. According to the Tehsildar of Banki, Mahima Swami left Kapilaś around 1856 and spent six years in Puri. Thus it seems that he began preaching in 1862.
12. 'Tehsildar of Angul to the Commissioner of Orissa', Cuttack, 12 August 1881, Board of Revenue Document No. 443, OSA, Bhubaneswar; Jagannath Temple Correspondence, Part 6, 1880–84, No. 513, RR, Board of Revenue, Cuttack, pp. 1328–33.
13. 'Banki Tehsil Office to the Commissioner of Orissa Division', Cuttack, 06 August 1881, Board of Revenue Document No. 441/1, OSA, Bhubaneswar; Jagannath Temple Correspondence, Part VI, 1880–84, No. 131, RR, Board of Revenue, Cuttack, pp. 1324–7.
14. The reports of the Tehsildar of Angul and Banki mentioned 1866 as the year of its construction. Board of Revenue documents Nos.443, 441/1, OSA, Bhubaneswar; Jagannath Temple Correspondence, Part VI, 1880–84, Nos. 131, 513, RR, Board of Revenue, Cuttack, pp. 1324–7, 1328–33.
15. 'Banki Tehsil Office to the Commissioner of Orissa Division', Cuttack, 6 August

1881, Board of Revenue Document No. 441/1, OSA, Bhubaneswar; Jagannath Temple Correspondence, Part VI, 1880–84, No. 131, RR, Board of Revenue, Cuttack, pp. 1324–7.

16. The report of the Tehsildar of Banki mentions that the Swami died in 1875. 'Banki Tehsil Office to the Commissioner of Orissa Division', Cuttack, 6 August 1881, Board of Revenue Document No. 441/1, OSA, Bhubaneswar; Jagannath Temple Correspondence, Part VI, 1880–84, No. 131, RR, Board of Revenue, Cuttack, pp. 1324–7. N. N. Vasu's *The Modern Buddhism and its Followers in Orissa* (Calcutta, U. N. Bhattacharya, 1911), also indicates that 1875 is when the Swami died. However, later scholars have come to regard 1876 as the year of Mahima Swami's death.
17. Asit Patnaik, *Socio-Religious Reforms in Orissa in the 19th Century* (Calcutta, Punthi Pustak, 2000), p. 36.
18. Babu Banamali Sing, Manager of the Dhenkanal State, to the Superintendent of the Tributary Mahals, Orissa, 4.10.1881, Board of Revenue Document No. 444, OSA, Bhubaneswar; Jagannath Temple Correspondence, Part VI, 1880–84, No. 40, RR, Board of Revenue, Cuttack, pp. 1334–8.
19. *Utkala Deepika*, 1 June 1867, Part 2, No. 22; *Utkala Deepika*, 6 September 1873, Part 8, No. 36.
20. 'Indian Report of the Orissa Baptist Mission for 1873–74', BMS Archives, Angus Library, Regent's Park College, Oxford.
21. Earlier, I have mentioned that B. B. Misra, a scholar from Sambalpur accepts the identification of Mahima Swami with Mukunda Das. Other scholars from the same region seem to be of the same opinion. See, for instance, Debendra Kumar Dash, 'Bhima Bhoi o Mahima Dharma', *Eshana*, 34, (June 1997), pp. 212–51. I thank Johannes Beltz for bringing this article to my notice. Dash, in fact, blames Biswanath Baba and his followers like Satrughna Nath for creating confusion by trying to deny that Mahima Swami was Mukunda Das. *Ibid.*, p. 214. This identification has also found its way into censuses and gazetteers.
22. Nagendranath Vasu, *The Archeological Survey of Mayurbhanja* (Delhi, Rare Reprints, 1981), vol. I, p. ccxxxvii.
23. *Ibid.*, p. ccxxxviii.
24. Biswanath Baba, *Satya Mahima Dharmara Itihasa* (Cuttack, Satya Mahima Dharmalochana Samiti, 4th edition, 1978, 1st edition, 1935), p. 2. Henceforth *Itihasa*.
25. Nagendra Dhara Sarman, *Sebakalara Katha* (Cuttack, 1941); Eschmann collections, SAI, Heidelberg.
26. Indeed, the *Itihasa* premised its veracity on the divinity of the founder, a point I will discuss at greater length in the fourth chapter. That Mahima Swami's divinity had attained a certain degree of credibility among scholars is reflected in the foreword written by Artaballabh Mahanti to the first edition of Bhima Bhoi's *Stuti Chintamoni*. Mahanti asserted that the propounder of the faith was Alekh Swami himself. Artaballabh Mahanti (comp.) *Bhima Bhoi Granthabali*, Part I, *Stuti Chintamoni* (Cuttack, Prachi Samiti, 1925), 'Foreword'.
27. B. Baba, *Itihasa*, pp. 44–9.
28. According to legends, it was king Indradumnya who took over the worship of the Lord from the Śavars. Jagannath became the state deity of Orissa in the twelfth century during the rule of the Ganga kings. It was Chodaganga Deva who constructed the temple of Jagannath at Puri. For a discussion of the myths associated with the evolution of Jagannath, see M. Mansinha, 'The cult of Lord Jagannath', in D. Panda and S. C. Panigrahi (eds) *The Cult and Culture of Lord*

Jagannath (Cuttack, Vidyapuri, 1984), pp. 17–37.

29. These oppositions have been analysed from distinct perspectives by a variety of authors. For a detailed discussion of the *vana* and the *kshetra* see Sontheimer, Guenther-Dietz, 'The Vana and the Ksetra: The tribal background of some famous cults' in G.C. Tripathi and H. Kulke (eds), *Religion and Society in Eastern India: Anncharlott Eschmann Memorial Lectures* (Bhubaneswar, Utkal University, 1987), pp. 117–64; an analysis of the diverse meanings and liminal characteristics of the *vana* in Vedic literature is contained in Charles Malamoud, *Cooking the World: Ritual and Thought in Ancient India* (Delhi, Oxford University Press, 1996). Vanadana Madan traces the genealogy of the opposition between *nagar/pura* (city/town) and *gram* (village) in V. Madan, 'Introduction' in V. Madan (ed.), *Village in India* (New Delhi, Oxford University Press, 2002), pp. 1–26. Kalpana Ram and Ajay Skaria provide imaginative accounts of the configurations of settled, inhabited space and fringe dwelling and forest. See Kalpna Ram, *Mukkuvar Women* (New Delhi, Kali for Women, 1997) and Ajay Skaria, *Hybrid Histories*.
30. A. K. Ramanujan, *Speaking of Siva* (Harmondsworth, Penguin, 1973).
31. It was by denying the services of the barber and the washerman that a caste or a village community would exercise its sanction over a family that had been ostracized.
32. Kenneth W. Jones assesses Mahima Swami's teachings in terms of its success in bridging 'not only the pre-colonial and colonial worlds, but also tribal and Hindu areas of Orissa'. K. W. Jones, *New Cambridge History of India (III. 1): Socio-Religious reform Movements in British India* (Cambridge, Cambridge University Press, 1989), p. 134.
33. *Utkala Deepika*, 1 June 1867, Part 2, No. 22.
34. *Utkala Deepika*, 6 September 1873, Part 8, No. 36.
35. 'Indian Report of the Orissa Baptist Mission for 1873–74', BMS Archives, Angus Library, Regent's Park College, Oxford.
36. *Ibid.*
37. *Ibid.*
38. *Ibid.*
39. *Ibid.*
40. It was around this time that detailed ethnographic surveys and censuses conducted by the colonial state were classifying the Indian population in relation not only to the castes and tribes to which they belonged but also in terms of the social position and characteristics of such castes and tribes. The Pans, to whom the Tehsildar makes special reference in his report, were categorized as belonging to a 'Criminal Tribe'. A detailed analysis of these processes can be found in I. Banerjee-Dube, 'Introduction: Questions of caste' in I. Banerjee-Dube (ed.), *Caste in History: Modern Indian Perspectives*, (New Delhi, Oxford University Press, forthcoming). For a critical analysis of the construction of the categories of criminal castes and tribes see, Sanjay Nigam, 'Disciplining and policing the "criminals by birth" part 1: The development of the disciplinary system, 1871–1900', *The Indian Economic and Social History Review*, 27, 1 (1990), pp. 131–62; and 'The making of a colonial stereotype part 2: The criminal tribes and castes of northern India', *The Indian Economic and Social History Review*, 27, 2 (1990), pp. 257–87.
41. 'Tehsildar of Angul to the Commissioner of Orissa Division', Cuttack, Board of Revenue Document No. 443, OSA, Bhubaneswar; Jagannath Temple Correspondence, Part 6, 1880–84, No. 513, RR, Board of Revenue, Cuttack, pp. 1328–33.
42. Babu Banamali Sing, Manager of Dhenkanal State, to the Superintendent of the

Tributary Mahals, Orissa, 4 October 1881, Board of Revenue Document No. 444, OSA, Bhubaneswar; Jagannath Temple Correspondence, Part VI, 1880–84, No. 40, RR, Board of Revenue, Cuttack, pp. 1334–8.

43. 'Banki Tehsil Office to the Commissioner of Orissa Division', Cuttack, 6 August 1881, Board of Revenue Document No. 441/1, OSA, Bhubaneswar; Jagannath Temple Correspondence, Part VI, 1880–84, No. 131, RR, Board of Revenue, Cuttack, pp. 1324–7.
44. I use Kali Yuga and Kali interchangeably.
45. The *malikas* very closely resemble the *smriti* literature of classical Hindu tradition. The *smritis* were attributed to vedic sages and their contents were reformulated by commentators. However, unlike the *malikas*, these texts were used by Brahmin priests and royal administrators to project the past as a model of truth and righteousness, a repository of epistemological power and a source of knowledge. See Mikael Aktor, 'Smritis and jatis: The ritualisation of time and the continuity of the past' in Ali, *Invoking the Past*, pp. 258–79.
46. Balaram Das, Jagannath Das, Achyuta (nanda) Das, Ananata Das, and Yaśobanta Das were the Panchasakhas.
47. *Report on the Administration of Bihar and Orissa during 1911–12* (Patna, Govt. of Bihar and Orissa 1913), p. 82.
48. The Paik rebellion of 1817 for the first time made the Company's government take note of the defects in revenue administration. Three reports of enquiry were drawn up, respectively, by Watson, fourth judge of the Cuttack High Court, W. Trower, Collector of Zillah Cuttack, and W. Ewer, Commissioner of Orissa, in 1818. They ascribed the rebellion primarily to economic hardships caused by a defective system of revenue. These problems — over-assessment, extreme rigour in the collection of revenue, punishment of defaulters and depreciation of the cowrie currency — were discussed by Ewer in his letter to Trower. W. Ewer, Commissioner, to W. Trower, Collector of Zillah Cuttack, 15 February 1818, Board Proceedings No. 17, Department of Revenue (6 December 1817 to 20 May 1818), OSA, Bhubaneswar. For a general review of the economic condition of Orissa in the first phase of Company rule, see M. Mahapatra, 'General economic condition of Orissa (1803–18)', *Orissa Historical Research Journal*, 1:2, 1952, pp. 171–7. A detailed survey of the socio-economic conditions in nineteenth-century Orissa is contained in K. C. Jena, *Socio-Economic Conditions of Orissa in the Nineteenth Century* (Delhi, Sundeep Prakashan, 1978).
49. Tapan Raychaudhuri, 'The pursuit of reason in nineteenth century Bengal' in Rajat Kanta Ray (ed.), *Mind, Body, Society: Life and Mentality in Colonial Bengal* (Delhi, Oxford University Press, 1995), p. 47.
50. The Baptist Missionary Society set up its first station in Cuttack in 1822.
51. The fifties, sixties and seventies of the nineteenth century were marked by the publication of several Christian tracts that criticized idolatry and established the superiority of Christ over Jagannath. See, for instance, Mukunda Dasa, *Jagannatha-pariksha* (Cuttack, Mission Press, 2nd edition, 1867); A. Sutton, *Devapuja: The Testimony of the Bible against Idolatry* (Cuttack, Mission Press, 2nd edition, 1874), *Vernacular Tracts*, India Office Library and Records (IOLR), London. Earlier, in the 1820s and 1830s the Baptist missionaries had conducted a very active campaign against the institution of pilgrim tax at the temple of Jagannath, which kept the government of the East India Company in direct and close connection with the management of the temple. The campaign had varying degrees of success. Finally, a combination of change of policy on the part of the Company's government and

missionary propaganda led to the abolition of the pilgrim tax in 1840. For details see, Ishita Banerjee-Dube, *Divine Affairs: Religion, Pilgrimage and the State in Colonial and Postcolonial India* (Shimla, Indian Institute of Advanced Study, 2001), p. 137; Nancy G. Cassels, *Religion and Pilgrim Tax under the Company Raj* (New Delhi, Manohar, 1988); M. Dhall, 'Activities of Christian missionaries and British policy towards them', *Our Documentary Heritage*, 4, (Government of Orissa, Bhubaneswar, OSA, 1988), pp. 14–23.

52. For an analysis of how caste came to be definitely defined as a 'religious' institution under colonial rule see, I. Banerjee-Dube, 'Introduction: Questions of Caste'. See also, P. Samarendra, 'Classifying caste: Census surveys in India in the late nineteenth and early twentieth centuries', *South Asia: Journal of South Asian Studies*, 26, 2, (2003), pp. 141–64. A distinct and provocative exploration of this interaction can be found in Ashis Nandy, *The Intimate Enemy: Loss and Recovery of Self under Colonialism* (Delhi, Oxford University Press, 1983).

53. This is characteristic of the entire province of Bengal in the early nineteenth century. For incisive analyses of the interaction of Indian society and colonial state see, for instance, Partha Chatterjee, *The Nation and its Fragments: Colonial and Postcolonial Histories* (Princeton, Princeton University Press, 1993); Lata Mani, *Contentious Traditions: The Debate over Sati in Colonial India* (Berkeley & Los Angeles, University of California Press, 1998).

54. In the area under direct British administration — Cuttack, Puri, Balasore, Angul and Banki — Hindus constituted 97.4 per cent of the total population and in the tributary states they accounted for 74.82 per cent, with the adivasis (designated as aborigines) constituting 24.72 per cent of the population. A. Bourdillion, *Report on the Census of Bengal 1881* (Calcutta, 1883), p. 76.

55. W. W. Hunter, *A Statistical Account of Bengal*, (reprinted Delhi, Concept Publishing, 1976), vol. XIX, p. 61.

56. *Ibid.*, p. 76.

57. Castes excluded from entering the temple: (i) Christians; (ii) Muhammedans; (iii) hill or forest races; (iv) Bauris; (v) Savaras; (vi) Panas; (vii) Haris (except to clear away filth); (viii) Chamars; (ix) Doms and Chandals; (x) Chiria maras (bird-killers); (xi) Sials (wine sellers); (xii) Gokhas (fishermen); (xiii) Siulas (fishermen); (xiv) Tiyars (fishermen); (xv) Nulias (Telenga boatmen); (xvi) Patras (low-caste cloth makers); (xvii) Kandaras (village watchmen); (xviii) common prostitutes; (xix) persons who had been in jail, but with right of expiation; (xx) washermen and (xxi) potters. The last two were allowed to enter the outer court. Hunter, *A Statistical Account of Bengal*, vol. XIX, p. 62.

58. L.S.S. O'Malley, *Bengal District Gazetteer: Puri* (Alipore, 1908). The list was revised on the basis on the information supplied by the manager of the Jagannath temple and included in the revised edition of O'Malley's Gazetteer. P. T. Mansfield, *Bihar and Orissa District Gazetteer: Puri* (1929), pp. 106–7. The revised list made one change: Jews were mentioned along with Christians. The Gazetteer also noted that caste distinctions were sometimes followed even in the sharing of *mahaprasad.*

59. For a critical analysis of the process of appropriation of Jagannath by the priests and rulers and the legends associated with it see, Banerjee-Dube, *Divine Affairs*; G. N. Dash, *Tribal Priests of a Hindu Shrine: Social Dynamics in Medieval Orissa* (Delhi, Radiant Publishers, 1998); Ruprecht Geib, *Indradumnya-Legende: Ein Beitrag zur Geschichte des Jagannatha-Kultes* (Wiesbaden, Otto Harrassowitz, 1975).

60. The use of the term was started by Anangabhima III in A.D. 1230, under whom Jagannath became State deity. The Ganga rulers who came after him gave varying

degrees of importance to the 'deputy ideology'. H. Kulke, 'Jagannath as the state deity under the Gajapatis of Orissa', in A. Eschmann, H. Kulke and G.C. Tripathi (eds) *The Cult of Jagannath and the Regional Tradition of Orissa* (New Delhi, Manohar, 1986), pp. 200–2; H. Kulke, 'Ksatriyaisation and social change', in S. D. Pillai (ed.), *Aspects of Changing India: Studies in Honour of Professor G.S. Ghurye* (Bombay, Popular Prakashan, 1976), p. 402.

61. *Ibid.* The term *sevaka* was used by the Suryavamsi rulers (1435–1540 C. E).
62. *Ibid.* It was the first Suryavamsi king, Kapilendra, a usurper, who called himself an elect of Jagannath and stressed that opposition to him was revolt against the deity.
63. Kulke, 'Ksatriyaisation and social change'. Marglin takes Kulke's argument to mean that 'divine kingship was not a part and parcel of the ancient ideology of Hindu kingship but is a relatively recent innovation'. She argues that Hindu kings have always been thought of as embodying divine power. The greater involvement of the rajas of Orissa with temple rituals was a new development connected with the loss of territory and political power. It did not necessarily involve a redefinition of the notion of kingship. F.A. Marglin, *Wives of the God-King: Rituals of the Devadasis of Puri* (Delhi, Oxford University Press, 1985), p. 126. However, one is not certain whether Kulke uses his material to establish the recent origin of divine kingship. The main thrust of his argument seems to concern the exploitative uses of religion in Orissa.
64. Katherine Prior, 'The Administration of Hinduism in North India, 1780–1900' (Ph.D. Dissertation, Cambridge University, 1990), p. 76.
65. A brief analysis of the causes and consequences of the famine is contained in P. Mukherjee, 'The Orissa famine of 1866', *Orissa Historical Research Journal*, 6:1, 1957, pp. 69–95.
66. *Utkala Deepika*, 20 July 1867, Part 2, No. 20, reported that the Governor General, while analysing the report on the Orissa famine in the Parliament in London, found no reason for the lack of caution, alertness, and foresight shown by the Government of Bengal. The daily also quoted the *Time* magazine as having accused the Bengal government of not taking any measures at the start of the famine.
67. The enquiries of the famine commissioners bear testimony to the furore that had been caused by the serving of cooked rice from the relief houses. The commissioners felt it necessary to find out whether the food was actually prepared by Brahman cooks. *Report of the Commissioners Appointed to Enquire into the Famine in Bengal and Orissa in 1866*, vol. I (Cuttack, 1867), p. 222. Moreover, several issues of *Utkala Deepika* in 1867–68 reported on the efforts made by the Hindu intelligentsia to bring back within the fold of Hinduism through *prayaścitta* (penance) those who had been rendered outcastes during the famine. A collection of these reports is found in S. Patnaik, *Sambadpatraru Odisara Katha*, and in S. Patnaik, 'Orissa in 1867', *Orissa Historical Research Journal*, 10:3, 1961, pp. 61–73; see also S. Patnaik, 'Orissa in 1868', *Orissa Historical Research Journal*, 10:4, 1961, pp. 44–58.
68. Treaty engagements were executed with 14 hill chiefs in November 1803: Narsingpur, Tigiria, Dhenkanal, Ranpur, Baramba, Khandpara, Nayagarh, Talcher, Daspalla, Athgarh, Nilgiri, Hindol, Banki and Angul. Mayurbhanj, Keonjhar and Baud entered into treaty negotiations with the Company soon after. They constituted the Tributary Mahals of Orissa. Banki and Angul were later brought under direct administration. C.V. Aitchison (comp.) *A Collection of Treaties, Engagements and Sanads Relating to India and Neighbouring Countries*, (Calcutta, 1892), vol. 1, p. 117; L.E.B. Cobden-Ramsay, *Bengal Gazetteers XXI: Feudatory States of Orissa* (Calcutta, 1910 [Microfiche, Nehru Memorial Museum and Library], New Delhi),

p. 24. The Sambalpur group of states (which comprised the district of Sambalpur) became a part of Garhjats of Orissa in 1817. On the death of the ruler without an heir in 1849, the district was annexed as an escheat and was administered by the Bengal government till 1862, when it was transferred to the Central Provinces. It reverted back to Orissa in 1905. F. Dewar, *Report on the Land Revenue Settlement of the Sambalpur District 1906* (Patna, 1920), pp. 6–7.

69. L.E.B. Cobden-Ramsay, *Bengal Gazetteers XXI: Feudatory States of Orissa*, p. 89.
70. The annual reports on the administration of tributary mahals of Orissa that I found in the India Office Library and Records relate to a slightly later period, from 1893–94 to 1924–25.
71. For a discussion of the uprisings in Orissa in the nineteenth century, see P.K. Mishra, 'Political Unrest in Orissa in the Nineteenth Century' (Ph.D. Dissertation, Utkal University, 1980). Mishra provides an account of the following uprisings: Khurda rising of 1817–24; Ghumsar rising of 1837–56; Kand rising of 1837–56; Sambalpur rising of 1857–64; risings in Keonjhar in 1867–68 and 1891–93; and risings in Nayagarh in 1849–52 and 1893–94. A discussion of the disturbed situation in the Garhjats in the second half of the nineteenth century is also found in S. Pati, 'Democratic Movements in the Feudatory States of Orissa (1905–48)', (Ph. D. Dissertation, Utkal University, 1984).
72. That *bethi* and *rasad* were common practices and that forced labour caused discontent even leading to rebellion is evident in the description of the Keonjhar uprising of 1891 in Fakirmohan Senapati, *Atmacarit* tr. Maitree Sukla, (New Delhi, Sahitya Akademi, 1977), pp. 224–55. An official report on one of the feudatory states described bethi as the 'worst feature in the revenue administration', *Final Report on the Land Revenue Settlement of the Patna State 1937*, p. 21.
73. 'Mansfield Papers', Box I A, vol. 2; letters written to his parents between 19 October 1919 and 19 July 1920, Centre of South Asian Studies, Cambridge.
74. The interest taken by the colonial administration in the rulers and internal affairs of the state is reflected in the compilation of detailed 'confidential histories'of all these states by Political Agents and Commissioners of the Orissa Feudatory States. These histories are contained in files of the Political Department, General Branch, IOLR, London.
75. All the important Oriya dailies and weeklies which came to be published from the 1860s and 1870s — *Utkala Deepika*, *Sambalpur Hitaishini*, *Utkala Putra* — commented on the deplorable condition of the Garhjats and urged the government and the educated Oriyas to come forward and take steps to improve the lot of the Garhjat population. For a cross-section of these articles see S. Patnaik (comp.) *Sambadpatraru Odiśara Katha*; G.C. Misra (comp.) *Sambadpatrare Unabingśa Śatabdir Odiśa* (Cuttack, J. Moahpatra & Co., 1972).
76. In his minute of 23 January 1847 on the Tributary Mahals, A.J. Moffat Mill, the Commissioner of Cuttack, stated: 'I have spared no exertion to put an end to the atrocious system of Suttee and Meriah sacrifice. The rules touching the former were separately notified to the Rajahs, and the notice was again repeated on receipt of the Honourable Court of Directors' despatch, 29 September 1841, enjoining its abolition.' *Selections from the Records of the Bengal Government*, No. III, Papers on the Settlement of Cuttack and on the State of the Tributary Mehals (Calcutta, 1851).
77. For a detailed and sensitive discussion of this theme, see Nicholas Dirks, *The Hollow Crown*.
78. Kulke, 'Ksatriyaisation and social change'.
79. Kulke has shown how the village gods and goddesses gradually became the *ista-*

devatas (personal gods) of the ruling chiefs of feudatory states. H. Kulke, 'Tribal deities at princely courts: The feudatory rajas of central Orissa and their tutelary deities (Istadevatas)' in S. Mahapatra (ed.), *The Realm of the Sacred* (Calcutta, Oxford University Press, 1992), pp. 56–78.

80. *Jagannath Temple Correspondence*, Part I, pp. 180–220, contains numerous petitions from the rulers of different feudatory states to the Collector of Cuttack and other colonial officials against their 'disrespectful treatment' by Mukunda Deva II. See also, Banerjee-Dube, *Divine Affairs*, pp. 55–7; H. Kulke, 'The struggle between the Rajas of Khurda', in *The Cult of Jagannath*, pp. 350–1.
81. H. Kulke, 'Legitimation and townplanning in the feudatory states of central Orissa' in H. Kulke, *Kings and Cults: State Formation and Legitimation in India and Southeast Asia* (New Delhi, Manohar, 1993), p. 109.
82. F. Dewar, *Report on the Land Revenue Settlement of the Sambalpur District 1906* (Patna, 1920), p. 7.
83. O'Malley, *Bengal District Gazetteer: Sambalpur*, p. 65.
84. Cobden-Ramsay, *Bengal Gazetteers XXI: Feudatory States of Orissa*, p. 166.
85. *Malikas* became prominent once again in Orissa after the devastating cyclone of 1999. An analysis of these recent *malikas* can be found in Bishnu N. Mohapatra, 'Fish will swim over the "Twenty-two Steps" of the Jagannath Temple: Time, order and cosmology', paper presented at the Second International Conference on Indic Religions and Civilization, New Delhi, 17–20 December 2005.
86. Resolution, Judicial, 12 October 1881. Board of Revenue Document, No. 449/1, OSA, Bhubaneswar.
87. The Deputy Magistrate, Kedarnath Datta, also included an abbreviated version of this anecdote in his autobiography, *Atmajibancharit*, which was reprinted in a collection of his writings, which I have used. Banrasi Nath Bharadwaj (ed.), *Anabishkrita Sahitya Pratibha Kedarnath Datta (Bhaktibinod Thakur)* (Calcutta, Sri Chaitanya Research Institute, 1989), pp. 74–5.
88. *Ibid.*, p. 74. Contempt and disapproval for founders of new religious sects claiming themselves to be incarnations was a feeling shared by all upper-caste, educated Bengalis. Jogendranath Bhattacharya comments in his 'general observations about the sect founders' that the absence of a strong central authority recognized by all as supreme in religious matters in Hinduism had enabled 'many a clever adventurer to play the role of "incarnations", and to carve out independent religious principalities'. Jogendranath Nath Bhattacharya, *Hindu Castes and Sects: An Exposition of the Origin of the Hindu Caste System and the Bearing of the Sects Towards Each Other and other Religious Systems*(Calcutta, Firma K L M, 1973, 1st edition, 1891), p. 278.
89. *Census of India 1911* (vol. V Bengal, Bihar and Orissa and Sikkim; Calcutta, 1913). Part I, Report by L. S. S. O'Malley, p. 214.
90. This would make Artatran Das a contemporary of Mahima Swami who started preaching his faith in the 1860s.
91. *Census of India 1911*, p. 214.
92. Patnaik, *Socio-Religious Reforms in Orissa in the 19th Century*, p. 33.
93. This success story was given great publicity in the journals published by the missionaries. See, for instance, *The Calcutta Christian Observer* (n.s.), vols. 10 and 18, December 1849, pp. 540–2. The reports on the Orissa Mission published in various missionary journals in the nineteenth century have been compiled by S. Chatterjee, typescript, Carey Library, Serampore. B.B. Misra, however, claims that Sundar Das eventually became 'a follower of the Alekha cult founded by Mahima Swami'. This is not borne out by facts. B. B. Misra, 'Rise and Growth of the Mahima Cult

in Orissa in the Nineteenth Century' (M. Phil. Dissertation, Sambalpur University, 1984), p. 7.

94. Kshitimohan Sen, *Medieval Mysticism of India*, tr. Manmohan Ghosh (London, Luzac and Company, 1930), p. 120. For detailed analyses of the *Nirguna Sant* Tradition of North India see, P. D. Barthwal, *Traditions of Indian Mysticism Based Upon the Nirguna School of Hindi Poetry* (New Delhi, Heritage Publishers, 1978); Daniel Gold, *The Lord as Guru: Hindi Sants in the North Indian Tradition* (New York, Oxford University Press, 1987) and the collection of essays contained in K. Schomer and W.H. Mcleod, *The Sants: Studies in a Devotional Tradition of India* (New Delhi, Motilal Banarsidass, 1987).
95. From A. Smith, Commissioner of Orissa, to the Secretary, Judicial Department, 1 November 1881, Board of Revenue Document No. 445/1, OSA; Bhubaneswar; 'A Sect of Hindu dissenters', *Proceedings of the Asiatic Society of Bengal 1882*, pp. 5–6.
96. *Ibid.*
97. Resolution, Judicial, Government of Bengal, Board of Revenue Document, No. 446/1, OSA, Bhubaneswar.
98. From the Commissioner of Orissa to the Secretary, Government, Judicial Department, 1 November 1881, Board of Revenue Document No. 445/1, OSA, Bhubaneswar; 'The sect of Hindu dissenters', *Proceedings of the Asiatic Society of Bengal 1882*, p. 2.
99. 'Banki Tehsil Office to the Commissioner of Orissa Division', Cuttack, 6 August 1881, Board of Revenue Document No. 441/1, OSA, Bhubaneswar; from the Assistant Secretary to the Chief Commissioner, Central Provinces, to the Under Secretary to the Government of Bengal, 23 May 1881, enclosing an extract from letter No. 11/15, dated 1 April 1881, from the Deputy Commissioner, Sambalpur, to the Deputy Superintendent, Census, Central Provinces, Board of Revenue Document No. 440/1, OSA, Bhubaneswar.
100. 'Banki Tehsil Office to the Commissioner of Orissa Division', Cuttack, 6 August 1881, Board of Revenue Document No. 441/1, OSA, Bhubaneswar; Jagannath Temple Correspondence, No. 131, RR, Board of Revenue, Cuttack, pp. 1324–7.
101. 'The sect of Hindu dissenters', *Proceedings of the Asiatic Society of Bengal 1882*, pp. 5–6.
102. 'Tehsildar of Angul to the commissioner of Orissa division', Cuttack, 12 August 1881, Board of Revenue Document No. 443, OSA, Bhubaneswar; Jagannath Temple Correspondence, Part VI, 1880–1884, No. 513, RR, Board of Revenue, Cuttack, pp. 1328–33.
103. For a critical discussion of the distinction and hierarchy between the Brahman renouncer and the Brahman priest and the lower status of the Brahman priest occasioned by the acceptance of *dana* (gift) see, Jonathan Parry *Caste and Kingship in Kangra* (London, Routledge and Kegan Paul, 1979); C. J. Fuller, *Servants of the Goddess: The Priests of a South Indian Temple* (Cambridge, Cambridge University Press, 1984) and Banerjee-Dube, *Divine Affairs*. For a critical discussion of the relative position of the Brahman, the king and the renouncer as laid out in texts see, Veena Das, *Structure and Cognition: Aspects of Hindu Caste and Ritual* (Delhi, Oxford University Press, 1977), pp.18–56.
104. From the Commissioner of Orissa to the Secretary, Government, Judicial Department, 1 November 1881, Board of Revenue Document No. 445/1, OSA, Bhubaneswar; 'The sect of Hindu dissenters', *Proceedings of the Asiatic Society of Bengal 1882*, p. 3.
105. For a discussion of transfer of inauspiciousness from patron to the client associated with *dana*, see Gloria Goodwin Raheja, *The Poison in the Gift: Ritual, Prestation, and the Dominant Caste in a North Indian Village* (Chicago and London, University of Chicago

Press, 1988); J.C. Heesterman, *The Inner Conflict of Tradition: Essays in Indian Ritual, Kingship, and Society* (Delhi, Oxford University Press, 1985), pp. 26–44.

106. *Utkala Deepika*, 18 December 1867, Part II, No. 50, reported that the Governor General had decided to confer on him the title of Maharaja in recognition of the special help accorded by him to the poor and the needy at the time of the famine. The issue of the daily dated 9 January 1869 gave an account of the 'durbar' held 'in great pomp', to confer the title on Bhagirathi Mahindrabahadur. The *Deepika* asserted that the ruler had well earned the title of Maharaja by dint of his learning, wisdom, behaviour, responsibility towards subjects, and proper expenditure, and disagreed with the critics who tried to say that he had 'bought' the title with money. 'Who else', asked the *Deepika*, 'has been able to buy title and respect with money so far?' *Utkala Deepika*, 9 January 1869, Part IV, No. 1. This issue carried an appendix that included the speech delivered by the British Commissioner on the occasion of the conferral of the title of Maharaja. This speech mentioned the *annachatra* and the cash donation.
107. The importance of healing in relation to the spread of a new faith, particularly Christianity, in South Asia and Africa has been discussed in several important studies. I discuss this more fully in chapter 5.
108. Kumbhipatia was the generic term used for all members of Mahima Dharma, even lay disciples, who wore cloth.
109. *Census of the Central Provinces 1881*, vol. II, p. 39. T. Drysdale, the Census Commissioner, commented that the exhibition of statistics throughout the final tables was a 'mistake', made during his absence on leave.
110. This census carried a detailed account of the sect and estimated the following at 'not less than 25,000 plus'. *Census of India 1911*, vol. V, p. 213.
111. Both the Tehsildar of Banki and Angul stated in their reports that the Kumbhipatia religion was dying out in their regions. They, however, mentioned that the faith was gaining in strength in Sambalpur.
112. 'It is said that Narsing Das is the principle [sic] follower of Mahima Swami is at present living at Dhenkanal. But he is not seen to have any superiority over other Kumbhipatias who are equally respected by each other and by the Ashritas. In fact the followers of Mahima appear to have no leader after the death of Mahima Swami.' From the 'Tehsildar of Angul to the Commissioner of Orissa Division', Cuttack, 12 August 1881, Board of Revenue Document No. 443, OSA, Bhubaneswar; Jagannath Temple Correspondence, Part VI, 1880–84, No. 513, RR, Board of Revenue, Cuttack, pp. 1328–33.
113. *Ibid.*
114. *Utkala Deepika*, 12 March 1881, Part 16, No. 11.
115. From the Magistrate of Pooree to the Commissioner of Orissa Division, Cuttack, 15 March 1881, Board of Revenue Document No. 438/1, OSA, Bhubaneswar; Jagannath Temple Correspondence, Part VI, 1880–84, No. 224, RR, Board of Revenue, Cuttack, pp. 1308–17.
116. From the Assistant Superintendent of Police in charge of Pooree District to the Magistrate of Pooree, 11 March 1881, Board of Revenue Document No. 438/2, OSA, Bhubaneswar; Jagannath Temple Correspondence, Part VI, 1880–84, No. 175, RR, Board of Revenue, Cuttack, pp. 1305–6.
117. Jagannath Temple Correspondence, Part VI, 1880–84, pp. 1312–15, RR, Board of Revenue, Cuttack.
118. I draw here upon Ranajit Guha's sensitive discussions of the language used in official records to characterize peasant insurgency, a language that make the

spontaneous, irrational, unconscious character of the act self-evident. Ranajit Guha, *Elementary Aspects of Peasant Insurgency in Colonial India*; and Ranajit Guha, 'The prose of counter insurgency' in R. Guha (ed.), *Subaltern Studies II: Writings on South Asian History and Society* (Delhi, Oxford University Press, 1983), pp. 1–40. This is worked out in the writings of other members of the Subaltern Studies collective, Gautam Bhadra, 'Mentality of subalternity: *Kantanama* or *Rajdharma*' in Ranajit Guha (ed.), *Subaltern Studies VI: Writings on South Asian History and Society* (Delhi, Oxford University Press, 1989), pp. 54–91, for instance. See also the first four volumes of *Subaltern Studies*.

119. *Utkala Deepika*, 26 March 1881, Part 16, No. 13.
120. The Pratiharees, temple servants, traditionally entrusted with keeping order inside the temple.
121. 'The deposition of B.B. Gupta', Civil Surgeon, Board of Revenue Document No. 438/8, OSA, Bhubaneswar.
122. 'Judgement of the Deputy Magistrate of Puri on Jagna Singh, Prosecutor vs. Dhani, Situ, Bhagat, Moyaram, Mallik, Bhanor, Dina, Hari, Mosad, Badhan, Thara, Bundah, Seekuara, Parbati and Reuti, Defendants', Board of Revenue Document, No. 438/5, OSA, Bhubaneswar; Jagannath Temple Correspondence, Part VI, 1880–84, p. 1314, RR, Board of Revenue, Cuttack.
123. Board of Revenue Document No. 438/7, OSA, Bhubaneswar; Jagannath Temple Correspondence, Part VI, 1880–84, p. 1315, RR, Board of Revenue, Cuttack.
124. Biswamoy Pati, 'The "high": "low" dialectic in Fakirmohan's Chamana Athaguntha: Popular culture, literature and society in late nineteenth century Orissa', *Occasional Papers on History and Society*, Second Series, 49, (Nehru Memorial Museum and Library 1993), pp. 33–4. A slightly revised version of the paper has been published in Biswamoy Pati, *Situating Social History: Orissa (1800–1997)* (New Delhi, Orient Longman, 2001), pp. 26–49.
125. The list of works that have discussed this issue is too long to bear citing. Ranajit Guha, 'Chandra's death' in Ranajit Guha (ed.), *A Subaltern Studies Reader 1986–1995* (Minneapolis, University of Minnesota Press, 1997), pp. 34–62; Shahid Amin, 'Approver's testimony, judicial discourse: The case of Chauri Chaura' in Ranajit Guha (ed.), *Subaltern Studies V: Writings on South Asian History and Society* (Delhi, Oxford University Press, 1987), pp. 166–203; Saurabh Dube, *Stitches on Time: Colonial Textures and Postcolonial Tangles*, indicate innovative ways of 'reading' and deploying court records by historians. For a critical engagement with colonial archives and categories see, Anand Pandian, 'Securing the rural citizen: The anti-Kallar movement of 1896', *The Indian Economic and Social History Review*, 42: 1, 2005, pp. 1–39.
126. *Ibid.*, Sabean, *Power in the Blood*, pp. 2–3.
127. I discuss the works of Bhima Bhoi in the following chapter.
128. An account of the 'suspicion' and confusion generated by the conduct of Bhima Bhoi among his followers is contained in the Resolution, Judicial, Calcutta, 21 October 1881, Board of Revenue Document No. 446/1, OSA, Bhubaneswar.
129. 'Dasa Ram, the leader of the party which proceeded to Pooree, and who was killed in the scuffle at the temple, thought that, if Jagannath were burnt, it would convince the Hindus of the futility of their religion, and the whole world would thereby embrace the true religion. This account is given by some Kumbhupatias who reside in Sambulpore; and it is not improbable that the man was actuated by dreams, in which the Kumbhupatias firmly believe.' Resolution, Judicial, Calcutta, 21 October 1881, Board of Revenue Document No. 446/1, OSA, Bhubaneswar.

130. This act possibly provides a brilliant example of 'liminality' discussed by Victor Turner — the in-between, threshold zone that comes into play in the 'ritual process' when the established structure is transcended, and the new, 'anti-structure' is yet to take shape. Victor Turner, *The Ritual Process: Structure and Antistructure* (Chicago, Aldine, 1969).
131. *Utkala Deepika*, 12 March 1881, Part 16, No. 11.
132. Board of Revenue Document No. 438/7, OSA, Bhubaneswar; Jagannath Temple Correspondence, Part VI, 1880–84, No. 224, RR, Board of Revenue, Cuttack, pp. 1312–3.
133. Sen, *Medieval Mysticism*, p. 120.
134. 'There can be no doubt that the violent demonstration against the worship of Jagannath at Puri was organised by some impetuous and irresponsible Kumbhipatias without any sanction of the Guru Bhima Bhoi'. B. Nepak, *Bhima Bhoi: The Adivasi Poet Philosopher* (Bhubaneswar, Publication Committee, 1987), p. 72.
135. A. Eschmann, 'Mahima Dharma', unpublished, Eschmann papers, Munich.
136. On the basis of fieldwork conducted in western Orissa, Johannes Beltz claims that the attackers were 'Ganda Panas', a caste mentioned in the in the list of castes excluded from entering the temple of Jagannath. Johannes Beltz, 'Disputed centres, rejected norms and contested authorities: Situating Mahima Dharma in its regional diversity', paper presented at Orissa Research Project Conference, Salzau, Germany, 2001.
137. Translated from the original cited in Das, *Odiśara Mahima Dharma*, p. 98.
138. Interview with sadhu Anakar Das, Karamunda, Barpali, 12 March 1992.

CHAPTER 3.

Poets and Texts

This chapter explores the interplay of heterogeneous yet coeval temporalities as shaping overlapping but distinct modes of reading and interpretation, understanding and apprehension of texts and pasts. My focus is on Bhima Bhoi, the main poet-philosopher of Mahima Dharma. The effort is to probe the contradictory relationship of Bhima Bhoi with Mahima Dharma occasioned by the polyvalent compositions and experimental lifestyle of a non-conformist poet. Through a detailed discussion of Bhima Bhoi's key works and a critical analysis of the diverse ways in which the poet and his compositions have been perceived in the twentieth century, I attempt to unravel the mutual imbrications of the spoken and the written, faith and reason, philosophy and theosophy, yogic meditation and pure devotion and legend and history.

Believed to have been born blind to poor Khond (*adivasi*) parents, Bhima Bhoi was initiated into Mahima Dharma by Mahima Swami. The Swami also endowed the *adivasi* with the gift of poetry to spread the message of the faith. Growing up with no formal education, Bhima Bhoi combined precepts of the Guru with aural comprehensions of popular religious texts and the epics to elaborate a philosophy–theosophy of Mahima Dharma. His rich compositions at once reflect an agglomeration of wide trends of religious thought current in Orissa, and underscore Bhima Bhoi's ingenuity in imbuing prevalent ideas and precepts with new meanings. Indeed, a creative genius, Bhima Bhoi's emotive chants of devotion could not be contained by the dictates of any one faith. A discrete blend of high philosophy and everyday metaphors, the spoken-written compositions of the poet produced a surfeit of meanings at collective readings/recitations in gatherings of non-literate followers.

If his creations were open to distinct apprehensions, Bhima Bhoi's life of a householder, which transgressed the unwritten rule of celibacy adhered to by many preachers, generated a host of legends and stories that led to his near deification in western Orissa. At the same time, the poet incensed the ascetic disciples of Mahima Swami by cohabiting with women and by allowing women to join the monastic order. This led to a parting of ways between the renouncers who constructed a memorial of the Guru at Joranda in Dhenkanal, and Bhima Bhoi who set up his own *ashrama* at Khaliapali in Sonepur. However, in the early twentieth century, when the ascetics themselves came to clash over interpretations of Mahima Swami's teachings, one group resorted back to Bhima Bhoi's works as the only authentic record of the founder's precepts. At this time, apocryphal texts in Bhima Bhoi's name began to circulate among the lay followers. Illustrating the tremendous hold of Bhima Bhoi over popular imagination, these texts prophesied a bright future as a way out of the difficult present. While his works have been to put to different use, Bhima Bhoi himself has been marginalized and canonized by renouncers and intellectuals over the twentieth century. As in the case of his teacher Mahima Swami, the story of Bhima Bhoi has been told and retold and yet remains open to further renderings.

Life

Bhima Bhoi rose from obscure beginnings and became a legend in his own lifetime. His birth, family and early life continue to be matters of debate and dispute. Several stories have developed around him, and scholars have attempted to assess the veracity of these stories. At least four villages scattered over different parts of Orissa — Joranda in Dhenkanal,[1] Gramadiha in Redakhol,[2] and Jatasinga and Paiksara in Bolangir[3] — have been listed as the birthplace of Bhima Bhoi. There is disagreement over whether Janardan and Maharagi or Danara and Gurubari were his parents, and whether he was born in 1845 or 1855 or on some date in between.[4] Bhima Bhoi's own works, which provide a considerable amount of autobiographical detail, are silent on these issues. What they repeatedly stress is the fact of his low birth. At the end of each chapter of his numerous works Bhima calls himself a 'kandha' (Khond). But his Khond status is also controverted. Stories are still current in the Redakhol-Sambalpur-Bolangir region about how the infant Bhima Bhoi was actually discovered by a Khond couple. This fact has found mention in several recent works on the poet.[5]

All accounts agree that Bhima Bhoi's childhood was unhappy. According to legend, his bad days started after the death of his father, when his mother remarried and gave birth to other children. Bhima was left to fend for himself.[6] Bhima Bhoi's *Stuti Chintamoni* depicts the plight of his youth when he roamed in the forest, tending cattle, and allayed the pangs of hunger and thirst by drinking water from streams.

> Day after day I wandered in the woods with the cattle.
> Overtaken by hunger and thirst, I drank water from the streams.[7]

Legends identify Chaitanya Pradhan of the village Kankanapada in Redakhol as Bhima Bhoi's employer. They also narrate how from an early age Bhima Bhoi showed signs of his future greatness.[8] Chaitanya Pradhan was a regular reader of the *Bhagabata*, the influential Oriya rendering of the life of Sri Krishna. Bhima the Khond did not have the right to enter either Chaitanya Pradhan's room or the village *bhagabata ghara* (an assembly hall where the *Bhagabata* was read). He stood outside, listened to the readings and memorized the entire text. Other signs of the boy's piety became visible soon after. One day Bhima Bhoi went out with his cows but did not return. Enquiries revealed that he had fallen into a well.[9] He refused all offers of help and maintained that he would remain there until the Lord, who had caused his fall, came to his rescue. The Lord heard his prayers. Mahima Swami came from Joranda, stretched out his hand, lifted Bhima out of the well, and then disappeared.

This incident brought about a significant change in Bhima Bhoi's life. Chaitanya Pradhan convinced that the cattle-tender was no ordinary mortal, took full charge of his well-being and left him completely free to spend his time meditating on the Guru. With this began Bhima Bhoi's elevation in stature. His employer, with whom he stood in a relation of subordination, became his friend and admirer and spared him the responsibility of earning his livelihood. The mediation of Mahima Swami transformed the lowly Khond into a pious disciple and effected a reversal of roles between the high caste master and the tribal servant.[10]

Bhima Bhoi's actual initiation into Mahima Dharma took place at the age of 16. With this also began his career as a poet. The Guru and his first disciple, Govinda Das, approached the *bhakta* Bhima to grant him initiation; this inspired Bhima Bhoi to spontaneously recite a *pada* (couplet) in honour of his Lord. Mahima Swami, pleased by Bhima's sincere devotion, granted him the gift of poetry. Bhima was filled with devotion for his master and his mind overflowed with songs in praise of the Lord that spread his message to all.

Bhima Bhoi's sufferings, however, did not end with his initiation into Mahima Dharma. His efforts to spread the new faith, that questioned and challenged many of the existing norms, met with opposition and ridicule. *Stuti Chintamoni* abounds in lurid descriptions of his tormented life.[11] A few excerpts are in order here:

> People are calling me a Christian and hurling abuses at me
> I am going through great suffering for taking the name of Alekh[12]
> Men and women in one voice are calling me names
> The people of three worlds are running away when I am approaching them.[13]

But the ardent *bhakta* persisted. Towards the end of his life he attained success. After the death of Mahima Swami, Bhima Bhoi emerged as the most prominent leader of the faith. He set up his own *ashrama* at Khaliapali near Sonepur and severed all links with Joranda.[14] Government reports on the sect written as a result of the incident of 1881, unanimously point to Sambalpur as the region that supplied the Dharma with most of its followers.[15] They also mention Bhima Bhoi as the person who composed a book of 'songs and dialogues interpreting the truth of Alekh' that was widely used by the followers of the faith.

We have noted that the Census of the Central Provinces of 1881 provided separate statistics on the Kumbhipatias of Sambalpur in its tables. A feature in the *Utkala Deepika* of 19 November 1881, entitled 'Kumbhipatia Babaji' mentioned the Kumbhipatias as 'a community that exists in Sambalpur district' and described Bhima Khond as their leader. The report affirmed that although first propounded in Banki by Alekh Swami, the Dharma very soon 'gained special spread in the district of Sambalpur' where people of all castes except the Brahmans adopted the faith.[16] The annual report of the Orissa Baptist Mission on Sambalpur for the year 1881–82 commented:

> 'The Kumpatias continue to gain adherents and we are glad to welcome this as a sign of continued reactionary [*sic*] movement against the grosser forms of idolatry'.[17]

Bhima Bhoi experimented with his life after he settled down at Khaliapali. His intimate connection with popular trends of yogic/tantric meditation prevalent in eastern India — a connection which has been forgotten or suppressed within the Mahima Dharma tradition — probably actuated Bhima Bhoi to take to the life of a householder. He cohabited with four women. One of them bore him a daughter, Labanyabati, and another a son, Kapileswar. He started celebrating a fair that rivalled the one held in Joranda on the full-moon of the month of *magh* (January–February), gave sacred thread to his disciples, and allowed women the freedom to join the monastic order — something not permitted by the renouncers at Joranda to this day. Finally, he let himself and his spiritual consort Annapurna[18] be deified and worshipped by his followers. This was possibly meant as a statement that the life of a householder in no way jeopardized the position of a spiritual leader.[19]

Bhima Bhoi's unusual lifestyle created tension among the followers of Mahima Dharma. The *sanyasis* at Joranda, threatened by the poet's rising popularity and incensed by acts which went beyond the precepts of Mahima Swami, felt that by adopting the life of a somewhat extraordinary householder Bhima Bhoi had forfeited the right to preach the faith. He was ostracized by the Mahima *samaj* (community) at Joranda, and *sanyasis* were instructed not to accept *bhiksha* at his *ashrama*. Some of his *bhaktas* were perhaps unnerved by the fact of his having fathered two children. At several places in *Stuti Chintamoni* Bhima justifies his marital status.

> I was destined to lead a happy life with wife, children and wealth.
> How does it affect anyone else if I enjoy the rewards of previous good deeds?[20]

The mix of opposites that characterized Bhima Bhoi — his capacity to compose works of great literary and spiritual merit despite his low birth and a lack of formal education, and his success as a religious leader who transgressed celibacy but allowed women to become ascetics — confounded middle-class critics and admirers. Contemporary reports reflect this uncertainty. Grudgingly, the *Utkala Deepika* acknowledged in its report of 19 November 1881 that 'he [Bhima Kandha] is born blind but very intelligent. He has had no formal education...but has composed some songs and hymns in praise of God whose beautiful style can hardly be matched by the most educated.'[21] The very next sentence stated that Bhima Bhoi had annoyed the Kumbhipatias by getting a woman pregnant through 'illicit love' (*papa pranaya*). Moreover, he had tried to deceive them by saying that the woman would give birth to Arjun, who would destroy all the non-believers. Bhima Bhoi was proved wrong when a daughter was born. Bhima now claimed that he had received order from the Lord that the daughter was to do away with the non-believers. But the baby died within a few days. At this, those 'who had even a little bit of intelligence' separated themselves from Bhima

Bhoi and formed a distinct sect. Bhima Bhoi thus, was simultaneously praised for his success in propagating the faith, and blamed for causing dissension among its adherents.

The same ambivalence characterized the reports of the Baptist missionaries. In 1881–82 the success of Bhima Bhoi in gaining adherents was a welcome sign that people were moving away from 'the grosser forms of idolatry'. But by 1887–88, the sign was no longer welcome. The people who had moved away from idolatry had not taken the next step — of adopting the true faith — Christianity. They remained faithful to Bhima Bhoi. The missionaries now described him as an 'impostor', a master of 'blasphemous pretensions', who gave himself out to be 'a new incarnation', an *anadi avatar* (incarnation without beginning), who had appeared on earth 'to inaugurate a new dispensation'.[22] According to the missionaries, Bhima Bhoi called his wife the *adi avatar*, the first incarnation, and named the village he established *agamya dham* (the inaccessible place). What irked the missionaries most was that this impostor could 'number his disciples by [the] hundreds, if not thousands.'[23] No doubt the messengers of Christ saw in the act of 'thousands of men giving divine honour to an ignorant man' a 'widespread disbelief in idolatry and an equally widespread restlessness of heart which was leading the people hither and thither for some way of salvation'.[24] But their sense of outrage and tone of contempt for this 'ignorant man' underscored their disappointment. The devotees of western Orissa, instead of seeing their destiny in Christ, had turned to Bhima Bhoi for solace. Clearly, the poet had greater appeal than the messengers of Christ and the divine dispensations of upper-caste Hinduism.

The above report leaves no doubt that, dissension notwithstanding, most followers continued to be guided by Bhima Bhoi, their Guru. Slowly but surely Bhima Bhoi came to take the place of Mahima Swami in the western part of Orissa.[25] The rise in his popularity, which had started with a change of heart on the part of Chaitanya Pradhan, reached its culmination in the merger of Bhima Bhoi's identity with that of his preceptor.[26] The supreme faith of Bhima Bhoi's disciples cemented the gap between the devotee and the master; in their eyes the *bhakta* became *bhagaban*. The report in the *Deepika*, that held Bhima Bhoi responsible for a 'sinful union' with a woman and for causing dissension among his disciples by telling lies, claimed that the followers who remained with him worshipped him like god. 'Every morning Bhima sits with his wife on a *bedi* [raised platform]. His disciples circumambulate the *bedi*, wash the feet [of Bhima Bhoi and his wife] with milk and drink it.'[27]

The same fact was repeated with greater flourish in the introduction to the published version of Bhima Bhoi's collected works:

> From 1876, after the disappearance of Mahima Swami, an annual fair started being held during the full moon of January–February in Bhima Bhoi's *math* at Khaliapali. His followers assembled there in the thousands and began worshipping him. At the fair 108 pitchers were placed and 108 lamps lit on a raised platform. *Bhakta* Bhima and his wife Annapurna sat on the platform. The people present there performed *arati* to the couple with flowers and sandal paste and offered them paddy and cow. [28]

Bhima Bhoi's deification was complete.

Bhima Bhoi died in 1895.[29] The veneration offered to him in life got transformed into legends. In 1908 a senior official of the court of Sonepur wrote an essay entitled 'Bhima Bhoi's acquisition of knowledge'. In parenthesis he called it a 'legend'. Published in the literary magazine *Mukur* in 1908, the essay wanted to make Bhima Bhoi and 'his religion' known to readers.[30] In a very interesting turn of events, Bhima Bhoi's fall into the well was stated to have happened after the disappearance of Mahima Swami. A distraught Bhima called out to the formless Alekh. He heard a voice near the well asking Bhima to hold his hand and climb out of the well to avoid death. For the ardent devotee, however, death was much less painful than the pang of witnessing the erasure of the name of Alekh from the world. The number of Alekh's devotees was painfully small and was dwindling day by day. There was no written text to help people concentrate on the worship of Alekh and earn peace of mind. 'Were all the efforts of the Guru going to be in vain?' Hearing these words the voice asked Bhima Bhoi why he, a pious devotee, was blaming others instead of trying to write the text himself? But for Bhima Bhoi it was an impossible task to carry out. He was ignorant, with no knowledge of the letters, and blind. How could he write about the glories of Alekh preached by the Guru which was even difficult for learned men to understand? At that moment, the owner of the voice lifted Bhima Bhoi out of the well, set him on the right path and addressed him as the 'guru of the bhaktas'. The eye of knowledge was conferred on Bhima. The voice announced that the precepts of 'Mahima Das' and the essence of his faith would blossom in Bhima's heart in the form of 'prakruta' songs. He needed only to recite, scribes would write them down. Mahima Dharma would gain fame and popularity through Bhima who would spend the last part of his life serving the feet of the Lord. Within a few years of his death then, Bhima Bhoi had become the key figure in the propagation of Mahima Dharma.

Mahima Das had preached it first, but it was Bhima Bhoi who saved the faith from extinction, and interpreted and spread its message so that he became its real leader.

Almost the same sentiment was echoed in an English text three years later. N. N. Vasu, the scholar-cum-administrator based his account of Mahima Dharma on *Kali Bhagabata*, *Yaśomati Malika* and *Alekh Leela*, 'scriptures' of the faith he had chanced upon in the state of Mayurbhanj.[31] Vasu's account, written 'only ten years' after Bhima Bhoi passed away, categorically identified Bhima Bhoi as the leader of the sect and claimed that his sons were in possession of the Gadi 'at Jurunda near the Dhenkanal state' where Bhima Bhoi 'used to sit.'[32] Vasu further affirmed, on the basis of *Yaśomati Malika*, that the 'revival of Buddhism in the name of Mahima Dharma took place in the twenty-first year of the reign of Divya-Simha, late king of Puri, i.e., in 1875. 1875 is the year when Mahima Swami 'left his mortal remains'.[33] By the first decade of the twentieth century then, Mahima Swami had become the incarnation whose only purpose in coming down to earth was to bless the blind Bhima Bhoi with the 'eye of knowledge'. The task of spreading the message of the true faith was left entirely to Bhima Bhoi. And *malikas*, which had identified Mahima Swami as the incarnation of the Absolute now identified Bhima Bhoi as his divine devotee. Bhima Bhoi's name had found its way into apocryphal texts and 'official' accounts in English. The process of canonization of Bhima Bhoi had begun.

Texts

Mahima Swami did not himself codify in writing what he preached. He entrusted the task to Bhima Bhoi, whom he endowed with the gift of poetry. He also arranged for four scribes to become Bhima Bhoi's constant companions and record his inspired utterances.[34] Bhima Bhoi, the poet-devotee, is believed to have composed four bhajans in one *raga* simultaneously. He began with the refrains for the scribes to note down, and followed them up by singing the *bhajans* (devotional songs) one by one.[35] These were then sent to Joranda for the Guru's approval, and passed on to the *bhaktas* to be sung and recited. After Bhima Bhoi's death palm-leaf manuscripts of his works were discovered at various places in Orissa. Researchers even now locate handwritten copies of his texts in the houses of the *gruhi bhaktas* of western Orissa.[36] All the manuscripts have not been printed. Instead there has been a careful selection of the works that are regarded as authentic.

Bhima Bhoi had received no formal education. He had imbibed and apprehended various traditions of religious and popular literature by the time he was initiated into Mahima Dharma. His imaginative and creative mind combined these received ideas with the teachings of Mahima Swami to produce original compositions. Consequently, his works reflect the rich assortment of religious traditions that flourished in Orissa: there are elements of Hinduism, Buddhism, Yoga/Tantra, mysticism and *bhakti*. This blend makes it difficult to place Bhima Bhoi within one particular tradition. His numerous *bhajans*, *stutis* and *janans* speak of an Absolute (Brahma), omnipresent and omniscient, who created the world out of his *mahima* (radiance, glory), but who is beyond attributes — formless and indescribable. He is the Lord of lords, the one and only Guru who had taken form and come down to earth to redeem humanity by establishing *satya dharma*. This Guru is accessible to all through devotion. His worship does not require priests, temples or pilgrimage. The pilgrim sites are located in the body. Indeed, the *pinda* (body) is a replica of the *brahmanda* (universe). Through proper concentration and control one can attain the Absolute in oneself. The worship of images and the mediation of priests and rituals thus become totally redundant in the path of salvation.

The currency of these ideas for centuries before the birth of Bhima Bhoi has led scholars to try and situate him in one or the other of several religious traditions. Discussions and analyses of his works have throughout been plagued by a hunt for possible lineages and genealogies, an attempt to pin down his ideas in their pristine, unadulterated form. In the process, the very ingenuity of the poet devotee, that made his inspired utterances defy categorization, has been left out of consideration. An examination of the assessments of Bhima Bhoi's works will help clarify my point.

The nature of the Absolute conceived by Bhima Bhoi has formed the focal point of the analyses. N. N. Vasu, who discovered texts of Mahima Dharma soon after Bhima Bhoi's death, was convinced that *śunya* — a descriptive attribute of the Absolute in Bhima Bhoi — was nothing but the *śunya* (void) of Buddhism.[37] This led him to characterize Mahima Dharma as 'crypto-Buddhism', a faith that derived its concept of the Supreme directly from that of Buddhism. Vasu's theory found ready subscribers. B. C. Mazumdar, who published his work in the same year as Vasu, while indicating the faith's affinity with Jainism reiterated that it was influenced by Buddhism.[38] Artaballabh Mahanti, in his Foreword to the first published edition of Bhima Bhoi's works, pointed to the clear traces of Buddhism in Bhima Bhoi's philosophy, noting at the same time that it was Buddhism so severely altered by mutations over time as to be hardly recognizable.[39]

It was left to Biswanath Baba, a prominent leader of the sect in the twentieth century, to draw a clear line of separation between Buddhism and Mahima Dharma.[40] Biswanath Baba, in turn, aligned the faith to the Advaita Vedantic tradition of Hinduism. Chittaranjan Das and Anncharlott Eschmann drew on Biswanath Baba's *Itihasa* to make a powerful case for the autonomy of Mahima Dharma.[41] Das forcefully asserted: 'only a stray similarity in words ought not to encourage us for an excessive comparison'.[42] Each religion, he argued, had to be viewed against its specific background. Yet, he found it pertinent to underscore the close resemblance in thought and language between Bhima Bhoi and the Panchasakhas.

Eschmann followed the same tack. In a published essay, she demonstrated the conceptual differences between the *śunya* of Mahima Dharma and the *śunya* of Buddhism.[43] In an unpublished article she identified the three crucial elements that Bhima Bhoi had drawn directly from the Panchasakhas. These were: 'the worship of the sunya, the theory of Pinda Brahmanda, and the idea of a future redeemer who will come and openly establish what is for the time being a secret doctrine'.[44] Other scholars continued the trend. Bijayananda Kar's detailed discussion of the philosophy of Mahima Dharma specified the differences between Mahima Dharma and Buddhism on the one hand and Advaita and Visistadvaita Vedanta on the other.[45] The 'religious movement', however, was seen as 'a wonderful attempt at synthesis.'[46] Nagendra Nath Pradhan carefully traced the *nirguna dhara* (line of *nirguna* thought) in Oriya religious literature from the Nath *yogis* through the Vaishnavas to the Mahima Dharmis. The line reached its culmination in Mahima Dharma, which granted widest circulation to the concept of a *nirguna* Supreme.[47]

These discussions bring to the fore the problems associated with understanding through translation,[48] and the accompanying tendency of co-opting the history of Bhima Bhoi and that of Mahima Dharma into a 'meta-history'. Particulars are sacrificed at the altar of a general history of thought; and Bhima Bhoi is sought to be understood only as the product of one tradition or, at best, as a synthesizer, an integrator of several trends. His specific understanding of current traditions and imaginative deployments through novel combinations and elaboration is hardly taken into consideration. In this section I attempt an analysis of three core works of Bhima Bhoi to bring into relief the key elements of his thought and the richness of his ideas, in order to make some sense of what he actually stood for.[49]

Stuti Chintamoni stands alongside the *bhajans* as the most widely read, recited, and cited of the works of Bhima Bhoi. The text consists of a 100 *bolis* (chapters), each containing 20 *padas* (couplets). An intensely personal text, *Stuti Chintamoni* charts the course of Bhima Bhoi's life as a *bhakta*, bringing into relief his unique relationship with the Guru — at once the indescribable Absolute and his human incarnation — the *diksha-guru* (preceptor who grants initiation) of the poet. In *Stuti Chintamoni* Bhima Bhoi communicates directly with his Lord: he sings the praises of the all-powerful master, narrates his private experiences and pours out his heart to him. According to Artaballabh Mahanti, all the three different kinds of Vaishnava *janans* — *sangprarthanamayi*, *dainya bodhika*, and *lalasamayi* are represented in *Stuti Chintamoni*.[50] At the same time, the poet addresses himself to the readers. There is an implicit perception of a community of followers — a bounded group marked out from the non-Mahima Dharmis. He warns them of impending disaster, urges them to listen to him and follow his example to take shelter in the one and only Guru of the world. Bhima Bhoi conducts a two-way conversation through the text, with his preceptor on the one hand and his followers and readers on the other.

The poet had the first vision of his future Guru at the age of four; but he could not recognize him. His life as *bhakta* had not yet begun, and a great gulf separated him from his master. The Swami, who had the marks of the conch and the discus on his arms, was roaming in the village with an earthen pot in his hand asking for food and water. Little Bhima stood and watched; all the people who had gathered around the *yogi putra* looked at each other; no one offered him food or water. The Swami left the place calling out 'dharma, dharma'.[51] Memories of that august day overwhelmed the poet with both sorrow and joy, and transported him into a different world.

> Thoughts of that time are making me burn with sorrow
> My body and soul are crying constantly, my consciousness is drowning.[52]
> Those thoughts are making my mind and body quaver with sudden emotion,
> They are touching me with great excitement.[53]

The poet had to wait 12 years to see his Guru again. By then his mind had undergone a transformation, he had felt the stirrings of devotion for his unknown Lord. The Guru attended to the devotee's need — he came to initiate him into *satya dharma*. From that day Bhima Bhoi devoted his mind and body solely to the contemplation of the Prabhu (Lord).

At the outset, Bhima Bhoi's relationship with the preceptor is one of total subordination. The Absolute is all-powerful and all-pervading — the master of the world — and all Bhima can do is recognize his smallness in front of him and plead repeatedly for his mercy.

> I am a small, insect-like being, trying to follow you
> I am praying to you with folded hands to have mercy on me.[54]

The Absolute is the sole wielder of all power and authority. He is the one and only saviour of humanity who holds the key to the joys and sorrows of the beings he has created. This master is compassionate: he has assumed human form and come down to earth to lead the *bhaktas* on the path to salvation.

> Prabhu is the sovereign of the earth composed of nine parts, he is in all bodies.
> He saves the followers and redeems the world; which is why he is called *biśwambhara*.[55]

The master is remarkably just in handing out his mercy; he is equally accessible to the high and the low, the pious and the sinner. No one is denied his compassion.

> He is large in a large body, small in a small one; equal in animate and inanimate objects
> He resides in a place that is completely free of all trouble and all differences.[56]
> He is the parent of all beings without and within,
> He takes equal care of the pious and the wicked, and is revered as the giver of food.[57]

Where then is the basis for gradation and hierarchy among human beings? All are creations of the Lord and all have equal claims to his mercy. The *karuna* of the Lord, however, is not to be easily obtained. The *bhakta* has to undergo a prolonged period of suffering, the intensity of which heightens the greatness of the mercy when it is finally granted. Bhima Bhoi's life seems to be plagued by woes: he is abused, humiliated and ridiculed in his efforts to preach the message of the true faith.

> I am wearing sin and abuse as my garment,
> Everyone is criticizing me for talking about *satya dharma*.[58]

The extent of his suffering is such that at times the poet gets angry and impatient at his master.

> Why do you remain so indifferent to my troubles, what wrong have I done?
> You are heartless, you have no kindness, you destroyer of your followers' hearts.[59]

The next moment Bhima realizes his mistake. Hasn't his Guru, the formless, undivided, all pervasive Absolute without beginning or end come down to earth to save the devotees?[60] After all a true *bhakta* is one who refuses to get dissuaded by the Guru's apparent apathy, the trials he makes him undergo; for the real Guru ultimately showers his kindness on his earnest disciple and saves him.

Throughout his life the devotee performs a journey: a journey toward salvation, towards merger with the *parama* (Supreme). *Stuti Chintamoni* takes the reader along the successful journey of Bhima Bhoi, the ideal *bhakta*. As the text proceeds, Bhima moves closer and closer to his preceptor. Starting off with no knowledge of the Guru, through his initiation and a relation of subservience and veneration, Bhima Bhoi moves, by dint of devotion and contemplation, from difference and distinction from the Lord to identity with him. While it is difficult to state with clarity whether this identity also corresponded to the state of *sahaja* or perfect equilibrium in which the *yogin* becomes one with the whole universe explained in certain schools of yoga like the Buddhist Sahajiyas and the Naths,[61] the allusion to bodily training cannot be ruled out altogether. Through mental and physical concentration Bhima comes to recognize the mutuality in the relationship between the *Guru* and the *śisya*, the incompleteness of the one without the other. The all-knowing, all-pervading and all-powerful *ananta purusha* has created the *bhakta* out of his limitless *mahima* to act as an instrument for the spread of true faith. The devotee complements the master; the *bhakta* and the Guru are inseparable and interdependent, neither being superior to the other. This idea finds expression in several *padas* of *bolis* 35, 36 and 37.

> It is not important who is the Guru and who the disciple.
> Remember that *bhakta* and *bhagaban* form one body and eat together at the same place.[62]
> Know that the master and the disciple are one and the same
> The disciple worships the feet of the Lord; the Guru worships the disciple.[63]

As the being and the Supreme lie undifferentiated in the body
So are the minds of Guru and disciple inextricably intertwined. [64]

The journey is rough; the end is not within easy reach. Time and again Bhima Bhoi is beset by doubt; he has to combat a sense of inadequacy and inability to grasp the limitless Absolute, who eludes description by language. In desperation he implores the all-knower to come to his rescue.

How will I recognize the one who has no form?
Oh, all-knowing, formless Lord please appear before me.[65]

The vision of the Supreme elicited in the text thus remains one of a powerful, all-conquering master, not a benevolent friend (*sakha*). His characterization as *karta* (master) and Prabhu (Lord) highlights the attributes of dominance. This Lord evokes fear and veneration rather than love. The devotee surrenders to him to beg and pray for mercy, not to revel in his company. The sense of ecstasy, exhilaration and total abandon in giving oneself to the Lord that characterizes *bhakti* in Gaudiya Vaishnavism is missing here. Comparable to the dark mood of the compositions of a blind saint of an earlier era — Surdas — the mood in *Stuti Chintamoni* is one of despondency, of pessimism.[66] A picture of gloom — of Kali Yuga, the era of evil — forms the backdrop of the text.[67] The sins and vices of Kali halt the progress of *satya dharma*, making the problems of the disciple almost insurmountable. The ignorant and despicable human beings refuse to listen to the voice of truth or recognize the saviour, and persist in their worship of useless, lifeless images of stone and wood.

In total ignorance men and women are worshipping the gods
They are falling at the feet of the idols, promising to offer them sweets if they save them.
Instead of surrendering themselves to the one who has created them
They are rushing to an image of wood, pleading him to save them[68]
Living beings are keeping company of inanimate objects, see their ignorance
They have no comprehension of the One who has produced life out of void[69]

Bhima Bhoi is moved to desperation as he foresees imminent disaster. The evil Kali has spread its tentacles all over. Humanity is steeped in sinfulness. The burden of sin has devastated the earth and destroyed the sanctity of pilgrimages. The end of the era, of the world, is drawing close; a devastating war and deluge are approaching fast. The saviour has come to Kapilas, the only pilgrim site, and established *satya dharma*. Human beings can no longer afford to be ignorant. *Nam bhajan* and surrender to the feet of the Lord have become imperative for their survival. An exaggerated sense of immediacy, of urgency, marks the last chapters of the text, the end of the text symbolic of the end of the era. And the caring poet, concerned not about his individual salvation but the wellbeing of all living creatures, urges everyone to listen to him.

The message is addressed directly to the community of believers, the implicit readers of the text, who are construed as an embattled community, making exigency greater for them. Later in the chapter we will note the significance of this sense of catastrophe generated by a combination of the growing evils of Kali Yuga and a community in danger in the perception of the present and the past for the followers of Mahima Dharma. They will deploy the urge to take refuge in true faith and to take action in order to deal with a difficult present in inventive ways to strive for a brighter future. The last couplet of *Stuti Chintamoni* sends out a fervent appeal to all — to take shelter in the true faith without further delay.

All who have taken form as beings of the endless universe
I urge you to take to the path of dharma.[70]

If *Stuti Chintamoni* recounts the suffering, yearning and aspirations of a poet devotee and expresses his appeal to all to join him on the journey of salvation, *Brahma Nirupana Gita* features a circumspect philosopher-devotee pondering on the nature of Brahma. The 14 chapters of the text, written in the form of a dialogue between Anadi and Nirakara, contain an exposition of the Absolute. Like *Stuti Chintamoni*, the chapters are composed of two-line verses that vary in number between 81 and 133. But here, two or three lines in prose at the end of each chapter give the gist of its contents. The text is difficult to follow. In the fourteen chapters Anadi proclaims his incomprehensibility to Nirakara. The introduction to the text in the *Granthabali*, written by *sadhu* Banchanidhi Das, informs the reader that the text is meant primarily for *sadhus* and *siddhas* (saints and self-realized beings). Scholars who have some familiarity with the philosophy of the faith may be able to make some sense of the text; it would be futile for ordinary men and women to attempt an understanding of it.

It is, however, important for ordinary mortals to hear the text. It would save them from the evils of Kali and absolve them of all their sins.

> The beings suffering in the hell of Kali
> Will be saved if they listen to *Brahma Nirupana Gita*.[71]
> A great sinner will be redeemed
> On hearing the meaning of *Brahmanirupana*.[72]
> Those who have committed the sin of stealing their mothers Will be absolved of it if they listen to this Gita[73]

It is interesting to note the importance ascribed to hearing/listening. A poet, who acquired his knowledge through listening, reiterates the efficacy of aural comprehension for knowledge, devotion and salvation upholding thereby the emphasis on the spoken. In the last section of this chapter, I will discuss how this emphasis on the hearing of text as a remedy for sin and suffering has been deployed by Bhima Bhoi's followers in recent times.

The indescribable, incomprehensible Supreme resides in a place which is inaccessible to all; it is *nigama bhubana*, where there is no light nor darkness, neither day nor night, neither sound nor colour, neither hunger nor thirst, neither creation nor destruction. There is complete cessation of all activities. It is a temple of soundlessness. Not action, nor prowess nor speech can find entry there. Even water or air cannot reach that place, which is why I call it *agamya* (a place which cannot be reached). There is no creation, maintenance or destruction; it is devoid of dreams and desires.[74] This Supreme, at the same time, belongs to all; he dwells in all human bodies. The poet divides the body into several sections — *cakras* — from the feet up to the brain, and tries to feel the presence of the Brahma in all the parts separately. The demarcation of the parts of the body into *cakras* and the location of the Supreme in them points to Bhima Bhoi's familiarity with and interest in tantric and yogic practices.[75]

Ana, explained as presence in absence, is the main feature that characterizes *parama*. *Ana* signifies the denial of all categories, positive and negative. Brahman is above and beyond all categories, he cannot be limited or defined or determined. This explains his presence in all beings, although he himself is beyond comprehension. He is *anarupa* (beyond form/beauty), *anakara* (beyond form/body) and *anakshara* (beyond word/language).

> Calling Nirakara to attention Śriguru avers that the divine supreme essence is formless
> It pervades the universe without being limited to any definite form.[76]

Bhima Bhoi strives for the impossible: he tries to conceptualize this Absolute. This is done through a clever use of language. Pairs of complementary terms, positive and negative, are juxtaposed to illustrate the inexplicability of Brahma. He is at once the preceptor and the disciple, the master and the servant, the all-knower and the ignorant, the parent and the child, the friend and the foe, the husband and the wife, the Supreme and the being, who unite and separate out of their own accord.

He is at once the disciple and the master
He becomes the tree and the plant, the mountain and the desert.[77]
He is the supreme possessor of the knowledge of Brahma; he is ignorant
He is thoughtful and thoughtless.[78]
He becomes the *parama* (supreme) and the *jiba* (individual).
He separates and unites on his own.[79]

The all-pervasive Brahma eludes description. He is at once the presence and the absence of the same quality. He is *arupa* yet has *rupa*; he is *adeha* yet has *deha*; he is *ajyoti* yet looks like *jyotilinga*. He is white but does not seem so; he appears to be dark without actually being dark.

Should any one even attempt to ascertain the nature of such a Supreme? Such an act would turn the world upside down, make stones turn to water, make mountains grow in size, make dry trees start blossoming, and make dead bodies come alive.[80]

None of the known modes of prayer and worship, the Vedas and other scriptures, *nambhajan*, *sadhana* are of any help in the task of comprehending the Supreme. He reveals himself only to the true *bhakta* in *asadhana*. Complete devotion is the only way to the attainment of the Absolute. The *bhakta* infers and feels his presence by concentrating his body and soul on the Supreme and by giving himself up to him totally.

The one on whom the Brahma has mercy will see him in *asadhana*
By following the path of inference and feeling.[81]

The *bhakta* has to remain steadfast in the path of the true faith. It is a difficult path. He has to rise above all passions, be tolerant, kind and merciful, have complete faith in the Supreme and be engrossed in Him. Once he achieves this he becomes indestructible; he transcends the destructive powers of disease and death.

What will death do to a person with whom Mahima is pleased?
He will move about in the world like a lion.[82]
What will disease do to the one who has Mahima's blessings?

> He will definitely enjoy the three worlds to the full.[83]

The sense of journey is evoked once again. Steadfastness is the chief criterion of the path of *bhakti*. By remaining firm in his devotion to the Supreme, the devotee progresses slowly but inevitably towards liberation. The final reward comes in his emancipation; he becomes one with the Supreme whom he has prayed to all his life. The poet declares: 'You will become one with the Brahma only if you succeed in drowning yourself completely in Him.'[84]

Stuti Chintamoni and *Brahma Nirupana Gita* portray the trials and triumphs, doubts and anxieties of an ingenious devotee trying to make sense of the incomprehensible Absolute, and groping for the way that will lead to emancipation. *Nirveda Sadhana* records his success and confidence. Bhima Bhoi has found his way. With great conviction he predicts the future and outlines the course that a *bhakta* has to follow in order to attain the Absolute. This task moreover has been assigned to him by Mahima Swami. Bhima Bhoi as the divinely ordained narrator explains the path of *nirveda-sadhana* to all by relating the story of Anadi (Absolute) and his first disciple, Govinda Das, who is none other than Lord Jagannath of Puri. The text is composed of twenty chapters written in the famous *dandi matra* (metre) of the Oriya *Bhagabata*. It closely follows the language and style of the text of the Panchasakhas, so much so that a reviewer of the manuscript of *Nirveda Sadhana* stated that Bhima Bhoi could easily be placed 'at least four centuries earlier than the time when he actually lived'.[85]

> *Nirveda Sadhana* opens with a vivid description of Bhima Bhoi's initiation.
> It is ten o'clock at night.
> *Anakarjyoti* (formless glow) appeared.
> Anadi Prabhu entered my bedroom, darkness melted away in his power.
> The luminous being called my name and asked me to behold the Anadi Brahma.
> I woke up from slumber to see the divine pair of *guru* and *śisya.*
> I bowed down to him and got his blessings.[86]

On Bhima Bhoi's request Anadi Prabhu disclosed the identity of his *śisya* to him. He was Jagannath Dasa, the Lord of Puri, who had left Nilachal on the appearance of Anadi Prabhu as an *avatar* to become his disciple. This act absolved Jagannath of the sins he had incurred in all his incarnations.[87] This is significant: Jagannath's presence is not denied, but his position of subservience to Anadi is stressed. His failure to keep the people on the path of *dharma* is implicitly stated to be the reason for the appearance of the great Prabhu, his master, on earth. Jagannath's departure from Puri to become the first disciple of the Lord was the next logical step.[88] This rendered the wooden image ensconced in the temple of Jagannath lifeless and Puri bereft of all sanctity as a place of pilgrimage.[89] Anadi Prabhu ordered Bhima to tell the world the tale of this divine pair and explain *nirveda-sadhana*. Then he disappeared. An obedient Bhima Bhoi started composing the text.

The second chapter predicts the future. A devastating war, that would fill the entire region from Jajpur to Sambalpur with blood, would bring about the end of Kali Yuga. The end of the era of evil would be brought forth by the descent of the Lord on earth, making her tremble. That would mark the beginning of preparations for the establishment of the sacred *dhuni* (flame/fire).

In his human form Anadi would be an *abadhut* (ascetic). He would roam from door to door with an earthen pot in his hand asking for *anna* (rice). His mind would be calm and happy, enriched with *atma-jñana* (self-knowledge). He would be kind to all. He would set up his *ashrama* at Bolasingha, where he would meet his *śisya*.

The text simultaneously engages different registers of time which is also conceived spatially. What has already happened is presented as the future and what is to happen where is presented as something which has occurred in the past. The past is used as a suggestion for the future. What Anadi advises Govinda Das to do, is actually intended for humanity as a whole; beings of the Kali Yuga are made aware of the fate that awaits them through a discussion of what happened in the past.

Govinda Das is the first to recognize the *abadhut* as the great Guru. He goes to Bolasingha, performs *śaran* to Anadi and begs him to show the way, to give him *jñana-mantra* (incantation of knowledge) and teach him the path of *nirveda-sadhana*. With the third chapter begins the actual dialogue between the master and his disciple.

The first step for a true disciple is to become aware of Arupa Brahma as the supreme object of the world. This Brahma is eternal. He is free from good and evil, action and non-action. Like air he fills the universe, and permeates all objects. Brahma *jñana-mantra* is present in both Veda and *nirveda*. To acquire the *mantra* the *bhakta* has to concentrate on the name of Brahma while combining his mind with air and placing *jñana* (knowledge) and its five companions — *sata* (truth), *kshama* (forgiveness), *śila* (conduct), *daya* (kindness) and *daksha* — in his heart.

The name is an invaluable asset
It is completely free of sins.
Sit in meditation of that name,
Blend mind and air and place the six companions in your lotus-heart.[90]

The path of meditation and its components bear very close resemblance to the practice of Yoga/Tantra. All through the text there is an undercurrent of yogic meditation that is never made explicit. The interface of time and space bears a special meaning in tantric or yogic sadhana in that they symbolize the journey of the *kundalini* (the source of energy that lies coiled up in the navel) from the navel upwards. The path of meditation that Bhima Bhoi followed probably came down to him from the Naths via the Panchasakhas. While Sashi Bhusan Dasgupta has shown the influence of the idea of *kaya-sadhana* (training of the body) of the Siddha school on the Panchasakha school of Orissa Vaishnavism,[91] Bettina Bäumer has pointed to Bhima Bhoi's clear references to Matsyendra Nath and Haripa in his *Adi-Anta Gita*.[92] According to Paritosh Das, in fact, the Panchasakha Dharma and the Mahima Dharma of Orissa are both 'outcomes of a popular assimilation of the religious ideas of the later Tantrik Buddhism with those of Gaudiya Vaishnavism represented by Chaitanyadev'.[93] Bhima Bhoi's use of an 'intentional' language or language bearing a double meaning was in line with a long tradition current in Bengal since the time of the Caryapadas (eighth to twelfth centuries). Here, a special language (*sandhya bhasa*) was used to express a particular type of practice (*sadhana*) centred on the body. Subsequently, from the medieval period onwards, traces of this *sadhana* made their way into the hand-written manuscripts of the practitioners of *sahaja sadhana*.[94] Over time, Bhima Bhoi's close links with this brand of non-conformist striving intimately connected with the attainment of an immutable body[95] have perhaps been suppressed by ascetics or forgotten on account of a lack of comprehension by lay followers.

After Govinda's ears are washed with *jñana-mantra* (incantation of knowledge) and his body purified with cowdung, he is initiated by *abadhut swami* (supreme ascetic). He is given *siddha basana*, pure garment — a *kaupin* (waistcloth) and *ada-bandha* (a rope-like thing to be tied around the waist to fix the *kaupin*) of *kumbhipat* (the bark of the *kumbhi* tree). The Guru impresses upon him the necessity of remaining calm and detached, of remembering the simple truth that the Lord is everywhere, and of not discriminating between human beings in accepting food from them.

Govinda sets out to follow the master's instructions. He moves from door to door talking about his Guru, the *anadi*, all-pervading *abadhut*; he stuns the villagers by asking for cooked rice in place of uncooked grain, and by not paying heed to distinctions of caste in accepting food.[96] His strange ways excite anger and ridicule. Govinda does not bathe or perform *sandhya tarpan* (rites performed twice a day in honour of the ancestors), he does not wear the *tilak* (sandalwood marks on forehead) nor touch garlands, wears the bark of a tree instead of clothes and carries matted locks on his head. Not only are human beings surprised and agitated, even the gods feel threatened. The spread of the word of the Absolute and the establishment of the sacred *dhuni* would jeopardize their position. People would stop worshipping them and take shelter in Anadi Prabhu. They decide to take Govinda Das away while he is asleep. But their plans get foiled. Their utmost efforts fail to lift Govinda from the ground. Govinda wakes up, and the gods run away.[97]

Govinda's mind, however, is troubled. He realizes that he has spent twelve years following the dictates of the Guru that has made him suffer at the hands of gods and men, but Anadi Prabhu has not appeared again to give him further instructions. Govinda falters. He decides to move towards the east, towards Kapilas, in search of his master. The Guru comes to know of the doubts in the *śisya's* mind. He leaves his place, comes and meets Govinda midway, and reprimands him. He makes the disciple go through a trial. Govinda Das is locked inside a temple. The Guru claps three times from outside and tells Govinda that he will be able to come out only if he is a proper *yogi-putra* (ascetic). Govinda realizes his mistake; he sits in meditation of *ekakshara* (non-dual letter). He mixes his mind and air and concentrates solely on Arupa (one without form). His body becomes the ground, the navel the *dhunikunda* (a metal pot in which the sacred fire is lit) — Govinda lights the sacred *dhuni* in his navel. Anadi is pleased. He comes to the temple, releases Govinda and takes him to a mountain cave, an idyllic place on which Mother Nature has lavished all her bounties. It is here that Govinda's doubts and queries are answered, and the theory of creation explained.[98]

At the beginning was *maha śunya*, from which evolved sound. From sound arose space. After several attempts spread over crores of *kalpas* (Brahma's time which lasts aeons of years), *maha śunya* succeeded in creating the woman figure Śruti, who could retain light without perishing. Air and water originated from light. *Sthiti* emerged when air came to rest in water, and it in turn produced *bindunada*. Veda or knowledge developed from *bindu*. The world arose from knowledge, living beings from air and water.

Brahma resided in Śruti's heart: their union resulted in the birth of Nirakara, who was half-male and half-female. Nirakara sat in meditation of Śunya Brahma for millions of years. Finally, Brahma descended from *śunya* into his heart and directed him to create. The earth, mountains, fire, heaven and hell were produced. But the creation of living beings had to wait. Thousands of years later a voice from *śunya* ordered the combination of objects. Brahma, Vishnu and Maheśwara were born out of the union of Nirakara and Mahalakshmi.[99] The same union produced Adimata.

Hara (Maheśwara/Śiva) committed the sin of cohabiting with his sister. Nirakara taught him Yoga to purify his body and mind.[100] The three brothers were then taught the Vedas, informed about the nature of space, air and other objects created before them and instructed to produce many from one. Specific tasks were assigned to them after this. Brahma was put in charge of creation, Vishnu of maintenance, and Maheśwara of the destruction of the world. These tasks, as is common knowledge, are traditionally assigned to the three gods in all Hindu mythologies.

The *srusti tattwa* (theory of creation) is a peculiar combination of the naturalistic theory of the Sankhya school and the theism of Visistadvaita and Vaishnavism in general. At the same time, it is inlaid with yogic terms and expressions, and contains traces of thought similar to the Kalacakra school of Mahayana Buddhism. This school, according to Artaballabh Mahanti, was a combination of the systems of Yoga and Vedanta.[101] Bhima Bhoi, while holding on to the theistic position that the world was created by the Lord's *mahima*, came close to the Sankhya position in explaining the origin of objects through the proximity (*sannidhi*) of *purusha* and *prakriti* (the two ultimate principles in Sankhya philosophy).[102] The origins of 16 *matras* and 32 *aksharas* (letters), the basic units of Yoga, are explained and stated to constitute the essence of the Vedas. Yoga becomes a panacea for the sin committed by Maheśwara, who cohabited with his sister. One is reminded of Govinda Das's meditation, where he lit the *dhuni* in his navel to atone for his mistake. As stated before, all along the text there are indications that the path of *sadhana* outlined is actually yogic, although the poet wishes to reveal it only to those special *bhaktas* who have taken the path of Govinda Das. Bhima Bhoi, once again, eludes categorization and location within one particular trend of thought. What is more, in *Bhajanmala* and *Stuti Chintamoni* he explains creation in significantly different terms.[103]

After all the scriptures are explained, Govinda requests Anadi to instruct him on the proper application of *nirveda-sadhana*. The Guru reiterates his earlier instructions: the disciple has to remain detached, dispassionate and calm, and rise above passion and violent emotion. He is directed to practice tolerance and to recognize the truth in every religion. This involves outward conformity to Vedic rules with internal concentration on *nirveda*.

True knowledge is a pre-requisite of this mode of conduct. Knowledge endows the true devotee with equanimity and confidence so that the outward observance of rites does not come in the way of the internal practice of *sadhana*.[104]

The two closing chapters of the text draw the picture of a happy future — the dawn of Satya Yuga (era of truth). Metaphorically, Satya Yuga marks the end of the journey: the triumph of truth and knowledge over evil and vice. The devotee's mind conquers passion and emotion, disease and death.[105] The era of truth wins over the era of evil. Honesty, peace and prosperity prevail. The Anadi Guru, who moves around in Kali Yuga like a destitute *abadhut*, becomes the king of kings in Satya Yuga. He reigns in regal splendour, commanding the service and devotion of all. The power of Anadi is symbolic of the power of knowledge and devotion, the total control that comes with cognition. Such a happy state of affairs, however, is not easy to attain. It is preceded by a serious combat, when deluge and destruction make the true devotees come together in great fear and pray to the Lord to come down to earth and save them.

Let us come back to the distinctive features of Bhima Bhoi's thought. The Absolute, in the imaginings of the poet, was all-powerful, all-pervading, formless and indescribable. At the same time, he was the human incarnation — the master and the personal god — of the poet. This Absolute, the creator of the world, was the only object of devotion and worship. We see here an unusual blend of the *nirguna* and *saguna* traditions of *bhakti*. Bhima Bhoi, the blind, unlettered poet, who had acquired the knowledge of popular religious texts through listening and memorization, drew upon concepts prevalent in Sarala Das's *Mahabharata* and the texts of the Panchasakhas, only to invest them with new meanings and dimensions originating from his understanding and imagination.[106] The Supreme thus, did not remain omnipresent, indescribable and formless — distant and inaccessible. He became the personal god — intimate and accessible, full of compassion and mercy — who had come down to earth to save suffering beings. Bhima's Ultimate Reality was at once dual and non-dual, difficult to conceive yet easy to apprehend. Furthermore, he was reachable through true devotion that produced spiritual knowledge, and not intellectual knowledge arising out of difficult reflection and introspection. These ideas made Bhima Bhoi's works distinct and distant from the high philosophical tradition of Advaita Vedanta, and close to the hearts of ordinary men and women.

Yet, the philosopher was not absent in Bhima Bhoi. With remarkable insight, he used *ana* (presence in absence) to define an Absolute who transcended all categories. The Supreme was *anakar*, *anarupa*, *anakshara*.[107]

He was both with and without attributes — at once *saguna* and *nirguna* and none of the two. In conceptualizing the Absolute thus Bhima Bhoi surpassed his intellectual predecessors, even his guru Mahima Swami. At the same time, he stressed the presence of this Reality in all living creatures, disregarding thereby all hierarchy and discrimination among human beings. This underscored the redundancy of gods, rituals and priests, and made the caste system irrelevant. Bhima Bhoi enjoined his followers to disregard norms of caste through the practice of strict interdining. Indeed, his creative mind spoke of a new order of castes, one determined by moral and mental acquirements.[108] Finally, the insistence that a true devotee was as important to the Lord as the Lord was to the devotee, conferred on the aspiring believers a sense of confidence and self-worth.

The constant reference to the era of evil as the main cause of misery and suffering, and the forecast of its destruction, also provided hope by projecting a bright future, while impressing upon men and women the urgency of taking recourse to true dharma to avoid disaster. A combination of a creative mind and a caring heart, of high philosophy and quotidian metaphors, of the oral and the written made Bhima Bhoi unique and common. Like the Panchasakhas, whose works had influenced the poet most, Bhima Bhoi became an everyday name in western Orissa.[109] His compositions — first uttered then noted down, and subsequently sung — gained wide circulation.

The use of the everyday metaphor of Kali Yuga invested Bhima Bhoi's works with the quality of the ever-popular *malikas*, whose circulation and use in nineteenth-century Orissa we have noted in the preceding chapter. The prophecies of the *malikas* are vague and general in nature. Their credibility rests on their connection with the Panchasakhas. At the same time, there is nothing that establishes their authorship with certainty. Indeed, *malikas* are products of the interface between orality and writing.[110] They circulate in times of distress. The ascription of authorship to the medieval mystics is an index of the success and popularity of these thinkers. It is of no surprise then, that *malikas* got composed in the name of Bhima Bhoi in the twentieth century. These texts at once underscored the hold of Bhima Bhoi on the imagination of the followers of Mahima Dharma and revealed the ways his works were read and understood. I focus on one particular text to illustrate this point.

Prophesies

Bhima Bhoi Malika ba Padmakalpa was published by the Cuttack Dharma

Grantha Store as late as 1971. The text was not included in the collected works of Bhima Bhoi, published by the same Store, because the ascetics at Joranda were dubious about its authenticity. The proprietor of the publishing house, a lay disciple of Mahima Dharma, finally had to publish it on 'popular demand'.[111] If this exposes the tensions within the faith among a section of lay disciples and the leading ascetics and underscores the problem of treating the subaltern as a homogenous category, it also opens vistas for understanding 'reading', apprehension and authorship of texts by its interpretive community.[112]

Moreover, the fact that the text got published in the late twentieth century asserts the lingering presence of Kali Yuga as a concept-metaphor defining time as well as the continued popularity of *malikas*. A close reading of *malika*s reveals the changing dimensions of the recurrent reference to Kali Yuga that make it possible for these texts to be variously understood and differently apprehended. What makes the idea of Kali amenable to multiple appropriations is the fact that it is not over. According to the Puranas, Kali Yuga is meant to last 432,000 years before it is brought to an end by the tenth and final incarnation of Vishnu who is yet to appear. Kali thus, is a ready source of an appropriable past that lives on and gives meaning to the present.

Let us turn to the content of *Bhima Bhoi Malika ba Padmakalpa*.[113] True to the tradition of the *malikas*, the text dwells on the miseries engendered by Kali, foresees its destruction through a devastating war lead by an *avatar*, and announces the establishment of *satya dharma* heralding Satya Yuga. The tract consists of 37 chapters, each made up of a varying number of *padas* (verses). The padas are two-line and three-line verses in which the number of words varies significantly. In the mode of *malikas* and *Nireveda Sadhana*, the text is composed in the form of a dialogue, in this case between Anadi (the eternal one) and Adi (mata), mother of the world, who is also called Sati. It is to satisfy Adi and to clear away her doubts that the Absolute unravels the mysteries of his *leela* (divine play) and the events of Kali Yuga. Bhima Bhoi figures as the narrator of this dialogue. From time to time, he interjects his own comments, addressing the reader directly. Like *Nirveda Sadhana*, *Padmakalpa* is composed in a language of time and timelessness. There is a constant shift in temporality as the dialogue moves back and forth between what has happened, what is happening, and what will happen.

Padmakalpa opens with Bhima Bhoi expressing his fear and helplessness at being surrounded by the evil ways of Kali and calling upon Śri Guru (the master), at whose feet he has taken shelter, to save him.

The ways of Kali Yuga make the heart tremble — terror holds sway
My soul of five elements finds no peace — Śriguru will show the way

This is followed by an account of Kali Yuga, when the sinful deeds of human beings make Mother Earth suffer immensely. She sends anguished cries of help to the Lord. The injustice of kings and Brahmans disgusts Jagannath so much that he leaves his abode to dwell secretly for 16,000 years.

The activities of several dynasties of rulers form an integral part of the account. The *soma* (lunar) dynasty reigns over the world at the beginning of the age; the British, who follow the Gurkhas and Turks, come to power toward the end of the era. All rulers of this age are oppressive. There is, however, a progressive degeneration in the nature of the rulers and in the condition of the earth. Hence the British are the worst. Their duplicity makes them particularly dangerous: with an outward show of speaking the truth they secretly oppress their subjects and destroy them gradually but thoroughly, in the manner of white ants destroying wood. This wile goes hand in hand with their dirty habits — they eat the flesh of cows and buffaloes and drink liquor every day. Is it surprising that they do not wash themselves after defecating?[114] Exploitation by these *mlechhas* (extreme outcastes) robs Mother Earth of her beauty and compels Lakshmi (goddess of wealth and prosperity) to seek shelter in *patal* (the nether world). Scarcity is a constant feature: floods, droughts, and famines regular happenings.

Sinfulness comes to characterize humanity in general. Brahmans give up the study of the Vedas, start eating flesh, cohabit with other men's wives, forget the *gayatri mantra* and adopt the tantric *garedi mantra*. Members of other castes follow suit: caste distinctions disappear leading to a situation of anarchy and chaos. Each man cheats the other and acquires wealth through lies. Even true devotees waver. They fail to recognize the redeemer, the Brahma *avatar* (incarnation of the Absolute) when he appears and refuse to pay heed to his precepts. Under the influence of Kali they behave like 'a host of blind men'.[115] The Guru leaves the earth. Kali holds sway. Fear and despair prompt the gods to come together and pray to the Absolute in a gesture of abject surrender. In response to their prayers Anadi comes to *yogaghara* (a place for meditation), sends his devotees to earth, commands Brahmarshis, Rajarshis, and Devarshis (saints who have attained self-realization) to sit in meditation, and finally saves the earth by destroying Kali, lighting the Brahma *dhuni* (eternal flame), and establishing true faith.

A fierce battle has to be fought and great sufferings undergone before Kali is annihilated. Bhima trembles and his heart fills with sorrow as he narrates the events of the future. Kalki will play the game of non-violence in the era of evil. He will be called Gandhi-Sankarsana. A *bhakta* called Madana Malabya will always be with Gandhi. Motilal Nehru, a very powerful man, will be born in the Chudanga dynasty. Narendra Natha (Vivekananda?), who had been imprisoned in *dwaparayuga* (the era that immediately preceeds Kali) will come and join these men and will be imprisoned again. Some other followers, both men and women, will start an agitation. They will disobey the king and preach truth. A river of blood will flow during the seventh and eighth year of reign of Ram Chandra Dev. Sunya Guru will be fighting then, flying his sunya *bana* (flag).[116] This agitation is a part of the Great War that paves the way for the beginning of a new world and a new era by rooting out evil and effecting a complete break with the past. References to the war abound in the text, references which by virtue of their frequency, magnitude and detail create an intimidating picture of anarchy, destruction, devastation and death.

The description is neither clear nor consistent. At times it approximates to a fight between Gandhi and his followers and the British, at times it assumes the massive proportions of the '*kurukshetra*' war of Kali. An uncertainty lingers. Is there one war or several battles? At the same time, the uncertainty adds to the picture of anarchy. The confusion in narration becomes a tool in the generation of the picture of total chaos, where the several descriptions function as building blocks to construct the whole.

The human form of Anadi leads the forces of truth against the forces of Kali in the Kurukshetra war. In course of his dialogue with Adi, he declares with remarkable clarity that he will appear during the reign of Ram Chandra Dev, in the year 1941.[117] He is Mahima Swami, Gandhi, and Kalki. His soldiers are many: the gods and goddesses, *nagantis*, *yogantis*, and *rishis* (super humans and saints), the great heroes of the past, the present and the future — Ramchandra and Hanuman, the five Pandava brothers, Gandhi and his followers, the followers of Anadi, troops from all over India and abroad. The soldiers of Kali, who include the British, are powerful both in terms of numbers and the sophisticated arms and ammunition they command. It requires the combined strength of gods and men, of mythical, legendary, and historical figures, to overpower and destroy them. The battle continues for twelve years and devastates the world thoroughly. Humanity faces destruction; countries disappear from the face of the earth. Mughals come to rule again in the new age and are assisted by brave men from the families of Dhruba and Prahlada, the favoured devotees of Vishnu. People prosper under able rule; famine and scarcity are erased from memory. Anadi Brahma returns to his own abode, after establishing *satya dharma* on earth.

Padmakalpa is a richly flavoured concoction. It is a novel text that draws upon a tradition that goes back to the Puranas, and uses a language that is at once simple and esoteric.[118] There is a remarkable similarity with the general motifs that characterize Kali Yuga in the Puranas. Exploitative foreign rulers feature prominently in the description. At the same time, the analysis of their cunning and culpability is ingenious. It reveals a familiarity with the rhetoric of the nationalist movement that finds easy expression through the language of the everyday. British rulers are dangerous because they are deceptive. They rob their subjects secretly but steadily like white ants destroying wood. Their habits cannot but be strange and dirty; they form an integral part of the picture of the vile *mlechha* who is immensely powerful.

Such a strong enemy requires a mighty saviour. He is one and many at the same time, a combination of mythical and national leaders, legendary and real characters. He is Mahima Swami, Gandhi, and Kalki. This mix-up and inconsistency again, displays a drawing upon of diverse traditions that are understood, used and combined in novel ways to churn out unique constructions. One the hand, Mahima Swami's identification with Kalki while establishing him as the divine incarnation who had appeared on earth to root out Kali and bring back *satya dharma*, indicates the place he had secured for himself in the minds of his adherents. On the other, the prominence accorded to Gandhi is a good example of the hold of the 'Mahatma' in popular imagination in a region that was never in the forefront of the nationalist struggle.[119]

In fact, a very recent work has pointed to the upsurge in popular Oriya literature on Gandhi — poems and *bhajans* that identified him with the *avatar* born to liquidate evil from earth — that followed Gandhi's call for Non-cooperation and *swaraj*.[120] Moreover, a new version of *Kali Bhagabata*, published in 1925 spoke of Gandhi as the conqueror of Kali. The stock of 'common knowledge' surrounding Kali and the prevalence of literature that foretold its annihilation made for an inimitable combination of Puranic and nationalist ideas collapsing the crisis of a faith with the enthusiasm generated by the millenarian understandings of the message of a saintly nationalist leader. The war against Kali thus got transformed into a battle against the British demonstrating with extraordinary clarity how a perception of time in terms of both religious and secular makes for an easy coalescing of the 'mythical' and the modern, the religious and the political in everyday arenas. It follows then that there is perfect coherence in the understanding of an epic battle against forces of evil as the nationalist struggle against foreign rule. Remarkably, defying the influential nationalist evocation of Ram *rajya* (rule of the god-king Ram) at the end of colonial rule, *Padmakalpa* invokes the revolt of 1857 by predicting the re-establishment of Mughal rule after the destruction of Kali. The Mughals, however, have Dhruva and Prahlada — the devotees of Vishnu — as their lieutenants, symbolizing the harmony and amity that is to prevail at the end of the era of evil. Once again, the play of distinct temporalities eludes easy classification. The subaltern subject, in imaginatively combining the mythical and the linear in ordering the past, present and the future, resists his/her celebration as the defiant non-modern.

This coupling of 'mythic' and 'modern' time runs all through *Padmakalpa*. Time here is simultaneously eternal, cyclical and linear. The events occur during the reigns of the four kings of Puri — Mukunda Dev, Ramchandra Dev, Birakishor Dev, and Dibya Singha Dev. These are titles adopted by the kings of Puri when they ascend the throne. Temporally then, the rule of these princes can cover centuries. At the same time, the year of appearance of Kalki is announced with remarkable precision. Moreover, Ramchandra Dev's rule features prominently in the discussion along with the activities of Mahima Swami, Gandhi, and their followers. This seems to suggest that the text was composed in the 1920s when Gandhi dominated the national political scene and when Ram Chandra Dev ruled over Puri. It is not of much surprise then that the *sanyasis* at Joranda rejected it as a Bhima Bhoi text and left it out of the authoritative version of Bhima Bhoi's collected works published by the Dharma Grantha Store. *Bhima Bhoi Malika* must have been constructed after Bhima Bhoi's death unless parts of it were interpolated. Indeed, the expressed concern with the disappearance of caste distinctions during Kali — another dominant motif of Kali Yuga in the Puranas and the *Mahabharata* — stands in direct contrast to Bhima Bhoi's ideas. Yet, the fact that the *Malika* is ascribed to Bhima Bhoi, and is widely regarded as his composition by the present day lay followers, simultaneously underscores his enormous appeal to the adherents of Mahima Dharma, and his rootedness in the rich popular tradition of Orissa.

Why did this text appear in the 1920s? Let us pick up the story of Mahima Dharma to find an answer to this question. The first chapter has shown how *malikas* played a crucial role in the legitimization and divinization of Mahima Swami. It has also discussed how a belief in his divinity caused the sect to suffer a setback after his death. The preceptor had not nominated any successor. The ascetics of the sect refused to accept Bhima Bhoi's leadership. They convened a meeting of followers at Joranda in Dhenkanal, where Mahima Swami had come to reside before his death.

The decision to construct a *samadhi*, memorial for the Guru at Joranda was taken at this meeting. This memorial gradually grew into the Gadi, the seat of the sect. The *sanyasis* fought amongst themselves over the interpretation of the Guru's teachings and for control over the memorial of Mahima Swami. Disagreements turned to dissension and the ascetics became entangled in a never-ending struggle that led to the intervention of the law courts and effected a final breach between the two groups.[121]

As the leaders fought, the lay disciples strove to grapple with the situation, to find ways of holding fast unto their faith. The incident of 1881 was one dramatic illustration of their attempt.[122] Mahima Dharma survived the death of Mahima Swami. But in the 1920s crisis came in the shape of division among the followers.[123] The hold of Kali had indeed become all encompassing. The devotees of the Guru were faltering precisely at a time when the struggle against evil foreign rule had acquired a new significance.[124] Once again, a coming together of the sense of a community in danger and general disaster occasioned by powerful foreign rulers engendered a sense of immediacy.[125] But was there no way out? Hadn't the *malikas* for centuries spoken of the dissolution of Kali Yuga through the appearance of a redeemer? Hadn't Bhima Bhoi told the true followers again and again that the Guru would not abandon them? Is it a surprise then that Bhima Bhoi's *malikas* made their appearance at this stage?[126] They foretold the reappearance of Mahima Swami in the new incarnation of a warrior. He was to lead the battle against the forces of Kali and cause their destruction.

The resemblance of *Padmakalpa* to *Yaśomati Malika* is striking. *Yaśomati Malika* had announced the appearance of the incarnation in the shape of Mahima Swami and his divine disciple Bhima Bhoi. With meticulous care, it had laid out the names and places of residence of the true devotees and indicated the places where the battles would be fought underlining the territoriality of temporality. It had also announced the precise year when the saviour was to appear.[127] *Padmakalpa* did the same. It announced the reappearance of the redeemer with clarity — in the year 1941. In a list spread over five chapters, Anadi disclosed to Adi the names of his devotees in different parts of Orissa.[128] The disciples in Sambalpur were the first to be mentioned. Significantly, in earlier chapters Anadi categorically told Adi that his disciples in Kali Yuga were to be born in the family of Viswabasu.[129] Viswabasu, it bears pointing out, was the Śavar chief from whom Nilamadhab was stolen by Brahmans and kings and reinstated in Puri as Jagannath. Jagannath, we are informed very early on in the text, went into hiding for 16,000 years, being disgusted by the activities of Kali. It is not only the redeemer who had to reappear. His real devotees had to take birth again in the family of Viswabasu to help him destroy Kali. Even at this stage Mahima Dharma was trying to work out its relationship with the cult of Jagannath, a relationship that will become less and less important in the course of the twentieth century.

Anadi was also to awaken his lay disciples, both male and female. Was this a reference to the men and women from Sambalpur who had marched to the temple of Puri in 1881? Alongside, Krupasindhu was mentioned as a special favourite of Anadi.[130] Poised on the brink of crisis and flux, *Padmakalpa* brought into critical relief imaginative understandings, by lay disciples, of the teachings of Mahima Swami and Bhima Bhoi engendered by a grounding of these teachings in concepts and ideas disseminated over centuries. It also highlighted what characterized for these followers the real disciple and the Master. The first appearance of Mahima Swami had not brought about the end of suffering. *Bhaktas* had failed to recognize the redeemer and had behaved like 'a host of blind men'. Kali had gained in strength. Evil rulers had become specially powerful and dangerous. On another front, 'fake' yogis posing as the disciples of Mahima Swami had started to create dissension among the few faithful followers. The situation was ominous indeed. But all was not lost. If the true devotees took shelter in the master without further delay, he would save them by annihilating Kali and heralding the era of truth by establishing true faith.

I had ended the last chapter with a discussion of how the preachings of Mahima Dharma as diffused through the compositions of Bhima Bhoi had inspired a group of very ordinary and very marginal men and women to take the initiative for a spectacular event. In *Bhima Bhoi Malika ba Padmakalpa*, I see another attempt by lay followers to take initiative, not to control the destiny of their faith as the renouncers at Joranda were trying to do, but to cope with their own destiny by making sense of a difficult present. It is significant that *Padmakalpa* appeared around the same time Biswanath Baba, a leading ascetic of Joranda, produced the first formal *Itihasa* of Mahima Dharma, an authoritative text that was to play a crucial role in the institutionalization of Mahima Dharma.[131] *Bhima Bhoi Malika*, in providing a distinct reading of the past and the present and inspiring householder devotees to action, demonstrates how the beginnings of institutionalization produced simultaneous tendencies to transcend homogenization, underscoring not only the diversity of the subaltern but also the immense import of popular constructions of temporality.

The *malikas* had, for long, provided hope. Containing vague and general prophecies and lacking a definite author, they had arisen at different points of crises, out of the interaction of the written with the oral, and an intertwining of classical and quotidian concepts, of sacred and secular time, further giving the lie to the rupture of time and space occasioned by the secularization of time. The popularity of the Panchasakhas was inscribed in the ascription of *malikas* to them. Bhima Bhoi was an equally successful successor. He formed part of a community that was predominantly oral. Thoughts and ideas travelled through recitations and readings in common gatherings.[132] Bhima Bhoi's compositions, first sung, then noted down, were disseminated orally through singing in the presence of an 'audience/readership'. This intermingling produced an equivocal situation in which the oral–written compositions could be variously appropriated and recurrently reworked.[133] The coming together of the audience and the reader in the narration of *malikas* situated reading 'strategically' at the point of application, where interpretation and 'appropriation' of the text occurred simultaneously.[134] The multitude of meanings that this form of 'reading' generated highlighted, in turn, the efficacy of social reading and the 'sociability' of reading as opposed to private, individual reading.[135]

What is particularly important is that *Padmakalpa* deployed with remarkable force a message contained in many texts of Bhima Bhoi — of the impending dissolution of Kali premised upon the action of true followers. Texts such as *Padmakalpa* thus stand in direct contrast to the Kali Yuga texts of late nineteenth century Bengal analysed by Sumit Sarkar, where the end of the era lay 'so far in the future as to be largely irrelevant'.[136] Bhima Bhoi's works and the *malikas* credited to him harped on the immediacy of destruction and on the urgency of followers in taking recourse to true faith. The morality of the time was to be recovered by the recognition of the true incarnation and an acceptance of the faith proclaimed by him, not by the 'ultimate recuperation' of Brahmanical norms of caste and gender.[137] The return to the era of truth was not going to be a simple repetition, an 'eternal return' but a new beginning. The new age would be marked by new features. Such predictions, rather than providing limited scope for rebelliousness to subordinate groups that ended up in their eventual subalternisation,[138] opened up for them great possibilities of thought and action.

During his lifetime, Bhima Bhoi had provided optimism to ordinary men and women by decrying discrimination and hierarchy, and speaking of devotion as a way out of misery and exploitation. After his death, his works lent themselves to differential perceptions and reconstructions to allow his disciples overcome situations of crisis. A mutual imbrication of the oral and the written went hand in hand with a conjoining of the politico-religious to generate courage and confidence. Mahima Swami had appeared to Dasaram in a dream to order him to lead the march to Puri. Bhima Bhoi, the divine devotee who had insisted that the master would save the true disciples, now prophesied the reappearance of the Guru. The first appearance of the preceptor had not been successful because the devotees had failed to recognize him. But the disciples had realized their mistake. They were ready. Anadi was to take form again to complete his incomplete task. The end of suffering was not far away.

Perceptions

Throughout this chapter I have tried to highlight the uniqueness of Bhima Bhoi as a poetic genius of ungoverned imaginings: a fact that at once makes it difficult to categorize him and engenders prolific possibilities of apprehension. *Bhima Bhoi's Malika ba Padmakalpa* provides one instance of the varied ways in which Bhima Bhoi has been perceived and set to work among the followers of Mahima Dharma. There are many others. Bhima Bhoi today is a significant presence in the obscure villages of Bolangir and Sambalpur as well as among the middle classes of Bhubaneswar and Cuttack. Here, I trace the different ways in which the nineteenth-century poet has been read, understood and put to use by posterity.

We have seen that Mahima Dharma, which suffered a setback after the death of Mahima Swami, began to flourish in the Sambalpur region under Bhima Bhoi's leadership. The poet emerged as a preacher in his own right after the death of his Guru. He set up his *ashrama* at Khaliapali near Sonepur, initiated his own group of followers and cut his links with Joranda. He came to be worshipped as god in his lifetime and after his death, his life became a legend. Among the *sanyasis* and *bhaktas* of western Orissa, Bhima Bhoi has come to take the place of Mahima Swami; the *bhakta* has become *bhagaban*; the mediator, the ultimate object of worship. The conflation of identity is revealed in simple statements that describe the poet as *ajoni sambhuta bhagaban* who appeared in Orissa in 1826.[139]

The lay disciples of western Orissa, especially, have woven a rich tapestry of tales and legends around the figure of Bhima Bhoi. Bhima Bhoi the baby was found in a palm grove by a Khond couple who adopted him. Bhima Bhoi, the poor child, was rescued from the well by Mahima Swami. Bhima Bhoi, the youth, was made a *bhakta* by the Guru of the world. Bhima Bhoi, the *bhakta*, had to face great hardship and opposition from the rulers of Redakhol, Baudh and Sonepur and from the ignorant people in general. He overcame them all. He remained steadfast in his devotion to the master. He was none other than *nityasthali* (eternal) Radha, who had appeared in the form of a blind poet[140] to sing the praises of the Lord in Kali Yuga. Imagination of ardent followers transformed the romanticized yearning of Radha for Krishna in Vaishnava poetry into the suffering of an empathetic poet-preceptor, and made it possible for them to spontaneously relate to and identify with their master.

The belief in the Radhahood of Bhima Bhoi went hand in hand with the popularity of a range of Dalakhai and Rasarakeli songs that are ascribed to Bhima Bhoi. These songs, which speak of the love of Radha and Krishna, have, however, nothing in common with the precepts of the faith he followed. Yet they are widely held to be creations of Bhima Bhoi. Lay Mahima Dharmis find no inconsistency in thinking of Bhima Bhoi as Radha and as the poet-philosopher of Mahima Dharma, and no difficulty in accepting the love songs and philosophical compositions equally as creations of the poet.[141] They find it easy to assimilate the different Bhimas, the one who had close ties with yogic/tantric practices, led the life of an extraordinary householder with four consorts and allowed women to join the monastic order as well as the one who poured his heart out to an indescribable Absolute. But scholars find it difficult to accept this apparent contradiction. They seek to find answers to the uncertainty. Artaballabh Mahanti cited works believed to have been composed by Achyutanada, one of the Panchasakhas, which spoke of the birth of Radha as a blind poet in Orissa. This blind poet was to propagate the teachings of the Śunya Purusha, who will appear as an *abadhut*.[142] Interestingly, *Padmakalpa* too, described the Sambalpur region as the abode of *nityasthali* Radha.[143] Yet another scholar described the love-songs as created by Bhima Bhoi in the 'first flush of his youth'. 'Here is no restriction of Mahima religion, no control of the senses, no mystery of the Brahman. Drawing Radha and Krishna into the vortex of earthly life, the poet expresses his hunger for flesh in the most naked, provocative, sensuous language.'[144]

Bhima Bhoi the preacher tasted success after the king of Sonepur, won over by his display of the powers of a *siddha*, granted him land at Khaliapali and aided the construction of his *ashrama*. His deification began. He performed miracles. He threatened non-believers by appearing in their dreams,[145] fulfilled the desires of his disciples, cured diseases, gave children to childless women and brought dead bodies back to life. Stories also account for Bhima Bhoi's life as a householder. They state that *bhagaban* Bhima got married in order to keep his vow. The ignorance of human beings in Kali, who refused to see the path of redemption had, at one point of time, moved the poet to desperation. He had decided to drink liquor and steal Brahman women if his Guru did not bring about a change in the situation. His Guru gave him *darśan* and told him that sins would disappear only gradually. There could be no immediate change. Bhima Bhoi, however, had to respect the oath he had taken. The poet married Annapurna, a Brahman woman. She bore him a son, Kapileswar, and a daughter, Labanyabati.[146]

Annapurna came to share the honours with Bhima Bhoi as Ma Annapurna symbolizing the equality granted to women by Bhima Bhoi in the path of meditation and salvation. During the *maghi purnima* (full moon in January–February) celebration at Khaliapali, Bhima Bhoi and Annapurna sat on a raised platform to give *darśan* to their followers. They offered prayers, services and gifts to the spiritual couple in a gesture of devotion and surrender, in the manner of devotees surrendering themselves to their gods.[147] At other times the poet sat on a decorated horse and toured the village like a king surveying his kingdom.[148] He commanded the same authority and veneration that Mahima Swami was said to have enjoyed at the dawn of *satya yuga*. There was nothing more Bhima Bhoi wished for in life. He decided to leave the earth. He announced his departure in advance so as to prepare the *bhaktas* for it.[149] His mortal remains were buried at Khaliapali. His *khatau* (wooden sandals) started being worshipped. His life became a legend.

The deification of the poet by lay disciples was complemented by a process of canonization began by intellectuals in the early twentieth century. The ambivalence about an unlettered poet of low birth that characterized the late nineteenth-century reports, changed into admiration at the turn of the century. Soon after the essay in the Oriya magazine *Mukur*, appeared the two influential texts of N. N. Vasu — *The Archeological Survey of Mayurbhanja*, and *The Modern Buddhism and its Followers in Orissa.* In these texts, Vasu categorically identified Bhima Bhoi as the leader of the sect and paid him glowing tributes:

> Ere long the fame of Bhima Bhoi spread far and wide. Hearing his immortal instruction helping in the attainment of real knowledge and illumining the head and the heart, the mighty pillars of the caste system stooped at his feet, though the blood of the low kanda ran in his veins. They considered him a spark from the Eternal Flame of truth and knowledge. Before several years had elapsed the Mahima Dharma could count its followers by thousands.[150]

B. C. Mazumdar, an official of the Sonepur court, also credited Bhima Bhoi with the leadership of the attack on the Jagannath temple. 'That he [Bhima Bhoi] had a charming and commanding personality can be fully appreciated from a fact which is on Government records. Bhima Bhoi considered the celebrated idol of Jagannath at Puri in Orissa a huge nuisance, and ordered his followers to proceed to Puri and burn the idol.'[151] Government records, we have seen, did not in any way connect Bhima Bhoi with the attack on the temple.[152] At the same time, it is difficult to deny that the works of Bhima Bhoi had inspired the 'attackers'. Moreover, the confident statements of Vasu and Mazumdar, whose books appeared in print within 15 years of Bhima Bhoi's death, are perhaps indicative of the elevated position the poet had achieved in popular memory, which later found its way into the realm of the written word.[153]

Vasu's texts set the tone for subsequent assessments of Bhima Bhoi. For Vasu, the poet's low birth heightened his greatness and his achievements. His immortal message made 'the pillars of caste system' forget themselves and stoop at his feet even though 'the blood of a low kanda ran in his veins'.[154] Vasu's point has been taken up by Oriya intellectuals and used to serve projects of Oriya nationalism. Bhima Bhoi has been seized upon and canonized as the 'authentic' voice of tribal Orissa. No scholar today can afford to leave out Bhima Bhoi and his compositions from a discussion of Oriya literature or Oriya poetry. Binayak Misra hails him as the national poet of Orissa who occasioned an awakening of the Oriya people,[155] while Mayadhar Mansinha declares him to be the greatest *adivasi* poet.[156] For Chittaranjan Das, Bhima Bhoi is the 'most precious gift of Mahima Dharma to Oriya literature and he should also be claimed as the most precious gift of Orissa and Oriya literature to the legacy that is India'.[157] Bhima Bhoi's low birth thus has been turned into an asset, a symbol of Oriya pride. Is it not, ask the Oriya scholars, a credit to Oriya society that it can produce such a great philosopher and scholar from among its backward 'tribals'?[158] This philosopher has also seen as a *biplabi* (revolutionary), a champion of social reform. Through his protest against idol worship and caste distinctions he sought to bring about a change in society.[159]

The innovative poet did not stop at that. He experimented with language and style, making fruitful use of Sanskrit, Prakrit and colloquial Oriya in his *bolis*. Not constrained by rules of grammar, Bhima Bhoi used 'impure' words — 'words used very commonly by the illiterate' — to great effect, enriching Oriya language in the process.[160] In his contribution to Oriya language he has been ranked with the great early poets of the vernacular whose new style of composition successfully set Oriya on a career of its own, effecting a rupture with Sanskrit.[161]

This celebration of Bhima Bhoi as the indigenous radical intellectual — perhaps overdrawn but not totally off the mark — has marginalized and somewhat subdued the appeal of the poet as a devotee and spiritual leader. His *padas* continue to be cited in meetings, conferences, articles and books as proofs of an advanced and progressive mind. The famous lines of *Stuti Chintamoni*, where he pleads for the redemption of the world even at the cost of his own salvation, have been turned into the *leit-motif* of the Oriya language in the Sahitya Akademi's list of languages. But a critical discussion of his role as the poet-philosopher of Mahima Dharma seems to have fallen out of the agenda.

Scholars coming from the more provincial Sonepur-Sambalpur region have recovered stories of Bhima Bhoi's life for totally divergent purposes. Seeking to share in the pride of a region that nurtured this great mind, these scholars have made strident efforts to establish the 'true facts' of Bhima Bhoi's life. Bhagirathi Nepak, in his numerous works on Bhima Bhoi has tried to provide the readers with hard facts, which have not been discussed so far because of the preoccupation of scholars with myths and stories.[162] Nepak thus sees himself as having performed the useful task of purging the narrative of Bhima Bhoi's life of legends and recapturing him as a historical character.[163] In the process, he has vigorously challenged the idea that Bhima Bhoi was blind. Others, following Nepak's lead, have combed the *janans* of *Stuti Chintamoni* to find proof that Bhima Bhoi had eyesight.[164]

Debendra Kumar Dash has taken the statement in the *Calcutta Gazetteer* that Bhima Bhoi is 'said to have been born blind, and afterwards endowed with sight by Mahima Swami' to mean that the poet was definitely not blind in 1881. To support his claim he has presented five other 'important documents' — reports of colonial administrators, features in the *Utkala Deepika*, letters published in Oriya magazines, and an account in the *District Gazetteer* — the proper analysis of which would reveal the 'truth' about Bhima Bhoi's life and works.[165] In trying to accord Bhima Bhoi's life, verse and work the dignity of 'facts', these authors have sought to counter the poet's attempted marginalization by the renouncers of Joranda. While this is a very valuable gesture, their search for truth has tended to rid Bhima Bhoi's life of all indeterminacy. A figure that eluded categorization has been firmly placed within the parameters of a historical account.

The ascetics of Mahima Dharma have matched the scholars in according varying degrees of importance to Bhima Bhoi. The charismatic poet proved to be a problem for the *sanyasis* at the helm of affairs at Joranda. He had not only set up a parallel institution at Khaliapali but was commanding greater veneration from a section of the followers. The poet-philosopher had become a threat. He was also an embarrassment. As a householder he was exercising the authority of preaching the faith, reserved for *sanyasis*. The leading group of Balkaldharis at Joranda tried to run down the poet's influence by relegating him to the position of a *gruhi bhakta*, a householder who composed texts on the faith with the blessing of the Guru. This became pronounced from the third decade of the twentieth century with the rise to prominence of a new generation of ascetics who were scholar-philosophers, and with the entanglement of the renouncers with the legal apparatus of the state. The collected works of the poet, published under the auspices of the Dharma Grantha Store, whose proprietor is an adherent of the dominant group at Joranda, was entitled *Bhaktakabi Bhima Bhoinka Granthabali* (the collected works of the poet-devotee Bhima Bhoi) — an emphatic statement of the devotee status of Bhima Bhoi. His *bhajans* continued to be sung and his *stutis* recited, but his works were no longer regarded as the lone authoritative source of the preachings of the Prabhu.

The contending group of renouncers at Joranda, on the other hand, valorized Bhima Bhoi as the philosopher of the faith and conferred on his works the dignity of scriptures. They made his texts their point of reference in interrogating the new interpretations of the faith provided by the new leaders at Joranda. The two processes fed each other: the poet's influence alternated between negligence and over-emphasis.

Like his compositions, Bhima Bhoi's life and preachings have lent themselves to differential perceptions and evaluations. Unrestrained but immensely accessible, Bhima Bhoi's message has got conjoined to messages not directly linked to his life or concerns, lending force to diverse projects. The twentieth century thus, has witnessed the rise of different Bhima Bhoi's, similar yet distinct. The undeterminable creative genius has let himself be apprehended but not grasped. Causing trouble to ascetics and scholars, the sensitive poet has not abandoned the lay disciples of western Orissa. Legends and stories about his life as well as his devotional lyrics continue to confer strength and solace.. Indeed, the bolis 71–7 of *Stuti Chintamoni* have increasingly acquired the power of serving as a cure from snake bites and many other diseases, illustrating the ever newer uses of Bhima Bhoi works for devotees.[166] Stories that circulate orally have been codified in simple narratives like the *Śriguru Mahatmya* of Rashbehari Das that speak of Bhima Bhoi's greatness. There is evidence that this unpretentious text has found its way into the homes of numerous *bhaktas* of the region. Oral narratives and written texts intermingle. Bhima Bhoi marches on.

Notes

1. N. N. Vasu, *The Modern Buddhism and Its Followers in Orissa*, p. 161.
2. B. C. Mazumdar, *Sonepur in the Sambalpur Tract* (Calcutta, A. C. Sarkar, 1911), appendix iv, pp. 226–36; Artaballabh Mahanti, 'Foreword' in Bhima Bhoi, *Stuti Chintamoni* (Cuttack, Prachi Samiti, 1925), preserved in India Office Library and Records (IOLR); Binayak Misra, *Oriya Sahityara Itihasa* (Cuttack, Utkal Sahitya Press, 1928), p. 278; Mayadhar Mansinha, *Oriya Sahityara Itihasa* (Cuttack, Grantha Mandir 2nd edition, 1976); neither Misra nor Mansinha is very certain about the poet's place of birth; Biswanath Baba, *Satya Mahima Dharmara Itihasa* (Cuttack, Satya Mahima Dharmalochana Samiti, revised 4th edition, 1978), p. 68.
3. Bhagirathi Nepak, *Bhima Bhoi: The Adivasi Poet Philosopher* (Bhubaneswar, Publication Committee, 1987), p. 31. Ramesh Samantarai, who extensively toured the villages in the Bolangir region, established Paiksara as the birthplace of Bhima Bhoi. He found 'no evidence' to support the claim that Bhima was born in Gramadiha in Redakhol. Bhima Bhoi moved to the Redakhol region after his mother remarried. Samantarai also dismissed the suggestion of Joranda as totally baseless, a 'figment of imagination'. Ramesh Samantarai, 'Bhima Bhoi', *Saptarshi*, 2:4, 1973, pp. 2–3. He repeated the same information in *Oriya Sahityare Bhima Bhoi* (Cuttack, Dharma Grantha Store, 1976), p. 7. Sria Ma, the niece of Bhima Bhoi's scribes Hari and Basu Panda, who became the proprietress of the Khaliapali *ashrama* after the death of Bhima Bhoi's daughter, also mentioned Paiksara as the birthplace of the poet in the interview she gave to Bhignaraj Patel on 17 May 1985. I am grateful to Bhringaraj Patel for letting me consult his field notes.
4. One scholar attempts to clear the confusion regarding Bhima Bhoi's parents by stating that Danara was also known as Janardan and Maharagi as Gurubari. S. C. Panigrahi, *Bhima Bhoi and Mahima Darshana* (Cuttack, Santosh Publications & Department of Philosophy, Utkal University, 1998), pp. 11–12.
5. The story closely resembles the legend associated with the birth of Kabir. Linda Hess and Sukhdev Singh, *The Bijak of Kabir* (New Delhi, Motilal Banarsidass, 1983), pp. 4–5.
6. P. M. Nayak quotes from a letter written to him by one A. N. Gartia of Sangrampur, in which it is claimed that Bhima Bhoi had certainly taken shelter in the Gartia household as a child for some years. His work was to clean the cowshed, offer a little *ghee* to the fire god every day before lunch, and prepare ropes from *sabai* grass. P. M. Nayak, 'A Study on the Contribution of Sonepur Durbar to Literature (1837–1937)' (Ph. D. Dissertation, Sambalpur University, 1984), p. 128.
7. *Buluthai bane niti prati dine batsaku sangate gheni*
   Kshudha trusha kale jibana bikale piuthai jhara pani.
   Bhima Bhoi, '*Stuti Chintamoni*' in Karunakar Sahu (comp.) *Bhaktakabi Bhima Bhoinka Granthabali* (Cuttack: Dharma Grantha Store, 1977), *boli* 22, *pada* 1. Henceforth, I shall name the actual texts of Bhima Bhoi's which have been cited and not the *Granthabali*.
8. Such legends form the subject matter of simple narratives like B. Nepak, *Kabi Kula Chanda Bhima Bhoi* (Bhubaneswar, Bhagirati Prakashan, 1974); U. C. Nayak, *Mahatma Bhima Bhoi* (Bhubaneswar, B. L. Nayak Publishers, 1984); K. L. Baral, *Santkabi Bhima Bhoi* (Cuttack, Rashtrabhasa Samavaya Prakashan, 1986).
9. The village Kandhara, near Redakhol, is regarded as the village where Bhima Bhoi had fallen into the well. When I visited it in March 1990 inhabitants of the village pointed to the place where the well was said to have been. Recently, Johannes Beltz

informed me that there is now a concrete structure where the well is believed to have been. This is a clear indication of the elevation in status of Bhima Bhoi and the effort on the part of the village to come into prominence by virtue of its association with Bhima Bhoi.

10. The reversal of roles between the master and the servant as a crucial first step to the establishment of the legitimacy of a new religious leader is not particular to Mahima Dharma. See Saurabh Dube, *Untouchable Pasts,* pp. 120–1, for a similar incident pertaining to the life of Ghasidas, the founder of Satnampanth.
11. Bhima Bhoi, *Stuti Chintamoni, bolis* 20, 50, 51, 52, 53.
12. *Kirastan boli deuchanti gali ninda karuchanti loka*
 Alekh Alekh bolibaku swami deucha durdanda dukha. Stuti Chintamoni, boli 20, *pada* 2. Christian as a special term of abuse may have been used for Bhima Bhoi after he came in contact with the Baptist missionaries. This allows a glimpse of how the activities of Protestant missionaries were perceived at the local level.
13. *Stiri purusha ekanta mata hoi ninda karuchanti mukhe*
 Pakhaku gale ada hoy planati tini bhubanara loke. Stuti Chintamoni, boli 51, *pada* 1.
14. The *ashrama* at Khaliapali was set up under the patronage of Raja Niladhar Sing Deo of Sonepur. P. C. Rath, *Kośala Itihas Katha*, Pt. 2, p. 37. This has also been mentioned by P. M. Nayak in his dissertation, 'A Study on the Contribution of Sonepur Durbar', p. 128, and in 'Bhima Bhoi: Poet Laureate of Mahima Religion', in M. Pati (ed.), *West Orissa: A Study in Ethos [Silver Jubilee Commemorative Volume, Sambalpur University*] (Sambalpur, Sambalpur University, 1992), p. 176.
15. 'From the Tehsildar of Angul to the Commissioner of Orissa Division', Cuttack, 12 August 1881, Board of Revenue Document No. 443, OSA, Bhubaneswar; Jagannath Temple Correspondence, Part VI, 1880–84, No. 131, R.R., Board of Revenue, Cuttack; C. E. Buckland, *Bengal under the Lieutenant Governors* (Calcutta, K Bose, 1902), vol. II, p. 735.
16. *Utkala Deepika*, 19 November 1881, Part 16, No. 46, cited in Devendra Kumar Dash, 'Bhima Bhoi o Mahima Dharma', *Eshana*, 34, June 1997, pp. 120–52.
17. 'Indian Report of the Orissa Baptist Mission for 1881–82', BMS Archives, Angus Library, Regent's Park College, Oxford, p. 48.
18. Although Annapurna is generally regarded as Bhima Bhoi's spiritual consort, according to Śria Ma their marriage had resulted from mutual attraction. In her words, Bhima Bhoi was a 'robust' man and Annapurna a 'beautiful' woman. B. R. Patel's interview with Sria Ma, Khaliapali, 17 May 1985.
19. Leaders of several other religious sects — the Satnamis and Ramanandis, for instance — lead the life of a householder. They thereby put a question mark on Dumont's distinction between the man-in-the-world and individual-outside-the-world, and interrogate the privileging of renouncers as founders of new religious orders by classical Hinduism. See Richard Burghart, 'Renunciation in the religious tradition of South Asia, *Man* (n.s.), 18, 1983, pp. 635–53, for a more elaborate discussion.
20. Bhima Bhoi, *Stuti Chintamoni*, *boli* 63, *pada* 10.
21. *Utkala Deepika*, 19 November 1881.
22. 'Indian Report of the Orissa Baptist Mission for 1887–88', Angus Library, BMS archives, Regent's park College, Oxford, p. 46.
23. *Ibid.*
24. *Ibid.*
25. According to Debendra Kumar Dash Bhima Bhoi's success in western Orissa was directly related to the restlessness created by the failure of Surendra Sai's Bhalu

Gulan. 'The political and social void paved the way for Mahima Dharma and Bhima Bhoi's poetry.' Debendra Kumar Dash, 'Bhima Bhoi o Mahima Dharma', p. 132.

26. We will explore this in greater detail in the final section of this chapter.
27. *Utkala Deepika*, 19 November 1881.
28. Karunakar Sahu, 'Foreword' in K. Sahu (comp.), *Bhaktakabi Bhima Bhoinka Granthabali*.
29. Bhima Bhoi, like Mahima Swami, did not nominate any successor. Ma Annapurna was selected by the followers to take charge of the *ashrama* after the poet's death. Labanyabati followed Annapurna, and after her Śria Ma was in charge until she was ousted in the late 1970s. At present the *ashrama* is being managed by a board of trustees. A brief account of the Khaliapali *ashrama* after Bhima Bhoi's death is contained in B. Nepak, *Bhima Bhoi, The Adivasi Poet Philosopher*, pp. 80–3.
30. Cited in Debendra Kumar Dash, 'Bhima Bhoi o Mahima Dharma', pp. 120–52.
31. The manuscript Vasu discovered first was *Kali Bhagabata* of Bhima Bhoi. Later scholars have not been able to locate this manuscript. However, *Sambalpur Hitaishini* published a portion of the text in 1889 without mentioning its source. *Sambalpur Hitaishini*, 24 July 1889, pp. 23–4.
32. N. N. Vasu, *The Archeological Survey of Mayurbhanja*, (Delhi, Rare reprints, 1981), vol. 1. A long chapter in this text on 'Modern Buddhism and its followers in Orissa' was published as a separate text in 1911, along with *The Archeological Survey*.
33. Vasu, *The Archeological Survey*, ccxlv.
34. Biswanath Baba, *Itihasa*, p. 69. This is generally accepted by scholars who work on Bhima Bhoi.
35. S. C. Panigrahi, *Bhima Bhoi and Mahima Darshana*, p. 13.
36. Both Bhagirathi Nepak and Ramesh Samantarai claim to have found several such manuscripts, which they cite in their works. I came across one in the house of a lay disciple in Mahimapali, near Sonepur.
37. N. N. Vasu, *The Modern Buddhism*, pp. 150–1.
38. B. C. Mazumdar, *Sonepur in the Sambalpur Tract*, Appendix iv, pp. 126–36.
39. Artaballabh Mahanti, 'Foreword' to Bhima Bhoi, *Stuti Chintamoni*. Vasu's influence was evident on other scholars of Bengal. Suniti Kumar Chatterjee defined Mahima Dharma as a 'form of protestant Hinduism, which appears to have absorbed a good deal of Buddhism'. S. K. Chatterjee, *The People, Language and Culture of Orissa: Artaballabha Mahanti Memorial Lectures* (Bhubaneswar, Orissa Sahitya Akademi, 1966), p. 72.
40. Biswanath Baba, *Mahima Dharma o Baudhha Dharma* (Cuttack, Dharma Grantha Store, 1980). Much earlier, Biswanath Baba's *Itihasa* had also pointed to the distinctiveness of Mahima Dharma.
41. Chittaranjan Das, 'Studies in medieval religion and literature of Orissa', *Visva Bharati Annals*, IV, 1951, pp. 107–94. Section III of the article is entitled 'a religious movement of nineteenth century Orissa', and is devoted to a discussion of Mahima Dharma. For a powerful affirmation of autonomy and distinction from Hinduism of an early 'religion' of India see, K. Ishwaran, *Speaking of Basava: Lingayat Religion and Culture in South Asia* (Boulder, Westview, 1992).
42. Das, 'Studies in Medieval Religion', pp. 164–5.
43. A. Eschmann, 'Spread, organisation and cult of Mahima Dharma' in D. Panda (ed.), *Mahima Dharma Darsan* (Koraput, Shankar Philosophical Society, 1972).
44. A. Eschmann, 'Mahima Dharma and Tradition', Eschmann Papers, Munich. Published in I. Banerjee-Dube and Johannes Beltz (eds),

Popular Religion and Ascetic Practices: New Studies on Mahima Dharma (New Delhi, Manohar, 2008), pp. 31–42.

45. Bijayananda Kar, 'The religious philosophy of Mahima Goswami and his school', *Bharati, Utkal University Journal of Humanities*, 3:4, July 1969, pp. 59–66.
46. *Ibid.*, p. 66.
47. N. Pradhan, *Prachin Oriya Sahityare Nirguna Dhara* (Bhubaneswar, Basanta Kumari Pradhan, 1986), p. 235.
48. Here I use translation in its everyday sense of trying to apprehend something unknown by drawing a parallel with something known and similar. For an insightful analysis of mutations generated by this kind of translation with regard to symbolic measures adopted by colonial rule see, Bernard Cohn, 'Representing authority in Victorian India' in Terrence Ranger and Eric Hobsbawm (eds), *The Invention of Tradition* (London,Cambridge University Press, 1983).
49. The *bhajans* probably best represent Bhima Bhoi's thought and creative ability. But they are too numerous and diverse for an easy analysis. Besides, they have been discussed and translated elsewhere. I focus on three works that reflect three different facets of Bhima Bhoi's creative capacity and give a good idea of his thought and philosophy and convey a sense of his own journey in life.
50. Mahanti, 'Foreword' to *Stuti Chintamoni.* He explains the three kinds thus: *sangprarthanamayi* — to open one's mind to the Lord; *dainyabodhika* — to realize one's smallness and let the Lord know; *lalasamayi* — prayer for the fulfillment of one's desires and aspirations.
51. Bhima Bhoi, *Stuti Chintamoni, boli* 21, *padas* 7–11.
52. *Se samaya katha hrude kari cinta jibana jauchi podhi*
    Pancabhuta atma nitya kandu achi cia caitan budi. Stuti Chintamoni, boli 21, *pada* 12.
53. *Se kathaman ebe mane padhile hrudaya heuchi jaha*
    Deha pulakita hoi utkanthita chamaka uthuchi hia. Stuti Chintamoni, boli 21, *pada* 13.
54. *Mu hina pamara kita jiba chara to payare anusari*
    Karapatra jodi binati karuchi sukrupa kara Srihari. Stuti Chintamoni, boli 1, *pada* 18.
55. *Ibid., boli* 6, *pada* 11.
56. *Ibid., boli* 47, *pada* 5.
57. *Ibid., boli* 6, *pada* 13.
58. *Basana paraya ghodaichi kaye kalanka papa bakala*
    Satya dharma satya dharma bolibaku nindu achanti sakala. Stuti Chintamoni, boli 20, *pada* 3.
59. *Kimpa nirapaksha karuachi mote keun dosa mane dhari*
    Nisthura to hia na base to daya bhakta pranakhia hari. Ibid., boli 2, *pada* 1.
60. *Ibid., boli* 6, *pada* 7.
61. S. B. Dasgupta, *Obscure Religious Cults* (Calcutta, Firma K L M, repr. 1976, 1st edition, 1946), p. 196.
62. *Stuti Chintamoni, boli* 35, *pada* 19.
63. *Ibid., boli* 36, *pada* 11.
64. *Ibid., boli* 37, *pada* 1.
65. *Arupa śarira rupa nahin jara kemante cinhibi muhin*
    Dayakari mote darśana dia antaryami śunya dehi. Ibid., boli 47, *pada* 1.
66. For a discussion of Surdas and translation of some of his compositions see J. S. Hawley and Mark Juergensmeyer (eds), *Songs of the Saints of India* (New York, Oxford University Press, 1988).
67. In the classical conception of time in Hinduism, Kali Yuga constitutes the last of the four progressively deteriorating epochs that complete the time cycle before a return to the pristine *satya/kreta* age. General disorder characterizes Kali: the different

castes do not perform their assigned functions, rituals are disregarded, heretical sects prevail, and non-Brahman and foreign rulers reign.
68. This is a direct hint at the inefficacy of the wooden image of Jagannath.
69. *Acetare sina jana pranimane karuchanti debapuja*
Pade padi rakshakara boluchanti debu khiri khaja.
Jehu gadiachi apana pinda taku samarpana nahin
Daru pratima murtiku bolichi pranaku bancao tuhi.
Manushya hoi nirjiba sange bhaba dakhanti kede ajnana
Śunyaru jehu pinda prana gadhila nahin taku anumana.
Stuti Chintamoni, boli 95, *padas* 12, 14, 15.
70. *Ibid.*, *boli* 100, *pada* 19.
71. *E kaliyugare kumbhinarke padi jibe*
Brahma nirupana Gita śunile taribe.
Bhima Bhoi, *Brahma Nirupana Gita*, Chapter 1, *pada* 5.
72. *Mahapapi svadehare hoiba mukata*
Brahmanirupana bheda śunile aratha. Ibid., Chapter 2, *pada* 42.
73. *Mataku harana karuthiba jeun loka*
E Gita śunile tara ksaya jiba papa. Ibid., Chapter 2, *pada* 43.
74. *Ibid.*, Chapter 1, *padas* 43–6.
75. It has been argued that Bhima Bhoi's division of the body into *cakras* was different from the yogic division. The *cakras* enumerated by the poet were greater in number than the six — *shada cakra* — used in *yoga*. The names he gave to them were also different. Balakrushna Misra, 'Brahma Nirupana Gitare Brahmanka Sthiti bichara', *Saptarshi* (Sambalpur University Journal), 78, July–August 1981, pp. 61–6. On the other hand, Daitari Baba, a *sanyasi* of the Kaupindhari *samaj*, who prepared a schematic pictorial division of the different parts of the body as discussed in Bhima Bhoi, showed that they corresponded with yogic divisions. Daitari Baba gave me a copy of this pictorial division when I met him in 1990.
76. *Śriguru boile babu śuna nirakar*
Anarupa Brahma ana akare behar. Bhima Bhoi, *Brahma Nirupana Gita*, Chapter 1, *pada* 40.
77. *Ape śisya hoithai apane Śriguru*
Ape taru truna hue ape giri meru. Ibid., Chapter 4, *pada* 4.
78. *Ape maha brahmajnani ape ajnani*
Apane anabibek ape anumani.Ibid., Chapter 4, *pada* 6.
79. *Ibid.*, Chapter 4, *pada* 41.
80. *Ibid.*, Chapter 2, *padas* 12–14.
81. *Jaku daya heba asadhanare dekhiba*
Anumana anubhaba pathare diśiba. Ibid., Chapter 3, pada 62.
82. *Mahima prasanna hele ki karibe kala*
Simha praya pheruthiba e mahimandala. Ibid., Chapter 10, *pada* 93.
83. *Mahima prasanna hele ki karibe roga*
E tini brahmanda nische kariba se bhoga.Ibid., Chapter 10, *pada* 94.
84. *Ibid.*, Chapter 12, *pada* 112.
85. P. C. Raut, 'Review of manuscripts', *Journal of the Kalinga Historical Research Society*, 1:3, December 1946, p. 275.
86. *Hoichi daśa ghadi ratri. Bijaye anakara jyoti.*
Prabesa śayana mandire. Timira phetila tejire.
Chira hoile dibyajyoti. Jajvalyamaya rupakanti.
Śrabane subhila dakile. Anadi prabhu ajna dele.

Boile uthasire bapa. Dekha Anadi Brahmarupa
Ceti uthili tataksana. Paruśe bije sunyabrahma.
Caksu malina deli cahin. Samana guru śisya dui.
Kali mun danda je pranam. Labhili punyamuktakam. Nirveda Sadhana, Chapter 1.

87. *Ibid.*
88. The second chapter has explored how this idea was understood and used by a group of followers to attempt to burn the image of Jagannath in the temple of Puri.
89. As we have seen in the previous chapter, this is exactly what the lay disciples from Sambalpur tried to proclaim through their act of 1 March 1881.
90. *Namati amulya ratana*
Na lage papa doshamana
Sehi namaku kara dhyana
Miśai e mana paban
Chada janaku eka mele
Sthapibu e hrudaya kamale. Nirveda Sadhana, chapter 2.
91. Dasgupta, *Obscure Religious Cults*, p. 228.
92. B. Bäumer, 'Tantric elements in Bhima Bhoi's oeuvre' in Banerjee-Dube and Beltz (eds), *Popular Religion and Ascetic Practices*, pp. 159–172.
93. Paritosh Das, *Sahajiya Cult of Bengal and the Pancha Sakha Cult of Orissa* (Calcutta, Firma K L M, 1988), p. 175.
94. S. N. Jha, 'Cari chandra bhed: Use of the four moons' in R. K. Ray (ed.), *Mind, Body, Society*, pp. 65–108.
95. For a discussion of these different cults centred on the training of the body see Rajat Kanta Ray 'Introduction' in R. K. Ray (ed.), *Mind, Body, Society*, pp. 1–44.
96. We have noted in the first chapter that this is exactly what Mahima Swami did. Again, there is a mix-up between the preceptor and his first disciple.
97. *Nirveda Sadhana*, Chapter 1.
98. The theory of creation is elaborated in chapters 5 to 15.
99. According to Artaballabh Mahanti, this is taken from the Kalacakra school of Buddhism which believes that Brahma, Vishnu and Maheśwar were born out of a union between Śunyapurush, who is Niranjan, and his half-body, Adyaśakti. Artaballabh Mahanti, 'Foreword' to *Stuti Chintamoni.*
100. Bhima Bhoi here displays ingenuity in pointing to Nirakara as Śiva's teacher. The general belief of the Siddha schools, particularly the Naths, is that Śiva is the first instructor of Yoga. S. B. Dasgupta, *Obscure Religious Cults*, pp. 195, 197.
101. Mahanti, 'Foreword' to *Stuti Chintamoni.*
102. I owe this explanation to my philosopher father, Sankari Prosad Banerjee.
103. In *Bhajanmala* it is explained thus: Alekha, the source of form and formless transforms himself, by his sheer will, into cruder and cruder elements. Ether is born out of sunya which in turn gives rise to air. Fire is born from air and water from fire. The phenomenal world arises out of water. *Bhajanmala*, 177, cited in S. C. Panigrahi, *Bhima Bhoi and Mahima Darshana*, p. 32. In *Stuti Chintamoni*, *Anam* (the unnamed one), rather than *sunya*, is held responsible for all creation. *Stuti Chintamoni*, *boli*, 88.
104. *Bajhyare veda acaribu.*
Manare nirveda sadhibu.
Cinhi karibu manya dharma.
Je tathya vedara bacan. Nirveda Sadhana, Chapter 18.
105. See J. Belt, 'Apocalyptic predictions prophecies, and a new beginning: Mahima Dharma and the arrival of the *satyayuga*' in Banerjee-Dube and Beltz (eds),

Popular Religion and Ascetic Practices, pp. 79–102.

106. Sarala Das' *Mahabharata*, a fifteenth-century Oriya rendering of the Sanskrit epic that has become the Mahabharata of Orissa over the centuries, speaks of the Śunya Purush, Alekh Brahma and Adimata, and the creation of the universe by them. The works of the five medieval mystics of the sixteenth century — in particular *Birat Gita* of Balaram Das, *Tula Bhina* of Jagannath Das and the works of Achyutananda Das — abound in references to a *nirguna* Absolute and display an interest in yogic practices.
107. The Panchasakhas do use *anakara* to describe the Absolute at places, but the concept is not at all well defined. For a discussion of the idea of the Absolute of the medieval mystics, see P. Mukherjee, *The History of Medieval Vaishnavism in Orissa* (Calcutta, R. Chatterjee, 1940), pp. 70–1.
108. P. C. Raut, 'Review of manuscripts', p. 272.
109. It was not only certain concepts that Bhima Bhoi took from the Panchasakhas. We have noted how a reviewer of *Nirveda Sadhana* had stated that Bhima Bhoi could be placed much before his actual time on grounds of his language which was 'archaic'. Raut, 'Review of manuscripts', p. 275.
110. Puranans, in fact, provide the first examples of texts that got constructed and reconstructed over time. It is interesting to note in this connection that the *Bhabishya Purana* contains references to Adam, Noah, Yakuta, Taimur Lang, Nadir Shah, and Akbar, a fact that makes it 'rather disappointing' to some and make others conclude that it is 'practically a new work'. See Ludo Rocher, *The Puranas*, pp. 152–3, and R. C. Hazra, *Studies in the Puranic Records on Hindu Rites and Customs* (New Delhi, Motilal Banarsidass, 1975), pp. 167–73.
111. Interview with Bidyadhar Sahu, Cuttack, March 1993.
112. For a strong advocacy of 'reading' as an inventive and creative exercise and of the importance of appropriation in reading see, Roger Chartier, *Forms and Meanings: Texts, Performances, and Audiences from Codex to Computer* (Philadelphia, University of Pennsylvania Press, 1995), pp. 88–97. A critique of the assimilation of reading to passitivity can be found in Michel deCerteau, *The Practice of Everyday life*, p. 169.
113. For a detailed and critical analysis of *malikas* in general and this text in particular see, Banerjee-Dube, 'Reading time: Texts and pasts in colonial eastern India', *Studies in History*, 19:1, 2003, pp. 1–17.
114. Bhima Bhoi, *Bhima Bhoi Malika ba Padmakalpa* (Cuttack, Dharma Grantha Store, 1971), chapter 1, verse 5, 7 and 8.
115. *Ibid.*, chapter 9, verse 12.
116. *Ibid.*, chapter 10.
117. *Ibid.*, chapter 22.
118. It is plausible that the several battles mentioned in the text represent the struggle of the *kundalini* — the source of energy that lies coiled up in the navel according to Yoga — in its upward journey to the head. The different sites of the battle may well correspond to the various parts of the body the *kundalini* crosses in its journey. I am grateful for this information to G. N. Dash of Berhampur University.
119. For insightful analyses of Gandhi's presence in peasant consciousness see, Shahid Amin, 'Gandhi as Mahatma: Gorakhpur District, Eastern UP, 1921–2'; and Sumit Sarkar, 'The conditions and nature of subaltern militancy: Bengal from Swadeshi to Non-cooperation, c. 1905–22', in Ranajit Guha (ed.), *Subaltern Studies III. Writings on South Asian History and Society* (Delhi, Oxford University Press, 1984), pp. 1–62 and

271–320.

120. C. P. Nanda, 'Mapping the Mahatma: Literary tracts and rumours in late colonial Orissa', in M. Brandtner and S. K. Panda (eds), *Interrogating History: Essays for Hermann Kulke* (New Delhi, Manohar, 2006), pp. 291–302.
121. A detailed discussion of the struggle, and the gradual institutionalization of Mahima Dharma through its interaction with the legal machinery of the state is contained in Banerjee-Dube, 'Taming traditions: Legalities and histories in twentieth century Orissa' in Gautam Bhadra, Gyan Prakash and Susie Tharu (eds) *Subaltern Studies X. Writings on South Asian History and Society* (Delhi, Oxford University Press, 1999), pp. 98–125.
122. For a critical analysis of this event see, Chapter 2 and Banerjee-Dube, 'Issues of faith, enactments of contest: The founding of Mahima Dharma in nineteenth century Orissa' in Hermann Kulke and Burkhard Schnepel (eds), *Jagannath Revisited: Studying Religion, Society, and the State in Orissa* (New Delhi, Manohar, 2001), pp. 149–77.
123. I will discuss this at greater length in the following chapter.
124. The concurrence of a crisis within Mahima Dharma with the high tide of nationalist fervour occasioned a remarkable amalgamation of religious and political ideas in the *malikas* produced in the 1920s. *Padmakalpa* repeatedly defines the fight as the battle of *kurukshetra*, the *Mahabharata* war of Kali Yuga, underscoring its epic proportions.
125. A fascinating analysis of peasant and ordinary peoples' negotiation with authority in times of crisis is contained in Sabean, *Power in the Blood*, pp. 61–93 in particular. Another absorbing discussion of the use and understandings of time and history, past and present in the construction of a particular community by the Sikhs is contained in Veena Das, 'Time, self and community: Features of Sikh militant discourse' in Veena Das, *Critical Events: An Anthropological Perspective on Contemporary India* (Delhi, Oxford University Press, 1995), pp. 118–136.
126. I refer to Bhima Bhoi's *malikas* in plural because apart from *Padmakalpa* Eschmann's papers also contain the translation of a short 'Malika of Bhima Bhoi'. However, I have not been able to locate the original Oriya version of this *malika.*
127. I base my arguments on the long citations from *Yasomati Malika* in N. N. Vasu's, *The Archeological Survey of Mayurbhanja.*
128. *Padmakalpa*, chapters 16–20.
129. *Padmakalpa*, chapter 7.
130. The following chapter will analyse the role played by Krupasindhu in charting the course of Mahima Dharma in the first half of the twentieth century.
131. I owe this point to Prabhu Mohapatra.
132. Roger Chartier, in a speech delivered in Mexico City in 2001 emphasized that the coming together of text and voice made the word come alive — 'palabra viva'. An interesting discussion of the different kinds and uses of written texts in India can be found in Wendy Doniger, 'Fluid and fixed texts in India' in Joyce B. Flueckiger and Laurie Patton (eds), *Boundaries of the Text: Epic Performances in South and Southeast Asia* (Ann Arbor, Michigan, Center for South and Southeast Asian Studies, University of Michigan, 1991), pp. 31-41.
133. Donoghue argues that writing has to observe a 'different decorum' since printed texts are read by people not known to the author. Readership thus, is distinct from 'audience'. This difference, according to him produces an ambiguous situation that is then used for the production and proliferation of 'anonymous pamphlets and pseudonymous squibs, a vital facility in years of religious and political vehemence'.

Denis Donoghue, *The Practice of Reading* (New Haven & London, Yale University Press, 1998), p. 116. While this is a valid point, Donoghue seems to accept uncritically the division between reading and writing, and takes the 'audience' to be in direct conversation with the 'composer'. He totally rules out the possibility of written texts being read aloud, and 'heard' and 'read' by people unknown to the author.

134. P. Ricoeur, *Time and Narrative*, cited in R. Chartier, 'Texts, printing, readings', in Lynn Hunt (ed.), *The New Cultural History* (Berkeley, L.A., University of California Press, 1989), p. 157.
135. R. Chartier, 'Texts, printing, readings', p. 158. It is interesting that Gurevich holds the existence of a common knowledge and the expectation to 'hear' the same things by the unlettered, conservative common people responsible for the monotony of medieval popular literature. A. Gurevich. *Medieval Popular Culture*, p. 20.
136. S. Sarkar, *Beyond Nationalist Frames, Relocating Postmodernism, Hindutva, History* (Delhi, Permanent Black, 2002), pp. 12–3; S. Sarkar, 'Renaissance and Kaliyuga: Time, myth and history in colonial Bengal' in S. Sarkar, *Writing Social History*, (Delhi, Oxford University Press, 1999), pp. 186–215.
137. S. Sarkar, *Beyond Nationalist Frames*, p. 14.
138. *Ibid.*, p. 15.
139. Interview with sadhu Dambarudhar Das, head of the Khaliapali *ashrama*, Khaliapali, 12 March 1992. Ramesh Samantarai, however, challenges this claim on the basis of Bhima Bhoi's own compositions.
140. It was widely believed that Bhima Bhoi was blind, although he himself did not speak of this in any of his works. Since the 1970s several scholars of western Orissa have sought to show that he was sighted. I will turn to this a little later.
141. Ramesh Samantarai quotes a phrase current in western Orissa, which asks a blind man to compose Dalakhai and Rasarakheli for the people to sing, to argue that this blind man is none other than Bhima Bhoi. Ramesh Samantarai, *Oriya Sahityare Bhima Bhoi* (Cuttack, Dharma Grantha Store, 1976).
142. Artaballabh Mahanti, 'Foreword' to Bhima Bhoi, *Stuti Chintamoni*.
143. *Bhima Bhoi Malika ba Padmakalpa*, chapters 7, 11.
144. P. M. Nayak, 'Contribution of the Sonepur Durbar', pp. 135–6.
145. Tangara, a servant of Kanchana Pradhan of Athmallik, had criticized his master for accepting the *padodaka* (water in which the toe had been dipped) of Bhima Bhoi. Bhagaban Bhima appeared in Bhismarupa in Tangara's dream. Tangara was terrified: he realized his mistake, asked for Bhima Bhoi's forgiveness and became his follower. Interview conducted by Eschmann with Nabaghana and Chaitanya Pradhan of Kankanapada, Redakhol on 24 April 1971; 'Eschmann's field diary No. 1 (1973–74)', Eschmann Papers, Munich.
146. This account, given by Nabaghana Pradhan of Kankanapada, has been corroborated by many *bhaktas* I have interviewed. They, however, assert that Annapurna was Bhima Bhoi's spiritual consort and that the son and the daughter were born to two other women who were also Bhima Bhoi's wives. Ramesh Samantarai claims that Sumedha bore Kapileswar when Bhima Bhoi put *mantraput bibhuti* (blessed ash) on Sumedha's forehead to fufil her mother's wish. In the same manner, Rohini gave birth to Labanyabati. Ramesh Samantarai, 'Bhima Bhoi', *Saptarshi*, 2:4, 1973, p. 15.
147. Resolution, Judicial, Calcutta, 21 October 1881, Board of Revenue Document No. 446/1, OSA; K. Sahu, 'Foreword', in K. Sahu (comp.) *Granthabali*, p. 37. This has been corroborated by several inhabitants of the Sonepur-Khaliapali region.
148. Interview with Maguni Patnaik, Sonepur, 5 February 1993. Maguni Patnaik was

originally a resident of Khaliapali. As a child he had played with Kapileswar. Maguni had been born with the blessing of Ma Annapurna.

149. According to Ramesh Samantarai Bhima Bhoi's *ghatatyag* (departing from the body) happened on the auspicious day of 'sibaratri'. He had announced it to his followers a month in advance. Samantarai, 'Bhima Bhoi', p. 16.
150. Vasu, *The Modern Buddhism*, p. 164.
151. B. C. Mazumdar, *Sonepur in the Sambalpur Tract*, Appendix iv, pp. 126–36.
152. It is surprising that the District Gazetteer of Bolangir published in 1968 credited Bhima Bhoi with the attack on the Jagannath temple which is stated to have taken place in 1880, N. Senapati and N. K. Sahu (eds), *Orissa District Gazetteers, Bolangir*, p. 109. A Census of Mayurbhanj also attributes the attack to Bhima Bhoi. Mohammed Laeequddin, *Census of Mayurbhanj State, vol.1: Reports*, 1931, p. 120.
153. Scholars from western Orissa take it upon themselves to disprove Vasu and Mazumdar's assertion that Bhima Bhoi headed the attack on the Jagannath temple. The basic assumption behind their attempt is that leadership in the incident in no way enhances the prestige or popularity of the non-violent, introspective poet. B. Nepak, *Bhima Bhoi, The Adivasi Poet Philosopher*, p. 71; Kasinath Pradhan, '"Puri Jagannathanka prati akraman" ghatanare santha Bhima Bhoinka samprikta ki?', *Saptarshi* (Sambalpur University Journal), 7–8, 1981, pp. 79–83. Surendra Nath Chinara, on the other hand, supports Vasu and Mazumdar in stating that if Bhima Bhoi did not actually lead the attack, he definitely inspired it. S. N. Chinara, 'The History of the Mahima Cult in Orissa' (Ph. D. Dissertation, University of Berhampur, 1982), p. 34.
154. N. N. Vasu, *The Modern Buddhism*, p. 164.
155. Binayak Misra, *Oriya Sahityara Itihasa*, p. 278.
156. M. Mansinha, *Oriya Sahityara Itihasa*, p. 206.
157. Chittaranjan Das, *A Glimpse into Oriya Literature* (Bhubaneswar, Orissa Sahitya Akademi, 1982), p. 158.
158. As an instance of this mode of thinking, see M. Mansinha, 'The greatest tribals', in M. N. Dash (ed.), *Sidelights on History and Culture of Orissa* (Cuttack, Vidyapuri, 1977), Chapter 18.
159. Numerous essays published in anthologies and journals bear titles like 'Bhima Bhoi the revolutionary' and 'Bhima Bhoi the radical social reformer'.
160. Bhagirathi Nayak, *Oriya Poets through the Ages* (Balasore, Grantha Bharati, 2002), p. 71.
161. S. Nayak, 'A note on the mystic poetry of Bhima Bhoi' in Banerjee-Dube and Beltz (eds), *Popular Religion and Ascetic Practices*, pp. 103–116.
162. See, for instance, B. Nepak, *Bhima Bhoi. Chinta, Chetana o Jibana* (Bhubaneswar, Publication Committee, 1973); *Mahima Dharmare Kabi Bhima Bhoinka Bhumika* (Bhubaneshwar, Publication Committee, 1976); *Bhima Bhoi Atma-pariciti o Anyanya Prasanga* (Bhubaneswar, Publication Committee, 1981); *Bhima Bhoi Adivasi Poet Philosopher* (Bhubaneshwar, Publication Committee, 1987); *Bhima Bhoi: His Life and Works* (Lacchipur, Bhima Bhoi Sanskrutik Sansad, 1998).
163. Interview with Bhagirathi Nepak, Bhubaneswar, May 1992.
164. See, for instance, the works of Udhhab Nayak and Ramesh Samantarai.
165. Devendra Kumar Das, 'Bhima Bhoi o Mahima Dharma', pp. 122–52.
166. This is a very recent phenomenon. I had not come across it during my field work in the early 1990s. However, a student of Delhi University who has worked on Mahima Dharma made a mention of the 'healing powers' of *Stuti Chintamoni* in the course of a conversation in 2003. This has been reiterated by Johannes Beltz and Bettina Bäumer, who worked on Bhima Bhoi between 2001 and 2004.

CHAPTER 4.

Ascetics, Histories and the Law

This chapter analyses different configurations of history — especially entailing mutual imbrications of state and community, religion and law and asceticism and modernity as they are played out in the career of Mahima Dharma between 1875 and 2000. It focuses on the struggles of leading ascetics to hold together a disparate group of followers after the death of the charismatic preceptor and their efforts at forging a community. The renouncers succeed in elaborating and maintaining a *samaj* (community). At the same time, the measures they adopt result in the evolution of the Dharma as an institutionalized, internally differentiated order. The long process, fraught with tensions and contradictions, brings in its wake dissension among renouncers over the interpretation of the Guru's teachings, the intervention of law courts and the construction of formal, authoritative histories of the 'sect' — modernist histories that premise their veracity on the divinity of the founder. While this renders the histories amenable to varied perceptions, the commanding presence of scholar ascetics and prolonged encounter with the legal machinery of the state engender significant shifts in emphases within the faith. Tracking these distinct yet overlapping stories, my narrative unravels discrete apprehensions of time and history, past and present and conjoined articulations of authority and resistance and uniformity and discordance that interrogate both singular constructions of the subaltern and the pervasive dominance of power.

The Samadhi and the Dispute

We have seen that the death of Mahima Swami in 1875 produced a crisis within Mahima Dharma. His followers had not expected him to die, and the Guru had made no arrangements for the continuation of the faith after his death. He had not nominated a successor. He had created a monastic order with two groups of renouncers, Kumbhipatias and Kanapatias (or Balkaldharis and Kaupindharis, as they came to be known in the twentieth century), but had not specified their positions in relation to each other. His insistence on absolute detachment and his rejection of property had prevented the acquisition of land and the construction of permanent structures by the faith. All that the sect possessed at the time of the Guru's death was an *ashrama* at Malbaharpur in Banki and the hut at Joranda in which the Guru had lived. The Commissioner of the Tributary Mahals sold off these two structures as intestate property. The belongings found in the *ashrama* were put to auction.[1] The disciples were left with no core structure and no authority. Many lay followers reverted to Hinduism.[2] Leadership and organization became crucial to the survival of the faith after the death of Mahima Swami.[3]

There were difficulties here. Govinda Baba, the first and the most respected disciple of Mahima Swami, had predeceased his Guru. There were more serious problems in relation to the second disciple, Nrusingha Baba. Stories current among the followers of Mahima Dharma indicate that he had been ostracized by Mahima Swami. Contemporary reports also hint at a scuffle that occurred during the performance of *dhuni* by Mahima Swami at Malbiharpur in Banki. Nrusingha Baba (Narsing Das in administrators' reports) was arrested in this connection. His expulsion from the community of followers possibly followed this incident.

Bhima Bhoi, the poet-philosopher, had roused the ire of the ascetics by cohabiting with women. He severed his ties with the renouncers who congregated at Dhenkanal after the death of Mahima Swami, set up his own *ashrama* in Khaliapali and established himself as the preacher in the region. The *sanyasis* refused to recognize Bhima Bhoi as their leader.[4] They were also unable to select someone from among themselves as the head of the sect. In the *dharma sabha* (religious meeting) convened at Jaka to decide on the future of the faith, the ascetics resolved to construct a *samadhi*, memorial of the Guru at Joranda in Dhenkanal, where he 'had left his mortal body'. This was to prove momentous for the crystallization of the loose body of followers of Mahima Swami — often designated by the generic term Kumbhipatia — into an organized, institutionalized order, Mahima Dharma.

The *sanyasis* had chosen a key symbol. The *samadhi* of the Guru at Joranda became the new rallying point for the followers of the faith.[5] The land for the construction of the memorial was acquired from the Raja of Dhenkanal. The Raja had offered 65 acres of land in and around Joranda to the Guru

Memorial of Mahima Swami, Jordana

during his lifetime. The followers of Mahima Swami now took over that land and gradually turned it into the main centre of the sect.[6] The initial construction of the *samadhi mandir* (memorial), the *śunya mandir* (temple in honour of the great Void/Absolute) and the *dhuni mandir* (shrine where the sacred fire is kept burning all the time) was completed by 1877.[7] The process of constructing new buildings and adding to and renovating old ones went on for decades.[8] A huge complex emerged: Joranda became Mahima Gadi, the headquarters of Mahima Dharma. The importance of the *samadhi* increased with the passage of time. As the disciples initiated directly by Mahima Swami passed away one by one, the bond of personal commitment weakened, and the memory of the preceptor receded into a dim and distant past. The *samadhi* became the locus of the Guru's authority, the pivot of the sect. In a process similar to the transformation of the sacred text — Granth Sahib — of Sikhism into Guru Granth Sahib following the termination of the line of gurus by Govind Singh, the *samadhi* of Mahima Swami became the *asthan*, the site invested with the authority of the founder. It laid the foundations for the growth of an institutionalized order. An annual pilgrimage to the *samadhi* came to constitute an important part of the activities of a member of the faith, a mode to assert his/her distinct identity. A static symbol replaced an extremely mobile preceptor — charisma became 'routinized'.[9] The *sanyasis* developed a set of ritual practices (*niti* and *sebapuja*) which were to be performed at the *samadhi/asthan*. This *niti* at the *asthan* became symbolic of service to and worship of the Guru. However, it also proved to be a source of friction.

The beginnings of tension lay in the ambiguous relationship between the Kumbhipatias or Balkaldharis (wearers of the bark of the kumbhi tree) and the Kanapatias or Kaupindharis (wearers of waist-cloth). Problems had arisen during the lifetime of the Guru. Indeed, Mahima Swami's ostracization of Nrusingha Baba had caused the first rift among his disciples. After the trouble at Malbiharpur resulting in the arrest of Nrusingha Baba, Mahima Swami is believed to have commanded him to wear silk cloth (*kanapat*) from this time on, as his *kumbhipat* had become polluted. He was also asked to found his own *ashrama* at Mahulpada. We do not know if the *ashrama* was set up under the direction of the preceptor.[10] We do know that it had become a flourishing centre by the early 1880s. Damodar Patnaik, a writer based in Cuttack and the editor of a journal, wrote a feature in the *Utkala Deepika* in 1883 to inform the readers of the beauty and tranquility of this *ashrama* that had reminded him of the *ashramas* of old and filled his mind with divine sentiments.[11]

This *ashrama* also acted as a rival institution of the Kanapatias. Reports on the sect, drawn up after the incident of 1881, noted that relations between the Kumbhipatias and the Kanapatias were not cordial: 'They do not eat with each other'.[12] There was a little more to the problem. 'Each sect [division] has a separate temple or place of prayer'.[13] Within five years of Mahima Swami's death, two groups of ascetics, differentiated by their garb, had demarcated their frontiers by establishing parallel institutions.

The picture was made muddier by Bhima Bhoi. A prominent disciple of the founder, he started leading the life of a householder. At the same time, he actively participated in the propagation of the message of his master through his compositions and brought more and more men and women within the fold of the faith. Shunned by the ascetics at Joranda, Bhima Bhoi nevertheless acquired the position of the Guru among his followers. In the preceding chapter I referred to a report published in the *Utkala Deepika* in 1881 that blamed Bhima Bhoi for causing dissension within the sect. Instead of joining hands with the ascetics at Joranda, the radical poet-propagator had established yet another parallel institution at Khaliapali in the state of Sonepur. Death of the founder had brought in its wake disorder and discord among the followers of Mahima Dharma.

The move to construct the *samadhi* at Joranda and to establish it as the main centre of the faith acquires special significance against this background. As long as the ascetics at Joranda managed to work together, the memorial steadily grew in importance and marginalized other *ashramas*. However, it was precisely its growing importance that brought about dissension. The Balkaldharis, by virtue of the fact that the Guru wore *balkal* and had made it the garb of his first disciple, Govinda Baba, claimed a status superior to the wearers of *kaupin* and sought to monopolize the right of ritual services offered at the *samadhi*. The Kaupindharis challenged this bid at leadership.

There was some truth in the claim of the Balkaldharis. Baptist missionaries, reporting on their interview with 'Dhulee Babajee', had felt it pertinent to comment on his attire. 'His dress was of the most primitive character, composed of a strip of the bark of a tree called Kumbhee.'[14] Mahima Swami, we may recall, had cut off his matted locks, discarded the *kanthi* and the *kaupin*, and started wearing *kumbhipat* before proclaiming himself as the founder of a new faith. He had also initiated his first disciple Govinda Baba by granting *balkal* to him. Govinda Baba in turn, is believed to have given *balkal* to the legendary 64 *siddhas* (self-realized beings). Undoubtedly, the generic name of Kumbhipatia acquired by the entire body of adherents of the Swami in the nineteenth century owed its origin to this garb of Mahima Swami and his prominent ascetic disciples.

A statement in the report of the manager of Dhenkanal corroborated the Balkaldharis' claim to superiority: [If a] 'Kanapatiya was considered fit to be Kumbhipatiya the Mahima Gosain used to favour him with a Kumbhipat… and from that time he would never wear cloth but only the bark of Kumbhi tree.'[15] But apart from these indirect references, there is nothing to suggest that the Swami had initiated the system of gradation among his disciples. Indeed, he had preached a radical religion that advocated equality and the removal of all divisions. Could he have introduced discrimination among his own disciples? The Kanapatias, who had been initiated by the founder and served him along with the Kumbhipatias, refused to accept an inferior status. From their point of view, the claim of the Balkaldharis militated against the spirit of the Guru's teachings.[16]

Matters came to a head when Nanda Baba, a *prathama-panthi* Balkaldhari *sanyasi* (renouncer of the first line) granted *balkal* to 56 Kaupindhari *sanyasis* who were his followers. We do not have an exact date for this incident, but there are indications that it happened some time in the early twentieth century.[17] This act of Nanda Baba was a defiant declaration of the superiority of the Balkaldharis: these ascetics had the exclusive right to promote the Kaupindharis to the higher status of the wearers of *balkal*. Nanda Baba had of course claimed that he was only obeying a *śunya adeś*[18] (command from the void), a manner in which the Guru made his wishes known to his followers. The veracity of the command was, however, challenged by another *prathama-panthi* Balkaldhari *sanyasi*. Krupasindhu Baba refused to accept the 'promotion' of Kaupindharis to Balkaldhari status and asked them to stay away from the Gadi. He even appealed to the ruler of Dhenkanal, who ordered the new wearers of *balkal* to reside at a distance of three miles from the compound wall of the *gadi mandir*.[19] Krupasindhu's success was short-lived. The new Balkaldharis got the better of him. They established themselves at the Gadi. Krupasindhu left Joranda on a long tour.

The induction of new members infused the Balkaldhari group with fresh vigour. It set about organizing the sect with great zeal. New norms and rules were drawn up through a reinterpretation of the teachings of the Guru, and novel ceremonies were initiated at the Gadi. It was during this time that the *maghi purnima* (an annual gathering of followers at Joranda on the full-moon of *magh*, January–February) started being celebrated on a grand scale. More land was bought and new buildings constructed at the Gadi complex with donations from *bhaktas*. All this went hand in hand with a drive to widen the numerical and social basis of the following. The *sanyasis* now wanted to draw people from the literate and urban strata into the fold of the Dharma. Little by little, Mahima Dharma reversed its early emphasis: the importance of the *vana* was substituted by the primacy of the *kshetra*. N. N. Vasu and B. C. Mazumdar, by providing detailed accounts of the new faith in their works in English, had aroused the interest of a section of Oriya intellectuals.[20] The *sanyasis* now wanted their support and involvement. Dharma *sabhas* (religious meetings) were organized and associations formed for the propagation of the faith.[21] The ascetics were successful in drawing in the literati and politicians. The joint secretary of the most significant association of Mahima Dharma, the Satya Mahima Dharmalochana Samiti (society for the discussion of Satya Mahima Dharma), for instance, was Naba Krushna Chowdhury, the then Chief Minister of Orissa. In the meetings of the Samiti leading Balkaldhari *sanyasis* explained the tenets of the faith and interpreted its ideas and practices to the members. They also sought to base their claims to leadership on their credentials as scholars.

The career of Biswanath Baba, who dominated the affairs of Mahima Dharma from the 1930s to the 1990s, typifies the shift in Mahima Dharma. Biswanath, born to adherents of Mahima Dharma at the turn of the twentieth century, had expressed his desire to become a renouncer at the very young age of eight. Dissuaded by his parents, he persisted in his dedicated learning of Hindu scriptures till the age of 11 when he was struck by a painful disease that could not be cured. Biswanath told his parents that the cure lay in his renunciation of the world. His parents were forced to grant him permission.[22] We have here the makings of a new kind of leader — at once a devoted ascetic and a dedicated scholar. At the same time, his life had the touch of the magical. His initiation into the monastic order was divinely ordained. The blessing and direction of the divine master were to accompany all his subsequent ventures.

Biswanath's rise to prominence was rapid. Still in his twenties, he was the most prominent of the 56 *sanyasis* granted *balkal* by Nanda Baba. The young ascetic was quick to grasp the urgency of consolidating his position and that of the newly ordained Balkaldharis once they got control of the Gadi. Equally, his group's claim that the Balkaldharis were superior to the Kaupindharis in spiritual achievement had to be substantiated. A demonstration of the scholarship Biswanath was known for became imperative. Oral modes of dissemination were deemed inadequate for this kind of knowledge: the written form acquired centrality. The absence of authoritative treatises that would make 'the movement meaningful, provide an intellectual base and maintain stable continuity of the principles' was sorely felt, both by the self-realized ascetics of Mahima Dharma and its sympathizers among the Oriya literati.[23] The task was undertaken by

Biswanath Baba in the early 1970's,
(courtesy of Charlott Eschmann)

different ascetics; all their efforts were in vain. The works produced failed to satisfy the learned *sanyasis* of Mahima Dharma. Prayers were offered to Mahima Swami to get the difficult task performed. Biswanath Baba's *Mahima Dharma Pratipadaka* saw the light of day owing 'to the grace of Mahima Mahaprabhu'.[24]

Mahima Dharma Pratipadaka, as the name suggests, was geared towards an exposition of the teachings of Mahima Swami and the main tenets of the faith. The exposition addressed scholars and people of intellect — the ones capable of judging the efficacy of the faith by testing it against reason and truth.[25] Consequently, the proof of each statement was corroborated by citations from scriptures and texts of Indian philosophy. The *Pratipadaka* began by carefully establishing the identity of Mahima Swami as *prabuddha avatar* (enlightened incarnation) and *iśwar purush* (god personified). This involved the enumeration of the special features of *avatars* and *iśwar purush* contained in Hindu scriptures and then establishing their presence in Mahima Swami. Quotations from the *śastras* were profusely used, citations were followed by translations. The author's mastery of Sanskrit was displayed along with his grasp of the scriptures. The discussion of the founder's manifest form was followed by an interpretation, cast eclectically in the categories of Hindu philosophy and religious traditions, of the terms *mahima* and *dharma*. The next six chapters provided a thorough analysis of the teachings of the Dharma and their implications for the various categories of followers. Brahma *upasana* (worship of the indescribable Absolute) was declared to be the highest form of worship and the primary principle of the Dharma. Prayers and supplication to gods and goddesses and their idols, it was argued with the help of the *śastras*, were inferior modes of worship.

The initiates in the path of the worship of Brahma belonged to two broad categories: the *gruhis* (lay disciples) and the *abadhutashrama sanyasis* (renouncers who would eventually become *abadhuts*, the highest form of being). Indeed, these were the only two of the four[26] to be found in Kali Yuga,[27] *brahmacharya* and *banaprastha* having been lost in this era. *Sanyasis*, the members of *abadhutashrama*, were undoubtedly higher beings than *gruhis*. They embodied qualities such as selflessness, modesty, mercy, simplicity, devotion, patience, calm, a pure body and mind and other virtues ascribed to them by the *śastras*. Mahima Swami again, had divided the members of *abadhutashrama* into two orders, *apara* and *para*.[28] An *apara sanyasi* was one who had shunned all craving for material wealth and had renounced the world. His elevation to the level of a *para sanyasi* occurred when he succeeded in internalizing the Guru's teachings and in understanding the *tattwas*, thereby attaining *siddhi* (self-realization). This realization dawned — very much in the Advaita Vedantic tradition of Sankaracharya — with the realization of 'I am Brahma'.[29] It was the culmination of Brahma-*jñana-bhakti yoga*. The *apara sanyasis* wore *kaupin*, the *para sanyasis* had the distinction of wearing *balkal*. The spiritually higher status of the Balkaldharis was established as a fact. There was no hint of any tussle, of the battle lines that stood clearly drawn. This was hardly surprising. Biswanath Baba could not afford any ambivalence about the matter. The Balkaldharis' credentials as the leaders of the faith were at stake.

A comparison of Biswanath Baba's *Pratipadaka* and Bhima Bhoi's writings brings the significant issues to the fore. The main teachings of Mahima Swami — belief in the one and only formless, un-written, indescribable Absolute as the sole redeemer of humanity, the abandoning of the worship of gods and goddesses and the rejection of the rules of caste — find a prominent place in the writings of both Bhima Bhoi and Biswanath Baba. But this is also where all similarities end.

The tone of the arguments and the tenor of writing diverge. Emotion is the key feature of Bhima Bhoi's *stutis*, *janans* and *bhajans* (praises, supplications, prayers) that evoke a sense of complete devotion and total surrender of a poet abandoning himself and pouring his heart out to his master. There is no display of scholarship, no appeals to individual reason, and no conscious effort to pose as the interpreter of the master's teachings. The emotive lyrical compositions of Bhima Bhoi, that stressed the significance of hearing and pure devotion and urged people to take refuge in the true faith to combat the evils of Kali, were meant for joint singing and recitation in communal gatherings of predominantly unlettered devotees. The *Pratipadaka*, on the other hand, conjures up a picture of a detached scholar guiding people along the path of salvation. There is no scope for collective readings here. What we have is a scholarly work that is devised to be read and reflected on privately and alone.[30] Although the author calls upon 'intelligent people' to hear the text, they are urged to use their intellect and power of reasoning to judge the truth of the statements in accordance with *pramana*, evidence.[31] A proper discussion of true faith is impossible without this prerequisite. Basing itself on this premise, the text gives precise instructions to its members, lays down standards they should strive to attain, and inscribes the milestones on the path to salvation. The sense of impending disaster related to Kali is totally absent. Mahima Dharma, the true faith of the era, was to guide its members to salvation if they followed its rules rigorously. Brahma-*jñana-bhakti* replaces Bhima Bhoi's *bhakti*; ascetics are ranked in accordance with the spiritual standard they have attained, promotion comes as a reward for the attainment of spiritual superiority, gradation becomes an integral part of the monastic order. Bhima Bhoi, on the other hand, had done no more than mention the two orders of *sanyasis*.

The most striking feature of the *Pratipadaka* is the central place occupied by *śrutis* (heard/narrated divine texts) and *śastras* (scriptures). They provide the crucial *pramana*, evidence that supplement, substantiate and justify Biswanath Baba's arguments. Equally, they also serve to display the extent of the Baba's scholarship. It is not surprising, then, that the table of contents of the *Pratipadaka* carries a list of the 185 *śrutis*, *śastras* and other works cited in the text. These include the entire corpus of Hindu texts starting from the Rig Veda, moving on through the classical texts of Indian philosophy to the Brahmanas, Upanishads and Puranas, the *samhitas* and *malikas*, works of the Panchasakhas, the biography of Chaitanya and the works of Bhima Bhoi. The *dohas* (couplets) of Kabir and Paltusaheb, the scripture of Sikhism, the Quran and the 'Christian Scripyuyures' are all mentioned in the list. The total number of *ślokas* cited is stated to be one thousand three hundred and two. Was all this not proof of the immense, indeed universal, knowledge of Biswanath Baba? Did he require any supplements to his scholarship, his wisdom and his credentials? Were not the Balkaldharis leading the Mahima Dharmis from the front?

Needless to say, this reliance on scriptures stood in marked contrast to Bhima Bhoi's writings. These writings had criticized, ridiculed and dismissed societal norms and rules laid down in the *śrutis* and *śastras* and instead advocated *nirveda sadhana*. It is not as if the *Pratipadaka* argued in favour of the reading of scriptures as a mode to achieve self-realization. Indeed, knowledge acquired from the *sastras* was declared to be useless once *atmajñan* (self-knowledge) and *Brahmajñan* (knowledge of Brahma) had been achieved. And prior to that, the performance of rituals and ceremonies for the acquisition of merit was of no avail. Of even lesser value was the worship of idols which was compared to the play with dolls by young, unmarried girls. If this helped retain the main tenets of the faith laid down by Mahima Swami, it also served to transform the terms of the discourse. Biswanath Baba, the intellectual, had, in the course of providing a reasoned explication of his faith, aligned it closely to high Hinduism.[32] He had drawn upon ideas from Indian philosophy and laid stress on the maintenance of purity and vegetarianism by the followers. As a corollary, he had secured the cooperation of people who, in Bhima Bhoi's view, were the perpetrators of oppression and social discrimination in an unequal society.

Biswanath Baba was perhaps not unaware of the changes set in motion by the new group of Balkaldharis and not unconcerned about the opposition of those who regarded Bhima Bhoi as the philosopher of the faith. In a dramatic move, the *Pratipadaka* warned the Mahima Dharmis against accepting a *gruhi* as guru.[33] A householder — attached to his family and the organic material world — who boasted of being one with the Brahma actually lost his *karma* (results of good deeds done) and his *brahmajñana* (knowledge of Brahma). He had to be shunned. For the scholar Biswanath, the experiments of Bhima Bhoi only made him inferior to the celibate ascetic — venerated for centuries in the Hindu tradition — as a spiritual leader. The *Pratipadaka* also reminded the readers of Mahima Swami's insistence that after initiation into *brahma-jñana-bhakti* yoga a follower had to give up his mortal guru and take shelter in the Guru of the world.[34] The changes engendered by new circumstances, the rise of leaders of a different order, their efforts towards the formation of a cohesive *samaj*, and the endeavour to gain recognition, legitimacy and publicity for the faith had produced new configurations of Mahima Dharma.

The Move to Law Courts

In the early 1930s, when Krupasindhu Baba returned to Joranda after his long travels, the Balkaldharis were firmly entrenched at the Gadi. The Mahima Dharma *samaj* functioned under their guidance. They had acquired new property and followers and constructed new structures near the *samadhi*; more importantly, they had got themselves registered as the *marfatdars* of Mahimagadi.[35] Literally, *marfatdars* are mediators who in this case meant persons who were in charge of the properties dedicated to the Guru and who represented the Guru in all affairs of the faith. The disaffected Krupasindhu refused to join them and started living separately within the *trutiya bedha* (third boundary) of the Gadi.[36] Krupasindhu commanded great respect. His presence at Joranda and the expression of his dissatisfaction with the existing state of affairs provided the Kaupindharis with a rallying point. The group had disagreed with the Balkaldharis and, consequently, had been left out of the management of the memorial. They now began to assert themselves. Krupasindhu's *tungi* formed the nucleus of a separate order, the Kaupindhari *samaj*.[37]

The Balkaldharis viewed this development with great concern. A rival order was emerging at the *asthan*, the nerve centre of the sect. In Balkaldhari perception this was a direct threat to the unity and solidarity they were trying to forge around the sacred legality of Mahima Swami, and a challenge to the authority of the Guru and the *samaj*. They did not wish to allow a visible breach to grow at Joranda and decided to resort to a higher authority. The Raja of Dhenkanal may have afforded a possibility. But the Raja had earlier stood behind Krupasindhu. It was once again with the Raja's support that Krupasindhu had shifted the Guru's *akhandabati* (undivided/eternal flame) close to his *tungi* upon his return to Joranda. The Raja then could not be relied upon. There were other methods of dispute settlement available. The Balkaldharis, well versed in the language of colonial law as the *marfatdars* of the Gadi, turned to the authority of the State's legal system. With this began a long, convoluted interaction with state power that contributed to the redefinition of Mahima Dharma within the universe of Hinduism.

The earliest document found in the court records[38] relates to a title suit of 1936 between Baba Dinabandhu Das of the Balkaldhari *samaj* and Baba Krupasindhu Das in the court of the subordinate judge of Dhenkanal.[39] Dinabandhu Das, the appellant, sued Krupasindhu for constructing a building and a *homa mandap* (a platform for the performance of fire sacrifice) within the Gadi compound. He pleaded that these buildings be demolished and asked for a permanent injunction against the raising of new ones by Krupasindhu. The verdict, unfortunately, is missing from the records. What is known, however, is that this verdict failed to resolve the problem. The dispute dragged on as members of both groups, individually and collectively, filed innumerable appeals and counter-appeals. From the court of the subordinate judge the dispute moved to the Cuttack High Court. The higher court eventually decreed that the matter fell within the jurisdiction of the Commissioner of Endowments, Orissa.[40] The entire process of litigation was accompanied by attempts at an amicable out-of-court settlement. These efforts involved arbitrators, interventions by the literati and politicians who sought to act as mediators, and the framing of schemes for the construction of a managing committee for Mahimagadi. The officials, intellectuals and politicians could not resolve the dispute. It was difficult to dispense with the law courts.

The intervention of the judicial machinery of the State helped to shape the sect's subsequent development. The requirements and resources of legal processes became crucial to the reworking of the norms and practices of Mahima Dharma. Indeed, the arguments of the lawyers of both groups of *sanyasis* and the awards and orders of judges ruled out methods of negotiation. The insistence of law courts on the collection of evidence and the display of proof prompted the ascetics, already convinced of the efficacy of written texts, to produce their own canonical formal histories of the sect. The lead, once again, was taken by Biswanath Baba. His *Satya Mahima*

Dharmara Itihasa appeared in 1935.[41] It gave the Mahima Dharmis an authentic past and a new present and accorded the Guru the dignity of chronology, temporality and a new historicity. The Guru, who had stood beyond history, was now situated in time and tradition. The *Itihasa* further consolidated Biswanath Baba's position as the leader of the faith.

Itihasa

The opening passage of *Satya Mahima Dharmara Itihasa* informed the reader that before Biswanath Baba embarked on the project of writing a history of the sect, several persons had taken up the task but had failed.[42] The failure had only one explanation: the Guru had not willed them to succeed. Clearly, Biswanath Baba was endowed with the *aśirvad* (blessing) of the Guru. He was also armed with the trust of the Mahima Dharmis. Finally, prominent citizens of Orissa, teachers of the prestigious Ravenshaw College at Cuttack, had urged him to take up the venture.[43] The credentials of the author stood established.

The *Itihasa* moved on to authenticate its contents. Fully subscribing to the view that 'historical' narratives have to be true, the *Itihasa* laid claim to a distinct standard of truth by premising its veracity on the divinity of the founder. The very content of the text made it inherently true. So much so, that the beginning of a new era, the age of Mahima (*Mahimabda*), was stated to begin in 1826, when Mahima Swami made his appearance in Orissa in the human form of an ascetic. 1826 heralded the beginning of the faith and a new temporality for its followers in multiple ways. It embodied the beginning of sacred chronological time, since the true faith which the divine founder was to preach would fundamentally guide and structure the life of the true devotees.[44]

At the same time, arguments in the text served to establish Mahima Swami as god incarnate. Simultaneously drawing upon faith and reason, Biswanath Baba's text acceded to and exceeded the concerns of rational historiography. It proffered a discrete blend of western history and the Indian tradition of *itihasa-purana*.[45] This made the *Itihasa* amenable to varied perceptions, even as the written form froze fluid events in time, presented a singular history by gathering multiple parts unto itself, often ruling out divergent and conflicting voices.

Biswanath Baba indicated that the material for the text — which described the life, activities and teachings of Mahima Swami — had been collated from the author's long association and detailed discussions with the first line of self-realized renouncers, the direct disciples and constant companions of Mahima Swami. This dialogue had cleared all doubts and ambiguities relating to the *nishkama leela*[46] (unattached sport) of the Prabhu.[47] These ascetics were also the source of information about the period that followed the death of the founder: the meeting convened after the Swami's death which took the decision of starting the Mahimagadi, and the functioning of the Gadi over the next several decades. Finally, Biswanath Baba was not a mere observer but an active participant in the affairs of the Gadi after the time of the *siddhas*. The *Itihasa* was an authentic record of what had been witnessed and experienced by the renouncers and lay followers of Mahima Dharma.[48]

This history took as its major task a description of the Swami's *nishkama leela* on earth: it highlighted his miraculous powers and his charismatic personality which overwhelmed all, high and low. Mahima Swami's *leela* was self-willed: but it was performed after the repeated entreaties of saints and pious beings and gods to re-establish *satya dharma* in the world.[49] The Swami, as *prabuddha narayana*, came down to earth, spent several years in self-meditation on top of Kailash and went down to the foothills of the Himalayas. There he commanded the *siddhas* to take birth again. They became the first initiates of *satya dharma*.[50] The Lord decided to preach in Orissa: the faith was to spread from there for the welfare of humankind.[51] All this involved a particular construction of the past and the present, a play with symbols embedded in diverse traditions of Hinduism. The Dharma had been founded by an immaculately conceived — *ajoni sambhuta* (one not born out of a womb) — incarnation of the Absolute; the *siddhas* of the Nath tradition were its first disciples; the human form of the *ajoni sambhuta* was *prabuddha narayana* (all-knowing Vishnu); Kailash, the abode of Shiva/Mahadeva, was the site of meditation of this incarnation of the Absolute. The figure of Mahima Swami was fashioned out of elements of the Vedantic, Vaishnavite and Saivite traditions within Hinduism. The *satya dharma* preached by Mahima Swami was the essence of *sanatan* (eternal) Hindu *dharma*. The new faith actually was pristine Hinduism as it existed before the advent of Kali Yuga.

The blending of distinct traditions of Hinduism present in the preachings of Mahima Swami and the compositions of Bhima Bhoi continue in Biswanath Baba. What is significant by its absence is the easy mix of 'high' and 'low', 'classical' and 'popular' trends of thought. The move is toward a 'modern' reformulation of the faith within the world of Brahmanical Hinduism. And, in following this track, Biswanath Baba came remarkably close to the elite reformers of mid and late nineteenth century and the Hindu nationalists of late twentieth century India. Just as they had sought to make Hinduism rational and manageable by declaring all its disturbing practices as later aberrations and posited an eternal Hinduism with an unchanging essence, Biswanath Baba redefined a radical faith which started its career by marking its difference from high Hinduism as 'pure' *sanatan* Hinduism unsoiled by the sins of Kali.

The *Itihasa* codified the teachings of the Swami and demarcated the different sets of rules he had established for the two categories of adherents, lay followers and ascetics. The instructions had initially been conveyed to Govinda Baba and were subsequently rehearsed before other disciples at different times in several places. The *Itihasa* had now brought them together for the benefit of followers and other readers.[52] The *gruhi*s were instructed to stick to their stations in life, warned against greed, falsity and immoral behaviour, and instructed to pray to the Lord in complete devotion at the *brahma muhurtas* of sunrise and sunset. They were also enjoined to keep good company and to show respect to the renouncers of Mahima Dharma. And as for life-cycle rituals, the *Itihasa* made it clear that the rites of passage had an important role in the lives of lay disciples. It prescribed detailed norms for the observance of birth and death impurities which bore a close resemblance to the orthopraxy of Brahmanical Hinduism.[53]

The monastic order had three layers. The lowest rung was made up of *bairagis* who had just renounced the world. They were to serve the *sanyasis*, stay on the path of renunciation, acquire knowledge of scriptures and develop their powers of meditation. The *apara sanyasis*, who constituted the intermediate layer, were obliged at each step to demonstrate their devotion to the *siddha para sanyasis*. Their minds had to be calm. These measures allowed them to learn the scriptures and understand the full import of the Guru's teachings. All this was supervised by the *para sanyasis*, their teachers and guides, who also decided on their eventual elevation to the rank of the *siddhas*. The *para sanyasis*, who represented the highest mode of being, were warned of the dangers of unjustly exploiting their superior status. They were to remain absolutely detached from all passions, aspirations and acquisitive instincts: they were prohibited from accumulating money, building their own *ashramas* and living there permanently as gurus or *mahantas*, and from starting their own *parampara*s (lineage). Their task was to teach the people to pray to the one and only Guru, the Absolute. Even as the *Itihasa* reinforced hierarchy and gradation it stated that all members of an order were equal; they were asked to display mutual respect and to honour each other.[54] Biswanath Baba's canonical text, in reiterating Mahima Swami's insistence on detachment, also decried the attempts of the Kaupindharis to create a rival community.

The *Itihasa* seized upon the decision to construct the *samadhi* of Mahima Swami as an act which fulfilled the wish of the Guru.[55] Anam Das Baba, a Balkaldhari sage, had a vision of the finished temple in his dreams: it was to be 12 cubits high, adorned with a seven-hooded snake on top and surrounded by four boundary walls.[56] The self-realized ascetics were to perform *niti* there by turns and congregate every evening for *nam bhajan*.[57] It was at the explicit desire of the Supreme Lord that Nanda Baba offered the first services at the *samadhi mandir*.[58] All this is significant. The vision of the temple, the right to offer ritual service and the order of precedence in the offering of the first service, all lay with Balkaldharis.[59] The present weighed heavily on the past.

We may recall here that it was Nanda Baba who had granted *balkal* to 56 sanyasis and stirred the dissension in the *samaj*. Was the Lord's desire that Nanda Baba offer the first service at the memorial an expression of the special place of the ascetic within Mahima Dharma? Did not the command prime and prepare Nanda Baba to initiate the second line of Balkaldharis? Was it then possible to doubt the veracity of the *śunya bani/adeś* mentioned in the *Pratipadaka* — that impelled Nanda Baba to give some Kaupindhari sanyasis the gift of *balkal*? The ground had been prepared. The grant of *balkal* to the 56 sanyasis was treated in the text as an ordinary incident.[60] One paragraph, devoid of rhetorical flourishes, referred to the message from void as a matter of course and went on to list the names of the new initiates. There was not even a hint at disagreement and dissension. Where, indeed, was the need? The preceptor himself had initiated the process of gradation and promotion among the renouncers. The reordered past legitimated the present.

The superior status and spiritual achievements of the Balkaldharis had put them in charge of the Mahima Gadi. They were entrusted with the supervision and management of the memorial, they alone had the right of entry to the inner sanctum of the *gadi mandir* and the *śunya mandir*, and they controlled the conduct of prayers and services. The task of the Kaupindharis, on the other hand, was to sweep and clean the outer compound. As for the inner compound, they could stand near the gate and supply the provisions needed for *niti* to the Balkaldharis. The Kaupindharis were enjoined to accept the self-realized *babas* (renouncers) as their spiritual guides and to honor and follow their preceptor's wishes and dictates in their day-to-day lives.[61] All this was implicit in their designation of *dasa* (servant). The *Itihasa* had firmly etched the norms and hierarchies of the Mahima Dharma *samaj*.

Decrees

The authoritative mode of inscription of the text meant that the Oriya literati came to accept it as an authentic history of the sect.[62] What is more important, it became the point of reference for practitioners of law. The court accorded the written *Itihasa* a superior position as evidence than it gave the oral testimony of witnesses. The Balkaldharis gained an edge over the Kaupindharis. This is evident in the first important award, dated 11 December 1947, found in the court records.[63] The award began by expressing the arbitrators' concern at the 'long-standing' disputes between the two groups at the Joranda Alekh Gadi and voiced their eagerness to resolve it, as the 'split' stood 'as an impediment to the progress of the religious order'.[64] The renouncers themselves were 'anxious to bring about peace and consolidation between them'. With this end in view, Ram Chandra Das on behalf of the Balkaldharis and Dharmananda Das on behalf of the Kaupindharis signed an agreement on 20 March 1947: all disputes were referred to the arbitrators and both parties agreed to abide by their award. The arbitrators in turn were satisfied that Ram Chandra Das and Dharmananda Das were proper representatives of their groups. The presence of lawyers and witnesses was sought both at the time of the agreement and at all stages of the hearing. The hearing commenced on 26 October 1947 and went on every day. The arguments of both sides were heard at length and 'due consideration' was given to their statements and to the 'evidence' they adduced. The arbitrators stated that they had taken great care to frame a just and proper award.[65]

The first clause vested sole authority over all property in the Mahima Gadi. This included 'all structures that exist or may be built on the lands belonging to the Gadi'; 'all structures built or to be built anywhere else'; and 'any other property that might have been or be acquired' by any of the Mahima Dharmi sanyasis. It further stated, 'No sanyasis should have any personal interest in the rights vested in the Gadi'. The ascetics were also forbidden to construct 'any separate Sunya Mandir, Dhuni Mandir or Gurupitha Gadi anywhere near or within the Joranda Math Compound'. If this was a clear warning to the Kaupindharis, their existing buildings and others which they had planned to construct were also declared illegal. The award ruled against the presence of rival institutions within the Gadi complex.

The prohibition on self-acquisition by *sanyasis* was stated to be 'one of the cardinal principles of Mahima Dharma'. The ascetics were permitted to collect *bhiksha* to meet emergencies: but they were not allowed to retain more than five rupees for themselves; the remainder was to be the property of the Gadi. At the same time, they were granted the right to 'make certain collections for purposes of Dharmasalas (lodging houses for pilgrims) to be erected for public purposes', which in turn would be the property of the Gadi. The Gadi was also to inherit the properties, if any, of all the *para* and *apara sanyasis* on their death: 'There can be no claim of personal inheritance or inheritance by disciples.'

The establishment of the *samadhi* — the Mahima Gadi — as the central institution of Mahima Dharma was complete. The process which had begun after the death of Mahima Swami had reached its culmination through the intervention of legal procedures. The Mahima Gadi had replaced the Guru as the prime authority. It managed the affairs of the faith and gave guidance to the adherents of the faith. The Gadi, propped up and legitimated by the award, became the sole owner of all properties that the ascetics of Mahima Dharma had acquired and would acquire in the future.

There were strong injunctions against the accumulation of wealth by individual members, but there was no ceiling on the extent of the Gadi's possessions. The ascetics were in fact encouraged 'to make certain collections' for public purposes. This was a consequence of the establishment of Mahima Dharma as an institutionalized monastic order. From the late 1870s the Dharma had gradually moved from practising absolute and complete detachment towards property to controlling and regulating the acquisitive tendencies of its members. The award formally recognized that property had become a critical contentious issue among the renouncers of Mahima Dharma.

The use in the award of the terms *para* and *apara*, first introduced in the *Pratipadaka*, revealed an uncritical acceptance of the categories introduced by Biswanath Baba. The primacy and the privileged position of the Balkaldharis was clearly recognized and inscribed in the award: 'Para sanyasis are exclusively held to be entitled to offer service at the Ashram of the Gadi Mandir to which none other should have access, but the other sanyasis are not to be debarred from rendering such assistance in services as they are carrying on at present'. The *para sanyasis* were, of course, the Balkaldharis; the Kaupindharis, the stragglers, were deemed the 'other sanyasis'. Similarly the injunction against the construction of 'any Sunya Mandir, Dhuni Mandir or Gurupitha Gadi' within or near the Joranda Math compound and the building of *tungis* or residences 'within 300 feet from the compound walls of the present Gadi Mandir' reiterated the claims of the Balkaldharis. The parallel contending constructions within 300 feet of the Gadi compound had been the cause of discord between Kripasindhu and Dinabandhu, Kaupindharis and Balkaldharis: the arbitrators decided the issue in favour of Dinabandhu's group in unequivocal terms. Biswanath Baba's texts, particularly the *Itihasa,* had succeeded in projecting the Balkaldharis as the true representatives of Mahima Dharma. The award underwrote the legitimacy of the norms, rules and practices developed by the Balkaldharis and gave unqualified support to their system of gradation, promotion and hierarchy within Mahima Dharma.

The other conditions of the award clarified and expanded on the stand of the arbitrators. All the *para sanyasis* were to have an equal status among themselves: they were 'entitled to reciprocal Saran Manya'. The story of the relations between *para* and *apara sanyasis* was a little different: 'We recommend that latter should show Saran Manya to the former and this should grow up as a practice by mutual consent'.

It is striking how lawyers, judges and arbitrators, in the course of their involvement with the dispute among the ascetics of Mahima Dharma, increasingly assumed the responsibility of defining and interpreting the nature and the rules of the faith. In this case the arbitrators recommended that a gesture of respect to the *para sanyasis* 'should grow up as a practice'. They went further when they stated:

> Future initiation of Para sanyasi status shall be subject to the following conditions:
>
> 1. The Apara sanyasi must have at least seven years' practice as an Apara sanyasi.
> 2. He must be versed in all the existing books of Mahima Dharma.
> 3. The opinion of the majority of Para sanyasis present at the annual congregation of Magha Purnima should be collected secretly in a process of ballot voting.
>
> As to initiation to Apara sanyasi status, a Bairagi must have seven years' practice as a First initiate and should have besides a fair standard of knowledge about Mahima Dharma.
>
> No initiation from one status to another except made in the aforesaid manner in the annual congregation at Gadi shall be valid and recognised.

The shift from one grade to another was made conditional upon rigid frames of time. Candidates for promotion were to be judged on the basis of a set standard: knowledge of 'all the existing books on Mahima Dharma' for *apara sanyasis* aspiring to be *para sanyasis*; and 'a fair standard of knowledge about Mahima Dharma' for the *bairagis* applying for *apara sanyasi* status. The system of gradation and promotion was not merely defined in clear terms, it was given the fixity of formal examinations. The practitioners of law colluded with and went beyond the ascetics to reform Mahima Dharma and provide it with a 'rational' footing.

The emphasis on textual knowledge highlights the mutation that the sect had undergone since the time of Mahima Swami. The preceptor had left no written records. He had endowed Bhima Bhoi with the gift of poetry for the propagation of his ideas and had sent scribes to the blind bard to note down his inspired utterances. Tenets and beliefs of the faith were disseminated through joint singing and 'reading' of Bhima Bhoi's lyrical creations. During Mahima Swami's lifetime and for a long time thereafter, they were the only written texts of the faith. The cultural world of Mahima Swami and Bhima Bhoi was grounded in the matrix of orality. The circulation and popularity of Bhima Bhoi's verses were premised on their oral recital and performance in the tradition of early Oriya texts. In less than a century the power of writing had triumphed over orality. The urban literati had become an important and influential support base for Mahima Dharma. Only a few became followers of the faith. The majority worked as advisors, consultants and mediators. They codified — and could create anew — the rules, rituals and practices of the faith. The fixity of the written form informed the regulations of Mahima Dharma.

After setting out detailed instructions on various aspects of the faith, the arbitrators entrusted Baba Dharmananda Das, Baba Biswanath Das and Baba Dinabandhu Das with the formulation of 'a code of rules not inconsistent with the provisions' of the award. This code was 'to be followed by the Mahima Dharmis of different status. If the aforesaid persons cannot come to an agreed solution on any particular issue, they shall be referred to the Board of Arbitrators for final decision'. The representatives of the neutral judiciary, as the overall arbiter in charge of the smooth functioning of 'religion', had taken over the initiative from the *sanyasis*, who were now being 'entrusted' with the authority to frame rules. The final decision, in case of disagreement on any issue, rested with the Board of Arbitrators. The members of the Board also had the authority, during an interim period of one year, to 'individually or collectively visit the Mahima institution, examine the accounts and look into the actual administration to assess the practicability of the present arrangement', and issue directions to the 'members of the parties to the arbitration on matters dealt with by them'. Any recalcitrance was to be met with 'forfeiture of all or any right of the non-observants to the Mahima Gadi'. As a corollary the arbitrators reserved the right to punish disobedient members of the faith. The ascetics who had managed the affairs at Mahima Gadi were no longer the decision-makers:

their role had been appropriated by the Board of Arbitrators.[66] The lack of unanimity regarding the running of Mahima Dharma and the intervention of law courts and arbitrators to settle matters had led the renouncers to forfeit, at least on paper, their rights of leadership and decision-making. In actual practice they often did not follow the dictates of the award.

The choice of lawyers as arbitrators demonstrated the sanyasis' preference for and faith in legal practitioners and underscored the critical presence of the state in the life of the community. The lawyers in turn applied themselves to their task with great zeal and sought to monopolize the authority of settling all disputes and differences among the Mahima Dharmi *sanyasis*. Their decision on all these matters was to be 'binding and conclusive'. The ascetics, however, had their own uses for the decrees of lawyers and arbitrators.

Other Histories

The Kaupindhari reply to the strategies of the rival order, particularly to Biswanath Baba's *Satya Mahima Dharmara Itihasa*, took the form of Mahindra Baba's *Satya Mahima Dharmara Sankshipta Itihasa*, which was published in 1958.[67] This marked the culmination of a series of measures adopted by the Kaupindharis to organize and strengthen their own *samaj*. In the 1950s energetic ascetics such as Mahindra Baba and Kasinath Baba assumed the leadership of the Kaupindharis. The struggle against the Balkaldharis was now taken up with renewed vigour. The Kaupindhari *samaj* became more tightly organized: it secured its identity and began to counteract the moves of the Balkaldharis. The Kaupindhari Mahima Samaj Satya Mahima Dharma Alochana o Prachar Sabha was set up, meetings were organized, and the tasks of propagation of the faith and proselytization were attended to in earnest.[68] Mahindra Baba and Kasinath Baba participated in the *Biśwa Dharma Sammelan* (World Religious Conference) held at Delhi in 1955 as representatives of Mahima Dharma. Mahindra Baba's speech was published in a booklet, *Biśwa Kalyan Pathe Satya Mahima Dharma*.[69] The Kaupindhari *samaj* asserted itself by attending to a sharp clarification of its difference with the *apara sanyasis* of the Balkaldhari *samaj*. The conventional *kaupin* (waistcloth) was replaced by a wider and longer piece of cloth which reached the knees and a *chadar* (piece of cloth), which covered the upper body. Similarly, the group played within the tenets of Mahima Dharma by identifying Bhima Bhoi's *ekakshara* (one/non-dual letter) with *omkar*, the first sound of Hinduism.

The appearance of Mahindra Baba's *Satya Mahima Dharma Sankshipta*

Itihasa in 1958 signalled the coming of age of the Kaupindhari *samaj*. The introduction to the text drew attention to the crucial role played by history in the existence of *samaj* and *jati* (nation).[70] An *itihasa* which recorded the life and deeds of *yogeśwara* (lord of yoga) Mahima Prabhu was of vital importance to the followers of the faith: a source of inspiration in times of distress, which enabled them to hold steadfast to the path of *satya dharma*. At the same time, Biswanath Baba's *Pratipadaka* and *Itihasa* and a host of other texts published until the 1950s had not fulfilled the expectations of the devotees. These texts lacked substantial and authoritative discussions of the faith, they were devoid of distinction, and their statements often contradicted the fundamental principles of the Dharma.[71] Mahindra Baba's short *Itihasa* filled these gaps and redressed the imbalance.

The account of Mahima Swami, from the moment of his appearance in Orissa in 1826 through to the time he started preaching the faith after a long meditation of 36 years, closely followed Biswanath Baba's *Itihasa*. At the same time there were significant variations. Mahima Swami was described as *ajoni-sambhuta* and *yogeśwara* ; but the term *iśwara purush* was left out. When he gained repute as Dhulia Gosain his garment was a *gairik kaupin* (a saffron waistcloth).[72] These variations tallied with Bhima Bhoi's description of the Swami in *Stuti Chintamoni*. At the age of four Bhima Bhoi had come across an ascetic travelling through villages. He wore a *kasa-kaupin* and his arms bore the signs of a *śankha* (conch) and *chakra* (disc).[73] We have noted that this ascetic is widely identified as Mahima Swami, the future Guru of Bhima Bhoi. Equally the *Sankshipta Itihasa* forgot to mention that the Guru started wearing *balkal* instead of *kaupin* when he started preaching. Was this a gentle reminder that there was little to distinguish between these garments? The details rehearsed by Mahindra Baba were part of a pattern.

If the text hinted that Mahima Swami's first disciple, Govinda Baba, was given *balkal*, it also provided an interesting vignette relating to the beginning of the Kaupindhari order which was absent in Biswanath Baba's *Itihasa*.[74] One day Nrusingha Baba, the second disciple of the Swami, planted a cotton tree in the Malbaharpur *ashrama* and made it produce cotton, from which he spun yarn and wove a white flag. The flag was hoisted on top of the *dhuni mandir* as *patit paban bana* (the flag of the redeemer of the fallen). When the matter was brought to the Guru's notice he reprimanded Nrusingha Baba for engaging in meaningless display. True faith was not to be propagated through magic and miracles — the instruments of lesser beings. He ordered Nrusingha Baba to transform the white flag into a *gairik kaupin* (saffron waistcloth), use it as his garment, and join the services at the *dhuni mandir*. Nrusingha Baba obeyed the Guru's order, discarded his *balkal* and started wearing *kaupin*. The twist to this tale was crucial: a Balkaldhari *sanyasi* gave up his *balkal* and adopted the *kaupin* as his mode of dress to honour the wishes of the Prabhu. It underscored the irrelevance of gradation among *sanyasis* and highlighted the reciprocal and interchangeable basis of the two orders.

A second vignette clinched the argument. Soon after the ascetics started wearing *kaupin*, squabbles arose between the Balkaldharis and the Kaupindharis regarding their relative status. The Balkaldharis claimed to be superior on the ground that they had the same *bana* (garment) as the Guru; the Kaupindharis reminded them that waistcloth was the Prabhu's *adi bana* (first/original garment) which made both garments equal. The matter reached the master. He was pained to see his followers bicker over such trivial issues. The *bhek* (dress), he said, was only an external symbol: a *sanyasi*'s status was to be judged by the quality of his *sadhana*; the renouncers were reminded that *paat* (cloth) and *pat* (bark) were the same.[75] The ascetics rejoiced over the verdict of the founder, forgot their differences and joined forces to propagate the faith. Bhima Bhoi had echoed the same sentiment in his *Brahma Nirupana Gita*: 'Adimahima's bana is *patita paban*, his *bana* is dress made from yarn; Maha Mahima's *bana* is the bark of a tree.'[76] Did all this not settle the issue conclusively?

The rules for initiation into the monastic order were unambiguous: one who desired to become an ascetic had to renounce the world, live with a *sanyasi* and develop his capacity for meditation, concentration and spiritual pursuits — *sadhan-bhajan* (meditation-prayer) — before seeking initiation. After the initiation his status as a Balkaldhari or Kaupindhari depended on the order of his preceptor: he was to wear a *kaupin* if the guru was a Kaupindhari and a *balkal* if he was a Balkaldhari.[77] The garment and the renouncer's status became fixed for life. The system of gradation and promotion among the ascetics was an unjust innovation of the second line of Balkaldharis. They were men of 'audacious character' (*ugra svabhav*) who had compelled their guru to grant them *balkal* and had relegated their equals, the other Kaupindharis, to a subordinate position. They had taken possession of the Gadi by force and had not hesitated to resort to law courts in order to evict Krupasindhu, a senior ascetic of their own order, from his separate living space within the Gadi compound. This was because Krupasindhu had refused to recognize the new wearers of *balkal*.[78] At the same time the text noted with relish that the devious ways of the Balkaldharis had failed to bring them success.[79]

The Kaupindharis had faced their fair share of problems. Their *samaj* had gone through a grave crisis when a Balkaldhari, in the guise of a friend, had attempted to align the *samaj* to that of the rival order. The Kaupindhari community had survived the threat. It reconstituted itself in 1953 and initiated the tasks of efficient management, the propagation of its faith and the extension of its support base. Since that time the Kaupindhari *samaj* had shown unmistakable signs of growth and development.[80] The triumph of Kaupindhari efforts to establish a separate order was proudly proclaimed. The split between the two orders was not perceived as an impediment to the growth of the Dharma. Instead the coming into being of rival group was hailed as the victory of right over wrong. The noble teachings of the founder had vanquished their subsequent misinterpretations.

Mahindra Baba's abridged *Itihasa* made it clear that the wrong practices of the Balkaldharis made any agreement with them impossible and turned the endeavours of law courts and arbitrators into caricature and parody. These deviations were presented in the form of a manifesto:

1. The practice of the new Balkaldharis to regard living beings rather than the Supreme Being as Brahma.
2. The practice of *śaranamanya*, which disregarded barriers of age and respectability.
3. The rejection of *ekakshara omkar*.
4. The practice of changing over from *kaupin* to *balkal*.
5. The use of *apara* and *para* in place of older terms.
6. The refusal to allow the Kaupindharis to perform *nitis* at the Gadi.
7. The resistance to an equal representation of the two *samajas* in the Mahima Dharma Parichalana and Prachar Samiti.[81]

The self-assertion of the Kaupindharis and its inscription in a text were an effective mode of intervention. With this assertion the dispute entered a new phase. There was a shift in the issues. The debate was no longer over whether it was possible or permissible for a separate Kaupindhari *samaj* to exist, it was over the status of Kaupindharis and their role in the management of the Gadi. The existence of the Kaupindhari *samaj* was accepted as an established fact. Further issues were premised upon it. The Kaupindhari point of view was granted recognition by the judges who handled the dispute. They eventually decreed that the matter fell within the jurisdiction of the Commissioner of Religious Endowments.[82] In 1966 these judges[83] handed over a comprehensive and well-chalked-out program to the Commissioner to help him prepare a scheme for the management of the Gadi.[84] A suitable scheme, in the opinion of the judges, required a careful consideration of three important points: Who were the ascetics who formed the Kaupindhari *samaj*? Was the Kaupindhari *samaj* a separate institution or was it to be treated as a part of the Balkaldhari *samaj* in which Balkaldharis were the be all and end all? If the Kaupindhari *samaj* was indeed a separate order, what status was it to be given in the proposed scheme for the better administration of the Gadi?

The judges turned to the history of Mahima Dharma since its inception to answer these questions. The Dharma was declared 'a part of the Vedic Sanatan Dharma in which idolatry has been discarded. The mantra is Ekakshara i.e., Omkar.' The judges, once again the interpreters of the faith, apart from locating Mahima Dharma in a linear history of religion as a part of Vedic *sanatan dharma*, presented Mahindra Baba's identification of *ekakshara* with *omkar* as an axiomatic truth.[85] Never mind that the identification of *ekakshara* with *omkar* engendered confusion in the Kaupindhari *samaj* and was eventually rejected by its members. Mahima Swami's garb, the judges claimed, consisted both of 'scarfs of cotton' and 'barks of Kumbhi tree': 'He gave balkal to 91 and kaupin to 68 sanyasis of whom 64 and 34 became siddhas respectively.' In the legally ordered past of Mahima Dharma it was during the lifetime of the founder that parallel orders had come into being. The different orders did not reflect any desire to create superior and inferior grades of renouncers on the part of the founder, since the status of an ascetic could only be achieved by meditation or self-realization. It came about rather because Mahima Prabhu had worn both the *kaupin* and the *balkal*.[86] The change of Mahima Swami's dress from cloth to bark when he started preaching was left out of the picture. This conveyed the impression that the founder picked up the *balkal* and *kaupin* alternately and at his will as his garb. The arguments of the judges emphasized the superfluity of the garment as a standard of assessment and, as a corollary, underscored the importance of meditation and self-realization as the real yardstick of the worth of an ascetic.

We have seen that Bhima Bhoi's devotion had been supplanted by Biswanath Baba's *jñana-bhakti* (knowledge-devotion) as the true path of Mahima Dharma. Now Mahindra Baba transformed this path further into *sadhana-bhakti-marga* (the path of meditation-devotion). This is significant because it brought back yoga centrally into the path of meditation, the palpable presence of which we have noted in the works of Bhima Bhoi. The primacy accorded to *sadhana* was evident, for instance, in the use of a new attribute, *yogeśwara*, for the founder. The judges incorporated Mahindra Baba's concerns in their arguments. They also supported his assertion that the procedure of promotion of *sanyasis* was 'an innovation of later days ... laid down by Baba Biswanath Das'.[87] The judges concluded that 'the

Kaupindhari sanyasis are equal in status with the Balkaldhari sanyasis of their level. They also did niti at the first bedha'.[88] The *sanyasis* 'who wear kaupin and serve the Balkaldharis are not representatives of the Kaupindhari Samaj, nor are they equal in rank. They are attendant sanyasis of the Balkaldharis who have created them since the time of the dispute between the two orders.'[89] This history of the faith was clear that the two orders were equal and complementary. Their separate and independent existence went back to the time of the founder. All attempts to lump them together as one hierarchically graded group were unjust impositions. The judges cautioned posterity to guard against 'the unfair domination of one party by another party.'[90]

The awards of the arbitrators and the arguments of the judges demonstrate the centrality of the legal process in the evolution of Mahima Dharma in the course of the twentieth century. Disagreements over the interpretation of the founder's teachings and the formation, organization and supervision of the Mahima Dharmi *samaj* came to be formalized in a proper legal battle. Two groups of renouncers, with divergent facts and arguments, became 'contending parties'. Judges and lawyers as arbitrators became decision-makers and came to speak for Mahima Dharma. The idiom of law and legal procedures effected a final breach between the two groups. There was a crystallization of two separate *samajas* with rigid and definite rules. In a bid to coordinate and supervise these orders and claim adherence from their followers, Parichalana Samitis were set up, presidents and secretaries elected. 'Management' of the Gadi gained precedence over the performance of ritual services at the memorial. The *sanyasis* ceased to talk about unity. They became advocates of peaceful coexistence. All this and more — new turns, fresh shifts — was to be seen in the depositions of the renouncers before the Commissioner of Religious Endowments that were made in 1961 and 1962.

Witnesses

My account begins with the deposition of Biswanath Baba, the controversial leader of the Balkaldhari *samaj* and a key figure in the dispute.[91] His statements were simple and clear. Mahima Dharma was a part of *sanatan* Hindu Dharma which incorporated, as its most important feature, 'Ek Advitiya Param Brahmanka Upasana' (worship of the one, non-dual Brahma), and practised non-violence, truth and celibacy. Mahima Swami had brought lay disciples and renouncers into the fold of the Dharma. He had categorized them into different orders and defined their respective positions. The two major divisions were into *gruhis* and *sanyasis*. The *sanyasis* in turn were hierarchically graded. A renouncer began as a *tyagi/bairagi*, rose to the status of an *apara sanyasi* and eventually, as he progressed spiritually, became a *para sanyasi*. During cross-examination, Biswanath Baba admitted that although the Balkaldharis had enjoyed a superior status since the time of the founder, the terms *para* and *apara* came into circulation with the publication of texts of Mahima Dharma in the 1930s.[92]

After the death of Mahima Swami the Balkaldharis started ritual services at the Gadi in accordance with the founder's instructions. They were assisted by the Kaupindharis. The problems within Mahima Dharma were rooted in the misdemeanour of Krupasindhu: he misused the offerings of money, *ghee* (clarified butter) and other objects made by lay disciples and created trouble when the other Babas objected to these practices.[93] Kripasindhu left the Gadi for several years and on his return started living separately within 300 feet of the Gadi compound. This was in stark violation of the Guru's orders. The Babas were compelled to find a way out of the impasse. They had to turn to litigation.

Mahindra Das, Biswanath Baba affirmed, was aligned with their group until a few years earlier, when he left Joranda because of a difference of opinion with his guru. He went to western Orissa and came into contact with Arya Samajis. This encounter resulted in his adoption of *om* as a *mantra* (incantation) of Mahima Dharma. On his return Mahindra Das faced severe criticism from the Balkaldharis, who refused to recognize *om* as a *mantra* of the faith. Mahindra Das joined the followers of Kripasindhu, who formed a rival group. 'They started a Kaupindhari samaj, printed books with om. All this is against Mahima Dharma'.[94] In his cross-examination Biswanath Baba admitted that Bhima Bhoi had used *omkar* at one or two places in his writings but added, 'our *samaj* cannot accept it.' Moreover, the works of Bhima Bhoi were 'not taken as books laying down our regulations or rules of conduct but they are accepted as books of religious worship along with the others'.[95] I shall return to the analysis of this deposition a little later.

The deposition of Brundaban Das, a leading member of the Kaupindhari *samaj*, began with a reiteration of the group's claim that there was no hierarchical difference between the Balkaldharis and the Kaupindharis. He pointed to the grant of *balkal* to 56 sanyasis in 1931 as the main cause of disharmony between the two groups. This act did not have the sanction of *guru-ajña* (order of the master). He lamented the damage to Mahima Dharma caused by the struggle between the ascetics and urged the Commissioner to formulate a proper scheme of management to help restore the faith to its earlier fame and glory. The ideal scheme, Brundaban Das felt, would be to divide the management of the Gadi for six months every year between the two *samajas*. All this was straightforward. However, in terms of legal procedure, Brundaban Das's cross-examination revealed uncertainties and ambivalence. He qualified his own statement that Mahima Dharma was a part of Hindu religion when he stated, 'I can't understand what Hindu religion is.'[96] Similarly, he was not quite clear about the position of *omkar* in the belief-structure of the Kaupindharis: 'We were not worshipping Omkar Mantra but were reading Bhima Bhoi's bhajan where omkar finds place. It is not a tap (worship). None of us do japa'.[97] Finally, he ended up contradicting the Kaupindhari assertion of the equality of all ascetics. 'According to the original Dharma which was in vogue before the difference, only Babas wearing balkal were doing puja and those wearing kaupin were doing cleaning, sweeping, etc. Now the Kaupindharis of our camp are not associating with the original Gadi. The Balkalis have got their own Kaupindharis who work.'[98]

A comparison of the two depositions makes for an interesting exercise, a lens to understand Mahima Dharma. Biswanath Baba, the vanguard of a new leadership and the author of *Pratipadaka* and *Itihasa*, had no hesitation in declaring that Mahima Dharma was a part of eternal Hindu Dharma. This is what the Balkaldharis, their advisors and followers had come to believe and propagate. Brundaban Baba was not so definite. He had witnessed a time when the association of the faith with Hindu Dharma was either tendentious or absent. The thought and writing of Bhima Bhoi, followed closely by Brundaban Baba, ruled out a close identification of Mahima Dharma with Hinduism. Biswanath Baba had moved beyond Bhima Bhoi: he was a self-realized renouncer, while Bhima Bhoi had been only a householder disciple. Biswanath Baba had no qualms in dismissing Bhima Bhoi's statements as unacceptable when they did not conform to the new rules and regulations formulated by his group. He asserted that the works of Bhima Bhoi were no longer 'taken as books laying down our regulations or rules of conduct but they are accepted as books of religious worship along with the others'. Biswanath Baba's confidence and directness gave proof of his place as the key interpreter of the Dharma and the leader of a sect which had clearly entered a new phase of development. In this phase one confident, authoritative voice had come to dominate; it had subdued multiple voices and overcome the plurality of views. The Baba's statements were also an index of his familiarity with law courts and his ease with legal procedures. He had the skill to present his arguments in direct, bold and precise terms. Questioning and cross-examination, lawyers and judges, did not unnerve him.

Brundaban Das, on the other hand, was used to less structured modes of dispute resolution. He was capable of participating in discussions with authority but was not adept at the art of answering questions in the blunt and fixed categories of clear affirmative and a firm denial.[99] His many hesitations and inconsistencies exhibited a profound unease with the method of dispute settlement followed in the arbitrating agency of the law courts. The shifts and turns, the ambiguities and difficulties, were marks of the interplay of the old and new within a faith in transition.

Contradictions did not find a place in Narendra Baba's deposition.[100] He was an 80-year-old Kaupindhari *sadhu* who had joined the *samaj* in his fifteenth year. Narendra Baba was certain that he would never wear *balkal*; there was no *guru-ajña* for it. In his view the Kaupindhari Samaj, which had existed all along, had fallen out with the Balkaldharis because the other order did not 'obey the Bhima Bhoi Grantha, Alekh Ekakshari Mantra'. The Balkaldharis had 'created false gradations' and coined terms such as *para* and *apara* to establish their supremacy over the *samaj*. At the time he joined the *samaj*, Balkaldharis and Kaupindharis were 'working together in perfect harmony' under the guidance of Paramananda Baba who was a Kaupindhari; but 'now there are separate institutions for the two orders'. The reason behind the discord was 'oppression' by Balkaldharis.[101]

The statements of scholars, lay disciples and inhabitants of Joranda recorded in court display interesting cross-currents of opinion. Laxmi Narayan Sahu[102] and Artaballabh Mahanti,[103] both members of the Utkal Sahitya Samaj, which had set up the Satya Mahima Dharmalochana Samiti, and key figures in the Prachee Samiti which published Bhima Bhoi's works, upheld the Balkaldhari position when they affirmed the existence of only one Mahima *samaj*. While Laxmi Narayan Sahu categorically denied an independent status to the Kaupindharis, Artaballabh Mahanti could not be sure if all the Kaupindharis whom he had met in the course of his research on the sect were followers of the Balkaldharis. The two scholars joined hands in rejecting the Balkaldhari claim that Mahima Dharma was *sanatan* Hindu Dharma. Mahanti was pedantic: he differentiated between two trends of Vedic worship to show that Mahima Dharmis were *brahmabadis* (believers of Brahma) but not *sanatanis*. They did not perform *yajña* (sacrifice) according to Vedic rites. Sahu categorized Mahima religion as 'a protest against Hindu religion', although he granted that some of its principles 'might have been taken from the Vedas and Vedanta'. The scholars, more concerned about the true nature of the faith and less about the dissension within it, displaced the issue. They had no hesitation in subscribing to the fiction of one Mahima *samaj* maintained by Balkaldharis;

they felt it necessary to challenge the Balkaldhari attempt to align the faith with *sanatan* Hinduism.

Abhiram Mohanty, who had 'read a lot of literature and eventually joined this Dharma' 15 years earlier, declared the worship of the non-qualified, supreme Brahma to be the main principle of the faith.[104] He had no doubt that all the ritual services at the Gadi were performed in accordance with the orders of the founder. The Balkaldharis formed the highest order in the *samaj*. They were the leaders of the Dharma and the only members entitled to be called Baba: 'Bhaktas, Bairagis or Kaupindharis are subordinate to the Balkaldharis and with their consent only they can be recognised in our samaj'.[105] The dispute, which cropped up four or five years after he had joined the *samaj*, was due to 'a desire for personal luxury and love of power'.[106] The difference was 'fomented by some local people, lawyers, political parties and bhaktas with selfish ends'.[107] The Kaupindharis, Abhiram Mohanty continued, sought to compete with the Balkaldharis on all counts: they published books, set up a Kaupindhari *adhyaksha sabha* (managing committee), and appropriated the right of preaching the faith. These activities were illegal and did not have the sanction of the *samaj*. Even Bhima Bhoi, who did not clearly indicate the relationship between the two orders, consciously differentiated between *balkal bana* and *sunya bana* and *kaupin bastra* and *gairik bastra*. Was this not a marker of the superiority of the wearers of *balkal*?

Govinda Naik[108] and Jagabandhu Sahu, [109] both residents of Joranda but not members of the faith, affirmed that they treated the Balkaldharis and Kaupindharis as equals. The Kaupindhari *samaj*, which had existed all along, was in no way inferior to that of the Balkaldharis. However, they were not clear about the precise time of the inception of separate worship by the two orders. Govinda Naik felt that it had started forty years earlier. In Jagabandhu Sahu's view it was of more recent origin. The issue, at any rate, was trivial. Separate worship only served to demarcate the two orders more clearly; it did not signify any new division. Had not the two groups come into being during the lifetime of the founder? This stance of extending support to the Kaupindharis adopted by the residents of Joranda was given concrete shape in their social boycott of the Balkaldharis in 1959 when Biswanath Baba's group shifted the *dhuni* to the present *dhuni mandir*.[110] The stance is held even today.

The long time span of the dispute, the innumerable appeals and counter-appeals and the widely divergent views, opinions and standpoints on various matters made it difficult for the Commissioners of Religious Endowments to frame workable schemes for the management of the Gadi. Three commissioners handled the issue and formulated three separate schemes. But they also concurred on certain points. First, all three were convinced that there was only one Mahima *samaj*. The Kaupindhari claim of a separate *samaj* was not tenable. Moreover, the commissioners accepted that the Mahima *samaj* was a part of Hindu religion: this also bestowed on them complete authority to examine and settle any problems that arose within this faith. Finally, in drawing up their schemes they paid careful attention to the awards and orders of the arbitrators. This becomes clear from the statement of the commissioner, L Panda, who conducted a prolonged enquiry into the dispute: 'The tenets of ... Alekh Mahima Dharma shall be per the rules laid down by the founder Sri Alekh Goswamy and as interpreted from time to time by several courts including the Dhenkanal High Court in Civil Suit No. 8 of 1943, the Award passed by the Arbitrators Sri Bichitrananda Das and others.'[111] The courts and the arbitrators were given precedence over the renouncers and accorded a position second only to Mahima Swami as interpreters and codifiers of Mahima Dharma!

Panda's scheme of management, drawn up in June 1965 under Section 7 of the Hindu Religious Endowments Act, provided for a committee of management which comprised seven members: four Balkaldharis, two Kaupindharis, and one lay disciple. The second commissioner, Mohapatra, while stating that there was but one Mahima Dharmi *samaj*, felt that since its groups were not pulling along together they should be given the right to manage their own committees and look into their own affairs.[112] The third commissioner, B K Misra, came down heavily on the Kaupindharis.[113] The group was denounced as rebels who had damaged the institutional order and were not to be granted any rights to the Gadi. The Kaupindharis were in fact denied the right to call themselves members of Alekh Dharma. They would gain that right only when they entered the main fold, which included the graded order of *tyagis*, Kaupindharis, Balkaldharis and *gruhi bhaktas*. It is not surprising that the Balkaldharis gained the upper hand.

> Since there is complete harmony in the genuine group, no scheme ... is called for. Thus they [the Balkaldharis] are free to form their own committee for peaceful conduct of their Dharma. Before concluding I may reiterate that the present Kaupindhari group or any members therefrom now are free to follow the original discipline, so as to be compulsorily accepted by the group, known as Balkaldhari ... In case some members of the Kaupindhari group accept the discipline, but require protection by having a scheme, for better management, a regular one, we will do so. For the time being, with the above decision

the matter is closed.[114]

Recent Developments

The order of the Commissioner did not settle the matter. The Balkaldharis and Kaupindharis defied legal decrees and continued to run their own institutions separately. The Additional Assistant Commissioner of Endowments observed in 1973, 'The two branches are now working independently without any regard to the schemes framed from time to time.'[115] If law and legal idioms have caused the Dharma to undergo mutations, definitive decrees have been disregarded or deployed in special ways by ascetics of Mahima Dharma. Once the division within the community was acknowledged, the two groups of renouncers went about the business of managing the Gadi separately without paying any heed to judgements and settlements.

By the 1970s the enterprising ascetics had found a new public forum and arena for conducting their battle. Oriya newspapers had started giving publicity to the statements of the two groups of *sanyasis*. They diligently reported the *dharmasabhas* and *balyalilas* (a ceremony that involves the feeding of children) that were organized. The tussle between the two orders surfaced when the *Samaj* (Oriya newspaper) of 14 January 1971 published a report in which Kasinath Baba and Sudarsan Baba were mentioned as the administrators of Mahima Gadi. This was a part of an announcement that the annual festival in the month of *magh* at the Gadi would be celebrated between 6 and 10 February 1971. Sadhus, *bhaktas* and religious-minded people from far-flung provinces — Nagaland, Tripura, Uttar Pradesh, Manipur, Meghalaya, West Bengal, Bihar, Madhya Pradesh, Andhra Pradesh, Madras, Bombay, Gujarat, Rajasthan, Punjab, Delhi and Orissa — were invited to congregate at the Gadi. The people were assured that the organizers were taking great care to manage the ceremony properly and that preparations were afoot to look after the well-being of the pilgrims. The government had also been approached to extend official help. This report did not only proclaim the Kaupindharis to be the leaders of the *samaj*, it also stressed the success of these leaders in the dissemination of the faith.

The Balkaldhari rejoinder was not slow to appear: it was published in the *Samaj* of 3 February 1971 and the *Prajatrantra* of 4 February 1971. A special meeting of the Mahima Dharma Parichalana Samiti was held at the Mahima Gadi on 29 January 1971. The meeting discussed the *maghi purnima* celebrations: a programme was chalked out and various measures adopted for the efficient observance of the festival. The meeting was presided over by *adhyaksha* (president) Sri Biswanath Baba and attended by four other members of the Parichalana Samiti. The report published in the *Samaj* of 14 January 1971 was read out at the meeting, and the Babas expressed concern at the false propaganda being carried out by persons who were not members of the Mahima *samaj*. The affairs of the Gadi were managed by the Balkaldharis. They were the highest order of *sanyasis* and constituted the Parichalana Samiti. The Kaupindharis, as their assistants, did not have the right of supervision. The Parichalana Samiti had been vested with the authority to coordinate the affairs of the *samaj* by the 'authorities', and the body had functioned for years with the full knowledge of the government. People were asked not to believe in the false statements of non-members, which were conjured up with the sole intention of creating confusion. The rejoinder was issued in the name of the secretary, Sri Satyabadi Baba, and the treasurer, Sri Kshetrabasi Baba.

This was not the first time that the Samiti was taking exception to the activities of the Kaupindharis. In the records of the meetings of the Samiti which cover the period between 1965 and 1972,[116] deliberations on the dispute and moves to counteract the devious measures of the *birodhi paksha* (opponents) feature prominently in the agenda. The law courts had transformed the two groups of *sanyasis* with divergent ideologies into contending litigants. The use of the term *birodhi paksha* in the Samiti record books is a reflection of how legal language and categories had come to inform the two groups' perception of each other.

Books and pamphlets produced by each group in the 1970s and 1980s discussed their differences in detail and attempted to reveal the deception, deviation and distortions effected by members of the other group. Biswanath Baba's *Mahimagadi Mahimadham Itihasa* devoted an entire section to an elaboration of the causes of the dispute, the various schemes formulated for its resolution and the features which made such schemes unacceptable.[117] The villainy of Kaupindharis was stressed at each point. The Kaupindharis, in turn, noted with contempt the deception practised by Biswanath Baba and his companions in becoming Balkaldharis.[118]

The gulf between the two groups widened into a chasm. Scholars working on Mahima Dharma felt it necessary to evaluate the veracity of Balkaldhari and Kaupindhari claims. Consequently, they came to be viewed by the renouncers as supporters of one camp or the other.[119] The battle continued: more and more texts and counter-texts appeared in print. The shift in emphasis from the oral/spoken to the written, already underway, became pronounced and established as ascetics and sympathizers accepted and worked out the importance given by law courts to written documents as proper evidence. Two groups of *sanyasis* who differed over the interpretation of the Guru's teachings became all-time enemies.[120]

Dissension became the order of the day. Several sub-groups emerged who owed nominal allegiance to the Balkaldharis or the Kaupindharis.[121] Internal strife at Joranda encouraged some resourceful renouncers to attempt to gain control of the Gadi. Judhisthir Baba of Jatannagar, Dhenkanal, organized the 'Adivasis and Harizans' to protest against 'untouchability' practised by the Balkaldharis.[122] He and his followers marched to Joranda on 17 February 1981 in a bid to gain control of the memorial. The attempt was abortive. Judhisthir Baba received no support from the Kaupindharis of Mahima Gadi who, in fact, ostracized him.

Trouble also came from an unexpected quarter. The Commissioners of Endowments, in the course of their enquiry into the dispute, gained knowledge of the income and expenditure of the Gadi. In accordance with the provisions of the Orissa Hindu Religious Endowments Act they demanded contributions for the Endowments Fund. This prompted the members of the Parichalana Samiti to draft a fresh set of petitions against the unjust demands of the Commissioners. The Gadi, they argued, had no income of its own: it was run entirely by donations from lay disciples. This was shown in the approximate budget for the year 1975–76, presented by the ascetics to the Commissioner. It showed the income and the expenditure to be absolutely the same.[123] The Commissioners did not relent. The petitions were dismissed.[124]

Coda

In a century and a quarter after the death of its founder, Mahima Dharma has slowly but steadily become 'sedentarized'.[125] The need to ensure the continuation of the Dharma and efforts to create a cohesive community of believers has resulted in the setting up of a counter structure by the ascetics of the faith. Property has necessarily become a part of this structure and a static memorial has come to assume the authority of the mobile preceptor. This has entailed a concomitant shift in emphasis from the periphery toward the center and from heterogeneity to uniformity, symbolized by an increasing importance accorded to the power of writing. The move from the spoken to the written has been considerably enhanced by the faith's long interface with the law. A new generation of scholar ascetics, convinced of the necessity of 'reasoned' explications of the faith and authoritative histories for the 'progress' of Mahima Dharma, have answered the requirement of law courts for evidence by producing written texts.

At the same time, these *Itihasas*, formal histories, have turned the concerns of modern historiography on their heads by positing their veracity and chronology on a different standard of truth — the divinity of the founder — and a new sacred temporality which begins with the appearance of the divine founder. The excess resulting from this blending of history and *itihasa*, and linear religious time has made these texts amenable to varied interpretations. While lawyers and judges have moved beyond the authoritative texts of the sect in elaborating their definitions of Mahima Dharma as a Hindu sect, ascetics have used their own texts to question the definitions of judges and connive at their rulings. Groups of lay followers have drawn upon both the texts of Bhima Bhoi and those of ascetics written in the twentieth century as 'scriptures' to formulate their own understandings. In particular, householder devotees have elaborated newer ideas of healing and relief from suffering and novel concepts of the end of the era. Such distinct apprehensions have destabilized forceful attempts to unify and standardize.

And yet, the imperatives of law and the urgency of creation and preservation of a bounded community have wrought significant changes within a radical religious order. Under the auspices of legal and ritual power and through ascetic negotiations of religion and modernity Mahima Dharma has evolved as a 'sect' within the universe of Hinduism. In the process, it has shed off its crucial but contradictory relationship with the cult of Jagannath and redefined itself as a timeless religion pertaining to eternal Hinduism. It is perhaps telling that the last mention of Kumbhipatia (one of the terms used for Mahima Dharma in the nineteenth century) as a separate religion in the Census was in 1951, which returned only 51 followers from Orissa. From the Census of 1961, Mahima Dharma or Kumbhipatia religion ceased to be recorded separately indicating the complete merger of the faith with Hinduism.

Indeed, the new stance of non-engagement and non-confrontation with Jagannath found expression in a debate carried out in the late 1990s in the journal *Economic and Political Weekly*. Satrughna Nath, a prominent lay disciple and a close follower of Biswanath Baba felt the need to write a rejoinder to an essay published in the journal titled 'Jagannath and Alekh: A study in juxtaposition',[126] precisely because it tried to explore the close relationship of Alekh (Mahima) Dharma with the cult of Jagannath. In his 'Plea for proper perception' of the Dharma, Nath tried to clarify that Mahima Dharma is opposed to idol worship, discrimination, caste in general and is 'neither a critique of nor it stands against increasing orthodoxy in the worship of Jagannath'.[127] A faith that found its way into official records on account of its 'dissent' has increasingly come to align itself with high Hinduism. The sense of urgency reinforced by a strong belief in the pervasive presence of Kali in the late nineteenth and early twentieth centuries that urged members to take refuge in a new Dharma has become more and more distant in the course of the twentieth century, with the declaration of a new beginning, a new era, starting with the arrival of Mahima Swami. Variously identified as Kumbhipatia Dharma and Alekh Dharma in the nineteenth century, an affective faith has evolved as Mahima Dharma, a 'sect' within Hinduism, though with multiple pasts and orientations. In the following chapter, I examine the deployments of these different pasts, histories and interpretations of the Dharma in the everyday lives of the members of the *samaj*.

Notes

1. 'Banki Tehsil Office to the Commissioner of Orissa Division', Cuttack, 6 August 1881, Board of Revenue Document No. 411/1, OSA, Bhubaneswar; Jagannath Temple Correspondence, Part 6, 1880–84, No. 131, RR, Board of Revenue, Cuttack, pp. 1324–7; Biswanath Baba, *Satya Mahima Dharmara Itihasa*, p. 287. None of the sources mention the buyers.
2. See Chapter 2.
3. Von Stietencron argues, following Weber, that original charisma linked to a person rather than an office is by nature unstable. This makes a 'routinization' of this charisma almost imperative since the community formed by the personality requires the continuation of the charismatic authority for its own survival and stability. H. von Stietencron, 'Charisma and canon: The dynamics of legitimization and innovation in Indian religions' in Vasudha Dalmia, Angelika Malinar and Martin Christof (eds), *Charisma and Canon: Essays on the Religious History of the Indian Subcontinent* (New Delhi, Oxford University Press, 2001), p. 24.
4. This has not been documented anywhere. It has been hinted at in Bhima Bhoi, *Stuti Chintamoni*, where he justifies his status as a householder, and in Biswanath Baba, *Itihasa*.
5. According to von Stietencron, in special circumstances, charisma can be experienced in things, 'things that have something divine about them'. The best illustration of this is provided by the Sikh community. Authority of the Guru came to rest in the scripture, the Granth Sahib, after the tenth Guru Govind Singh, closed the line of spiritual succession. Von Stietencron, p. 25. This process has been discussed in detail in W. H. McLeod, *The Evolution of the Sikh Community: Five Essays* (Delhi, Oxford University Press, 1975), pp. 1–19. A recent analysis of the canonization of the Grant Sahib is contained in Gurinder Singh Mann, *Evolution of Sikh Scriptures* (New Delhi, Oxford University Press, 2002).
6. It is generally believed that the land for the construction of the Gadi was donated by the Raja of Dhenkanal. Eschmann, however, claims — on the basis of a suit in the court of the subordinate judge of Dhenkanal — that the land was bought by a follower. A. Eschmann, 'Mahima Dharma: An autochthonous Hindu reform movement', in A. Eschmann, H. Kulke and G. C. Tripathi (eds), *The Cult of Jagannath*, p. 388, pp. 375–410. The case — Title Suit No. 13/31 of 1960/62 —

deals with one particular plot of land, not the huge area that the Gadi complex occupies.

7. Biswanath Baba, *Mahimagadi Mahimadham Itihasa* (Cuttack, Satya Mahima Dharmalochana Samiti, 1984), pp. 8–10 (henceforth *Mahimagadi Itihasa*). It is interesting that Biswanath Baba characterizes the Gadi also as *dham*. *Dham* is a term used in Vaishnavism in relation to the four main abodes of Vishnu geographically located at the four extremities of the south, north, east and west of India. The use of *dham* for the headquarters of Mahima Dharma is a further indication that the authority of the wandering founder had become static and had come to rest at one spot.
8. The annual administration report of Dhenkanal for 1945–46 mentioned, for the first time, 'a big three-layered temple' constructed 'over the sacred grave of Mahima Goswami'. The reports for 1943–44 and 1944–45 spoke of Joranda as the seat of the Mahima cult but made no mention of the temple. Dhenkanal State Administration Report for 1945–46, p. 3. The construction of the present *dhuni mandir* was completed and the *dhuni* shifted there, in 1955. Biswanath Baba calls the earlier *mandir* the *asthai* (temporary) *dhuni mandir*. Biswanath Baba, *Mahimagadi Itihasa*, pp. 10–11.
9. See note 5.
10. This *ashrama* is not mentioned as forming part of the 'possessions' of the sect at the time of Mahima Swami's death.
11. Cited in Debendra Kumar Dash, 'Bhima Bhoi o Mahima Dharma', pp. 120–52.
12. Banki Tehsil Office to the Commissioner of Orissa Division, Cuttack, 6 August 1881, Board of Revenue Document No. 441/1, OSA, Bhubaneswar; Jagannath Temple Correspondence, Part VI, 1880–84, No. 131, RR, Board of Revenue, Cuttack, pp. 1324–7.
13. Government of Bengal, Resolution, Judicial Department, Calcutta, 21 October 1881, Board of Revenue Document No. 446/1, OSA, Bhubaneswar.
14. Indian Report of the Orissa Baptist Mission for 1873–74, BMS Archives, Angus Library, Regent's Park College, Oxford.
15. From Babu Banamali Sing, Manager of the Dhenkanal State to the Superintendent of the Tributary Mahals, Orissa, 4 October 1881, Board of Revenue Document No. 444, OSA, Bhubaneswar; Jagannath Temple Correspondence, Part VI, 1880–84, No. 40, RR, Board of Revenue, Cuttack, pp. 1334–8.
16. The census of 1911, which carries a detailed account of the sect, indirectly supports the Kaupindhari position. The 'Mahima Guru', it states, 'is said to have told his 64 disciples that they could wear cloth instead of bark. After his death the followers of Bhima Bhoi and Gobind Das (another disciple) took to clothes dyed yellow, while others kept the old custom.' *Census of India 1911*, vol. V, p. 214.
17. Biswanath Baba's *Itihasa* places the event between 1912 and 1914, while court records indicate that it occurred in 1931. My own guess, formed on the basis of a study of various documents, is that it happened in the 1920s. *Bhima Bhoi Malika ba Padmakalpa* also seems to have appeared in the 1920s.
18. Biswanath Baba, *Itihasa*, p. 306.
19. Mahindra Baba, *Satya Mahima Dharmara Sankshipta Itihasa*, (Mahimagadi, Kaupindhari Mahima Samaj Alochana o Prachar Sabha, 1958), p. 53.
20. Vasu, *The Modern Buddhism and Its Followers in Orissa*; Mazumdar, *Sonepur in the Sambalpur Tract*.
21. The Satya Mahima Dharmalochana Samiti was set up under the auspices of the Utkal Sahitya Samaj in 1926.

22. Ghanashyam Das, 'Foreword' in Biswanath Baba, *Mahima Dharma Pratipadaka* (Bhubaneswar, Satya Mahima Dharmalochana Samiti, 1931). I have used the Bengali translation published in 1953. Satrughna Nath, *Mahima Bhakti Rasamruta* (Cuttack, Mahima Dharmlochana Parishad, 1992) also contains details of Biswanath Baba's life and dwells at length on his philosophy and efforts to spread the faith.
23. Satrughna Nath, *A Saint, Self-realised in Mahima Faith Biswanath Baba* (Cuttack, Dharma Grantha Store, 1977), pp. 2–3. Satrughna Nath, a retired teacher, is a prominent lay disciple of Mahima Dharma and was a close associate of Biswanath Baba.
24. *Ibid.*, p. 4. 'Reason' and 'truth' would feature repeatedly in this and other texts of Biswanath Baba.
25. *Ibid.*, p. 2.
26. The reference obviously is to the four classical *ashramas* of *varnashramdharma*, viz. *brahmacharya*, *garhasthya*, *vanaprastha* and *sanyas*.
27. Biswanath Baba, *Pratipadaka*, p. 293. The point is substantiated by a citation from the *Mahanirban Tantra*.
28. *Ibid.*, p. 385.
29. *Ibid.*
30. I have discussed the differences involved in the strategies of 'collective' and 'individual' reading in the last chapter.
31. *Ibid.*, p. 2.
32. All this was to culminate in the production of the magnum opus — the two volumes of *Sarva Veda Vedanta Saratattva Śiromni, Alekh Parambrahma Darśanam* vol 1, (Bhubaneswar, Utkal University, 1968) and vol. 2, (Cuttack, Satya Mahima Dharmalochana Samiti, 1973). The two volumes were written by Biswanath Baba with the help of Ananta Charan Baba. These texts provided detailed analysis of the various yogas starting with the yoga of pure knowledge through the yoga of cosmology and the ultimate first principle, to a discussion of the qualified and unqualified nature of Brahman, to *atmajñan* and *bisudhha nishkamkarma* yoga to *grihasthashram dharmaniti* yoga, *brahmabadhutashram sanyas* yoga terminating in *jibanmukti bibek* yoga. Needless to say, these analyses were accompanied by detailed instructions to practitioners of the monastic and lay orders. The first volume was translated into English as *The Philosophy of Mahima Dharma* (*Philosophy of Unalloyed Non-Dual Supreme Being*) (Cuttack, Mahima Dharmalochana Samiti, 1987). In the preface to the first edition and the English translation Biswanath Baba thanked the chief minister of Orissa, the Vice Chancellor of Utkal University and several other eminent personalities, including Anncharlott Eschmann, the late scholar from Germany who had worked on Mahima Dharma in the early 1970s. In 1974, on being invited to the Religious Conference at Puri in 1974, Biswanath Baba delivered a published speech entitled *Philosophy of Mahima Dharma*. (Cuttack, Satya Mahima Dharmalochana Samiti, year not mentioned). In this lecture Biswanath defined Mahima Dharma as *viśuddha Advaitabad* — pure non-dualism with 'supporting evidence from Vedanta and other Shrutisastras'. See Satrughna Nath's introduction to the published speech. Biswanath Baba's numerous works sequentially portray the gradual reworking of Mahima Dharma's relationship with high Hinduism.
33. *Ibid.*, p. 304.
34. *Ibid.*
35. According to Biswanath Baba, the Balkaldharis were recorded as *marfatdars* in the

first *bandobasta* (settlement) carried out during the rule of Maharaja Bhagirathi Bhramarbar Bahadur, soon after the construction of the Gadi mandir. *Mahimadham Itihasa*, pp. 70–1.

36. Mahindra Baba, *Sankshipta Itihasa*, p. 55.
37. *Ibid.*
38. The records of the dispute are now difficult to locate. I came across a typescript of the records up to the 1970s in the archives of the Orissa Research Project in South Asian Institute, Heidelberg. They are entitled 'Joranda — Selections from Religious Endowments'. The typescript, however, does not contain complete references with regard to all the documents.
39. Civil Suit No. 215 of 1936. We do not know if this was the first suit.
40. This happened in 1962. Order on Miscellaneous Appeal No. 58 of 1960 and Civil Revision No. 190 of 1960. The Orissa Hindu Religious Endowments Act was passed in 1951.
41. The literal meaning of *itihasa* is 'thus it has been' — *iti-hi-asa*. While it cannot be ascertained if the law suits had started before the publication of the *Itihasa*, there is no doubt that the decision to move the courts had been taken earlier.
42. Biswanath Baba, *Itihasa*, Abataranika (Preface), p. 1.
43. *Ibid.*, pp. 2–3.
44. The *Itihasa* and all other texts of Biswanath Baba as well as those of other renouncers and prominent lay disciples like Satrughna Nath gives the year of publication in terms of the *Mahimabda*, asserting the importance of the new era for the aficionados of the Dharma.
45. As stated before, Romila Thapar argues that *itihasa-purana* 'veers between perceived past and historicity.' Thapar, 'Society and historical consciousness', p. 154.
46. It is not surprising that Biswanath Baba describes Mahima Swami's activities as *leela*, a word used widely in Vaishnavism to signify the divine sport of Lord Krishna. It is self-evident that Mahima Swami was no ordinary human being. The term finds no place in Bhima Bhoi's works.
47. Biswanath Baba, *Itihasa*, Abataranika, pp. 2–3.
48. This was reiterated by Biswanath Baba when I interviewed him in February 1990.
49. Biswanath Baba, *Itihasa*, p. 1.
50. It is of crucial importance that Bhima Bhoi's claim that Lord Jagannath had left Puri to become Mahima Swami's first disciple is omitted here. The faith was in the process of reworking its relationship with Hinduism and any hint of superiority over the central cult of Orissa was not in order.
51. Biswanath Baba, *Itihasa*, pp. 1–2.
52. *Ibid.*, p. 41, footnote.
53. I discuss this in the following chapter.
54. The *Itihasa* gives a detailed account of the rules, norms and practices in its first chapter, under the sub-section 'Satya Mahima Dharmara Upadeś' (Advice of Satya Mahima Dharma), pp. 13–41.
55. Biswanath Baba, *Itihasa*, pp. 288–9.
56. The seven-hooded snake on top is meant to act as a remembrance of Mahima Swami's meditation at Kapilas, where such a snake protected and sheltered him. Biswanath Baba, *Mahimagadi Itihasa*, p. 227.
57. For a discussion of the rules and ritual services, see Biswanath Baba, *Itihasa*, p. 280; Biswanath Baba, *Mahimagadi Itihasa*, pp. 13–21.
58. Biswanath Baba, *Itihasa*, p. 289.
59. Baishnab Charan Baba's *Satya Mahimadharma Mahimagadi Samachar* (Sambalpur,

Sadhu Birendra Kumar Das, 1978), pp. 134–5, supported this claim in a different way. It stated that Mahima Swami stopped granting *balkal* with Nanda Baba, who was to start it again. Mahima Swami also created Kaupindharis so that they could help in the propagation of Mahima Dharma under the guidance of the self-realized ascetics. But he did not confer any special responsibility or assign any special task to the Kaupindharis.

60. *Ibid.*, pp. 306–7.
61. *Ibid.*
62. The account of Mahima Dharma in the Gazetteer of Dhenkanal, for instance, closely followed the *Itihasa*. Not only were the terms *para* and *apara* used, the system of promotion of renouncers from one grade to another was stated to be an inherent feature of the Dharma. The Gazetteer described Biswanath Baba as a philosopher 'who in future will probably rank among other eminent philosophers'. N. Senapati and P. Tripathy (eds) *Orissa District Gazetteers: Dhenkanal* (Cuttack, 1972), p. 1. The account of the Dharma is to be found in the Appendix, pp. 443–7. Biswanath Baba's numerous texts and his participation in various religious meetings did succeed in getting intellectuals interested in Mahima Dharma. At the same time, the faith itself was shaped by the intervention of middle-class Oriyas. The success of the Baba in roping in intellectuals as instruments for the propagation of the faith has been proudly proclaimed by Satrughna Nath. S. Nath, 'Mahima Movement in Cuttack City' in K. S. Behera, J. Patnaik and H. C. Das (eds), *Cuttack: One Thousand Years* (Cuttack, Cuttack City Millennium Celebrations Committee, 1991), p. 267.
63. This award was framed by the arbitrators, Swami Bichitrananda Das, Sri Satyanarayan Sengupta and Sri Jaykrushna Misra (later replaced by Sri Paresh Mahanti), who were all advocates from Cuttack. This award, with slight modifications, was incorporated in a second award announced on 13 January 1950 and was executed on stamp paper on 25 August 1950 by the same arbitrators; 'Joranda — Selections from Religious Endowments', SAI, Heidelberg.
64. The same view, that the 'progress' of the institution was being 'retarded owing to litigation between two sections of the cult', was expressed in the Dhenkanal State Administration Report for 1945–46, *Crown Representative's Records*, Pt.1, Eastern States Agency, IOLR, London.
65. The main conditions laid down by the Award were prefixed by 'all parties agreed and we also decide'.
66. This record of the prolonged interaction between Mahima Dharma and the legal apparatus of the state tends to substantiate Marc Galanter's argument that representatives of the neutral judiciary in independent India made zealous use of their power of overall arbitration in matters of religion to sponsor reform within Hinduism. See Marc Galanter, *Law and Society in Modern India* (Delhi, Oxford University Press, 1989), pp. 237–58, and Galanter, 'Hinduism, secularism and the Indian judiciary', in Rajeev Bhargava (ed.), *Secularism and its Critics* (Delhi, Oxford University Press, 1998), pp. 268–93. This does raise questions about the nature of secularism in India. What I intend to do, however, is to extend Galanter's analysis and examine how the requirements of law and legal verdicts have been deployed by the renouncers of Mahima Dharma. This will help improve our understanding of the power and the reach of the legal machinery of the state and their manipulations by groups that seek redress in the law.
67. Mahindra Baba, *Satya Mahima Dharmara Sankshipta Itihasa* (Mahimagadi, Kaupindhari Mahima Samaj Alochana o Prachar Sabha, 1958).
68. The Alochana o Prachar Sabha was set up in 1954.

69. Mahindra Baba, *Biśwa Kalyan Patha Satya Mahima Dharma* (Mahimagadi, Kaupindhari Mahima Samaj Alochana o Prachar Sabha, 1957).
70. *Sankshipta Itihasa*, p. 11.
71. *Ibid.*, p. 65.
72. *Ibid.*, p. 6.
73. Bhima Bhoi, *Stuti Chintamoni, boli* 21, cited in *Sankshipta Itihasa*, p. 6.
74. *Sankshipta Itihasa*, pp. 18–9.
75. *Ibid.*, p. 19.
76. Bhima Bhoi quoted in *Sankshipta Itihasa*, p. 20.
77. *Ibid.*, p. 35.
78. *Ibid.*, p. 55.
79. *Ibid.*
80. *Ibid.*, pp. 55–6.
81. *Ibid.*, p. 57.
82. This view was expressed in the verdict which dismissed Miscellaneous Appeal No. 58 of 1960 and Civil Revision No. 190 of 1960 on 12 November 1962. For a detailed analysis of the role of the Commission of Religious Endowments in independent India see, J. D. M. Derrett, *Religion, Law and State in India* (London, Faber and Faber, 1968).
83. The honourable Chief Justice and the honourable Justice S. Burman.
84. Argument by the honourable Chief Justice and the honourable Justice S. Burman; 'Joranda — Selections', SAI, Heidelberg.
85. Apart from the fact that Biswanath Baba's texts had stated that Mahima Dharma was a part of *sanatan* Hindu Dharma, it was vital for the judges to insist that the faith formed an integral part of Hinduism. That is what gave them the power to define it and legislate over it.
86. *Ibid.*
87. *Ibid.*
88. *Ibid.*
89. *Ibid.*
90. *Ibid.*
91. Before the Commissioner of Endowments, Orissa, Cuttack, deposition by Abadhut Biswanath Baba, 28 March 1962, 'Joranda — Selections', SAI, Heidelberg.
92. Biswanath Baba's *Mahima Dharma Pratipadaka* and *Satya Mahima Dharma Itihasa* were published in 1931 and 1935, respectively. These texts used the terms *para* and *apara*.
93. The same opinion has been expressed in Biswanath Baba, *Mahimagadi Mahimadham Itihasa*, p. 150.
94. Deposition by Abadhut Biswanath Baba, 'Joranda — Selections', SAI, Heidelberg.
95. *Ibid.*
96. Before the Commissioner of Endowments, Orissa, Cuttack, deposition by Brundaban Baba, 21 November 1962, 'Joranda — Selections', SAI, Heidelberg.
97. *Ibid.*
98. *Ibid.*
99. Bernard Cohn has shown how the procedure of law courts, which insisted on coming to a decision, wrought a change in the traditional method in which discussion and arbitration were given greater importance. A settlement in which some of the differences of the contenders were compromised was arrived at, not a definite decision. Bernard Cohn, 'Some notes on law and change in North India', *An Anthropologist among the Historians and Other Essays* (Delhi, Oxford University Press, 1987), pp. 554–74.

100. Before the Commissioner of Endowments, Orissa, Cuttack, deposition by Narendra Nath Baba, 9 May 1962, 'Joranda — Selections', SAI, Heidelberg.
101. *Ibid.*
102. Form of heading of deposition Case No. 13/14 of 1960, deposition of witness No. 16, 10 December 1961, 'Joranda —Selections', SAI, Heidelberg.
103. Form of heading of deposition T.S. No. 13/14 of 1960, deposition of witness No. 17, 24 December 1961.
104. Before the Commissioner of Endowments, Orissa, Cuttack, deposition by Abhiram Mohanty, 9 May 1962, 'Joranda — Selections', SAI, Heidelberg.
105. *Ibid.* Here we have a clear instance of the influence of Biswanath Baba's works on a lay follower.
106. *Ibid.*
107. *Ibid.*
108. Before the Commissioner of Endowments, Orissa, Cuttack, deposition by Govinda Naik, 9 May 1962, 'Joranda — Selections', SAI, Heidelberg.
109. Before the Commissioner of Endowments, Orissa, Cuttack, deposition by Jagabandhu Sahu, 9 May 1962, 'Joranda — Selections', SAI, Heidelberg.
110. Mention of this boycott was made by several residents of Joranda and teachers of the Mahima Mahavidyalaya during interviews. This has been hinted at in Biswanath Baba, *Mahimagadi Itihasa*, p. 10.
111. Court of the Commissioner of Endowments, Orissa, Cuttack, in the matter of Sri Joranda Mahima Gadi, Dhenkanal, Order 607/858, 6 April 1965, 'Joranda — Selections', SAI, Heidelberg.
112. Sri Mahima Gadi, Joranda, Order of C. Mohapatra, Commissioner of Endowments, 4 October 1967.
113. Sri Mahima Gadi, Joranda, Order of B.K. Misra, Commissioner of Endowments, 6 April 1970, 'Joranda — Selections', SAI, Heidelberg.
114. *Ibid.*
115. To the Commissioner of Endowments, Orissa, Bhubaneswar, from the Additional Assistant Commissioner of Endowments, 22 January 1973, Management File No. 607, Office of the Commissioner of Endowments, Bhubaneswar, pp. 60–1.
116. These records form a part of the Eschmann Collections, SAI, Heidelberg.
117. Section 3 of *Mahimagadi Mahimadham Itihasa* is entitled 'siddhasadhu parampara suraksha pain apatti manantar o bicar' (objections, disagreements and trials regarding the preservation of the tradition of siddha sadhus), *Mahimagadi Itihasa*, pp. 118–57.
118. The story told by the Kaupindharis is that two of the 56 sanyasis climbed a tree and ordered Nanda Baba to grant *balkal.* Nanda Baba, whose eyesight had become poor by then, heard the voice and took it to be the śunya adeś of the Guru. This story is recorded in *Kaupindhari Mahima Samaj Mahima Gadir Barshik Bibarani o Mukhapatra* (Annual report and description of the of the Kaupindhari Mahima *samaj* of Mahima Gadi, Mahimagadi, 1977), pp. 4–5; Raj Kisore Baba, *Mahimadham Sankshipta Itihasa* (Mahimagadi, 1984), p. 11.
119. Uddhab Nayak's *Mahima Dharma Biśwa Itihasa* (Bhubaneswar, Bijaylaxmi Nayak, 1980) displayed a clear leaning towards the Kaupindharis. Gopal Charan Sahu, a sympathizer of the Balkaldharis, sought to expose the 'misinterpretations' and 'misstatements' of this text in a tract entitled *Mahima Dharma Biśwa Itihasa Lekhakanku Satarka Bani* (Chakrapur, G C Sahu, 1981). In 1982 appeared *Mahima Dharma Bidveshinku Ek Khola Cithi* (Dhenkanal, Orient Publications, 1982) by Atanu Debatirtha, which countered the arguments advanced by Sahu.

120. It would, however, be wrong to assume that all the *sanyasis* had totally ruled out the possibility of the two *samajas* becoming one again. Baisnab Charan Baba, a Balkaldhari *sanyasi* of the Lata *ashrama*, which owes allegiance to Biswanath Baba's group, stated in a text that a reunification is possible provided that the ascetics forget their pride and differences and devote themselves to the task of carrying forward the great work began by the founder. Brahmaabadhut Baisnab Charan Baba, *Satya Mahima Dharma Mahimagadi Samachar* (Cuttack, 1978), pp. 167–8. This book is not sold by the Dharma Grantha Store or by any of the bookstalls set up during the *maghi purnima* celebrations. I obtained this book as a gift from an ascetic of the Lata *ashrama* who happened to have it in his possession.
121. In the vicinity of the memorial itself there are about five *ashramas* of Mahimadharmi *sanyasis* which are not a part of the main complex.
122. This was an ingenious way of presenting the Balkaldhari prohibition of entry to all but the Balkaldharis into the Gadi *mandir*. Judhisthir Baba wrote to the Chief Minister of Orissa and sent copies of the letter to the Prime Minister and the Speaker of Parliament to seek the abolition of this practice of untouchability. Management File, No. 607, Office of the Commissioner of Endowments, Bhubaneswar, pp. 57–8.
123. Management File No. 607, Office of the Commissioner of Endowments, Bhubaneswar, p. 68.
124. Original Jurisdiction Case No. 1281 of 1979 decided on 14 December 1987, present the Honourable Chief Justice Mr. R.C. Patnaik and the Honourable Chief Justice Mr. K.P. Mohapatra, Management File No. 607, Office of the Commissioner of Endowments, Bhubaneswar, pp. 111–16.
125. The term 'sedentarization' has been used by Peter van der Veer to explain the process of settling down of the wandering Ramanandi ascetics. P. Van der Veer, *Gods on Earth: The Management of Religious Experience in a North Indian Pilgrimage Centre* (Delhi, Oxford University Press, 1988).
126. Subhakanta Behera, 'Jagannath and Alekh: A study in juxtaposition', *Economic and Political Weekly,* 32:3, 16–23 August 1997, pp. 2096–7.
127. S. Nath, 'Mahima Dharma: Plea for proper perception', *Economic and Political Weekly*, 33:4, 24–31 January 1998, pp. 191–2.

CHAPTER 5.

Contemporary Contours

What are the experiential dimensions of religion? Why do people get initiated into a new faith? What are the implications of initiation into a distinct religious order? How are the tenets of a faith understood and set to work by its members in the everyday arenas? What impact does all of this have on relations of caste, sect and gender? This chapter addresses such issues by focusing primarily on the lay followers of Mahima Dharma. It examines the reasons that have drawn these people to the Dharma and probes the significance of the precepts of the faith in the fashioning of distinct identities by its members. Stressing that the new orientations occasion significant transformation of caste and sect, I question singular conceptions of conversion as foundational rupture as well as query exclusive arguments emphasizing endless continuities within Hindu civilization. Here, explorations of the workings of caste and sect, of incorporation and disjunction, in the everyday lives of ordinary members of Mahima Dharma are accompanied by analyses of the monastic order as well as of important rituals and ceremonies that hold together the community of believers. In tune with such emphases, the chapter explores the meanings of pilgrimage centring on an annual ceremony at the memorial of the Guru and at Bhima Bhoi's *ashrama* in Khaliapali. The huge congregation of devotees at Joranda on the occasion of Guru *purnima* in the month of *magh* (January–February) as well as the smaller affair at Khaliapali reinforce the identity of a Mahima Dharmi and enable lay disciples to articulate their sense of belonging to a bounded community.

Gruhi Bhaktas

The rules for the initiation of *gruhi bhaktas* (householder devotees), as codified by Biswanath Baba, are simple. An individual who feels drawn to the faith starts praying to Alekh (unwritten, indescribable Absolute) and begins to follow the prescribed code of conduct. The prescriptions include getting up before sunrise, going without food after sunset, total devotion to the Absolute in place of all other deities, and the leading of an honest, truthful life. The person then asks to be initiated by the itinerant Mahima *sanyasi* who comes to his neighbourhood. If the *sanyasi* is satisfied that the applicant has imbued the true spirit of the faith he grants him *diksha*. Initiation can take place at the initiate's area of residence, in which case it has to be sanctified and recognized by the appropriate *samaj* at the annual congregation at Joranda on the occasion of *guru purnima*. At times the *bhakta* waits until *maghi purnima* to be initiated. The aspirant rises early on the day of initiation, cleanses his body by bathing and goes and stands near the *sanyasi*'s *tungi*. The *sanyasi* purifies the *bhakta*'s body with *pabitra* (a mixture made up of the excretions of the cow) and grants him a cloth the colour of red-earth which the *bhakta* wears after offering it to the Lord. He then stands facing east in his new garment to hear the *upadeś* (advice) of the *diksha-guru* (preceptor who will initiate him). The ascetic's task is to explain the greatness of the formless Absolute, who created the world out of his *mahima*. The *bhakta* is repeatedly asked to surrender his mind and body to this Supreme Absolute, the master of the world, and to think of no other gods and goddesses. The main tenets of the faith and the procedure of *śaran-darśan* are explained. The devotee invokes the name of Mahima Alekh and performs *śaran*. After this the new initiate bows down to the *diksha-guru* and all other Mahima *sanyasis* present at the ceremony. He returns home after requesting all the *sanyasis* to come to his house for *bhiksha*. The initiation ceremony concludes with the grant of *bhiksha* to the *sanyasis*. The *bhakta* returns to his normal life with a pledge to follow the path of the Dharma he has adopted and with the belief that he has the maker of the world as his friend and guide.[1]

Why do people get initiated into Mahima Dharma? The reasons are many. At the same time, it is striking that belief in the faith as the only one capable of guiding the follower through the evils and perils of Kali Yuga figure prominently among the answers. If this validates somewhat Sudhir Kakar's point that the individual as only a part of a stable network of relationships in a hierarchically ordered Indian society retains the child in him and continually looks for support,[2] it shows with much greater force the significance of different meanings of a difficult world and the modes in which the 'therapeutic' acquires prominence in specific circumstances. It is not just the continued presence of the child in the individual and his constant search for security that leads to a preoccupation with the 'therapeutic' in 'traditional' Indian society.[3]

At this point, it will make sense to look into the range of opinions expressed by the followers of Mahima Dharma as responses to my queries carried out in the 1990s and those of Anncharlott Eschmann and her assistants in the 1970s.[4] A few representative examples:

40-year-old Hari Behera of Ghantapada, Dhenkanal, had taken *diksha* for the liberation of his soul and for the cure of his blindness. He had not regained his eyesight but he persisted in his faith to escape from the cycle of births and deaths.

70-year-old Prasadi Jena of Mangarajpur, Balasore, felt the need for *dharma-palan* (conduct of *dharma*) as he grew old. He looked for *aśray* (refuge) and *sahay* (friend) and found it in Nirakar Prabhu.

Tulsi Dei of Banamalipur, Puri, had a vision while offering water to Surya *devata*. She began her quest for the Lord and was ultimately guided to the true Lord by Biswanath Baba.

60-year-old Rama Barik had, in his early fifties, criticized Mahima Dharma in front of a *sanyasi* who was preaching the faith. An angry Prabhu appeared in his dream, struck him and directed him to beg forgiveness from the *sanyasi* and become a *bhakta*.[5]

Bhikari Giri of Dhanarajpur, Keonjhar, had been induced to become a Mahima Dharmi by the sheer numerical strength of the faith's following in his village. 'I have taken to this faith because all the people in my area follow it.'[6]

Benudhar Misra arrived at Bhima Bhoi's *ashrama* in Khaliapali in the early 1990s in search of care and protection. He had traversed several miles through heat and dust to reach the *ashrama*. He arrived there emaciated and exhausted with a request to be allowed entry into the faith. He had come to surrender himself with total abandon at the feet of Bhima Bhoi, to implore him to apply the therapeutic touch and keep life's miseries away from him.[7]

Some followers are born into families of Mahima Dharmis. They are initiated into the faith at an age when they are not capable of exercising free will. Fathers persuade sons to take to the Dharma in several instances. The bonds of kinship are wide enough to include relations by marriage. In quite a few cases, a daughter-in-law who is an initiate has managed to persuade her husband and in-laws to join her faith. We will examine the implications of daughters from families of Mahima Dharmis marrying into families that are not members of the Dharma a little later. Here, I shall focus on the reasons offered by the householder devotees in general.

Many members find the principle of equality of all before the Lord and the simple path of liberation of the soul very attractive. Several others declare without hesitation that their faith is by far the best, the only one capable of leading a devotee to salvation in Kali Yuga. Moreover, the austere style of life of the itinerant *sanyasis* and their preaching carry the force of conviction. Several householders mentioned that they had been drawn to the faith by the teachings of the renouncers. They are happy to follow the dictates of the faith and are not overtly concerned with liberation.[8] Some stated that they were just content with being devotees of the great Prabhu, the Absolute. Whether or not they will get salvation was for the Lord to decide.[9] Belief in the Master sustains them through the ups and downs of life.

The desire to possess a strong, healthy body comes out as a very strong reason for initiation into Mahima Dharma. A large number of followers disclosed that they had become *bhaktas* following prolonged illnesses. Prabhu had acted as the panacea for their ailments when all other remedial measures had failed. We have noted that belief in the healing powers of Mahima Swami was vital for his elevation in status to that of an ascetic with divine powers. The integrated healing he offered — of cure for the body and solace for the mind — lay at the heart of his success as a religious preacher. In the case of Bhima Bhoi, the recent phenomenon of trust in the restorative powers of his couplets offer the newest mode of his canonization and deification. Together, they illustrate the acute relevance of bodily cure in the continuation of belief in preachers and doctrines.

Indeed, several important studies of diverse peoples and cultures have emphasized the importance of healing in the spread of new faiths. The success of evangelical missionaries in converting people they cured has also been documented.[10] It has been further pointed out that a disease free, healthy body has often been used by subordinate peoples as a device to resist oppression and exploitation.[11] Sensitive analyses of untouchable religions have indicated how these faiths have challenged the core of hierarchy premised on the principle of purity and pollution by reconstituting the untouchable as pure — possessed of a pure body and self.[12] Moreover, I have indicated before that there has been a long tradition of training for the attainment of an immutable body among different groups and cults. This trend, starting with the classical Yoga school of Indian philosophy has continued with mutations and newer nuances and emphases through Tantra and the secret practices of several 'non-conformist' Vaishnava and Buddhist tantric and sahajiya cults in eastern India. The Bauls of Bengal are a living proof of this tradition. Although there are no detailed studies of such cults in Orissa, the strong undercurrent of yoga emanating from the Naths has been noted by various scholars.

We have discerned the elements of yogic *sadhana* in Bhima Bhoi's compositions. The *malikas* are also believed to contain a secret language which communicates a different meaning to the initiated few. It is unlikely that the householder followers of Mahima Dharma are familiar with the path and practice of yoga. However, the reasons they adduce for the necessity of commanding a disease-free body reveal an intricate combination of some or all of the distinct ideas outlined here. Further, the importance of the body is acknowledged in the faith in its practice of *śaran-darśan*, which involves complicated bodily gestures as a mode of offering prayers to Alekh. We will turn to this soon.

At a more mundane level, the powers of the divine preceptor are assumed to be conveyed through his followers on rare occasions. Eschmann recorded an interesting case in 1974.[13] In Kuska, Gauranga Nayak, a practising homoeopath, proved to be a source of inspiration for the conversion of patients whom he cured. The doctor prayed to Alekh Prabhu before treating his patients and announced that whoever had faith in the Master would be cured. It was Alekh Prabhu who conferred efficacy on homoeopathic medicine. His curative power acted through the mediation of the doctor, his earnest devotee. Faith in the Prabhu healed bodies, medical treatment proved effective only when the Guru's blessings were bestowed on it.

Trust in the miraculous power of their distinctive faith is validated again and again in the life of the devotees. Two women followers recounted an interesting anecdote to me. In 1991, the inhabitants of a small colony in Bhubaneswar, where both these women lived, were plunged into a situation of excitement, tension and crisis: a young girl of the colony became possessed by a witch. All attempts to drive away the witch proved futile. As a last resort a Mahima Dharmi beseeched his Prabhu to come to their rescue. The witch left the girl, Mahima Dharma triumphed. Many inhabitants of the colony became convinced of the greatness of the Dharma and started following it.[14]

A study conducted among the Mahima Dharmis by the Tribal Research Bureau of Orissa in 1967 summed up its findings thus: 'Opinion of forty converts regarding reason of conversion — 35% to be cured from diseases; 32.5% persuaded by *sanyasis* and 10% by other converts; 15% to be blessed with a child; 7.5% for some other reasons. Two persons converted before attaining ten years.'[15] The real reason for conversion, the report stated, revealing its caste Hindu bias, was the desire of low-castes and untouchables to gain the right to worship gods of the Hindu pantheon. 'Members of untouchable castes like Panas readily accept the faith as it helps improve their social position and gives them access to Brahma, the supreme Lord of

Hinduism. The same holds true for Hinduised tribes like the Saoras and Desia-Kandhas, who are accorded a very inferior status in the caste system and denied the right to worship Hindu gods and goddesses.'[16]

The conclusions of this study reveal the influence of the concept of Sanskritization, in vogue in the 1960s. Sanskritization, formulated by M. N. Srinivas in the 1950s and elaborated in the early 60s, highlighted a tendency among lower castes to accept and absorb the 'customs, ritual, belief, ideology and style of life' of an upper-caste and, in particular, of a twice-born (*dwija*) caste. Such changes were generally followed by a claim to a higher position in the caste hierarchy than was traditionally granted to the claimant caste by the local community. Often, lower castes would follow the norms of their immediate superiors in the caste hierarchy, but the ideal role model was the Brahman who belonged to the highest caste. Again, since Brahmans did not have any superiors to imitate, 'Brahmanical customs and way of life spread among all Hindus'.[17] While it interrogated the powerful idea of a static caste system by pointing to the dynamism of it, Sanskritization reinforced the ritual preeminence accorded to the Brahman by Dumont.

Clearly, the concept of Sanskritization homogenizes and oversimplifies. By identifying a few symbols and markers and encapsulating all activities through them, it misses out completely on the novelty and ingenuity in the use, appropriation and application of those signs by untouchable and low-caste people. As critical studies of lower caste movements have pointed out, adoption of upper-caste norms and practices result in significant transformation in meanings. The 'acceptance' of upper-caste symbols by lower castes and untouchables is often guided by 'an ideology of protest' which ends up divesting these symbols of their special significance.[18]

Lay members of Mahima Dharma, who still pertain primarily to low-castes, do not display an overt tendency to subvert the caste system. Neither does upward mobility in the ritual hierarchy of purity and pollution feature prominently in their frame of reference. Moreover, they do not associate themselves with the *dalit* politics of contemporary India.[19] These devotees derive strength from the belief that by becoming Mahima Dharmis they gain the support and blessings of the omnipotent and omnipresent Absolute, Alekh Prabhu. They do not identify this Absolute with the supreme god of Hinduism, despite Biswanath Baba's efforts to align the faith with the tradition of Vedanta. The message of the faith which gives equal opportunities to all to attain salvation and implicitly rejects discrimination—probably makes it easy for these householders to accept their low ritual status as members of society. This might account for the absence of direct challenge to the caste system on their part.

All this raises important issues regarding the implications of belonging to a distinct faith. Literature on conversion in general and on South Asia in particular has tended to understand the phenomenon only in the sense of a complete break with the prior faith which in turn signals a total displacement of religious affiliation. While it has been shown that the new faith is understood in terms of the old, bringing forth overlaps among the two, initiation into religious formations such as Mahima Dharma is not taken to be conversion. The fashioning of separate identities and transformations of caste and sect resulting from such initiation are generally contained through 'aggrandizing notions of essential continuities with an overweening Hindu civilization', moves that elide the disjunction underlying the meanings of sect and caste.[20] It is to such issues that I now turn.

Caste, Sect, Community

The act of initiation enjoins lay Mahima Dharmis to follow a well-defined code of conduct. In addition to the prescriptions noted above, these include the daily performance of *śaran* and *darśan*, the wearing of *geru-basan* (cloth dyed the colour of red-earth), service and hospitality to all the *sanyasis* of the faith, and the exercise of strict control over sexual urge. For married *gruhi bhaktas* sexuality is meant to be geared toward the sole purpose of procreation. Husband and wife are enjoined to sleep together on particular days of the wife's menstrual cycle. Restraint is the key word in dealings with the opposite sex, members of which are to be addressed as *bapa* (father) and *ma* (mother) irrespective of their age. Norms of fidelity and loyalty are stricter in case of women. They are to dutifully serve and obey their husbands and parents-in-law, look after the running of the household, and take care of their children.[21]

The rules regarding waking up before sunrise, wearing a special garment for prayer, of lying prostrate on the ground praying to the Absolute at sunrise and sunset and of not eating after sunset, though not very easy to follow do not bring the followers of Mahima Dharma into conflict with anyone else. At the same time, *śaran-darśan*, a principal element of the everyday rituals of Mahima Dharma ascetics and devotees, is distinctive in terms of the actual practice and the meanings it embodies. The prayer expresses religious devotion to Mahima Alekh through the language of the body. Before sunrise ascetics and devotees prostrate seven times on the earth (*śaran*); before sunset they pray five times (*darśan*). The sequences of the prayer are put together with invocations of the name of the God and complex movements of arms and legs. In this mode of praying, right movement of the body is symbolic of the 'right' ideas and right conduct of Mahima Dharma, an internalised 'moral' purity with individual steps towards salvation. The prayer is also regarded as a medicine for body and mind with great importance attached to its correct performance.[22] Apart from stressing the importance of physical communication with the Lord, this ritual gives a significant twist to '*darśan*', defined as the composite action of going into the presence of the deity, of 'seeing/viewing' and being 'seen'.[23] Since the object of devotion in Mahima Dharma is the formless, all-pervading Absolute, the act of 'seeing' occurs through the medium of the pure body. Correct execution of the prayer in turn, inscribes the norms of the true faith into the body of the devotee.

Śaran-darśan, even though it marks out a follower as belonging to a distinct community, does not generate tension. What causes trouble is the injunction against the acceptance of *prasad* — the graced leftovers of a Hindu deity — or of not paying heed to the norms of caste in accepting or offering food. This may result in the exclusion of householder devotees from certain collective festivals of the village and from invitations to ceremonies in the houses of upper or dominant castes. It might also mean that fellow villagers do not accept invitations from the followers of the sect. On such occasions, the different but overlapping identities of Mahima Dharmis as adherents of a separate religion and as members of the village community come into conflict.

The ways these tensions are worked out often depend on the size and organization of the village[24] and the numerical strength and social and economic standing of the Mahima Dharmis in it.[25] Another crucial factor is the presence or absence of a *tungi* or any other typical structure of the Dharma, a *dhuni ghar* (a room where the sacred fire is kept lit) or a *śunya mandir* (temple in honour of the Absolute), in a village. The *tungi* demonstrates that members of the faith are significant in terms of number and have the resources at their disposal to construct a special structure for the faith. It also marks the presence of Mahima Dharma in the religious and cultural life of the village. Initiates and non-initiates regularly gather at the *tungi* in the evenings to light the *dhuni* and to sing *bhajans* in praise of the Absolute. Wandering ascetics of Mahima Dharma spend a night at the *tungi* from time to time. This provides an occasion for the preaching of the faith, the singing of *bhajans* and the holding of simple ceremonies such as the *balyalila*.[26] All this can contribute to the predominance of Mahima Dharmis in the village. The distinct practices of the adherents are not frowned upon in these villages and they are accepted as full-fledged members of the village community.

The absence of a *tungi*, on the other hand, indicates that either the followers of the Dharma are few in number, or that they are socially or economically not prominent enough or both. In such villages, the faith is often treated with derision as one meant for the low-castes and untouchables and the members of the village ignored and excluded from collective festivals unless they conform to the general norms of conduct.[27] In an attempt to cope with this, followers spread over a few neighbouring villages come together to build a *tungi* or an *ashrama* or a *dhuni ghar*. Interestingly, they appeal to and draw upon their sectarian identity that cuts across village boundaries in order to improve their position within the village. This results in a simultaneous and symbolic transgression and consolidation of village frontiers.

On rare occasions, the presence of a *tungi* but its disuse and state of disrepair reflect the gradual decline of the faith in the village. Mahimapali, a small village in the district of Bolangir in western Orissa, originally settled by Mahima Dharmis provides an instance. The few Mahima Dharmi households in the village have gradually lost their importance as other Hindu families have come to live there and the descendants of the initiates have lost their fervour for the faith. The *tungi* no longer commands importance as a centre of religious activity and has virtually fallen apart. Followers of Mahima Dharma, lamented Paramananda Sahu, the senior-most member of the faith in the village, were losing their sense of belonging in Mahimapali, a village settled, named after, and dedicated to Mahima Dharma.[28] His sense of loss was heightened by the fact that Mahimapali has ceased to be important for Mahima Dharma. It is no longer a regular halt of ascetics. It is as if the village has dropped off the map of a faith that fashioned its contours with reference to villages peopled by followers.

What role do norms of caste play in determining the inclusion or exclusion of Mahima Dharmis in the collective ceremonies of the village? It is important to note in this connection that a large number of lay disciples belong to the extremely vague and large category of *chasa*, which literally means a cultivator, but has come to be accepted as a caste in Orissa. People pertaining to this category are connected to agriculture, either as peasant cultivators with very small plots of land or as agricultural labourers. *Chasas* form the large majority in many villages. Given that the term itself is fuzzy and ample, there is hardly any distinction between followers of the Dharma and the *chasas* who are non-initiates. The same is true of the artisanal castes of potter (*kumbhar*) and smiths (*kamar*). Even if they belong to different sects (Vaishnava being very common in Orissa), Mahima Dharmi and non-

Mahima Dharmi *chasas* and artisans live in harmony, jointly participating in festivals and ceremonies of the village.

The presence of initiates from among the ex-untouchables along with initiates from other 'touchable' castes in the same village can cause tension. In Orissa, it is still common to find ex-untouchables living in separate quarters at the edge of the village.[29] *Dalit* followers of Mahima Dharma are thus almost compelled to live like untouchables, even though their faith rejects social discrimination. These members again, can pose a problem for their coreligionists who are not untouchables. Dictates of the faith demand that these Mahima Dharmis not only invite the *dalit* initiates to their houses but also share meals with them. But the entry of untouchables into households within the village can generate tension and even result in the ostracization of the Mahima Dharmi household. Rather than run such a risk, followers of the faith wait for occasions where festivals of the sect bring them together at one of the centers of the Dharma outside the village. As stated before, householder devotees do not display any explicit intention of subverting caste rules, even though both Mahima Swami and Bhima Bhoi openly flouted norms of caste and commensality and the *sanyasis* of Mahima Dharma do not mention their caste or observe distinctions of caste.[30] In ceremonies particular to the faith, of course, caste ceases to become a concern and all members offer and take food from each other as well as participate in a common meal to cement this feeling of solidarity and equality.

An important ritual that often occasions the transgression of the frontiers of a bounded community and adherence to caste norms is marriage. Theoretically, in a negotiation between two families of *bhaktas*, caste should not be a concern at all. But in practice, in most marriages bride and groom come from the same caste. Householders account for this ambiguity in diverse ways. Some dodge the issue by stating that in matches arranged between families of followers caste is never taken into consideration. For instance, Sanatan, an old man from Cuttack, affirmed, 'My son who is a Khandayet has married a Brahman girl. No question of caste was raised about the marriage.'[31] It is interesting that this marriage of a Brahmin woman with a man from a lower caste is *pratiloma* (hypogamous, literally 'against the hair') and hence an object of censure according to the laws of Manu.[32] Others claim that even though they, as members of Mahima Dharma, do not believe in caste, non-initiates with whom the wedding is arranged believe in it and see to it that the bride or the groom taken from a Mahima Dharmi family belongs to the same caste.[33] For some again, it is imperative for people who have not renounced the world to accept caste rules.

Indeed, a follower from Baud was surprised that I was asking the obvious.

He posed a counter-question: '*sansare rahi jati manibana* (won't the people who have not renounced the world observe caste)?'[34] This incredulous statement from an ordinary devotee is extraordinary for the understanding of classical conceptions it offers. Implicit here is an acknowledgement of the distinction between the societal self and the individual self — the man-in-the-world and the individual-outside-the-world — stylishly posed by Dumont. For the French sociologist, the individual-outside-the-world, the renouncer, contributes to innovations in Indian religion which the man-in-the-world aggregates, adds and absorbs only to reproduce caste as structural practice. Here the single guiding principle for understanding the two intersecting worlds is provided by the overriding continuity of the caste order. Hence eventually, most radical sects 'degenerate into castes'.[35] If the statement of a lay Mahima Dharmi partly reinforces Dumont's formulation of the distinction between the renouncer and the householder, the diverse perceptions, applications, accommodations and interrogations of principles of caste and sect by the members of Mahima Dharma give the lie to Dumont's argument that sects end up upholding the caste order.

Let me cite two examples in order to portray the wide divergence in approach to caste — among the ascetics of the faith — with regard to lay followers. The *sadhus* of Paschimashrama (western *ashrama*) of the Balkaldhari group affirmed in unison that observance of caste rules did not come in the way of *dharma palan* in the case of *gruhi bhaktas*. '*Jati kula raksha kari se mane dharmapalan karuchanti*' — they are following their faith while preserving their caste and lineage. Anakar Das, a Kaupindhari *sanyasi* from the Barpali region, an earnest follower of Bhima Bhoi, was furious when my senior friend Renudidi casually asked the woman disciple at the Karamunda *ashrama* about her caste.[36] She belonged to '*stri jati*, (the woman caste) like all other women', the *sadhu* snapped. It was typical of upper-caste non-initiates like us to enquire about *jati*. 'It will take long for us to get over our superstitions and hangovers,' he added angrily.

On our way back from the *ashrama* our rickshawpuller thought it fit to inform us that the Anakar Das had originally been a Harijan (*dalit*). He had taken *diksha* a long time back and was a very sincere devotee of the Prabhu. He had also initiated several Harijan and low-caste people into Mahima Dharma.

How are we to understand this? Is the fact that only untouchables and low-caste persons had become disciples of Anakar Das indicative of caste bias of the followers? Or is it that the ascetic had consciously decided to preach only among ex-untouchables and lower caste people? It is true that *sanyasis* of Mahima Dharma do not mention their caste and parentage, nor do they go back to their own villages to preach. Disciples are therefore generally unaware of the caste status and family background of their *diksha-gurus*. The position and esteem of *sanyasis* depend on their force of personality, style of living, knowledge and the capacity to reach out to people. On the other hand, it is not totally wrong to assume that if a renouncer decides to spread the message of the faith in villages close to his own, his caste background will not remain unknown to his initiates. Once more, we are faced with the constitutive mix-ups and inconsistencies of social worlds that make categorical formulations impossible.

Gender and Kinship

Marriages between families of initiates and non-initiates produce intriguing consequences. Women from Mahima Dharmi families married into non-Mahima Dharmi ones, frequently face an uphill task trying to remain true to the commands of their faith. The greatest challenge here is posed by the injunction against the acceptance of *prasad*, particularly the *mahaprasad*, the great graced left-over of Jagannath, the Lord of the Universe. Nirmalprabha, now a resident of Bhubaneswar, recounted a poignant story.[37] Nirmalprabha was born into a family that has followed the faith for generations. Her natal village, she stated proudly and nostalgically, has found mention in Biswanath Baba's *Itihasa*, an obvious proof of its importance. However, she was married into a family of Jagannath devotees in a village where Mahima Dharma had hardly any presence.

Life was not easy for Nirmalprabha; she had great trouble trying to observe the code of conduct prescribed by her faith. The situation reached a crisis when her mother-in-law returned from a trip to the temple of Jagannath in Puri carrying the *mahaprasad*. Nirmalprabha refused to have it. Her mother-in-law was outraged. How dare the wife of her only son, got as a blessing of Jagannath, not take the *prasad* of the great Lord? The situation became tense. Nirmalprabha, resigned to her fate, relented. It was perhaps the wish of the Absolute she told herself that she take *mahaprasad*. Why else had the Supreme led her parents to marry her into a family of Jagannath devotees? She prayed silently to the Absolute and ate the *prasad*. The next day she fell ill. Days and weeks passed, different doctors and medicines were tried, but her fever did not subside. Her worried parents-in-law finally sought the help of her father. Her father, incensed at the injustice done to his daughter, asked the in-laws to pray to the Absolute, beg for his mercy and offer *ghee* for the sacred fire. The in-laws obeyed. The following day, the fever left Nirmalprabha. Since then, there have been no unjust impositions on Nirmalprabha nor obstructions to her path of Dharma. What is more, some residents of her affinal village, astounded by the force of her faith, have become Mahima Dharmis.

This romanticized tale of trial and triumph invokes faith and affect in poignant ways. A dramatic contrast between an ideal village mentioned in the official history of the sect and a village with very initiates stands for the vicissitudes — the pleasure and pain — in Nirmalprabha's life before and after her marriage. Her natal village here is both 'an ideal and an idyll', its idyllic qualities enhanced by the pleasurable experience of her maiden days, made powerful and palpable by nostalgia.[38] Nirmalprabha emerged successful by dint of pure devotion after a tough ordeal. What set the seal on this achievement was her success in persuading her hostile in-laws to accept the efficacy of her faith. Resolute trust in her Dharma provided the 'hidden transcript' for the outwardly submissive daughter-in-law.[39]

Pramila, a resident of a village near Bhubaneswar, bore a son after repeated prayers to Mahima Prabhu.[40] She lost her mind after the birth of the child, forgot her Prabhu and did not get the son initiated. The boy died. Pramila realized her mistake. She repented and began to follow the instructions of the faith with great sincerity. She was blessed with another son. She has taught her son and daughters to pray to the Lord, but has had no success with her husband so far. She lives in fear of the loss of her son and prays to the Master constantly, *dibaratra* (day and night), begging for forgiveness.

Shakuntala, a spirited, unmarried woman from a village in the district of Sundargarh, had to deal with the constant hostility of her father and brothers after she decided to accept Mahima Dharma.[41] The male members of her family were dubious — how could a woman have her own independent views on which religion to follow? Moreover, they argued, it was difficult for a householder to abide by the rules of Mahima Dharma. Shakuntala refused to yield. Four years passed between the time she got attracted to the faith following the visit and preaching by an ascetic, and the time she got initiated, years of perennial tension and conflict. When I met her in Joranda in 1990, she had been a devout Mahima Dharmi for seven years. Her family, she said, had finally come round. She did, however, occasionally face ridicule from fellow-villagers. But, stated Shakuntala with a twinkle in her eye, 'I give it back to them.' Her strength and her resolve had also borne fruit. Parvati, another woman from her village had got initiated. This woman was her source of support in the village and her companion on her annual visits to Joranda. Together, hoped Shakuntala, they would gradually be able to induce a change of attitude toward their 'true faith' on the part of other villagers.[42]

These anecdotes of women are remarkable not only for insights into relations of kin and gender within the family but also for glimpses into the triumphs and troubles that underpin the process of being and becoming a follower of Mahima Dharma. Liminality inheres in the lives of the women who carefully navigate the push and pull of gender inequality and belief in a faith that advocates equality, in addition to the frictions produced by the specific norms of a distinct faith. It is evident that there are wide variations in the diligence and care with which the daily rituals are performed and prescribed code of conduct adhered to by householder devotees. While Shakuntala proudly affirmed the strength of her belief by stating that not for once since her initiation had she failed to wake up early and perform the *śaran* in the *brahma muhurta* and Santosh, a government employee from Sonepur smilingly lifted his shirt to reveal the *geru basan* for evening *darśan* he wore underneath — forcefully asserting the separate yet similar ways in which each strictly followed the precepts of the faith, they also admitted that there were others who were very lax in their ways. This discrepancy notwithstanding, for the lay members as a whole, the difficulties of abiding by the rules of faith while not directly challenging the norms of caste, of being a member of the village community and belonging to a special community of believers, engenders a self-awareness that bolster their belief in a separate Dharma which in turn sustains them through the ups and downs of life.

Rituals

It is in order here to track the interface of prescription and practice through a survey of the rules pertaining to important life-cycle rituals as codified by Biswanath Baba.[43] An exposition of them helps us understand the standard of life the Balkaldhari *samaj* wants its followers to attain.

Life begins at birth and the period of birth impurity continues for 21 days regardless of the sex of the child. At the end of this period the parents throw water mixed with cowdung (*gomaya*) over their bodies, bathe and drink *pabitra*. Their purification is complete. They bathe the child with *gomaya jala* and then perform *śaran*. Later in the day a gathering of *sanyasis* and *bhaktas* is organized in a nearby *ashrama*. *Akhandabati* is lit with *ghee* and sadhus and *bhaktas* invoke Mahima Alekh through *bhajans*. *Balyalila* is performed the next morning and Kaupindhari *sanyasis* are given new *kaupins*. *Ghee* is offered at Prabhudwar and Balkaldhari Babas are offered *bhiksha*. A suitable name for the newborn is chosen by the Babas. The parents bear the cost of all this.

The grandeur and magnitude of the ceremony depend on their resources. In the absence of *sanyasis*, *gruhi bhaktas* are invited. The *nam-karan* (naming) then has to wait for the appearance of a Baba in the area or for the *mela* at Joranda.

The *annaprasan* ceremony involves a similar function. Along with *bhaktas* and *sanyasis*, relatives of the parents are also invited. *Saptamruta* — a mixture of milk, curds, ghee, honey, sugar, sandal and camphor — is prepared the previous day. Before sunrise on the morning of the *annaprasan* the *saptamruta* is poured into a new earthen pot and kept outside the house or in front of a *tungi* in an area which has been swept clean and plastered with *gomaya* (excretions of the cow). Sandal and camphor are poured on the pot, which the Mahima Dharmis then offer to Mahima Prabhu. The child is fed with the mixture and all others present get a share. It is significant that all the articles used in Hindu worship and rituals feature in the *saptamruta*. The Balkaldharis have also done away with the founder's rejection of the barber and washerman. The barber is called to shave the child's head at an early age (*mundan*).[44] He, however, has no role to play in the marriage ceremony.

Brahma bibaha, the prescribed mode of wedding, is quite unique in style. Widely prevalent during the time of Mahima Swami, it is observed rarely now, only in cases where both the bride and the groom belong to Mahima Dharmi families. At each stage, starting with the negotiations and extending to the time the bride and groom start their new life, the devotees of the faith play an important role. A *bhakta* is chosen by all the members involved to officiate at the wedding. The parents of the bride and the groom pray at the *tungi* once the negotiations come through, and they also organize *nam-bhajan* before the wedding. The ceremony takes place in the bride's house early in the morning. The site of the ceremony is swept clean the day before and purified with cowdung. *Saptamruta* is prepared. On the day, a lamp and two vessels full of water are placed near the wedding *bedi* (platform). The lamp is lit with *ghee*. The bride and groom, their parents and all others present finish *snana-śauca* (morning oblation) at the prescribed hour and come to the *bedi*. The ceremony begins with a prayer to Alekh by the officiating *bhakta*. It is followed by the prayers of the bride's and groom's parents and those of the bride and groom. The groom's hand is placed on one of the vessels, the *bhakta* joins to it the hand of the bride — and they are declared man and wife. All the participants pray to the Lord again for the health, happiness and prosperity of the couple and for the welfare of humanity.[45] *Saptamruta* is drunk by the partners and shared by the other unmarried invitees. The earthen pot which contained it is then broken. A feast follows. The feast consists only of vegetarian dishes. Flesh is forbidden to Mahima Dharmis.[46]

The total absence of *purohit*, *śastras*, *nai* and *dhobi* in the *Brahma bibaba* is remarkable. The *bhaktas* place their sole reliance in Mahima Prabhu; nothing but his blessings is required to make the union happy. Another significant feature is the respect given to the partners, whose parents ask for their consent before the wedding is decided upon. It is in this ceremony that one gets the glimpse of a parallel structure, notwithstanding the fact that it occurs rarely.

Mahima Dharmis do not burn their dead but bury them instead. The period of death impurity is eleven days if the dead person was married and nine days if he was not. At the end of it, the earthen pots in the house are thrown away, the house is purified with *gomaya*, while the members of the family clean themselves with *snana-śauca* and drink *pabitra* to be free of all impurities. They are now fit to pray to the Prabhu.

Ceremonies

Ceremonies and festivals revive and reinforce the identity of *bhaktas* as members of the Mahima *samaj*. The visit of a *sanyasi* occasions a gathering of disciples from nearby villages. The Baba takes shelter in a *tungi* for the night if there is one, or in a village schoolroom or *sabhaghar* (meeting hall). The *bhaktas* collect there in the evening. Non-initiates are welcome to listen to *dharmopodeś* (religious instruction). The *dhuni* is lit, Mahima Alekh is invoked, and *bhajans* begin. The group gets immersed in passionate singing which continues until late at night.

A simple ceremony held regularly and frequently is *balyalila*.[47] It is celebrated on its own or as part of a *brahma-bibaha* or the *śukla caturdaśi* (fourteenth day of the bright fortnight) celebrations. An individual member or a group of adherents of a particular locality take the initiative in organizing *balyalila* as an independent ceremony. It carries with it the desire of wish-fulfillment. Kshetrabasi Baba lucidly describes *balyalila* in simple verse:

Balyalila drabya samarpi Brahme
Balake bantan samata jñane
E bara utkrushta dharma dhamare
Śisu atma seba dharma dandare
Sahaje prabhata kal
Brahmanka prasada balaka badane debaku barnibe phal.

[The offering of *balyalila* is distributed to children without any discrimination. Service of children is a superior mode of *dharma palan*. *Phal*, reward, will accrue if Brahma's *prasad* is given to children in the early morning.][48]

The ceremony takes place at dawn on any *purnima* (full moon). Followers begin gathering at the *ashrama* from the afternoon of *caturdaśi*, the previous day. A common meal is taken before sunset. After it the followers change into their garment for *darśan* and pray to Alekh in unison facing west. They lie prostrate. Their heads, chests, hands and feet touch the ground. The posture changes: the body contracts, the outstretched arms joined together come to rest on the forehead, the right foot rests on the back of the left kneecap. The body stretches and contracts five times in a similar manner while the *bhaktas* change from right to left foot and back to the right.[49] Prayers are offered silently with the movements of the body (*kayik* and *manasik darśan*).[50] They are interspersed with cries of 'Mahima Alekh'. In the end, all the *bhaktas* stand up and pray to the Lord, looking upwards and holding their folded hands over their heads. The presiding Baba lights the *bati* (lamp) and holds it up.

The *darśan* over, the *dhuni* is lit and the *bhajans* begin. Men sing, women sit nearby and listen. Participation in singing is not obligatory. Several followers sit scattered in the *ashrama* compound in small groups and exchange news. The air is one of 'pervasive friendliness', the mood that of a family gathering on a festive occasion. A feeling of affinity and amity temporarily subsumes individual identities and distinctions and highlights the unity and solidarity of the followers of Alekh. The participants stay up until well after midnight, making arrangements for the next day's ceremony.

On the day of the *purnima*, everyone present at the *ashrama* is up long before dawn. They purify their bodies with *snana-śauca* and perform *śaran*. A particular spot is swept clean and purified with cowdung. A mixture of puffed rice, flaky rice, milk, curds, *ghee*, honey, sugar, coconuts and bananas is prepared in a new earthen pot and carried to the spot which has been cleaned. The *bati* is lit and the Baba offers the food to Brahma. *Sanyasis* and *bhaktas* stand around and pray. Children from neighbouring areas are called to the *ashrama*, made to stand in rows and take the name of Mahima Alekh. Each child is fed a handful of the mixture and the rest is distributed among the followers. The children go away while the *bhaktas* stay on for another meal, which consists of rice, lentils, vegetables, *chutney*, and *payesa*. The meal marks the end of the ceremony. The participants start to disperse and go back to their homes and their routine lives with renewed vigour, having restated their faith in the Prabhu.[51]

Sanyasis

The last chapter has discussed the processes that led to the establishment of two groups of *sanyasis* who lead separate *samajas* — the Balkaldhari *samaj* and the Kaupindhari *samaj* — at the Mahima Gadi at Joranda. The division has become a matter of history. There is now little talk of a unified Mahima Dharma. The rival orders are engaged in consolidating and strengthening their organizations and institutions, formalizing the rules and regulations that are codified in writing, and extending the numbers of their *bhaktas*, *tungis* and *ashramas*. The sedentarization of the two orders of Mahima Dharmi renouncers works in tandem with the competition between them.

The entire Gadi complex, with its *samadhi mandir*, *dhuni mandir*, *śunya mandir*, *dharmaśalas* and other constructions, covers about a hundred acres of land spread across three villages, Joranda, Natima and Patna.[52] The Balkaldhari group controls the key institution of Mahima Dharma: the *samadhi mandir*, the *asthan* of the Guru. The members of this group are locally referred to as the owners of the *bara matha* (the larger, older *matha*). The *bara matha*, in terms of landed property and prestige, scores over its rival, the *sana matha* (the younger, smaller *matha*) of the Kaupindhari group. Apart from the three key institutions mentioned above, the Balkaldhari *samaj* has its own *sabhaghar* (assembly hall), *koshagar* (treasury), *granthagar* (library), *niti mandir* (a place were all the articles needed for services at the *gadi* are kept), *ghantaghar* (bell room), a compound for *satsanga goshthi*, and numerous *tungis* and *ashramas* which house the renouncers and lay disciples during ceremonies and festivals (see the Appendix for a plan of Mahima Gadi). The *tungis* and *ashramas*, like the other buildings, have been constructed with donations from *bhaktas*.[53] All this speaks of a structurally well-ordered group of renouncers.

The *sanyasis* of the *samaj* are divided into three clearly defined hierarchical grades. The lowest rung is formed by *bairagis* or *fokodias*, new initiates to the monastic order. The Kaupindhari *sanyasis*, numerically the largest group among the ascetics, form the intermediate stratum. The highest grade is made up of Balkaldharis.[54] The affairs of the Balkaldhari *samaj* are conducted by a Parichalana Samiti composed of five senior Balkaldhari *sanyasis*. In practice, for five decades, Biswanath Baba played a crucial role as the *adhyaksha* of the Parichalana Samiti. His death in 1992 saw the end of one-man leadership. From that time on, the Parichalana Samiti came to be composed of four *adhyakshas*.

The *sanyasis* of the *samaj* are expected to conform to strict rules of conduct which were formalized and codified by Biswanath Baba. The *bairagis* function under the tutelage of the Kaupindharis and the Balkaldharis. They are meant to serve the senior *sanyasis* while studying the texts of Mahima Dharma and conducting their lives along the precepts of the faith. Their itinerant movements are tuned to the wanderings of the Kaupindhari and Balkaldhari *sanyasis*. These renouncers are enjoined to be constantly on the move, spend but one night at a village, travel only on foot, live exclusively on alms and, of course, not possess any kind of property. The acquisition of knowledge by the Kaupindharis must include the tenets and the philosophy of Mahima Dharma as well as the *śastras* (scriptures). The Balkaldhari Babas, the spiritual guides, command total devotion. These Babas, who embody the highest form of human existence, are entrusted with the spiritual welfare of their followers. The norms of behaviour which govern their lives are rigorous: they sleep on the bare ground; own nothing except their *balkal bana*, a garment made up of a girdle, a piece of bark worn around the waist and another bit flung across the left shoulder; eat one meal a day, which consists of cooked food obtained as *bhiksha* in a broken earthen pot. They do not touch money or precious metal.[55] Their lives are constructed as models for others to follow: existential examples of the ways of the self-realized.

There are, of course, gaps between precepts and practice. At a mundane and somewhat trivial level the *sanyasis*, particularly the Kaupindharis, use buses whenever they are available. Similarly, in the last years of his life infirmity had forced Biswanath Baba to ride a rickshaw which was pulled by Kaupindharis. Narayan Baba, the *sampadak* (secretary) of the Parichalana Samiti, had also taken recourse to the same mode of transport.

More significantly, the process of setting up a well-structured and institutionalized sect and the maintenance and efficient management of the Gadi complex have diluted the principles which had once so markedly struck a note of renunciation. Property in land, we have seen, has been and is being acquired for construction, which also necessitates the collection of money. Donations in cash and kind are also taken for the various ceremonies and for the sustenance of those *sanyasis* whose duties require them to spend considerable lengths of time at Joranda. The performance of regular *niti* at the *mandirs* demands the constant presence of *sanyasis* at Joranda. The responsibility for conducting ritual services devolves on the Balkaldharis. These Babas are assisted by Kaupindharis. The persons in charge of *niti* serve for a month at a time, and for that period cannot move out of Joranda. Consequently, the practice of *bhiksha* becomes merely symbolic for them. They do go out to the neighbouring villages to collect alms, and they eat food cooked in the *ashramas*. In Joranda the phrase '*Baba bhiksha karuchanti*' has almost become synonymous with 'Baba is eating'.

The resourceful renouncers have hit upon an ingenious solution to conform to the rule of constant mobility. The huge area that the Gadi now occupies straddles three villages. There are *ashramas* in all the three. The ascetics rotate from one *ashrama* to the other for the entire time they stay at the Gadi, never staying more than one night in a village yet never moving out of the Gadi compound. The perpetual movement of a dynamic preacher has come to be replaced by a static memorial which stands at the locus of a sedentarized sect. Formal conformity to rules has superseded respect for the spirit behind the founder's principles. Many Balkaldhari *sanyasis* have followed the example of the *niti* Babas. They have roughly demarcated their zone of movement, their spheres of influence. They have come to be loosely regarded as the proprietors of particular *ashramas* or *tungis*. They reside there frequently, preach in the neighbouring areas, and preside over all the functions of the *ashrama*.[56]

Biswanath Baba's powerful personality and his long leadership of the *samaj* had made his case unique: he had very nearly come to be regarded as the Guru.[57] This had caused further shifts. During the *guru purnima* celebrations Biswanath Baba sat outside his *tungi* with a *bhikshapatra* in front of him.[58] Old age had constrained his movements considerably. But the fact of his supreme position lent a new quality to the act. For the *bhaktas* to see and be seen by the Baba constituted an act of piety. It was *darśan*, not of the Absolute through intricate movements of the body and mind, but *darśan* in the sense of 'seeing' and 'being seen', of going into the presence of a human Guru. Physical proximity to Biswanath Baba was nearly tantamount to proximity to the great Guru. Money and food offered to Biswanath Baba were a token of the devotion of the disciple, of his humble service to the Lord. The Baba did not touch the currency notes and coins, which went straight to the treasury of the *samaj*. But the fact that money was offered to the *adhyaksha* highlighted the mutations the sect has undergone over time. Property and establishment have replaced poverty and movement; there are strictures on the acquisition of property by individual members but increase in the Gadi's possessions is actively encouraged.

These changes and shifts in emphasis, however, are regarded as necessary adjustments engendered by the need for the maintenance and proper functioning of the *samaj*. The overarching construct of the *samaj* confers on the sect an idea of sameness and stability and makes it seem as if the community of Mahima Dharmis has been operating in exactly the same way from the time of its inception by the founder. This explains in part the rigour and rigidity with which rules are observed in the *bara matha*.

At the Joranda complex (as well as for other followers of the faith) the day begins very early. The inhabitants get up long before sunrise and perform *snana-śauca*: They relieve themselves and then take a bath which purifies their bodies.[59] The mind is sought to be purified by concentrating on Alekh. The renouncers change into the *bhek* (garment) specially reserved for *śaran* and *darśan* and go the memorial for *śaran*. They face east and prostrate themselves seven times, praying to Alekh Prabhu for the welfare of the world. Then the morning *niti* begins.[60] A siren kept in the *ghantaghar* is sounded well in advance to alert the Babas. Kaupindhari *sanyasis* sweep clean the compound outside the innermost sanctum. Only the Balkaldhari Niti Babas have the right to enter the *samadhi* (the enclosed area within the first boundary wall). They sweep it clean, throw water in and around it (*jala phetiba*), spray camphor and sandalwood, and perform *camar seba* and *arati* at the *samadhi*. During the services huge lamps are lit with *ghee*; four bells posted at the four doors of the sanctum are rung, conches are blown, and *bhajans* of Bhima Bhoi are sung as the Babas circumambulate the *samadhi* waving *camar* and praying to Alekh. Half of the water, camphor and sandal are poured into a small drain inside the *mandir* which leads to a *kunda* (receptacle) outside. The mixture is given to the *bhaktas* along with sweets made from gram flour as *prasad*. The same services are performed at the *śunya mandir* and at the *dhuni mandir*. Ritual services are offered at the *mandirs* at noon. The same procedure is repeated except for the lighting of lamps and the singing of *bhajans*. An important addition is the breaking of coconuts by Kaupindharis outside the first *bedha*. These coconuts are offered to Alekh by followers who want particular wishes to be fulfilled.

Singing is an important part of the evening *niti*. This service starts after *darśan*. At *darśan* the *sanyasis* prostrate themselves five times, facing the west. In the afternoon the siren reminds the renouncers to get ready for the service. Brass lamps are lit again and conches and bells are sounded. A group of Kaupindharis and lay disciples go round the compound within the second boundary singing the compositions of Bhima Bhoi and others to the accompaniment of the *gini* and *khanjani* (cymbal and tambourine). The singing continues for a long time. *Arati* is performed with great care. The *niti* provides a good example of the shifts within the faith entailed by an acceptance and appropriation of the traditions of dominant Hinduism by Mahima Dharma. The close resemblance of these services with those offered at the temple of Jagannath and other Hindu temples is striking. For Eschmann, the *niti* at the Gadi was 'an obvious adaptation of the worship of Jagannath which is likewise termed as *niti*'.[61] *Seva* (service) is an inherent feature of *niti*. The concept of *seva* is tied to the idea of a personal god. The performance of *arati*, the waving of the *camar*, the *pradakshin* (circumambulation), all symbolize the devotee's sincerest wish of serving his Lord, of taking care of him.[62] In Hindu temples the *camar* is waved in front of the deities to keep dirt and flies away from them. The Sikhs wave it over the Granth Saheb. The ascetics of Mahima Dharma treat the *samadhi* of Mahima Swami as the representative of the Guru and offer services that befit a personal god.

The time between the ritual services is taken up by *bhiksha*, preaching and the learning and interpretation of the scriptures. Evenings are spent in group singing, discussion and contemplation. Kaupindharis, *bairagis* and *gruhi bhaktas* gather near the Balkaldhari Babas. Texts of the faith and other scriptures are read out, their meanings are explained and analysed, the doubts and queries of the *bairagis* and Kaupindharis are cleared. A structure of paradigmatic knowledge is established, the path of spiritual advancement is expounded before the lower orders of renouncers, the learners. A definite mode in which these renouncers have to conduct their lives is set forth. Great importance attaches to the acquisition of 'knowledge': command over the *śastras* is used as the criterion of assessment in the promotion of a renouncer from one grade to another. Strict observance of the prescribed code of conduct is a corollary to the acquisition of knowledge. This insistence on rigorous observance of rules has made the Balkaldhari group fall more and more in line with and established order.

The Kaupindhari *samaj* presents a different picture. The atmosphere here is more relaxed; conformity and discipline are not imposed with great rigour. The room of the secretary of the *samaj*, Raj Kishore Baba, has fluorescent lights and wooden bookcases with glass fronts which display the texts of Bhima Bhoi, the Upanishads and other Hindu scriptures. Raj Baba moves around with a cigarette in his mouth. This, however, cannot be regarded as a contravention of rules: Mahima Swami is known to have been very fond of smoking tobacco. Raj Baba wears a *gairik bastra* which comes down to the knees and a *chadar* which covers the upper part of the body. This is an innovation of Mahindra Baba which the group has retained. Raj Baba is a very busy man. He is a member of the governing body of Mahima Mahavidyalaya, a college sponsored by the *sana matha*, he has close ties with the people of Joranda and takes an active interest in the affairs of the village. He also practises astrology, an ability which brings him closer to the inhabitants of the locality. The Kaupindhari *samaj* is liberal enough to allow its secretary to devote time to individual pursuits which have nothing to do with Mahima Dharma. Raj Baba takes no money from the people for telling them their futures; he earns prestige and esteem through the practice.[63]

The structures of the Kaupindhari *samaj* are situated in a spatially compact area. The office, library, *sabhaghar*, treasury, *dharmaśalas*, and *ashramas* stand next to one another inside one large compound near the entrance to the *gadi mandir*. The *akhanda bati mandir*, the *guru purnima dhuni mandir* and the *śunya mandir* are situated in another compound, just outside the boundary wall of the *gadi mandir*. These two compounds make up the Kaupindharis' holdings within the Gadi complex. The acquisition of property is an on-going process.

The norms of behaviour prescribed for the members derive from the works of Bhima Bhoi. They do not differ much in content from those applicable to all categories of renouncers of the Balkaldhari *samaj*. All the renouncers are of equal status, follow the same code of conduct, and adhere to the same rules and regulations. Recognition of altered social conditions has made the Kaupindharis pragmatic in their approach: they feel no qualms in accepting cash donations or in using vehicles for transport. Rather, they regard their open acceptance of new codes as statements of their honesty and frankness. 'The Balkaldharis have such impractical rules only on paper, they dishonour them in action.'[64] This practical outlook and open-mindedness has left the *samaj* free to engage in experiments; it also accounts for the presence of a certain degree of laxity and lack of discipline among the Kaupindharis.

As stated before, in their day-to-day practices the *sanyasis* of this *samaj* claim to have not deviated from the precepts of Bhima Bhoi. They get up before sunrise, perform *śaran* at *brahmamuhurta* and then proceed to do *niti* at their *śunya mandir*. They go out to collect alms, read religious texts, offer the midday ritual service and gather again for *darśan* and the evening *niti*. This service lasts longer than that of the Balkaldharis. *Bhajans* are sung for a long time with great fervour. Here again, the insistence on rigour and strict adherence that permeates the practices of the *bara matha* gives way to a somewhat casual attitude.

The best instance of the open-mindedness of the *samaj* is its grant of recognition to the Matas (mothers/women ascetics) of the Mata *matha*. In the Balkaldhari group, women are strictly forbidden to enter the monastic order.[65] The Balkaldharis view women who have left their families to become *sanyasinis* and have taken the initiative to build a *matha* with great suspicion as those who have moved away from the path outlined by the Dharma. Under no condition is the *bara matha* prepared to recognize them as true followers of the faith. The Kaupindharis do not allow women in their monastic order, but they accept the *sanyasini* status of the Matas and are ready to guide and advise them.[66] This lends credence to their claim of being the true followers of Bhima Bhoi. The poet, we know, had not only

Main entrance to the Balkaldhari Ashrama, Jordana

granted *diksha* to women who had left their homes for his *ashrama*, he had raised his spiritual consort to the position of a *devi* (goddess). Ma Annapurna sat alongside Bhima Bhoi on a raised platform and received the same services that were offered to the poet-propagator of Mahima Dharma.[67]

A significant section of the Kaupindhari *samaj* consists of *sanyasis* who live and preach in the western part of Orissa. They owe allegiance to the *sana matha* at Joranda but congregate at the Khaliapali *ashrama* on festive occasions. To this day the group has retained the spirit of militancy and of the questioning of authority that was central to Bhima Bhoi's life and teaching.[68] Its members are troubled by the social inequalities which a faith like Mahima Dharma and a personality like Bhima Bhoi have not yet succeeded in removing. They are concerned about the ignorance of the people, which prevents them from coming into the fold of *satya dharma*, and at the high position and authority which the Brahmans continue to enjoy in society. They urge their disciples and the people among whom they preach to draw inspiration from the life and the numerous creations of Bhima Bhoi, the divine *śisya* of the divine master.

There are other sub-groups of renouncers within the two main *samajas*. Some of them have established their own *ashramas* outside the Gadi complex. The Lata *ashrama* is one such. Till the early 1990s, it asserted its autonomy by refusing to come within the fold of the Parichalana Samiti even while recognizing the authority of the Balkaldhari *samaj*. The death of Biswanath Baba and the increase in the number of *adhyaksha* induced the members of Lata *ashrama* to rejoin the *bara matha* as full-fledged members. The inmates of the Jamusara *ashrama* continue to maintain their separate existence although they owe allegiance to Biswanath Baba's group. The followers of the late Jatia Baba, a leader of the Kaupindharis, established an *ashrama* at Natima, while Kasinath Baba, another leader of the *Kaupindhari* group, resided in an *ashrama* of his own. The *ashrama* at Angarbandha in Angul, under the *sana matha*, started celebrating its own *guru purnima*, and a few others followed suit. A group of Mahima Dharmis settled at Chiplima in Sambalpur district had begun their search for a new Alekh and adopted a new *mantra* for the purpose — 'nutan tarak Brahmanam'.[69] The sect is now not one but many.

Pilgrimage

A pilgrimage to the Guru's memorial at Joranda on *maghi purnima*, constitutes a very significant activity in the life of a lay disciple. This huge annual congregation of renouncers and householders, the most important event in the ritual calendar of the faith, provides a crucial juncture for the reinforcement and consolidation of Mahima Dharmis as a bounded community. All rituals and practices at the site reaffirm the identity of a believer. The circumambulation of the memorial, the performance of prayer to the Absolute together with thousands of other devotees, and the joint singing of *bhajans* in the evenings bolster the sense of belonging to Mahima Dharma. Initiations performed by the ascetics in different villages are ratified at the time of *guru purnima*, a ceremony that creates a common bond among all new initiates. And meetings of renouncers and lay followers bring the householder disciples in direct contact with their *diksha-gurus*, preceptors who have initiated them into the faith. It is a time when the identity as a Mahima Dharmi blurs and takes precedence over all others.[70] In short, the congregation at Joranda provides the best example of the concretization of the Mahima Dharmi *samaj* and a resurgence and revitalization of the beliefs of the *bhaktas*. For the ascetics at the helm of affairs, the pilgrimage provides the best occasion to ensure the effective functioning of the *samaj*. Direct interaction with a large number of lay disciples enables them to insist on the necessity of conforming to the path outlined by their special faith. The annual congregation recreates and reinforces the bounded community through an employment of the us/them dichotomy, a demarcation of the frontiers between initiates and non-initiates.[71]

The gathering at Joranda is a grand event: it is at once an *utsav* and a *mela*, a combination of pilgrimage and fair. Hordes of *bhaktas* travel long distances to reach the *asthan* of the Guru, to offer their prayers at the *asthan* and perhaps to get their wishes fulfilled. For them it is also an occasion to interact with other members of their Dharma and to draw sustenance from the extensive activities of the Mahima Dharmi *samaj*. Non-initiates come in large numbers to gain *punya* (merit) by visiting a sacred site. The explicit meaning of pilgrimage, the accumulation of merit, holds true in their case.[72] Many come to enjoy the *mela*. Numerous private buses plying between Joranda and Cuttack during the celebrations bring in pilgrims and tourists.[73] *Bhaktas* and non-initiates from distant places come in buses which they specially hire. Oriya newspapers announce the date of the *utsav* well in advance to help people make proper preparations for the trip.

The ceremony starts on *caturdaśi* (the day before the full moon) and continues for four days, while the *mela* lasts about a week. A large compound around the Gadi is taken up for the fair. Stalls sell all possible items ranging from texts on Mahima Dharma and other religious texts to baby's rattles. Blaring loudspeakers hold out the temptation of Oriya *naca* (folk theatre), circuses and magic shows. Several food stalls are set up to cater to the needs of the tourists. Students and teachers from the Mahima Mahavidyalaya provide first aid. Photo studios sell photographs of the *mandirs*.

The interior of the Gadi complex comes agog with activity. *Tungis* and *ashramas* overflow with *sanyasis* and *bhaktas* and the *sabhaghar* and courtyards of *ashramas* become the centre of meetings. The compound of the Gadi *mandir* offers a remarkable sight at *brahmamuhurtas*: hundreds of Mahima Dharmis and devoted non-initiates lie prostrate, praying to Alekh in unison. In the mornings coconuts offered by lay disciples are broken by Kaupindhari *sanyasis* outside the *samadhi mandir*: each carries a personal wish of the devotee to the Maker. In the evening huge brass lamps are lit to dispel darkness, while *bhaktas* pour *ghee* on them with prayers to Alekh. Renouncers and lay disciples congregate in several groups to sing *bhajans* and *stutis* in honour of Mahima Prabhu until late at night. In the general mood of empathy and sharing, individual identities get blurred, generating an 'altered consciousness'.[74]

For the *sanyasis* of both the *samajas*, particularly those in leadership, it is a busy time. They have to take proper care of the devotees, hold meetings with the *bhaktas*, grant initiation, draw up the budget for the coming year in consultation with other important *sanyasis*, and perform *niti* with meticulous care. The *adhyakshas* of the Parichalana Samiti of the Balkaldhari group have the added responsibility of holding the *Satsanga Goshthi*.[75] The *Goshti*, which generally takes place two days after the full moon, marks the culmination of the celebrations.

Satsanga Goshthi literally translates as an assembly of *sat* (good/honest) people. The Balkaldhari *samaj* takes great care to ensure that only the worthy and the deserving are granted the right of participation in the *Goshthi*. All the householders and renouncers who take part are interviewed individually. They are carefully questioned on their behaviour in the preceding year and are allowed to join the *Goshthi* only when the members of the Parichalana Samiti are satisfied that they have conformed to the rules of the faith and have been guided by the spirit of the Dharma in their everyday activities. Lay disciples and *sanyasis* come up on their own to confess lapses in their behaviour. Minor offenders are let off with a warning or a fine; but if the nature of the offence is deemed to be serious, the person is ostracized temporarily. There was no excommunication in the years I visited the *mela*; during Eschmann's time a Kaupindhari *sanyasi* was expelled for good for violating the code of chastity and a Balkaldhari *sanyasi* was expelled for three years for visiting his own village and spending more than one night at a village.[76] This thorough questioning reflects the Balkaldharis' great concern with maintaining discipline and of keeping alive the notion of the devotee's accountability to the Lord. At the same time, the *Goshthi* exemplifies the ideal of equality of all the disciples of Mahima Swami. It is a statement of their unity and commonality. As such, members of the Parichalana Samiti are doubly careful in assessing the honesty and sincerity of the participants.[77]

The *Goshthi* is held in the morning in a compound specially reserved for the ceremony. The entrance to the compound is vigilantly guarded by Kaupindhari *sanyasis* of the *bara matha*, and no 'outsider' is allowed to enter. *Satsanga Goshthi* is a common meal in which the different grades of ascetics and lay disciples belonging to the Balkaldhari group sit and eat together in a gesture of equality, unity and brotherhood. The well-ordered sitting arrangement, however, hints at the maintenance of hierarchy. It also shows the Balkaldharis concern with order. The *adhyakshas* head the line followed, by Balkaldharis, Kaupindharis and *bairagis*. Last of all sit the male *gruhi bhaktas*. Women and new initiates are denied the right of participation. They are allowed to sit or stand at a distance and watch.

Once the participants sit down, plates made of *śal* leaves are distributed by a few Balkaldhari and Kaupindhari *sanyasis* and food is served. It is a sumptuous meal consisting of *bhat* (rice), *mitha bhat* (sweet rice), *dal* (lentils), two kinds of *tarkari* (vegetables), a sweet made from *kanca kadali* (green plantain), and *payesa* (a sweet dish). After all the participants are served, a few Balkaldhari Babas start feeding them with a mouthful of *payesa*, taking in return a mouthful of food from their plates. This is called *laga lagi*. This practice strikes at the root of discrimination and the rules of commensality set by caste society. Food and touch, the two carriers of pollution, are used as tools to break barriers and diffuse boundaries. Solidarity and equality within the *samaj* are underscored and reinforced each year through this symbolic act of reciprocal feeding. It provides a fitting end to the annual congregation, a ceremony designed to sustain, consolidate and rejuvenate the Mahima Dharmi *samaj*. The adherents set off on the return journey content and reassured: their faith is indeed the only true faith in the evil era of Kali.

Compared to the gathering at Joranda, the *mela* at Khaliapali is a small affair.[78] Till the late 1990s, Khaliapali was a remote village; there were no bus or train connections to it. *Bhaktas* and non-initiates, who came there, had to come on foot. This greatly reduced the number of participants. The *ashrama* was a site of pilgrimage for the followers of Bhima Bhoi, who inhabit a limited space in the western part of Orissa. Khaliapali could not boast of receiving visitors from places as far away as Andhra Pradesh, Mysore, West Bengal and Assam. This fair held out very few attractions. There were a handful of sweet stalls, one bookstall and one tent for *naca*. Inhabitants of the village, other than the ones in the trust of the *ashrama*, display no special involvement.

Community meal, Jordana

At the time I visited the fair, matters were in a state of turmoil. The proprietor of the *ashrama* had been ousted on a charge of defalcation, and there was no recognized leader to manage the ceremony. This defect was more than made up by the enthusiasm of those who had gathered there. *Maghi purnima* for them is a special day, the only day of the year on which the doors of the *samadhi mandir* of Bhima Bhoi and Ma Annapurna are opened. *Bhaktas* cherish the privilege of going into the presence of the *bhagaban*, of offering prayers to him directly. They worship the sandals of Bhima Bhoi and Annapurna, which are housed in another *mandir*, and pray for their guidance and support in life's trials and struggles. Devotees speak nostalgically of the grand old days when members of the faith climbed to the top of the *samadhi mandir* to tie a *kalas* (pitcher) at its golden pinnacle in the hope of wish-fulfillment, when Bhima Bhoi and later his son Kapileswar toured the village like a king mounted on a decorated horse and when Bhima Bhoi and Ma Annapurna sat on a raised platform and allowed their followers to worship them. Those were the days when the divine couple removed the sufferings of the followers and led them on the path of salvation.

Khaliapali, like Joranda, served to generate a feeling of fraternity and commonness among the participants. Worship and prayers at the *mandirs*, the singing of *bhajans* on the night of *caturdaśi*, conversations, exchange of stories of joy and woe and the collective presence at a sacred sight brought the participants together as members of a distinct group. The common meal which concluded the *utsav* lacked the sombre tenor of the *Gosthi*. At the same time, the meal did not mark out the members of Mahima Dharma from its non-members. It was a feast for all who had come to Bhima Bhoi's *ashrama* — men, women and children, renouncers and householders, devotees and non-initiates.

Indeed, my octogenarian Brahman host in Sonepur had railed against the gathering at Khaliapali, describing it as merely an occasion for poor low-caste and untouchable people to transgress Hindu norms by eating together with higher castes, (unsuccessfully) instructing me, a *Brahmanara jhiya* (a girl of a Brahman family), not to eat at the feast. Unknown to my host, the participants at the feast had efficaciously reiterated the teaching of Bhima Bhoi, dispersing at the end with a sense of well-being that *bhagaban* Bhima was ever present to help them tread the tortuous path of life.

Notes

1. For a detailed description of initiation, see Biswanath Baba, *Gruhasthashrama Subhakarmavidhana* (Mahimagadi, 2nd edition, 1985), pp. 22–6.

2. Sudhir Kakar, *The Inner World: A Psychoanalytic Study of Childhood and Society in India* (Delhi, Oxford University Press, 1978), p. 124.
3. Sudhir Kakar, *Shamans, Mystics and Doctors: A Psychological Inquiry into India and its Healing Traditions*. (Delhi, Oxford University Press, 1982), p. 272. It is remarkable how Kakar uncritically accepts Dumont's formulation of 'traditional' Indian society as hierarchical and governed entirely by the caste system in which the parts — the individuals, are subordinate to the whole.
4. Ten field diaries of Eschmann were given to me by her mother in Munich in February 1991. Six of them deal mainly with Mahima Dharma: field diaries No. 1 (1971–72), No. 2 (April–May 1974), No. 3 (May 1974), No. 4 (May 1974), No. 5 (June 1974) and No. 6 (no date).
5. These responses are taken from surveys conducted by Eschmann and her associates between 1971 and 1973. Eschmann Papers, Munich.
6. Excerpt from survey conducted by Eschmann and her assistants between 1971 and 1973, Eschmann Papers, Munich.
7. Benudhar Misra arrived at the Khaliapali *ashrama* in my presence on 7 March 1992.
8. These devotees simply accept the hierarchy of the renouncer and the householder without showing much knowledge of the inversion implied by the teachings of Mahima Swami. The founder had preached that anyone could gain salvation through pure devotion.
9. Interview with Sricharan Sahu, Khaliapali, 11 March 1992.
10. Saurabh Dube, *Stitches on Time*, p. 58.
11. Jean Comaroff, *Body of Power, Spirit of Resistance: The Culture and History of a South African People* (Chicago and London, University of Chicago Press, 1985).
12. Saurabh Dube, *Untouchable Pasts*; Sekhar Bandyopadhyay, *Caste, Protest and Identity in Colonial India: The Namasudras of Bengal, 1872–1947* (Richmond, Curzon Press, 1997); Mark Juergensmeyer, *Religion as Social Vision: The Movement against Untouchability in Twentieth Century Punjab*, (Berkeley and Los Angeles, University of California Press, 1982).
13. Eschmann's interview with Gauranga Nayak, Kuska, 27 April 1974. Eschmann's field diary No. 2, Eschmann Papers, Munich.
14. Interview with Nirmalprabha and Saudamini, both residents of the colony, Khandagiri *ashrama*, 16 March 1992.
15. 'Impact of Satya Mahima Dharma on Scheduled Castes and Scheduled Tribes in Orissa', *Adivasi*, 10:1, 1968–69, pp. 44–76. The study covered selected areas: Nayagarh of Puri district, Athgarh of Cuttack district, Rairakhol (Redaakhol) of Sambalpur district and Bhawanipatna of Kalahandi district. The number of tribal converts was assumed to be greater in these areas. The *bhaktas* studied constituted 1.1 per cent of the total population of 23 villages.
16. *Ibid.*
17. M. N. Srinivas, *Caste in Modern India and Other Essays* (Bombay, Asia Publishing House, 1962), p. 44. A critique of the concept is found in, among other works, David Hardiman, *The Coming of the Devi: Adivasi Assertion in Western India* (Delhi, Oxford University Press, 1987), pp. 157–63, Saurabh Dube, *Untouchable Pasts*, p. 128; Hermann Kulke, 'Ksatriyaisation and Social Change'.
18. See Sekhar Bandyopadhyay, *Caste, Protest and Identity*, introduction.
19. There is a huge corpus of literature on *dalit* politics. A few representative examples are, Gail Omvedt, *Dalits and the Democratic Revolution: Dr. Ambedkar and the Dalit Movement in Colonial India* (New Delhi, Sage Publications, 1994); Eleanor Zelliot,

From Untouchable to Dalit: Essays on the Ambedkar Movement (New Delhi, Manohar, 1996); Christophe Jaffrelot, *Analysing and Fighting Caste: Dr Ambedkar and Untouchability* (Delhi, Permanent Black, 2005).

20. A detailed discussion and critical analysis of conversion understood in the context of incorporation in distinct religious formations is contained in Saurabh Dube and Ishita Banerjee-Dube, 'Spectres of conversion: Transformations of caste and sect in India' in Rowena Robinson and Sathinanath Clarke (eds), *Conversion in India* (New Delhi, Oxford University Press, 2002), pp. 222–54.
21. The only text I have come across so far which is devoted entirely to instructions for women is a slim booklet entitled *Naridharma Śiksha Manjari* (2nd edition, Rahania, 1983). It is written by one Ma Sita who is stated to be the daughter of *bhakta* Lakhmidhar Nayak. Ma Sita addresses all women as *bhagini* (sister) and dwells on the virtues of a 'Sati Stri' (exemplary wife). Service, devotion, duty, loyalty — all the traditional virtues of married women are extolled, and women are asked to practise them in their lives. The booklet is kept in the library of the Balkaldhari group.
22. I draw extensively upon L. Guzy, 'Translocal rituals of Mahima Dharma: the fire and the prayer' in Banerjee-Dube and Beltz (eds), *Popular Religion and Ascetic Practices*, pp. 43–60.
23. Diana Eck and Lawrence Babb provide us with detailed discussions *darśan*. Eck considers *Darshan*, 'seeing' to be a 'passive' act, not initiated by the worshipper, where the worshipper is 'seen' by the deity. Lawrence Babb, on the other hand, stresses the reciprocity of the act. D. L. Eck, *Darshan: Seeing the Divine Image in India*, (Chamberburg, PA, Anima, 1981). Lawrence A. Babb, 'Glancing: Visual interaction in Hinduism', *Journal of Anthropological Research*, 37:4 (1981), pp. 387–401. For a critical analysis of *darśan* and of the positions of Eck and Babb see, Banerjee-Dube, *Divine Affairs*, pp. 39–42, 51.
24. It is important to bear in mind that villages in India vary widely in size, composition and internal organization. S. C. Dube stressed the wide difference in the structure and composition of villages, indicating that Indian languages often used different words to signify different kinds of settlements, all of which are grouped under the generic village. S. C. Dube, *Indian Village* (New York, Harper Colophon Books, 1967), p. 3.
25. The general picture I provide here is based on extensive fieldwork carried on in Orissa over the past decade and a thorough reading of the field-notes of Anncharlott Eschmann who worked on Mahima Dharma in the early 1970s.
26. I discuss *balyalila* in a later section.
27. M. N. Srinivas provides an incisive analysis of the different connotations of 'exclusion' in a village in different situations. See M. N. Srinivas, 'The Indian village: Myth and reality' in M. N. Srinivas, *The Dominant Caste and Other Essays* (Delhi, Oxford University Press, 1987), pp. 20–59, 47–51 in particular.
28. Interview with Paramananda Sahu, Mahimapali, 7 March, 1994.
29. When Stephen Huyler, an American photographer cum ethnographer toured the villages of Orissa in the early 1980s, he was surprised by the 'strict caste delineations' observed there. He writes: 'most villages are laid out in such a way as to physically separate the low-caste and Harijan members from the high-caste villagers.' Stephen P. Huyler, *Village India* (New York, Harry N. Abrams, 1985), p. 155.
30. There is some indication that this was so even at the time of the founder. See, for instance, extract from letter No. 11/15 dated 1 April 1881, from the Deputy Commissioner, Sambalpur, to the Deputy Superintendent, Census, Central

Provinces, enclosed in the letter from the officiating Assistant Secretary to the Chief Commissioner to the officiating Under Secretary to the Government of Bengal, Judicial, Political and Appointment Departments, Calcutta, Nagpur, 23 May 1881, Board of Revenue Document No. 440/1, OSA, Bhubaneswar.

31. Interview with Sanatan, Jamusara *ashrama*, 9 February 1990.
32. See Dube, *Untouchable Pasts*, pp. 190–2, for an analysis of the uses of hypogamy (*pratiloma*) and hypergamy (*anuloma*) by untouchables. A detailed discussion of the implications of *anuloma* and *pratiloma* marriages for caste ranking can be found in Stanley J. Tambiah, 'From varna to caste through mixed unions' in Tambiah, *Culture, Thought and Social Action: An Anthropological Perspective* (Cambridge Mass. & London, Harvard University Press, 1985), pp. 211–51.
33. I summarize here the results of several interviews with lay disciples.
34. Interview with Sricharan Sahu, Khaliapali *ashrama*, 11 March 1992.
35. Louis Dumont, 'World renunciation in Indian religions', first published in French in 1959 and in English in 1960, reproduced as Appendix B in L. Dumont, *Homo Hierarchicus: The Caste System and Its Implications* (The Hague, Mounton, 1970), pp. 267–86.
36. Interview with Anakar Das, Karamunda *ashrama*, Barpali, 12 March 1992.
37. Interview with Nirmalprabha, Khandagiri *ashrama*, 17 March 1992.
38. I draw upon Dipesh Chakrabarty, 'Memories of displacement: The poetry and prejudice of dwelling', in D. Chakrabarty, *Habitations of Modernity: Essays in the Wake of Subaltern Studies* (Chicago, University of Chicago Press), pp. 115–37.
39. For a discussion of 'hidden transcripts' see, James C. Scott, *Domination and Arts of Resistance: Hidden Transcripts* (New Haven, Yale University Press, 1990). For an exploration of 'hidden transcripts' in speech and songs of women in India see, Gloria Goodwin Raheja and Ann Grodzins Gold, *Listen to the Heron's Words: Reimagining Gender and Kinship in North India* (Berkeley and Los Angeles, University of California Press, 1994).
40. Interview with Pramila, Khandagiri *ashrama*, 16 March 1992.
41. Interview with Shakuntala, Mahimagadi, 10 February 1990.
42. Here I draw upon insights offered by Rosalind O'Hanlon's discussion of how it is not enough to locate 'enclaves of women's autonomy or women's resistance' in order to make women visible as subjects but rather to uncover how gender relations intersect with and shape wider social relations. Rosalind O'Hanlon, 'Issues of widowhood: Gender and resistance in colonial western India' in Douglas Haynes and Gyan Prakash (eds), *Contesting Power: Resistance and Everyday Social Relations in South Asia* (Delhi, Oxford University Press, 1991) pp. 62–108.
43. Biswanath Baba, *Mahima Dharma Pratipadaka*, *Satya Mahima Dharmar Itihasa*, *Gruhasthashrama Subhakarmavidhana*.
44. Biswanath Baba, *Gruhasthashrama Subhakarmavidhana*, p. 15.
45. For a description of the ceremony during Mahima Swami's time see Chapter 2.
46. *Ibid.*, pp. 26–60. That non-vegetarian items do not form a part of Mahima Dharmi feasts was reiterated by a follower from Nadda, a village near Sonepur. Interview with Dhaneswar Rana, Nadda, 10 March 1992.
47. Eschmann felt that this ceremony of the feeding of children is a variant of the practice introduced by Chaitanya Deva. A. Eschmann, 'Mahima Dharma: An autochthonous Hindu reform movement', p. 398.
48. Kshetrabasi Baba, *Guruajña Niyam Nistha* (Mahimagadi, 1985), p. 96.
49. This corresponds with the description of *śaran* given in Bhima Bhoi's *Nirveda Sadhana*, Chapter 1.

50. For a description of *śaran* and *darśan* and their usefulness, see Satrughna Nath, *Mahima Dharmadhara* (Bhubaneswar, Hemlata Nath, 1990). Appendix 1, pp. 89–94.
51. This discussion is based entirely on my observation of a *balyalila* ceremony held at the Khandagiri *ashrama* on 16–17 March 1992. The Khandagiri *ashrama* is aligned to the Balkaldhari group and its presiding Balkaldhari *sanyasi* is Joykrushna Baba. According to a scholar who has worked on the spread of Mahima Dharma in and around Bhubaneswar, the Khandagiri *ashrama* has played a vital role in proselytisation. Mamata Bisoi, 'Mahima Dharma in the temple city', *Orissa Historical Research Journal*, 32: 3–4, 1987, pp. 32–48.
52. *Census of India 1961, District Census Handbook-Dhenkanal*, p. 55.
53. The *tungis* and *ashramas* take their names from the trees under which they are located, such as the *panashamula ashrama*. They are also named after the geographical directions — for instance *paścimashrama* — *bhaktas* from which have aided in their construction.
54. In the 1990s the Balkaldharis numbered between 150 and 200.
55. These rules derive directly from the practices of Mahima Swami. See the reports of the Baptist missionaries and *Utkala Deepika*, discussed in Chapter 2.
56. For instance, the Balkaldhari *sanyasi* Joykrushna Baba had become the proprietor of the Khandagiri *ashrama* for all practical purposes.
57. For a discussion of the role and power of the 'living guru' in the *Sant* tradition see Daniel Gold, *The Lord as Guru*, pp. 104–10.
58. I observed this during my visits to Joranda on the occasion of *guru purnima* in February 1989 and 1990.
59. The *snan-śauca* is meant to take place at 2 a.m. in summer, at 2:30 a.m. during the monsoon and at 3 a.m. in winter. Biswanath Baba, *Mahimagadi Itihasa*, p. 13.
60. A detailed description of the ritual services is contained in Biswanath Baba, *Mahimagadi Itihasa*, pp. 13–21.
61. A. Eschmann, 'Mahima Dharma: An autochthonous Hindu reform movement', p. 401.
62. For a detailed discussion of the ritual services offered to Jagannath see, Banerjee-Dube, *Divine Affairs*, pp. 44–6.
63. Of course, several residents of Mahimagadi mentioned that Raj Kishore Baba and several other *sanyasis* had secret bank accounts with huge balances.
64. Interview with Raj Kishore Baba, Joranda, 10 February 1993.
65. The practice is said to have come down from the time of the founder. However, the report on the sect in the *Proceedings of the Asiatic Society of Bengal 1882*, which was based on the report of the Commissioner of Orissa, mentioned the presence of Matas in the monastic order.
66. The Mata *matha* at the Gadi complex was constructed under the auspices of Labanya Mata, who came from the district of Cuttack. Her own disciples bought the plot of land and bore the cost of construction. Other *sanyasinis* came to live there when Labanya Mata was alive. With her death the *math* has fallen on bad days. The number of its inmates has dwindled along with the number of followers. The present Matas receive no financial aid from the Kaupindhari *samaj*.
67. See Chapter 3.
68. This is not to say that concerns of property and establishment do not feature at all in their lives. From the 1970s, when Śria Ma, the niece of Hari and Basu Panda, was forced out of the *ashrama*, the *math* at Khaliapali has been plagued by strife over its management. In the 1990s, it was run by a board of trustees composed of five members, most of whom are important local residents who were not Mahima

Dharmis. The management file No. 607 at the office of the Commissioner of Endowments contains appeals made to Commissioners by the proprietor of the Khaliapali *ashrama*, supported by Raj Kishore Baba and a politician of the area for the appointment of an efficient board of trustees for the Khaliapali *ashrama*. The *ashrama* has about thirty acres of land which are cultivated, in contravention of the rules of the Balkaldhari *samaj*.

69. I could not collect a lot of information on the group. B.B. Misra gave me a pamphlet of the group in Sambalpur in March 1993. He could not throw much light on its beliefs and practices. The group finds mention in Eschmann's field diary. The leader of the group, the proprietor of the Kardula *ashrama*, whose name is not mentioned, is stated to have been ordered by the Guru to spread the new *mantra* as Kali Yuga had come to an end and Satya Yuga had begun. The *mantra* found in the field diary is identical to the one given in the pamphlet: Haraya Ananta Haraya Ananta Ananta Ananta Haraya Haraya Haraya Alekha Haraya Alekha Alekha Alekha Haraya Haraya. Eschmann's field diary No. 2, Eschmann Papers, Munich. Johannes Beltz, who conducted some research on the group in 2001–2002, more or less confirms this information.
70. Although I draw upon Victor Turner's analysis of pilgrimage, I do not wish to essentialize his idea of 'liminality' or 'communitas', or the pilgrim's 'confrontation' with other individuals that eventually engenders 'communitas'. The feeling of affinity with other members is always present among the followers of Mahima Dharma. Pilgrimage only provides an occasion to re-state it. Moreover, the community created at Joranda results more from a 'spilling over', an idea taken from the Vaishnava theory of *rasa*, than from 'confrontation' used by Turner. Victor Turner, *The Ritual Process*.
71. Several studies have discussed how individuals and communities define themselves with reference to a 'significant other'. It is this contrast that provides a community or a culture with its essential character. See, for instance, Anthony P. Cohen, *The Symbolic Construction of Community* (London, Routledge, repr. 1989), pp. 115–18.
72. For a detailed analysis of the explicit and implicit meanings of pilgrimage in India, see E. A. Morinis, *Pilgrimage in the Hindu Tradition: A Case Study of West Bengal* (Delhi, Oxford University Press, 1984). It is, however, difficult to accept a general theory on the implicit meaning of pilgrimage that is based mainly upon a particular reading of Indian tradition.
73. I discuss the problems associated with clear classification and demarcation of pilgrims and tourists in Banerjee-Dube, *Divine Affairs*.
74. For a vivid description of 'altered consciousness' and an analysis of the 'assault' of the crowd on individual identity, see the portrayal of a Radhasoami *satsang* in Sudhir Kakar, *Shamans, Mystics and Doctors: A Psychological Enquiry into India and its Healing Traditions*, (Delhi, Oxford University Press, 1982), pp. 128–30.
75. The description of the *goshthi* is based on my observation of the ceremony in 1990 and 1993, once before the death of Biswanath Baba and once after it. There did not seem to be any significant variation between the two occasions. The *Goshthi* of 1993 appeared to have greater number of participants. In 1990 there were about six hundred participants, while in 1993 there were about eight hundred.
76. A. Eschmann, 'Mahima Dharma: An autochthonous Hindu reform movement', p. 400. Eschmann's field diary mentions the expulsion of one Kaupindhari *sanyasi* for a year for wishing to construct his own *matha*. Field diary No. 3, Eschmann Papers, Munich.

77. The Kaupindhari *samaj* also has a *goshthi*, but it is a simple affair of a common meal for all members at the end of the *purnima* celebrations.
78. I joined the *utsav* at Khaliapali on 6 February 1993.

CHAPTER 6.

Epilogue

On 17 May 1992, the daily *Prajatantra* reported that Biswanath Baba, 'the *adhayksha* of Mahima Dharma *samaj* and an eminent religious preacher, philosopher and writer of Orissa' breathed his last in his *ashrama* in Cuttack at the auspicious *brahmamuhurta* on 16 May. The Baba's death had cast a spell of sorrow on all followers of Mahima Dharma. He was said to be of 108 years of age at the time of his death.[1] A towering figure who had governed the affairs of the dominant group of the faith for decades in order to steer the institutionalization of Mahima Dharma, it was claimed that Biswanath Baba's death signalled the start of a new phase (and probably a novel era) in the life of the faith.

Actually, Biswanath Baba's departure has only speeded up some of the changes that have accompanied the Dharma since its inception. Emerging with a clear message of protest in the midst of turbulent times, the polyvalent tenets and practices of the faith have resisted exclusive understandings and interpretations. The prominent presence of scholar ascetics and prolonged interactions with the law have shaped the elaboration of Mahima Dharma as an institutionalized religion with a central seat in Joranda, Dhenkanal, possessing properties in land and permanent built structures. The beginning of the process was marked by a parting of ways between the Mahima Dharmi ascetics and Bhima Bhoi. It has been followed by a falling out of two groups of renouncers, urging both to take decisive steps toward forging uniform and cohesive *samajas*, generating further dissension. Today, apart from the existence of competing groups of *sanyasis* with their own establishments in and around Mahima Gadi, the heterogeneity of the Dharma is underlined by the assertive presence of different regional centres and a rapid increase in the interest of scholars and politicians in Bhima Bhoi as the true 'revolutionary' of the

Dharma.

Johannes Beltz's fieldwork in western Orissa at the beginning of the twenty-first century confirms that local politicians are increasingly getting involved in the management of the Khaliapali *ashrama* and all villages associated with Bhima Bhoi are fast transforming themselves into pilgrim sites for the followers of Mahima Dharma. While these moves have emerged as conscious attempts to counter the authority and establishment that has come to characterize the Mahima Gadi, the measures of politicians, scholars and lay followers of western Orissa are actually leading to a canonization and institutionalization of Bhima Bhoi, transgressing thereby the poet's own defiance toward forms of classification.

In the Koraput region of southern Orissa studied by Lidia Guzy, Mahima Dharma displays a 'locally specific tribal profile of asceticism'.[2] While professional ascetics from Dhenkanal visit Koraput about once a year to initiate new devotees, teachings of the faith are spread and given new meanings in the 'ecstatic vocal rituals of the Alekh Gurumayi'. These singing sessions by women ascetics are particularly potent as a mode of communication with Alekh and for healing.[3] The 'shamanic sessions', as Guzy calls them, portray remarkable refractions and appropriations of distinct emphases in the practices of Mahima Swami and Bhima Bhoi. Here, in the emphases of the Gurumayi, Mahima Swami's legendary steps of resorting to the temple of Śiva at the dead of night, of interceding with the deity on behalf of his devotees and of curing sick pilgrims at Kapilaś (and later his own followers) are combined with Bhima Bhoi's accent on singing and on aural comprehension of his compositions as a way of redemption. Imaginatively combining singing and healing, these women ascetics serve to affirm affect and emotion as vital elements of faith(s).

The Mahima Dharmis of Chiplima, Sambalpur, briefly referred to earlier, provide in turn another new and innovative deployment of Bhima Bhoi's doctrines. Disregarding Biswanath Baba's inauguration of the *Mahimabda*, these followers of the faith engage and extend Bhima Bhoi's emphasis on the immediate recourse to Mahima Dharma as the only way to avoid destruction along with Kali. They announce that Kali Yuga has come to end. It came to an end in 1965, when Satya Narayana Baba, the deceased founder of this new group and the proprietor of the Kardula *ashrama*, declared himself to be a religious preacher. Satya Narayana Baba is believed to be an incarnation of Bhima Bhoi. Satya Narayana Baba's wife — the current head of the Kardula *ashrama* — is said to be an incarnation of Annapurna.[4] The end of Kali Yuga legitimized the spiritual couples' search for a new *mantra*, incantation, for a new Yuga, the Sri Swadhin, Satya,

Bhogyayuga. The new mantra 'Haraye Ananta, Haraye Ananta, Ananta Ananta Hare Hare' (exactly the same as the one passed on to me by B. B. Misra) is an invocation of the eternal Vishnu — the Brahma of the new age — and follows the traditional chants of Vishnu's names in sequence and rhythm. At the same time, it is taken to be the new redemptive name of the Brahma appropriate for the new Yuga — *nutan tarak Brahma nam.*

However, what I find even more striking is the name of the new age, disclosed by Satya Narayana Baba's son to Johannes Beltz. The age is called *swadhin*, independent. It is independent both of classical temporalities as well as of the new beginning invoked by Biswanath Baba. It is *satya*, marked by truth and fairness and *bhogya*, to be enjoyed. Here, the self-evident definition of the Yuga embodies all the qualities that characterize an ideal age for these followers. Indeed, a new group of followers of an affective and acquiescent, modern and ageless faith today experiment with its teachings and configure novel temporalities. Through all of this they articulate the effective and enduring presence of a potent and multifaceted religion, Mahima Dharma, in the life of its adherents.

Notes

1. *Prajatantra*, 17 May 1992, p. 8.
2. L. Guzy, 'Translocal rituals…' in Banerjee-Dube and Beltz (eds), Popular Religion and Ascetic Practices, p. 57.
3. *Ibid.* See also L. Guzy, *Baba-s und Alekh-s — Askese und Ekstase einer Religion im Werden. Vergleichende Untersuchungen der asketischen Tradition Mahima Dharma in Orissa/östliches Indien* (Berlin, Weissensee Verlag, 2002).
4. J. Beltz, 'Apoclayptic predictions prophecies, and a new beginning: Mahima Dharma and the arrival of the *satyayuga*' in Banerjee-Dube and Beltz (eds), *Popular Religion and Ascetic Practices*, p. 94.

BIBLIOGRAPHY

Oral Testimonies

In course of my extensive fieldwork in Orissa between 1989–1994 and 1999–2001, interviews were conducted on a formal and informal basis with numerous lay followers and important ascetics of the different orders of Mahima Dharma as well as with residents of Joranda, Sonepur, Bhubaneswar and Cuttack and teachers of the Mahima Mahavidyalaya (college). I had the opportunity of speaking to Biswanath Baba on two occasions, in Joranda in 1989 and in Cuttack in 1990. I also interviewed the secretary and other members of the executive committee of the Balkaldharis and have had several conversations with Raj Kisore Baba, the secretary of the Kaupindhari *samaj*, apart from speaking to many Kaupindhari *sanyasis* of both the groups. The lay followers I interviewed during the annual congregation at Mahima Gadi were from Orissa, Bengal, Assam, Madhya Pradesh and Andhra Pradesh. I toured the Bhubaneswar–Khandagiri region of central Orissa and the Bolangir (Patna)-Redakhol-Sonepur-Sambalpur region of western Orissa, visiting *ashramas*, including Bhima Bhoi's *ashrama*, and villages inhabited by Mahima Dharmis. While all these oral testimonies helped provide an overall picture, the most significant of the interviews have been mentioned in the notes and the text.

Unpublished Records

Private Papers

Eschmann Collection, South Asian Institute (SAI), Heidelberg.
Eschmann Papers, Munich.
Mansfield Papers, Centre of South Asian Studies, Cambridge.

Government Records

Annual Reports on the Administration of the Bengal Presidency, 1850–1900.
Bengal Government Selections.
Board of Revenue Documents, Government of Bengal relating to the Attack on the Jagannath Temple, nos. 438–46.

Confidential Histories of the Feudatory States of Orissa.
Crown Representatives Records, Part I: Eastern States Agency.
Dhenkanal State Administration Reports.
Feudatory States Survey and Settlement Reports.
Jagannath Temple Correspondence.
Records of the Commissioner of Endowments, Bhubaneswar.
Proceedings of the Board of Revenue Cuttack.

Other Collections

Baptist Missionary Society Archives (BMS), Angus Library, Regent's Park College, Oxford.
Orissa Baptist Mission Records, Carey Library, Serampore.
Orissa Research Project Archives, South Asia Institute (SAI), Heidelberg.
Vernacular Tracts, India Office Library and Records (IOLR), London

Government Publications

Ahmed, M, 1965, *Census of India 1961, vol. 12: Orissa, District Census Handbook,* Dhenkanal.
Bourdillion, A, 1883, *Report on the Census of Bengal 1881*, Calcutta, *vol. XII: the Central Provinces and Feudatories*, Bombay, 1893.
Cobden-Ramsay, L E B, 1910, *Bengal Gazetteers XXI: Feudatory States of Orissa* (Calcutta, 1910 [Microfiche, Nehru Memorial Museum and Library, New Delhi]).
Dewar, F, 1920, *Report on the Land Revenue Settlement of the Sambalpur District 1906*, Patna.
Drysdale, T, 1883, *Census of the Central Provinces 1881*, Bombay.
Final Report on the Land Revenue Settlement of the Patna State 1937, Patna.
Gait, E A, 1902, *Census of India 1901*, vol. VI: Bengal, Calcutta.
Kuanr, D, 1977, *Orissa District Gazetteers: Puri,* Cuttack.
Laeequddin, M, 1937, *Census of the Mayurbhanja State 1931.*
Mahanti, B, 1971, *Orissa District Gazetteers: Sambalpur,* Cuttack.
Mansfield, P T, n.d., *Bihar and Orissa District Gazetteers: Puri*, Patna.
O' Donnel, C J, 1893, *Census of India 1891, vol. III: The Lower Provinces of Bengal and their Feudatories*, Calcutta.
O'Malley, L S S, 1913, *Census of India 1911, vol. V: Bengal, Bihar and Orissa and Sikkim*, Calcutta.
______, 1908, *Bengal District Gazetteer: Puri,* Calcutta.
______, 1909, *Bengal District Gazetteer: Sambalpur*, Calcutta.
Report on the Administration of Bengal 1888–89: Relations with Tributary States and Frontier Affairs, Calcutta, 1889.
Report of the Commissioners Appointed to Enquire into the Famine in Bengal and Orissa in 1866, vols 1 and 2, Cuttack, 1867.
Selections from the Records of the Bengal Government, No. III, Papers on the Settlement of Cuttack and on the State of the Tributary Mehals, Calcutta, 1851.
Senapati, N; Tripathy, P (eds), 1972, *Orissa District Gazetteers: Dhenkanal,* Cuttack.

Newspapers and Journals

Utkala Deepika

Sambalpur Hitaishini
Prajatantra
Samaj
The Calcutta Christian Observer

Vernacular Texts

Baba, B, 1968, *Sarva Veda Vedanta Saratattva Śiromni, Alekh Parambrahma Darśanam*, vol. 1, Bhubaneswar, Utkal University.

______, 1973, *Sarva Veda Vedanta Saratattva Śiromni, Alekh Parambrahma Darśanam*, vol. 2, Cuttack, Satya Mahima Dhramalochana Samiti.

______, 1978, *Satya Mahima Dharmara Itihasa*, Cuttack, Satya Mahima Dharmalochana Samiti. [1st edition, 1935.]

_____, 1980, *Mahima Dharma o Baudhha Dharma*, Cuttack, Satya Mahima Dhramalochana Samiti.

_____, 1984, *Mahimagadi Mahimadham Itihasa*, Cuttack, Satya Mahima Dharmalochana Samiti.

_____, 1985, *Gruhasthashrama Subhakarmavidhana*, Mahimagadi, 2nd edition.

Baba, B C, 1978, *Satya Mahimadharma Mahimagadi Samachar*, Sambalpur, Sadhu Birendra Kumar Das.

Baba, K, 1985, *Guruajña Niyam Nishtha*, Mahimagadi.

Baba, M, 1957, *Biśwa Kalyan Patha Satya Mahima Dharma*, Mahimagadi, Kaupindhari Mahima Samaj Alochana o Prachar Sabha.

_____, 1958, *Satya Mahima Dharmara Sankshipta Itihasa*, Mahimagadi, Kaupindhari Mahima Samaj Alochana o Prachar Sabha.

Baba, R K, 1984, *Mahimadham Sankshipta Itihasa*, Mahimagadi, Kaupindhari Mahima Samaj.

Baral, K L, 1986, *Santkabi Bhima Bhoi*, Cuttack, Rashtrabhasa Samavaya Prakashan.

Bhadra, G, 2002, *Jal Rajar Katha: Bardhamaner Pratapchand*, Calcutta, Ananda Publishers.

Bharadwaj, B N (ed.), 1989, *Anabishkrita Sahitya Pratibha Kedarnath Datta (Bhaktibinod Thakur)*, Calcutta, Sri Chaitanya Research Institute.

Bhoi, B, 1971, *Bhima Bhoi Malika ba Padmakalpa*, Cuttack, Dharma Grantha Store.

_____, 1977, 'Stuti Chintamoni' in Sahu, K (comp.), *Bhaktakabi Bhima Bhoinka Granthabali*, Cuttack, Dharma Grantha Store.

Chatterjee, P, 1991, 'Itihaser Uttardahikar', *Baromas*, 12: 2, (pp. 1–24).

Das, C, 1992, *Odiśara Mahima Dharma*, Cuttack, Dharma Grantha Store, 2nd edition.

Das, G, 1931, 'Foreword', in Baba, B, *Mahima Dharma Pratipadaka*, Bhubaneswar, Satya Mahima Dharmalochana Samiti.

Dash, D K, 1997, 'Bhima Bhoi o Mahima Dharma', *Eshana*, 34, June, (pp. 212–51).

Debatirtha, A, 1982, *Mahima Dharma Bidveshinku ek Khola Cithi*, Dhenkanal, Orient Publications.

Mahanti, A (comp.), 1925, *Bhima Bhoi Granthabali*, Part I, *Stuti Chintamoni* Cuttack, Prachi Samiti.

________, 1925, 'Mukhabandha' [Foreword] in Bhima Bhoi, *Stuti Chintamoni*, Cuttack, Prachi Samiti.

Mansinha, M, 1976, *Oriya Sahityara Itihasa*, Cuttack, Grantha Mandir, 2nd edition.

Misra, B, 1928, *Oriya Sahityara Itihasa*, Cuttack, Utkal Sahitya Press.

Misra, B, 1981, 'Brahma Nirupana Gitare Brahmanka sthiti bichara', *Saptarshi*, Sambalpur University Journal, 78, (pp. 61–6).

Misra, G (comp.), 1972, *Sambadpatrare Unabingśa Śatabdir Odiśa,* Cuttack, J. Mohapatra & Co.

Nayak, U C, 1980, *Mahima Dharma Biśwa Itihasa,* Bhubaneswar, Bijaylaxmi Nayak.

________, 1984, *Mahatma Bhima Bhoi,* Bhubaneswar, B. L. Nayak Publishers.

Nepak, B, 1973, *Bhima Bhoi. Chinta, Chetana o Jibana,* Bhubaneswar, Publication Committee.

________, 1974 *Kabi Kula Chanda Bhima Bhoi*, Bhubaneswar, Bhagirati Prakashan.

________, 1976, *Mahima Dharmare Kabi Bhima Bhoinka Bhumika,* Bhubaneshwar, Publication Committee.

________, 1981, *Bhima Bhoi Atma-pariciti o Anyanya Prasanga,* Bhubaneswar, Publication Committee.

Patnaik, S, 1972, *Sambadpatraru Odiśara Katha,* Cuttack, Grantha Mandir. vol. 1.

Pradhan, K, 1981, '"Puri Jagannathanka prati akraman" ghatanare santha Bhima Bhoinka samprikta ki?', *Saptarshi* (Sambalpur University Journal), 7–8, (pp. 79–83).

Pradhan, N N, 1986, *Prachin Oriya Sahityare Nirguna Dhara,* Cuttack, Basanta Kumari Pradhan.

Rath, P C, 1942, *Kośala Itihasa Katha*, Bolangir.

Sahu, G C, 1981, *Mahima Dharma Biśwa Itihasa Lekhakanku Satarka Bani,* Chakrapur, G C Sahu.

Sahu, K, 1978, 'Foreword' in Sahu, K (comp.) *Bhaktakabi Bhima Bhoinka Granthabali*, Cuttack, Dharmagrantha Store, new edition.

Sarman, N D, 1941, *Sebakalara Katha,* Cuttack.

Samantarai, R, 1973, 'Bhima Bhoi', *Saptarshi*, 2: 4, (pp. 2–17).

________, 1976, *Oriya Sahityare Bhima Bhoi,* Cuttack, Dharma Grantha Store.

Senapati, F, 1977, *Atmacarit,* tr. Maitree Sukla, New Delhi, Sahitya Akademy.

Sutton, A, 1870, *Dharmar Vishayare Kathabarta*, Cuttack, Mission Press.

Books and Articles

Aitchison, C V (comp.), 1892, *A Collection of Treaties, Engagements and Sanads Relating to India and Neighbouring Countries*, Calcutta, vol.1.

Aktor, M, 1999, 'Smritis and jātis: The ritualisation of time and the continuity of the past', in Daud Ali, *Invoking the Past: The Uses of History in South Asia*, Delhi, Oxford University Press, (pp. 258-79).

Amin, S, 1984, 'Gandhi as Mahatma: Gorakhpur district, eastern UP, 1921–22', in Guha, R (ed.), *Subaltern Studies III: Writings on South Asian History and Society*, Delhi, Oxford University Press, (pp. 1–55).

_______, 1987, 'Approver's testimony, judicial discourse: The case of Chauri Chaura', in Guha, R (ed.), *Subaltern Studies V: Writings on South Asian History and Society,* Delhi, Oxford University Press, (pp. 166–203).

_______, 1996, *Event, Metaphor, Memory: Chauri-Chaura, 1922–1992,* Princeton, Princeton University Press.

_______, 2004, 'They also followed Gandhi' in Saurabh Dube (ed.), *Postcolonial Passages,* Delhi, Oxford University Press, (pp. 132–58).

Appadurai, A, 1981, 'The past as a scarce resource', *Man* (N.S.), 16:2, (pp. 201–19).

Asad, T, 1993, *Genealogies of Religion: Discipline and Reasons of Power in Christianity and Islam*, Baltimore, The Johns Hopkins University Press.

_______, 1993, 'The construction of religion as an anthropological category' in Asad, T, *Genealogies of Religion: Discipline and Reasons of Power in Christianity and Islam*, Baltimore,

The Johns Hopkins University Press, (pp. 27–54).
Asiatic Society of Bengal, 'The Sect of Hindu dissenters', *Proceedings of the Asiatic Society of Bengal 1882,* Calcutta.
Axel, B K (ed.), 2002, *From the Margins: Historical Anthropology and its Futures,* Durham, Duke University Press.
Baba, B, 1987, *The Philosophy of Mahima Dharma* (*Philosophy of Unalloyed Non-Dual Supreme Being*), Cuttack, Mahima Dharmalochana Samiti.
_______, n.d., *Philosophy of Mahima Dharma*, Cuttack, Satya Mahima Dharmalochana Samiti.
Babb, L A, 1975, *The Divine Hierarchy: Popular Hinduism in Central India,* New York, Columbia University Press.
_______, 1981, 'Glancing: Visual interaction in Hinduism', *Journal of Anthropological Research,* 37:4, (pp. 387–401).
Bandyopadhyay, S, 1997, *Caste, Protest and Identity in Colonial India: The Namasudras of Bengal, 1872–1947,* Richmond, Curzon Press.
Banerjee-Dube, I, 1999, 'Taming traditions: Legalities and histories in twentieth century Orissa', in Bhadra, G; Prakash, G; Tharu, S (eds), *Subaltern Studies X. Writings on South Asian History and Society,* Delhi, Oxford University Press, (pp. 98–125).
_______, 2000, *Divine Affairs: Religion, Pilgrimage, and the State in Colonial and Postcolonial India,* Shimla, Indian Institute of Advanced Study.
_______, 2001, 'Issues of faith, enactments of contest: The founding of Mahima Dharma in nineteenth century Orissa', in Kulke, H; Schnepel B (eds), *Jagannath Revisited: Studying Religion, Society, and the State in Orissa*, New Delhi, Manohar, (pp.149–77).
_______, 2003, 'Reading Time: Texts and pasts in colonial eastern India', *Studies in History,* 19:1, January–June, (pp. 1–17).
_______, forthcoming, 'Introduction: Questions of caste', in Banerjee-Dube, I (ed.), *Caste in History: Modern Indian Perspectives*, New Delhi, Oxford University Press.
Barthwal, P D, 1978, *Traditions of Indian Mysticism Based Upon the Nirguna School of Hindi Poetry*, New Delhi, Heritage Publishers.
Bäumer, B, forthcoming, 'Tantric elements in Bhima Bhoi's oeuvre', in Banerjee-Dube, I; Beltz, J (ed.), *Routinization of Charisma: New Studies on Mahima Dharma*, New Delhi, Manohar.
Behera, S, 1997, 'Jagannath and Alekh: A study in juxtaposition', *Economic and Political Weekly,* 32:3, 16–23 August, (pp. 2096–7).
Beltz, J, 2001, 'Disputed centres, rejected norms and contested authorities: Situating Mahima Dharma in its regional diversity', paper presented at *Orissa Research Project Conference*, Salzau, Germany.
_______, forthcoming, 'Apocalyptic predictions, prophecies, and a new beginning: Mahima Dharma and the arrival of the *satyayuga*' in Banerjee-Dube I Beltz, J (eds), *Routinization of Charisma: New Studies on Mahima Dharma*, Delhi, Manohar.
Bhadra, G, 1989, 'The mentality of subalternity: *Kantanama* or *Rajdharma*', in Guha, R, (ed.) *Subaltern Studies VI: Writings on South Asian History and Society,* Delhi, Oxford University Press, (pp. 54–91).
Bhargava, R (ed.), 1998, *Secularism and its Critics,* Delhi, Oxford University Press.
Bhattacharya, J, 1973, *Hindu Castes and Sects: An Exposition of the Origin of the Hindu Caste System and the Bearing of the Sects Towards Each Other and other Religious Systems* (Calcutta, repr. Firma K L M, 1973, 1st edition, 1891).
Bisoi, M, 1987, 'Mahima Dharma in the temple city', *Orissa Historical Research Journal,* 32: 3–4, (pp. 32–48).
Bloch, M, 1953, *The Historians Craft*, tr. Peter Putnam, New York, Vintage, 1st French

edition, 1949.

Borofsky, R, 1987, *Making History: Pukapukan and Anthropological Constructions of Knowledge*, Cambridge, Cambridge University Press.

Buckland, C E, 1902, *Bengal under the Lieutenant Governors*, vol. 2, Calcutta, K Bose.

Burghart, R, 1983, 'Renunciation in the religious tradition of South Asia, *Man* (n.s.), 18, (pp. 635–53).

Cassels, N G, 1988, *Religion and Pilgrim Tax under the Company Raj*, New Delhi, Manohar.

Chakrabarty, D, 1989, *Rethinking Working Class History: Bengal 1890–1940*, Delhi, Oxford University Press.

———, 1997, 'Postcoloniality and the artifice of history: Who speaks for the "Indian" pasts?', in Ranajit Guha (ed.), *A Subaltern Studies Reader, 1986–1995*, Minneapolis, University of Minnesota Press, (pp. 263–93).

———, 2000, *Provincializing Europe: Postcolonial Thought and Historical Difference*, Princeton, Princeton University Press.

———, 2002, 'Memories of displacement: The poetry and prejudice of dwelling', in Chakrabarty, D, *Habitations of Modernity: Essays in the Wake of Subaltern Studies*, Chicago, University of Chicago Press, (pp. 115–37).

Chartier, R, 1989, 'Texts, printing, readings', in Hunt, L (ed.), *The New Cultural History*, Berkeley, L.A., University of California Press, (pp. 154–75).

———,1995, *Forms and Meanings: Texts, Performances, and Audiences from Codex to Computer*, Philadelphia: University of Pennsylvania Press, (pp. 88–97).

Chatterjee, S K, 1966, *The People, Language and Culture of Orissa: Artaballabha Mahanti Memorial Lectures*, Bhubaneswar, Orissa Sahitya Akademi.

Chatterjee, P, 1993, *The Nation and its Fragments: Colonial and Postcolonial Histories*, Princeton, Princeton University Press.

———, 1994, 'Claims on the past', in Arnold, D; Hardiman, D (eds), *Subaltern Studies VIII: Essays in Honour of Ranajit Guha*, Delhi, Oxford University Press, (pp. 1–49).

Cohen, P, 1989, *The Symbolic Construction of Community*, London, Routledge.

Cohn, B, 1980, 'History and anthropology: The state of play', *Comparative Studies in Society and History*, 22:2, (pp. 198–221).

———, 1983, 'Representing Authority in Victorian India', in Ranger, T; Hobsbawm, E (eds), *The Invention of Tradition*, London, Cambridge University Press, (pp. 165–211).

———, 1987, 'Some notes on law and change in north India', in *An Anthropologist Among he Historians and Other Essays*, Delhi, Oxford University Press, (pp. 554–74).

Comaroff, J, 1985, *Body of Power, Spirit of Resistance: The Culture and History of a South African People*, Chicago and London, The University of Chicago Press.

Comaroff, J; Comaroff, J, 1992, *Ethnography and the Historical Imagination*, Boulder, Westview.

Coronil, F, 1997, *The Magical State: Nature, Money, and Modernity in Venezuela*, Chicago, University of Chicago Press.

Das, C, 1951, 'Studies in medieval religion and literature of Orissa', *Visva Bharati Annals*, IV, (pp. 107–94).

———,1982, *A Glimpse into Oriya Literature*, Bhubaneswar, Orissa Sahitya Akademi.

Das P, 1988, *Sahajiya Cult of Bengal and the Pancha Sakha Cult of Orissa*, Calcutta, Firma KLM.

Das, V, 1977, *Structure and Cognition: Aspects of Hindu Caste and Ritual*, Delhi, Oxford University Press.

———, 1995, 'Time, self and community: Features of Sikh militant discourse', in Das,V, *Critical Events: An Anthropological Perspective on Contemporary India*, Delhi, Oxford University Press, (pp. 118–36).

Dasgupta, S B, 1976, *Obscure Religious Cults*, Calcutta, Firma K L M, 1st edition, 1946.

Dash, G N, 1998, *Tribal Priests of a Hindu Shrine: Social Dynamics in Medieval Orissa*, Delhi, Radiant Publishers.

Davis, N Z, 1977, *Society and Culture in Early Modern France: Eight Essays by Natalie Zemon Davis*, Stanford, Stanford University Press.

Derrett, J D M, 1968, *Religion, Law and State in India*, London, Faber and Faber.

Dhall, M, 1988, 'Activities of Christian missionaries and British policy towards them', *Our Documentary Heritage*, 4, Government of Orissa, Bhubaneswar, OSA, (pp. 14–23).

Dirks, N, 1987, *The Hollow Crown: Ethnohistory of an Indian Kingdom*, Cambridge, Cambridge University Press.

Doniger, W, 1991, 'Fluid and fixed texts in India', in Flueckiger, J B; Patton, L (eds), *Boundaries of the Text: Epic Performances in South and Southeast Asia*, Ann Arbor, Michigan, Center for South and Southeast Asian Studies, University of Michigan.

Donoghue, D, 1998, *The Practice of Reading*, New Haven & London, Yale University Press.

Dube, S C, 1967, *Indian Village*, New York, Harper Colophon Books.

Dube, S, 1998, *Untouchable Pasts: Religion, Identity, and Power among a Central Indian Community, 1780–1950*, Albany, State University of New York Press.

_______, 2004, *Stitches on Time: Colonial Textures and Postcolonial Tangles*, Durham, Duke University Press.

_______, forthcoming, 'Anthropology, history, historical anthropology', in Dube, S (ed.), *Historical Anthropology*, New Delhi, Oxford University Press.

Dube, S; Banerjee-Dube, I, 2002, 'Spectres of conversion: Transformations of caste and sect in India', in Robinson, R; Clarke, S, (eds), *Conversion in India*, New Delhi, Oxford University Press, (pp.122–54).

Dumont, L, 1970, 'World renunciation in Indian religion', in *Religion/Politics and History in India: Collected Papers in Indian Sociology*, Paris and The Hague, Mouton.

_______, 1970, *Homo Hierarchicus: The Caste system and its Implications*, The Hague, Mouton.

Eck, D L, 1981, *Darshan: Seeing the Divine Image in India*, Chamberburg, PA, Anima.

Eliade, M, 1954, *The Myth of Eternal Return*, tr. Willard R. Trask, Tennessee, Pantheon.

Eschmann, A, 1972, 'Spread, organisation and cult of Mahima Dharma', in Panda, D (ed.), *Mahima Dharma Darsan*, Koraput, Shankar Philosophical Society, (pp. 7–11).

_______, 1986, 'Mahima Dharma: An autochthonous Hindu reform movement', in Eschmann, A.; Kulke, H; Tripathi, G C (eds), *The Cult of Jagannath and the Regional Tradition of Orissa*, New Delhi, Manohar, (pp. 375–410).

_______, forthcoming, 'Mahima Dharma and tradition', in Banerjee-Dube, I; Beltz, J (eds), *Routinization of Charisma: New Studies on Mahima Dharma*, New Delhi, Manohar.

Fabian, J, 1983, *Time and the Other: How Anthropology Makes its Object*, New York, Columbia University Press.

Farris, N M, 1987, 'Remembering the future, anticipating the past: History, time and cosmology among the Mayas of Yucatan', *Comparative Studies in Society and History*, 29: 3, (pp. 566–93).

Finnegan, R, 1988, *Literacy and Orality: Studies in the Technology of Communication*, Oxford, Blackwell.

Foucault, M, 1977, *Discipline and Punish: The Birth of Prison*, New York, Vintage, 1st edition, 1975.

Fuller, C J, 1984, *Servants of the Goddess: The Priests of a South Indian Temple*, Cambridge, Cambridge University Press.

Galanter, M, 1989, *Law and Society in Modern India*, Delhi, Oxford University Press.

_______, 1998, 'Hinduism, secularism and the Indian judiciary', in Bhargava, R (ed.), *Secularism and its Critics*, Delhi, Oxford University Press.

Geib, R, 1975, *Indradumnya-Legende: Ein Beitrag zur Geschichte des Jagannatha-Kultes*, Wiesbaden, Otto Harrassowitz.

Genovese, E D, 1974, *Roll Jordan Roll: The World that Slaves Made*, New York, Pantheon.

Ginzburg, C, 1980, *The Cheese and the Worms: The Cosmos of a Sixteenth Century Miller*, tr. by John and Anne Tedeschi, Baltimore, Johns Hopkins University Press, 1st Italian edition, 1976.

Gold, D, 1987, *The Lord as Guru: Hindi Sants in the North Indian Tradition*, Delhi, Oxford University Press.

Gold, A G; Gujar, B R, 2002, *In the Time of Trees and Sorrows: Nature, Power and Memory in Rajasthan*, Durham, Duke University Press.

Guha, R, 1983, *Elementary Aspects of Peasant Insurgency in Colonial India*, Delhi, Oxford University Press.

_______, 1983, 'The prose of counter insurgency', in Guha, R (ed.), *Subaltern Studies. Writings on South Asian History and Society*, Delhi, Oxford University Press, (pp. 1–40).

_______, 1997, 'Chandra's death', in Guha, R (ed.) *A Subaltern Studies Reader 1986–1995*, Minneapolis, University of Minnesota Press, (pp. 34–62).

Gurevich, A, 1990, *Medieval Popular Culture: Problems of Belief and Perception*, tr. Janós M. Bak and Paul A. Hollingsworth, Cambridge, Cambridge University Press.

Guzy, L, 2002, *Baba-s und Alekh-s—Askese und Ekstase einer Religion im Werden. Vergleichende Untersuchungen der asketischen Tradition Mahima Dharma in Orissa/östliches Indien*, Berlin, Weissensee Verlag.

_______, forthcoming 2006, 'Translocal rituals of Mahima Dharma: The fire and the prayer', in Banerjee-Dube, I; Beltz, J (eds), *Routinization of Charisma: New Studies on Mahima Dharma*, New Delhi, Manohar.

Hardiman, D, 1987, *The Coming of the Devi: Adivasi Assertion in Western India*, Delhi, Oxford University Press.

Hawley J S; M Juergensmeyer (eds), 1988, *Songs of the Saints of India*, New York, Oxford University Press.

Hazra, R C, 1975, *Studies in the Puranic Records on Hindu Rites and Customs*, New Delhi, Motilal Banarsidass.

Heesterman, J, 1985, *The Inner Conflict of Tradition: Essays in Indian Ritual, Kingship, and Society*, Delhi, Oxford University Press.

Hess, L, 1983, *The Bijak of Kabir*, tr. Singh S, Delhi, New Delhi, Motilal Banarsidass.

Hunter, W W, 1976, *A Statistical Account of Bengal*, reprinted Delhi, Concept Publishing.

Huyler, S P, 1985, *Village India*, New York, Harry N. Abrams.

Ishwaran, K, 1992, *Speaking of Basava: Lingayat Religion and Culture in South Asia*, Boulder, Westview.

Jaffrelot, C, 2005, *Analysing and Fighting Caste: Dr Ambedkar and Untouchability*, Delhi, Permanent Black.

Jena, K C, 1978, *Socio-Economic Conditions of Orissa in the Nineteenth Century*, Delhi, Sundeep Prakashan.

Jha, S N, 1995, 'Cari chandra bhed: Use of the four moons', in Ray, R K (ed.), *Mind, Body, Society: Life and Mentality in Colonial Bengal*, Delhi, Oxford University Press, (pp. 65–108).

Juergensmeyer, M, 1982, *Religion as Social Vision: The Movement Against Untouchability in Twentieth Century Punjab*, Berkeley and Los Angeles, University of California Press.

Jones, K W, 1989, *The New Cambridge History of India (III. I): Socio-Religious Reform Movements in British India*, Cambridge, Cambridge University Press.

Kakar, S, 1978, *The Inner World: A Psychoanalytic Study of Childhood and Society in India*, Delhi, Oxford University Press.

_______, 1982, *Shamans, Mystics and Doctors: A Psychological Enquiry into India and its Healing Traditions*, Delhi, Oxford University Press.

Kar, B, 1969, 'The religious philosophy of Mahima Goswami and his school', *Bharati, Utkal University Journal of Humanities*, 3:4, July, (pp. 59–66).

Kulke, H, 1976, 'Ksatriyaisation and social change', in Pillai, S D (ed.), *Aspects of Changing India: Studies in Honour of Professor G.S. Ghurye,* Bombay, Popular Prakashan, (pp. 398–409).

_______, 1986, 'Jagannath as the state deity under the Gajapatis of Orissa', in Eschmann, A; Kulke, H; Tripathi, G C (eds), *The Cult of Jagannath and the Regional Tradition of Orissa,* New Delhi, Manohar, (pp. 199–208).

_______, 1992, 'Tribal deities at princely courts: The feudatory rajas of central Orissa and their tutelary deities (Istadevatas)', in Mahapatra, S (ed.), *The Realm of the Sacred,* Calcutta, Oxford University Press, (pp. 56–78).

_______, 1993, 'Legitimation and townplanning in the Feudatory States of Central Orissa', in H. Kulke, *Kings and Cults: State Formation and Legitimation in India and Southeast Asia,* New Delhi, Manohar, (pp. 93–113).

Lal, V, 2003, *The History of History,* New Delhi, Oxford University Press.

Landes, D, 1983, *Revolution in Time: Clocks and the Making of the Modern World,* Cambridge, Mass., Harvard University Press.

Le Goff, J, 1992, *History and Memory*, tr. Steven Rendall and Elizabeth Claman, New York, Columbia University Press.

Levine, L W, 1993, *The Unpredictable Past: Explorations in American Cultural History,* New York, Oxford University Press, 1993.

Lorenzen, D N, 1987, 'Traditions of non-caste Hinduism: The Kabirpanth', *Contributions to Indian Sociology*, 23:1, (pp. 263–83).

_______, 1995, *Bhakti Religion in North India: Community Identity and Political Action,* Albany, NY, State University of New York Press.

Lowenthal, D, 1985, *The Past is a Foreign Country*, Cambridge, Cambridge University Press.

Lüdtke, A,1995, 'Introduction: What is the history of everyday life and who are its practitioners?', in Lüdtke, A (ed.), *The History of Everyday Life: Reconstructing Historical Experiences and Ways of Life*, tr. William Templer, Princeton, Princeton University Press, (pp. 3–40).

Madan, V, 2002, 'Introduction', in Madan, V (ed.), *Village in India*, New Delhi, Oxford University Press, (pp. 1–26).

Mahapatra, M, 1952, 'General economic condition of Orissa (1803–18)', *Orissa Historical Research Journal*, 1:2, (pp. 171–7).

Malamoud, C, 1996, *Cooking the World: Ritual and Thought in Ancient India,* Delhi, Oxford University Press, 1996.

Mani, L, 1998, *Contentious Traditions: The Debate over Sati in Colonial India*, Berkeley & Los Angeles, University of California Press.

Mann, G S, 2002, *Evolution of Sikh Scriptures,* New Delhi, Oxford University Press.

Mansinha, M, 1977, 'The greatest tribals', in Das, M N (ed.), *Sidelights on History and Culture of Orissa*, Cuttack, Grantha Mandir.

Mansinha, M, 1984, 'The Cult of Lord Jagannath', in Panda, D; Panigrahi S C (eds), *The Cult and Culture of Lord Jagannath,* Cuttack, Vidyapuri, (pp. 17–37).

Marglin, F A, 1985, *Wives of the God-King: Rituals of the Devadasis of Puri,* Delhi, Oxford University Press.

Mazumdar, B C, 1991, *Sonepur in the Sambalpur Tract,* Calcutta, A C Sarkar.

McLeod, W H, 1975, *The Evolution of the Sikh Community: Five Essays,* Delhi, Oxford

University Press.
Medick, H, 1995, 'Missionaries in a row boat'? Ethnological ways of knowing as a challenge to social history', in Lüdtke, A (ed.), *The History of Everyday Life: Reconstructing Historical Experiences and Ways of Life*, tr. William Templer, Princeton, Princeton University Press, (pp.41–71).
Michael, R B, 1992, *The Origins of Virasaiva Sects: A Typological Analysis of Rituals and Associational Patterns in the Sunyasampadane,* New Delhi, Motilal Banarsidass.
Mohapatra, B N, unpublished, 'Fish will swim over the "Twenty-two Steps" of the Jagannath Temple: Time, order and cosmology', paper presented at the Second International Conference on Indic Religions and Civilization, New Delhi.
Moore, R L, 2003, *Touchdown Jesus: The Mixing of Sacred and Secular in American History,* Louiseville, Kentucky, Westminster John Know Press.
Morinis, E A, 1984, *Pilgrimage in the Hindu Tradition: A Case Study of West Bengal,* Delhi, Oxford University Press.
Muir, E; Ruggiero, G (eds), *Microhistory and the Lost Peoples of Europe*, tr. Eren Branch, Baltimore, Johns Hopkins University Press.
Mukherjee, P, 1940, *The History of Medieval Vaishnavism in Orissa,* Calcutta, R. Chatterjee.
_______, 1957, 'The Orissa famine of 1866', *Orissa Historical Research Journal*, 6:1, (pp. 69–95).
Munn, N, 1992, 'The cultural anthropology of time: A critical essay', *Annual Review of Anthropology*, 21, (pp. 93–123).
Nanda, C P, 2006, 'Mapping the Mahatma', in Brandtner, M; Panda, S K (eds), *Interrogating History: Essays for Hermann Kulke,* New Delhi, Manohar, (pp. 291–302).
Nandy, A, 1983, *The Intimate Enemy: Loss and Recovery of Self under Colonialism*, Delhi, Oxford University Press.
_______, 1995, 'History's forgotten doubles', *History and Theory*, 34, (pp. 44–66).
Nath, S, 1977, 'Mahima Dharma', in Dash, M N (ed.), *Sidelights on History and Culture of Orissa,* Cuttack, Grantha Mandir, (pp.450–1).
_______, 1977, *A Saint, Self-realised in Mahima Faith Biswanath Baba,* Cuttack, Dharma Grantha Store.
_______, 1990, *Mahima Dharmadhara*, Bhubaneswar, Hemlata Nath.
_______, 1991, 'Mahima movement in Cuttack City', in Behera, K S, Patnaik, J; Das H C (eds), *Cuttack: One Thousand Years*, Cuttack, Cuttack City Millennium Celebrations Committee.
_______, 1992, *Mahima Bhakti Rasamruta,* Cuttack, Mahima Dharmlochana Parishad.
_______, 1998, 'Mahima Dharma: Plea for proper perception', *Economic and Political Weekly*, 33:4, 24–31 January, (pp. 191–2).
Nayak, B, 2002, *Oriya Poets through the Ages,* Balasore, Grantha Bharati.
Nayak, P M, 1992, 'Bhima Bhoi: Poet laureate of Mahima religion', in Pati, M, (ed.) *West Orissa: A Study in Ethos [Silver Jubilee Commemorative Volume, Sambalpur University*], Sambalpur, Sambalpur University.
Nayak, S K, forthcoming 2006, 'A short note on the mystic poetry of Bhima Bhoi', in Banerjee-Dube, I; Beltz, J (ed.), *Routinization of Charisma: New Studies on Mahima Dharma,* New Delhi, Manohar.
Nepak, B, 1987, *Bhima Bhoi Adivasi Poet Philosopher,* Bhubaneshwar, Publication Committee.
_______, 1998, *Bhima Bhoi: His Life and Works,* Lacchipur, Bhima Bhoi Sanskrutik Sansad.
Nigam, Sanjay, 1990, 'Disciplining and policing the "criminals by birth" part 1: The development of the disciplinary system, 1871–1900', *The Indian Economic and Social*

History Review, 27, 1, (pp. 131–62).
______, 1990, 'The making of a colonial stereotype part 2: The criminal tribes and castes of northern India', *The Indian Economic and Social History Review*, 27, 2, (pp. 257–87).
Obeyesekere, G, 1984, *The Cult of the Goddess Pattini*, Chicago, University of Chicago Press.
O'Hanlon, R, 1991, 'Issues of widowhood: Gender and resistance in colonial western India', in Haynes, D; Prakash, G (eds), *Contesting Power: Resistance and Everyday Social Relations in South Asia,* Delhi, Oxford University Press, (pp. 62-108).
Ohnuki-Tierney, E, 1990, 'Introduction: The historicization of Anthropology', in Ohnuki-Tierney, E (ed.), *Culture through Time: Anthropological Approaches*, Stanford, Stanford University Press, (pp. 1–25).
Omvedt, G, 1994, *Dalits and the Democratic Revolution: Dr. Ambedkar and the Dalit Movement in Colonial India,* New Delhi, Sage Publications.
Pandey, G, 1984, '"Encounters and calamities": The history of a north Indian Qasba in the nineteenth century', in Guha, R (ed.), *Subaltern Studies III: Writings on South Asian history and Society*, Delhi, Oxford University Press, (pp. 231–70).
______, 2001, *Remembering the Partition: Violence, Nationalism and History in India,* Cambridge, Cambridge University Press.
Pandian, A, 2005, 'Securing the rural citizen: The anti-Kallar movement of 1896', *The Indian Economic and Social History Review*, 42: 1, (pp. 1–39).
Panigrahi, S C, 1998, *Bhima Bhoi and Mahima Darshana,* Cuttack, Santosh Publications & Department of Philosophy, Utkal University.
Parry, J, 1979, *Caste and Kingship in Kangra*, London, Routledge and Kegan Paul.
Pati, B, 1993, 'The "high": "low" dialectic in Fakirmohan's Chamana Athaguntha: Popular culture, literature and society in late nineteenth century Orissa', *Occasional Papers on History and Society*, Second Series, 49, Nehru Memorial Museum and Library, (pp. 33–4).
______, 2001, *Situating Social History: Orissa (1800–1997),* New Delhi, Orient Longman.
Patnaik, A, 2000, *Socio-Religious Reforms in Orissa in the 19th Century*, Calcutta, Punthi Pustak.
Patnaik, S, 1961, 'Orissa in 1867', *Orissa Historical Research Journal*, 10:3, (pp. 61–73).
______, 1961, 'Orissa in 1868', *Orissa Historical Research Journal*, 10:4, (pp. 44–58).
Raheja, G G, 1988, *The Poison in the Gift: Ritual, Prestation, and the Dominant Caste in a North Indian Village,* Chicago and London, University of Chicago Press, 1988.
Raheja, G G; Grodzins Gold, A, 1994, *Listen to the Heron's Words: Reimagining Gender and Kinship in North India,* Berkeley and Los Angeles, University of California Press.
Ram, K, 1997, *Mukkuvar Women,* New Delhi, Kali for Women.
Ramanujan, A K, 1973, *Speaking of Siva*, Harmondsworth, Penguin.
Rao, V, 2002, *Living Traditions in Contemporary Contexts: The Madhava Matha of Udipi*, Hyderabad, Orient Longman.
Raut, P C, 1946, 'Review of manuscripts', *Journal of the Kalinga Historical Research Society*, 1:3, December, (pp. 271–7).
Ray, R K, 1995, 'Introduction', in Ray, *Mind, Body, Society: Life and Mentality in Colonial Bengal,* Delhi, Oxford University Press, (pp. 1–44).
Raychaudhuri, T, 1995, 'The pursuit of reason in nineteenth century Bengal', in Ray, R K (ed.), *Mind, Body, Society: Life and Mentality in Colonial Bengal*, Delhi, Oxford University Press, (pp. 47–64).
Redfield, R, 1956, *Peasant, Society, and Culture*, Chicago, University of Chicago Press.
Rosaldo, R, 1980, *Ilongot Headhunting 1883–1974: A Study in Society and History*, Stanford,

Stanford University Press.

Sabean, D W, 1984, *Power in the Blood: Popular Culture and Village Discourse in Early Modern Germany,* Cambridge, Cambridge University Press.

Said, E, 1978, *Orientalism*, London, Routledge and Kegan Paul.

Samarendra, P, 2003, 'Classifying caste: Census surveys in India in the late nineteenth and early twentieth centuries', *South Asia: Journal of South Asian Studies*, 26, 2, (pp. 141–64).

Sarkar, S, 1984, 'The conditions and nature of subaltern militancy: Bengal from Swadeshi to Non-cooperation, c. 1905–22', in Guha, R (ed.), *Subaltern Studies III. Writings on South Asian History and Society,* Delhi, Oxford University Press, (pp. 271–320).

_______, 1998, 'Renaissance and Kaliyuga: Time, myth and history in colonial Bengal', in Sarkar, S, *Writing Social History,* Delhi, Oxford University Press, 1998, (pp. 186–215).

_______, 2002, 'Colonial times: Clocks and Kaliyuga', in Sarkar, S, *Beyond Nationalist Frames: Relocating Postmodernism, Hindutva, History*, Delhi, Permanent Black, (pp. 10–37).

Schomer K; Mcleod, W H (eds), 1987, *The Sants: Studies in a Devotional Tradition of India,* (New Delhi, Motilal Banarsidass).

Scott, J C, 1990, *Domination and the Arts of Resistance: Hidden Transcripts*, New Haven, Yale University Press.

Sen, K, 1930, *Medieval Mysticism of India,* tr. Manmohan Ghosh, London, Luzac and Company.

Sen, S, 1999, 'Imperial orders of the past: The semantics of history and time in the medieval Indo-Persianate culture of north India', in Ali, D (ed.), *Invoking the Past,* Delhi, Oxford University Press, 1999, (pp. 231–57).

Sibbler, I, 1984, 'Dissent through holiness: The case of the radical renouncer in Thervada Buddhist countries', in S. N. Eisenstadt; R. Kahane; David Shulman (eds), *Orthodoxy, Heterodoxy and Dissent in India*, Berlin and New York, Mouton Publishers, (pp. 85–104).

Singh, K S, 1966, *The Dust Storm and The Hanging Mist: A Study of Birsa Munda and His Movement 1874–1904,* Calcutta, Firma K L M.

Skaria, A, 1997, 'Writing, orality and power in the Dangs, western India, 1880s–1920s', in Amin, S; Chakrabarty, D (eds), *Subaltern Studies IX: Writings on South Asian History and Society,* Delhi, Oxford University Press, (pp. 13–58).

_______, 1999, *Hybrid Histories: Forests, Frontiers and Wildness in Western India,* Delhi, Oxford University Press.

Sontheimer, G D, 1987, 'The Vana and the Ksetra: The tribal background of some famous cults', in Tripathi, G C; Kulke, H (eds), *Religion and Society in Eastern India: Anncharlott Eschmann Memorial Lectures* Bhubaneswar, Utkal University, (pp. 117–64).

Srinivas, M N, 1952, *Society and Culture Among the Coorgs of South India,* Oxford, Clarendon Press.

_______, 1962, *Caste in Modern India and Other Essays,* Bombay, Asia Publishing House, 1962.

Srinivas, M N, 1987, 'The Indian village: Myth and reality', in M N Srinivas, 1987, *The Dominant Caste and Other Essays,* Delhi, Oxford University Press.

Sutton, A, 1874, *Devapuja: The Testimony of the Bible against Idolatry*, Cuttack, Mission Press, 2nd edition.

Tambiah, S J, 1985, 'From varna to caste through mixed unions', in Tambiah, *Culture, Thought, and Social Action: An Anthropological Perspective,* Cambridge, Mass. & London, Harvard University Press, (pp. 211-51).

Thapar, R, 1986, 'Society and historical consciousness: The *itihasa-purana* tradition', in, Bhattacharya, S; Thapar, R (eds), *Situating Indian History for Sarvepalli Gopal,* Delhi,

Oxford University Press, (pp. 353–83).
______, 1996, *Time as a metaphor of History: Early India*, Delhi, Oxford University Press.
Thompson, E P, 1963, *The Making of the English Working Class*, New York, Vintage.
______,1967, 'Time, work-discipline and industrial capitalism', *Past and Present*, 38, (pp. 56–97), [reprinted in Thompson, E P, 1993, *Customs in Common*, New York, The New Press, (pp. 354–403)].
Tribal Research Bureau, 1968–1969, 'Impact of Satya Mahima Dharma on Scheduled Castes and Scheduled Tribes in Orissa', *Adivasi*, 10:1.
Trouillot, M R, 1995, *Silencing the Past: Power and the Production of History*, Boston, Beacon Press.
Turner, V, 1969, *The Ritual Process: Structure and Antistructure*, Chicago, Aldine, 1969.
Van der Veer, P, 1988, *Gods on Earth: The Management of Religious Experience in a North Indian Pilgrimage Centre*, Delhi, Oxford University Press.
Vansina, J, 1985, *Oral Tradition as History*, London, James Currey, 2nd edition.
Vasu, N N, 1911, *The Modern Buddhism and Its Followers in Orissa*, Calcutta, U N Bhattacharya.
______, 1981, *The Archeological Survey of Mayurbhanja*, vol. 1, Delhi, Rare reprints.
Veyne, P, 1971, *Writing History*, tr. Mina Moore-Rinvolucri, Middletown, Wesleyan University Press, 1st French edition, 1971.
Von Stietencron, H, 2001, 'Charisma and canon: The dynamics of legitimization and innovation in Indian religions', in Dalmia, V; Malinar, A; Christof, M. (eds), *Charisma and Canon: Essays on the Religious History of the Indian Subcontinent*, New Delhi, Oxford University Press, (pp. 14–38).
Weber, M, 1969, *The Sociology of Religion*, tr. by Ephraim Fischoff, Boston, Beacon Press.
Zelliot, E, 1996, *From Untouchable to Dalit: Essays on the Ambedkar Movement*, New Delhi, Manohar.

Unpublished Dissertations

Chinara, S N, 1982, 'The History of the Mahima Cult in Orissa', Ph. D. Dissertation, University of Berhampur.
Mishra, P K, 1980, 'Political Unrest in Orissa in the Nineteenth Century', Ph. D. Dissertation, Utkal University.
Misra, B B, 1984, 'Rise and Growth of the Mahima Cult in Orissa in the Nineteenth Century', M. Phil. Dissertation, Sambalpur University.
Nayak, P M, 1984, 'A Study on the Contribution of Sonepur Durbar to Literature (1837–1937)', Ph. D. Dissertation, Sambalpur University.
Pati, S, 1984, 'Democratic Movements in the Feudatory States of Orissa (1905–48)', Ph. D. Dissertation, Utkal University.
Prior, K, 1990, 'The Administration of Hinduism in North India, 1780–1900', Ph. D. Dissertation, Cambridge University.
Rana, F C, 1991, 'Socio-Economic Life of Orissa in the Nineteenth Century as depicted in Contemporary Literature', Ph. D. Dissertation, Sambalpur University.

APPENDIX
Plan of Mahima Gadi

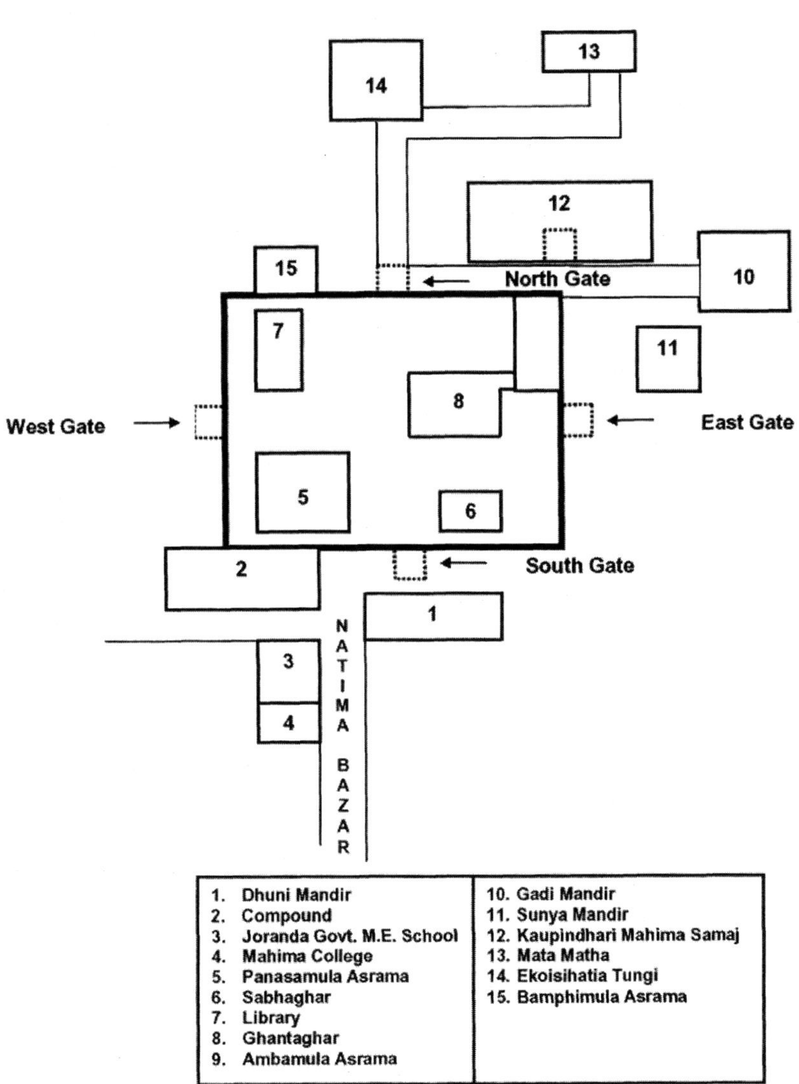

GLOSSARY

abadhut	Highest grade of a renouncer
abadhutashrama	Highest stage to which a renouncer can belong
ada-bandha	Girdle
adeś	Command
adharma	Sin, vice
adhyaksha	Head
adi bana	Original dress of the founder
ahimsa	Non-violence
akhandabati	Lamp which is never extinguished
alekh	Indescribable
alekhprabhu	Indescribable absolute
anadi	Without beginning
anadi avatar	Incarnation who has no beginning
anakara	Beyond form
apara	Imperfect
apara sanyasi	Renouncer who is yet to attain perfection
arupa	Formless
ashrama	Sacred place where ascetics and lay disciples gather
aśray	Shelter
aśrita	Lay disciple, one who has taken shelter in the faith
asthan	Sanctum where the founder lies buried
bairagi	Lowest grade of renouncer
balkal	Bark of a tree
balyalila	Ceremony in which children are fed
bana	Garb, flag
bara thakur	Great Lord, Jagannath
bedha	Fence, boundary
begar	Unpaid forced labour
bethi	Paid forced labour
bhagaban	God
bhajan	Devotional songs
bhakta	Devotee, follower

bhakta-kabi	Poet-devotee
bhakti	Devotion
bhek	Garb
bhiksha	Practice of asking for alms
bhoga mandap	Construction in which offerings to god are kept
boli	Chapter
brahma-jñana	Knowledge of absolute
brahmanda	Universe
chatra	Relief house
darśan	Mode of praying to absolute at dusk
darśan bastra	Garment worn during the offering of prayers to absolute
dasa	Lord's servant, designation of Kaupindhari ascetics
dharma	Faith, religion
dharma palan	Following the path of piety
dharmaśala	Rest house for pilgrims
dhuni	Sacred fire
dhuni mandir	Temple in which sacred fire is kept
diksha	Initiation
diksha-guru	Preceptor who grants initiation
dukha	Sorrow, suffering
dvaja	Flag
ekakshara	Non-dual letter
gadi	Sacred site of the sect
geru basan	cloth dyed with red earth
ghantaghar	Bell-room
gomaya	Cowdung
granthagar	Library
gruhi	Householder
gruhi bhakta	Lay disciple
guru	Master, founder of the sect
guru purnima	Festival in memory of founder at full moon of January-February
iśwara	God
iśwara purusha	Human Lord-incarnate
jiva	Human being, individual soul
kali yuga	Present era of evil
kanapat	Loincloth
karuna	Mercy, compassion
kaupin	Loincloth

koshagar	Treasury
kshetra	Field
kumbhipat	Bark of kumbhi tree
maghi purnima	Full moon in January-February
mahaprasad	Unpollutable food of Jagannath
mahima	Radiance, glory
mantra	Incantation
marfatdar	Mediator who represents the founder
mela	Fair
mleccha	Person outside caste Hinduism
nam bhajan	Singing/recitation of divine name
nirguna	Beyond attributes
nishkama leela	Non-attached sport
niti (seva)	Ritual service
pabitra	Purifying mixture of cow's excretions
pada	Couplet
pancamruta	Purifying mixture of five ingredients
para	Perfect
para sanyasi	Renouncer who has attained perfection
parama	Supreme
paramatma	Supreme (soul)
parampara	Line of successors, tradition
parichalana samiti	Managing committee
panda	Body
prabuddha avatar	All-knowing incarnation
prathama-panthi	Of the first line
sabha	Meeting
sabhaghar	Meeting hall
sadhana	Meditation
sadhu	Saint
saguna	With attributes
sahay	Friend, support
sakha	Friend
samadhi	Memorial
samadhi mandir	Temple built on mortal remains of founder
samaj	Community
sampadak	Secretary
sanatan	Eternal
sanyasi	Renouncer
saptamruta	Purifying mixture of seven ingredients

śaran	Mode of offering prayer to absolute at dawn
śaran manya	Showing respect through prostration
śastra	Scripture
satsanga goshthi	Common meal of devout followers
satya yuga	Era of truth
seva puja	Worship, divine service
siddha	Self-realized
siddhi	Self-realization
śisya	Disciple
snana-śauca	Purification through bath after defecation
stuti	Verse in praise of Lord
śunya	Void
śunya adeś	Order from void
śunya mandir	Temple in honour of void, Absolute
tattva	Doctrine, tenet, theory
utsav	Festival
vana	Forest
yogeśwara	Lord of meditation

Index

A

A Statistical Account of Bengal 38, 204
abadhut 44, 86, 87, 88, 90, 101, 123
Advaita Vedantic tradition 55, 77, 124
ajoni sambhuta 32, 100, 129, 137
akhandabati 127, 172
Alekh 12, 28, 30–2, 44–5, 50, 53–54, 57n.6, n.26, 58, 72, 75, 107n.12, 111 n.103, 132, 144, 146, 150–3, 160, 163–5, 172–3, 175, 179, 182, 184, 191n.69, 194
Alekh Brahma 26, 31, 112n.106 (*see also Śunya*)
Alekh (Kumbhipatia) Dharma (cult) 12, 44, 66n.111, 118, 146, 150, 151(*see also* Mahima Dharma)
Alekh Leela 31, 75
Alekh Prabhu (Swami) 30–2, 45–6, 50, 53–4, 57, 58n.26, 72, 75, 107, 146, 163–4, 179
Alltagsgeschichte 7, 15, 22n.40–1
    ana 84, 91
    anakara 84, 111–2
    anakshara 84
    anarupa 84
Anadi (Prabhu) 83–6, 88, 90, 92–5, 98, 100, 11n.86 (*see also* Alekh Prabhu)
Anthropology 1
    and history, vii, 3, 5, 7, 14, 19, 22
Asad, Talal 21 n.30, 24 n.57, 200
ascetic viii, 8–18, 25–8, 32–5, 44–8, 53, 56–7, 70, 73, 86, 87–8, 92, 97–8, 105, 117–43, 147–50, 155, 158, 160–71, 176, 178, 180–5, 193, 194 (*see also sanyasi*)
ashrama viii, 11, 12, 19, 70, 72–3, 86, 100, 102, 106–8, 114, 118–20, 130, 137, 152–3, 158–61, 167, 169, 172, 175–8, 181–184, 186, 193–4
aśritas 29, 36, 45, 46 (*see also gruhi bhaktas*)
asthan 119, 126, 176, 183 (*see also samadhi* and Mahima Gadi)
Athgarh 28, 44, 62
atma-jñana 86
authority 6, 12, 15, 25, 33–4, 39, 46–8, 54–5, 64, 102, 105, 113, 118–9, 126–7, 132–3, 135–6, 144, 146, 149, 151–2, 182, 194
    and power 79
    and resistance117
    and establishment 9, 34
    and State power 24

B

Baba, Biswanath 31–4, 77, 98, 122–5, 127–30, 133–7, 140–3, 145, 148, 150, 159, 161, 164, 170, 172, 176–8, 182, 193–5
    Pratipadaka 124–6, 131, 133, 137, 143

Satya Mahima Dharmara Itihasa 31, 127, 128, 136.
Baba (Das), Govinda 31, 53, 56, 87–8, 90,118, 120, 130, 137,152 (*see also* Mahima Swami and Govinda Das)
Baba, Kasinath 136, 147, 182
Baba, Krupasindhu 121, 146, 142
Baba, Kshetrabasi 148, 174, 199
Baba, Mahindra 136, 137, 140, 180
Satya Mahima Dharma Sankshipta Itihasa 136, 199
Baba, Nanda 121–2, 131, 155, 157n.118
Baba, Nrusingha 118–9, 137 (*see also* Narsing Das)
Baba, Raj Kishore 180, 190n.63, 199
Mahimadham Sankshipta Itihasa 157n.118, 199
Babb, Lawrence 23n.45, n.46, 188n23, 201
bairagi(s) 130, 134, 142, 144–5, 176, 180, 185
Balkaldhari (s) 105, 118–27, 131–49, 153n.35, 157n.119, 158n.120, n.122, 169, 172–3, 176–82, 184–5, 188n.21, 190 n.51, n.54, n.56, 191n.68, 197
samaj 127, 136, 140–1, 172, 176, 181–4, 191n.68
bara thakur 39, 50, 54 (*see also* Jagannath)
Baud 31, 62, 101, 168
Bäumer, Bettina 87, 201
Beltz, Johannes 55, 58n.135, n.136, 107n.9, 112n.105, 116n.166, 191n.69, 194–5, 201
Bengal viii, 38, 43, 45, 49, 50, 55, 57, 61, 62, 64, 87, 99, 113, 147, 162, 185
bethi 41, 42, 63
Bhagabata 44, 45, 71, 75, 85
bhajans 76–8, 105, 109, 124, 166, 172, 174, 175, 179, 181–4, 186
bhaktas 30, 37, 54, 73, 75, 76, 79, 89, 98, 100, 102, 106, 114n.146, 121, 145, 147, 159, 162, 168, 169, 172–6, 178–9, 183–6, 187n.15, 190n.53
bhandari 35
bhiksha 28, 35, 47, 73, 132, 160, 172, 177, 180
Bhima Bhoi viii, 10–13, 17–19, 23, 49, 53–8, 67–106, 118, 120, 124–6, 135, 140–51, 159, 161, 163, 168, 169, 179, 180–2, 186, 193, 194
and Ma Annapurna 73, 75, 102, 107n.18, 108n.29, 115n.147, n.148, 182, 186, 194
and missionaries 73, 74
and Yoga and Tantra 77, 87, 89, 94, 110n.75, 113n.118, 140, 163
Adi Anta Gita 87
Bhajanmala 89
Bhaktakabi Bhima Bhoinka Granthabali (*Granthabali*) 83, 105, 107n.7, 199
Bhima Bhoi Malika ba Padmakalpa (*Padmakalpa)* 92,93, 95, 96, 97, 98, 99, 100, 101
Brahma Nirupana Gita 83, 85, 138
Nirveda Sadhana 85–6, 90, 93, 125
Stuti Chintamoni 71, 72, 73, 78, 79, 80–5, 89, 104, 105, 137
bhog 27, 49 (*see also mahaprasad*)
Bloch, Marc 7, 21, 201
Bolangir 70, 100, 106, 115, 167
Brahma 83–7, 89, 110n.71, 112n.106, 123–6, 139, 141, 144–5, 163, 175, 195
Brahman (s) 8, 23, 27, 34–6, 42, 43, 46, 47–8, 53, 55, 65, 72, 84, 93, 98–9, 101, 102, 110, 156, 164, 168, 182, 186
British administrators 2, 25, 38
Buddha 31, 32, 39, 43

Buddhism 23, 32, 76, 77, 78, 87, 89, 102, 111
Kalacakra school 89

C

caste 8, 18–19, 23–7, 30–40, 44–7, 52, 55, 59, 61, 68, 72, 88, 93, 96, 99, 103, 110, 124, 150, 159, 163–70, 185–9
and kingship 8
and religion 51
low-caste 9, 25, 33, 35–6, 38, 41, 46, 52, 53, 61, 62, 163, 164, 167, 169, 186
out caste 35, 51, 62, 93
upper-caste 33, 36, 38, 40, 42, 53, 54, 64, 71, 74, 164
Census of India 44, 198
Chaitanya 44–5
chatras 40
chatrakhiyas 40
Christianity 26, 31, 36, 38, 44, 66, 74
Colonial rule 5, 61, 96, 109
Colonialism 2, 4, 21, 37
Community vii, 6, 8, 11, 12, 14, 15, 16, 17, 18, 19, 36, 72–3, 79, 82, 92, 97, 99, 113, 118, 130, 136, 139, 147, 149, 150, 151, 159, 164, 165, 166, 167, 168, 172, 178, 183, 191
and state 2, 13, 117
Coronil, Fernando 6, 21n.34, 202
Cuttack ix, 26, 33, 41, 51, 60, 63, 64, 92, 100, 119, 127, 128, 168, 183, 193

D

darśan 29, 102, 165, 166, 172, 175, 178, 179, 181, 188, 190 (*see also śaran*)
Das (Baba) Dinabandhu 127, 135
Das, Banchanidhi 83
Das, Chittaranjan 77, 103, 199, 202
Das, Dharmananda 132, 135
Das (Baba) Govinda 28, 71, 85, 86, 88, 89
Das, Jagannath 45, 86, 112n.106 (*see also* Panchasakhas)
Das, Krupasindhu 127
Das, Mukunda 9, 32, 57, 58 (*see also* Mahima Swami)
Das, Narsing 28, 29, 66, 118 (*see also* Nrusingha Baba)
Das, Paritosh 87,111, 202
Das, Rashbehari 106
Sriguru Mahatmya 106
Das, Sarala 44, 90, 112
Das, Sundar 44
and *Kujibar Patra* 44
Dasgupta, Sashi Bhusan 87, 202
Dash, Debendra Kumar 58, 104, 107–108, 152, 199
Davis, Natalie Zemon 7, 203
Derrett, J D M 156n.82, 203
Dev, Ram Chandra 94, 96
Deva II, Mukunda 39
Dharma Grantha Store 92, 96, 105
dharma 8, 10, 12, 16, 17, 18, 25, 26, 32–5, 44, 46, 49, 72, 79, 82, 86, 91, 123, 129, 137, 139, 140, 141, 143, 145, 161, 167, 171, 193
dharma sabha 118, 122, 147
Dhenkanal 12, 26–7, 29–31, 33, 36, 42, 44, 47–8, 57–8, 66, 70, 76, 97, 118, 121, 127, 146, 149, 151–2, 155, 161, 193–4
Dirks, N 22n.41, 63n.77, 203
dhulia babaji(gosain), *see* Mahima Swami
dhuni 29, 47, 86, 88, 89, 90, 118–9, 132, 137, 145, 152, 166, 167, 174, 175, 176, 179, 181
Dhuni Mandir 119, 132–133, 146, 152, 176, 179, 181
dhunikunda 88

Dube, S ix, 19n.2, 21n.32, 22n.41,107n.10, 188n.20, 189n.32, 200, 203
Dube, S C ix, 188n.24, 203
Dumont, Louis 18, 24n.54, 107n.19, 164, 169, 187n.3, 203

E

Eck, D188n.23, 203
East India Company 38, 60
ekakshara 88, 136, 139–40
Eliade, Mircea 3, 20, 203
Enlightenment, 1, 2, 4, 5
Eschmann, Anncharlott 77, 153, 161, 188, 203
Europe 1–3
event 6, 7, 9, 10, 16, 25, 49, 55, 56, 75, 92, 94, 96, 98, 113, 128, 183

F

faith viii, 8–19, 25–9, 31, 33, 36, 37, 43–56, 66, 69–77, 80–5, 92–101, 105, 117–30, 133–51, 154–6, 159–72, 175, 177–85, 193–5

G

Galanter, Marc 13, 155n.66, 203
Gandhi 11, 94–6, 113
Garhjats 28, 33, 36, 39, 41–2, 63 (*see also* tributary states)
Genovese, Eugene D. 7, 204
ghee, 47, 106, 142, 170, 172, 173, 175, 179, 184
Ginzburg, Carlo 22–3, 204
grama 33, 42
gruhi bhaktas 45, 76, 105, 146, 173, 180, 185, 212 (*see also aśritas*)
  and rules of caste 167–70
  and rules of initiation 159–60
  and rules of sex 165
  brahma bibaha 173–4
Guru 11, 12, 17, 30, 33, 36, 46–55, 68–90, 93, 97, 100–5, 117–21, 126–33, 137, 138, 142, 148, 151, 157, 159, 160, 163, 176, 178, 180, 182, 183, 190, 191
Guzy, Lidia 188, 194, 204

H

Herrschaft 14, 18, 24 (*see also* state power) and community 18
Hinduism, 3, 6–14, 18, 23, 28, 33, 34, 37, 38, 44, 45, 49, 55, 64, 74, 77, 110, 118, 125–130, 136, 143, 145, 150–151, 154, 156, 164, 179
Hindu Religious Endowments Act, 146, 149
History, 2–10, 13–19, 26–32, 55, 56, 77, 117, 128, 129, 132, 140, 141, 150, 171
  and anthropology, vii, viii, 1, 3, 5, 7,14, 22
  and *itihasas*, 3–5, 13, 17, 18, 20, 31, 32, 34, 67, 98, 127–132, 136, 137, 139, 143, 148
  and memory, 10
  and reason, 1
  and religion, 8
householder (devotees or disciples), 9–11, 14–18, 23–24, 29, 46, 49, 54, 70–73, 99, 101–102, 105, 107, 120, 126, 143, 150–151, 159, 161–164, 166–169, 171–172, 182–187 (*see also aśritas* and *gruhi bhaktas*)
Hunter, W. W., 38, 204

I

Incarnation, 3, 9, 11, 17, 28–32, 37–47, 53, 64, 74, 76, 78, 86, 90, 92, 95, 97, 99, 123, 129, 194

India, vii, 2–5, 8, 12, 13, 18, 20–23, 32, 38, 52, 72, 94, 103, 112, 113, 129, 155, 162, 164
Indian philosophy, 123, 125, 162
Indian religion, 24, 151, 169, 189
iśwara, 26, 137
  iśwar purusha, 31, 123

J

Jagannath, 8, 9, 10–12, 17, 25, 27, 31–34, 38–42, 44, 49–56, 58, 60–62, 64, 67–68, 85–86, 93, 98, 103, 110–111, 150, 154, 170, 179, 190, 197, 200–201, 203, 205–206, 211, 213
  and Govinda Das, 31, 53, 56, 85
  cult of, 10, 12, 31, 39, 55, 61, 64, 98, 150, 151, 203, 205
  temple of 9, 10, 17, 25, 27, 32, 38–9, 41–2, 44, 49–50, 52–3, 55–6, 58, 60–61, 68, 86, 103, 115, 170, 179, 197, 206
Jagannath Temple Correspondence 57–60, 64–8, 107, 151–2, 198
Joranda viii, 12, 29, 70–3, 76, 92, 96–8, 100, 104–6, 118–21, 126–27, 132, 133, 142, 144, 145, 149, 152, 154, 155, 159–60, 171, 173, 176–78, 180, 182–83, 185–86, 190–91, 194

K

Kabir 24, 45, 106, 125
Kali Bhagabata 31, 45, 75, 95
Kalki 11, 94–6
kanthi 28, 120
Kapilas 26, 27, 28, 31–3, 82, 88, 194
kaupin 28, 88, 120, 124, 136–141, 143.
Kaupindhari(s) 56, 110, 118–22, 126, 130–3, 136–49, 155, 169, 172, 176–7, 179–82, 185
Khandagiri 32, 33
Khond 69, 70–2, 101
Khurda 28, 29, 32, 39, 41–2, 44, 63
Kingship 8, 34, 62.
knowledge 5, 7, 22, 65, 76, 81–91, 95, 103, 114, 122, 125–6, 130, 134, 135, 140, 147–9, 153, 163, 170, 177, 180, 187
kshetra 9, 33, 58, 122
Kulke, Hermann viii, 42, 62n.63, 63n.79, 205, 208
kumbhipat 28–9, 88, 119, 120
Kumbhipatia 12, 44, 45, 46, 49, 55, 72, 73, 118, 119, 120, 121, 151
kundalini 87, 113

L

Lal, Vinay 4, 20, 205
law 6, 12–13, 15, 17–18, 97, 118, 126–7, 132–44, 147–50, 154–6, 168, 193
  and history 16
  and power vii, ix, 6, 8
  and order 36, 41, 50
legality 8, 126
Lorenzen, David ix, 20, 23n.45, 24n.54, 205

M

Mahabharata 3, 44, 90, 96, 112–13
Mahadev 27, 28, 50, 129 (*see also* Siva)
Mahanti, Artaballabh 58, 77, 79, 89, 101, 111, 144, 202
Mahima Alekh 160, 165, 172, 174–5
  mahima, 13, 19, 28, 29, 81, 85, 89, 123, 128, 135
Mahima Dharma
  and Buddhism 76–8
  and caste 8–9, 18–19, 26–7, 30–1, 33–7, 46–7, 72, 88, 91, 103, 124, 150, 164–5, 167–70, 172

and Hinduism (and Jagannath) 8, 10, 12–14, 18, 28, 33–4, 37–8, 49, 52–6, 98, 150–1, 170, 179
and Kali Yuga 37, 43, 194
and law 126–8, 132–6, 141, 144–7, 149
crisis 49, 73, 97, 117
Mahima abda 13, 18, 128, 154, 194
tenets and practices 34–5, 44–7, 136, 177
Mahima Gadi (Mahimagadi) 119, 126–7, 129–3, 135, 147–9, 157, 176, 193–4, 197
Mahima Gosain 28, 37, 121
Mahima Mahavidyalaya viii, 180, 184
Mahima Prabhu, 32, 137, 140, 171, 173–4, 184
Mahima Swami (*see also* Mahima Gosain), 8, 9, 10, 11, 13, 17–19, 23, 25–36, 43, 45, 47–9, 53–4, 56–9, 64, 66, 69–76, 85, 91, 94–8, 100–2, 104, 108, 111, 117–20, 123–6, 128–30, 133, 135, 137, 140–2, 146, 151–2, 154–5, 162, 168, 173, 180, 185, 187, 189–90, 194
and Bhima Bhoi, 10–11, 49, 53, 69, 71–2, 74–6, 78–2, 85–6, 90–1, 97–8, 100–1
and Govinda Baba (Das), 31, 53, 71, 85–88, 90
and missionaries 26, 30–31, 34–6, 48, 120
phalahari sanyasi 26, 27, 30, 34
Malbaharpur 29, 118, 136
malikas 9, 11, 37, 40, 43–5, 76, 91–2, 97, 99, 112–3, 125, 163
Yasomati Malika 31, 46, 75, 76, 97
Mansinha, M 58n.28, 103, 106n.2, 115n.158, 199, 205
Mansfield, P T 41, 198
Maratha 37, 39, 40
Mayurbhanj(a) 31, 43, 58, 62, 76, 102, 108, 113, 115, 198, 209
Mazumdar, B. C. 77, 103, 106, 108, 115,122, 152, 205
Misra, B. B. 57n.6, 58n.21, 64n.93, 191n.69, 195, 209
Misra, Binayak 103, 199
Missionaries 19, 26, 31, 34–40, 48, 74, 162
Baptist 30, 44, 60, 73, 107, 120
Protestant 17, 25, 38
Mobility 9, 28–30, 34, 164, 178
modernity 1, 2, 5, 15, 117
and history 4
and religion 150
western 2.
movement 34, 36, 39, 56, 72, 78, 95, 122, 164, 166, 175, 177, 178
Mukunda Das (see Mahima Swami)
Mughals 39, 40, 95–6
myth 1, 3, 5, 16, 27, 54, 56, 104.
and history 2, 11, 17, 21, 27

N

nagar (or pura) 33, 59
Nandy, Ashis ix, 4, 206
narration 6, 10, 17, 26, 45, 55, 94, 99
Nath *yogis* 40, 78
nation 4, 5, 137
Nepak, Bhagirathi 104, 108n.36, 116n.163, 200
Nirakara 83, 89.
nirguna 64, 78, 90, 91, 112

O

O'Malley, L.S.S. 38, 198
Gazetteer, 38
Omkar 139, 140, 142, 143
orality 8, 16, 21, 91, 135
Orientalist scholars 3, 38
Orissa viii, ix, 8–17, 25, 29–4, 48, 50–76, 87, 91, 96, 98–105, 108, 109,

112, 114, 115, 122, 127–9, 137, 142, 147–50, 153–158, 162–63, 167–68, 182, 185, 188, 193, 194

P

pada 71, 78, 81, 92, 104
Panchasakhas 37, 43, 44, 60, 78, 85, 87, 90, 91, 99, 101, 112, 125.
Pandey,Gyanendra ix, 207
Pati, Biswamoy 53, 67, 207
pilgrimage 9, 19, 32, 77, 82, 86, 159, 182, 183, 185, 191
pinda 77, 78, 110
politics 16, 35, 39, 164
    and religion 2, 14, 25, 35
power 5, 6, 10–17, 21–5, 28–31, 34, 35, 41–3, 54, 55, 60, 62, 79, 85, 90, 93, 105, 117, 124, 135, 145, 149, 150, 155, 163
prabuddha narayan 31, 33, 129
Pradhan, Chaitanya 71, 74
Pradhan, Nagendra Nath 78, 200
prayaścitta 35, 62
prayers 28, 32, 61, 94, 102, 123, 124, 131, 163, 171, 172, 175, 183, 184, 186 (*see also darśan* and *śaran*)
Puranas 3, 37, 43, 92, 95, 96, 125
  puranetihasa (or *itihasa–purana)* 3–5, 13, 18, 20, 128, 154
Puri 9, 11, 18, 25, 28, 31, 32, 33, 38–42, 44, 49, 50–6, 76, 85–9, 96, 98, 100, 103, 125, 153, 154, 161, 170

R

Raja 27, 33, 35, 36, 37, 41, 43, 48, 55, 127
    of Dhenkanal 27, 33, 47, 48, 118, 127, 151
    of Puri 42
    of Orissa 62–3
    Khurda rajas 39, 40, 41, 42 (*see also* Raja of Puri),
reason 2, 16, 45, 62, 86, 124, 144, 162, 163
    and faith vii, 8, 11, 16, 17, 26, 69, 128
    and history 1
    and truth 123
Redakhol 70, 71, 101, 106, 107, 114
Redfield, Robert 23, 207
religion vii, ix, 2, 6, 8, 12–16, 24, 25, 28, 35–40, 51, 62, 66–8, 75, 78, 90, 101, 109, 117, 121, 135, 140–4, 150–1, 155, 159, 162, 166, 169, 171, 193, 195
    and law vii, 6, 8
    and power 15, 25
ritual 1, 2, 13, 18, 25, 34–5, 39, 42, 46, 59, 119–20, 131, 141–42, 145, 150, 164, 168, 177–83

S

Sabean, David Warren 24n.55, 53, 113n.125, 208
Sadanand (*see* Savar)
Sahu, Laxmi Narayan 144
Said, Edward 21n.34, 208
samadhi 33, 97, 117, 118, 119, 120, 126, 133, 176, 179, 180, 184, 186 (*see also* Mahima Gadi).
samaj 73, 117, 126, 127, 131, 136–48, 160, 172, 174–185, 193
sanatan (Dharma or Hinduism) 12, 129, 130, 140, 141, 144, 145, 156, 168
Sanskrit 3, 23, 42, 45, 48, 104, 112, 123, 164
sanyasi 26, 29, 30. 33, 35, 45–6, 73, 96–7, 100, 105, 110, 118, 119–27, 130–42, 147–48, 158, 160–65, 168–78, 181–82, 184–85, 193 (*see also* ascetic),

śaran, 86, 134, 160, 165, 172, 175, 179, 181 (*see also darśan*)
Sarkar, Sumit 21, 99, 208
Satsanga Goshthi, 166, 184, 185
Satya Mahima Dharmalochana Samiti, 122, 144
satya–dharma 28, 32, 33, 37, 53, 77, 79, 80, 82, 92, 95, 129, 137, 182
Savar (s) 33, 56, 61
sect 9, 12–14, 18–19, 24, 31–2, 36, 38, 40, 43–4, 49, 55–7, 64, 66, 72–3, 76–7, 97, 102, 107, 110, 117–21, 126–8, 132, 135, 143–4, 150–2, 159, 165, 166–7, 169, 171, 178, 182, 188, 190
Secularization 1, 2, 14, 99
Sikhism 119, 125
Singh, Govind 119, 151
Siva 26–8, 89, 111, 194 (*see also* Maheswara)
  Mahadev 27, 28, 50, 129
society viii, 33, 38, 48, 51, 55, 61, 125, 160, 161, 182, 185
Srinivas M. N., 23, 164, 188, 208
state vii, viii, ix, 2, 8–9, 12–13, 18, 31, 33, 34, 39–42, 44, 48, 49, 58–64, 76, 81, 105, 120, 127, 136
  and community 13, 117
state power 13, 14, 24, 127
Subaltern Studies 7, 15, 22n.40, n.41, 53, 67n.118, 200–204, 207, 208
Śunya (Brahma, Guru or Purusha) 26, 77–8, 89, 94, 101, 110n.65, 111n.86, n.99, n.103, 112n.104, n.106 (*see also* Alekh Brahma)
śunya adeś (bani) 121, 131, 157 n118

T

temporality vii, 1, 2, 8, 13, 14, 93, 97, 99, 128, 150.
Thompson, E. P. 7, 209
time vii, viii, 1–6, 10–21, 26–7, 30, 32, 35– 40, 42–5, 47–56, 59–62, 66, 70–1, 76–81, 85–99, 102–3, 110–13, 117–22, 128–9, 132, 133–50, 155, 160, 165–6, 169, 171, 173, 176–86, 189, 193, 195 (*see also* Yuga Kali)
  and history, 1, 14, 20, 113, 117.
  and temporality, vii, 1, 14.
  and tradition, 128.
  cyclical time, 3, 21
  linear time, 3, 21
  linear–cyclical time, 3, 21
  Universal time, 2.
tradition, 3–7, 12–16, 23–7, 32–8, 43–4, 45, 47, 55, 60, 72, 76–8, 87, 90–2, 95, 123–4, 126–9, 135, 161, 162, 164, 179
  Vaishnavite, 3, 37
tribal peoples, 25, 34, 40, 42
tributary states, 9, 28, 40, 41, 61 (*see also* Garhjats)
tungi, 28–30, 47, 126–7, 133, 160, 166–7, 173–4, 176, 178, 184, 190

U

untouchable (dalits), 8, 9, 35, 56, 162, 163, 164, 167, 168, 186.
Upanishads 125, 180
Utkala Deepika 26, 30, 32, 34–5, 50, 51, 72, 73, 104, 119–20, 198

V

vana 9, 33, 58, 59, 122
Vasu N.N, 31–2, 43, 75, 77, 102, 122
  The Archeological Survey of Mayurbhanja 102, 209
  The Modern Buddhism and its Followers in Orissa 102, 209
Vedanta 78, 89, 91, 144, 153, 164
Vedas 33, 84, 89, 93, 144
veracity 4, 8, 18, 58, 70, 117, 121, 128, 131, 148, 149

Vishnu 27, 39, 43, 53, 89, 92, 95–6, 111, 119, 152, 195
Von Stietencron viii, 151n.3, n.5, 209

W

Weber, Max 24n.54, 209
worship 8, 26–8, 33–6, 38, 41–6, 52–3, 56, 58, 68, 73–5, 77–8, 81–4, 88, 90, 100, 102–3, 119, 123–5, 141–5, 150, 163–4, 173, 179, 186, 188

Y

Yoga (Tantra) 77, 81, 87, 89, 94, 110, 113, 124, 126, 137, 140, 153, 162, 163
Yuga 3, 4, 9, 11, 17, 21, 37, 43, 45, 81–2, 86, 90, 92–3–95, 98–9, 101–2, 110, 112–3, 123, 129, 160, 162, 191, 194–5 (*see also* time and temporality)
  Dwapar 3, 94
  Kali 3, 9, 11, 17, 20–1, 37, 40, 42–3, 45, 60, 81–3, 86, 90–102, 113, 123, 124, 129, 130, 150, 160, 162, 185, 191, 194
  Satya 3, 31, 37, 90, 92, 110, 191, 195
  Treta 3